JAMES JOYCE'S CATHOLIC CATEGORIES

SECOND EDITION

FR. COLUM POWER S.H.M.

Wiseblood Books

Copyright © 2023 Wiseblood Books

Published by Wiseblood Books
www.wisebloodbooks.com

All rights reserved, including the right to reproduce this book or any portions thereof in any form whatsoever except for brief quotations in book reviews. For information, address the publisher.

                    P.O. Box 870
            Menomonee Falls, WI 53052

Printed in the United States of America

Set in Baskerville Typesetting

Cover Design: Dominic Heisdorf

Second Edition

Paperback ISBN-13: 978-1-951319-17-5

Hardcover ISBN-13: 978-1-951319-18-2

CONTENTS

Introduction by Declan Kiberd · v

James Joyce's Catholic Categories

Introduction

   1: Content and Method · 1

   2: Contours of the Debate · 21

Chapter I: James Joyce: Relativist or Realist?

   I.1: Introduction · 31

   I.2: The Aesthetics Debate · 33

   I.3: Joyce on Scholasticism and the Enlightenment · 46

   I.4: Ratzinger on Theology and Aesthetics · 55

   I.5: The Case for Joyce as Relativist · 63

   I.6: The Case for Joyce as Realist · 83

   I.7: Conclusion of Chapter I · 107

Chapter II: Agape without Eros

   II.1: Introduction · 111

   II.2: "Eveline" and Irish Catholicism · 113

   II.3: The Irish Context · 119

   II.4: The Eros Controversy · 130

   II.5: A Theological Hiatus · 162

   II.6: Conclusion of Chapter II · 165

Chapter III: Joycean Individuation

   III.1: Introduction · 169
   III.2: Dubliners · 172
   III.3: A Portrait of the Artist as a Young Man · 208
   III.4: Ulysses · 235
   III.5: Conclusion of Chapter III · 276

Chapter IV: Judeo-Christian Individuation

   IV.1: Introduction · 279
   IV.2: Joyce's Interest in Moses · 284
   IV.3: Joyce's Interest in Saint Augustine · 289
   IV.4: Joyce's Interest in Aquinas · 296
   IV.5: Joyce's Interest in Saint Ignatius · 303
   IV.6: Tradition as Continuity and Creativity · 311
   IV.7: Conclusion of Chapter IV · 321

Chapter V: Eucharistic Mutations and Permutations

   V.1: Introduction · 325
   V.2: Key Moments in the Joycean Trajectory · 330
   V.3: The Eucharist in Portrait and Ulysses · 338
   V.4: Body and Blood in Ulysses · 373
   V.5: Joyce's Theological Intentions · 384
   V.6: The Eucharist as Culmination of Eros and Agape · 398
   V.7: Conclusion of Chapter V · 405

Final Summary and Conclusion

   1: Apostasy and Afterwards · 409
   2: Vestigial Belief according to Aquinas · 420
   3: Joyce and the Faith-Culture Dialogue · 422

Bibliography · 427

Notes · 445

Index · 503

Acknowledgments · 519

INTRODUCTION BY DECLAN KIBERD

The practice of literary criticism has been, for well over a century, a resolutely secular activity—and this despite the fact that modern literature has often opened up sacred spaces not much explored in everyday life. It is not difficult to understand why this has been so. Ever since the "higher criticism" threw certain forms of biblical narrative into question, critical practice has prided itself on its unmasking, this-worldly quality. A further factor is the location of most critical endeavours within the university system, at a time when academia no longer sees itself as refereeing the debate between religion and science but as pursuing wisdom in a purely secular form. The fact that many modern forms of physics have reopened many scientists to the possibilities of the numinous has not changed that prevailing orthodoxy.

The decline of institutional religious practice in the western world has been accompanied by an openness to the numinous among artists. This has little of the credal about it. Nevertheless, from D.H. Lawrence's priesthood of love to Samuel Beckett's insistence that poetry is a form of prayer, the history of modernism has been a story of spiritual exploration. Perhaps this is merely to confirm Matthew Arnold's suggestion that the role of the priest would be assumed by the artist. The two greatest exponents of Irish Modernism certainly saw it so. W.B. Yeats said that in his church there would be an altar and no pulpit. Far from upholding the higher claims of criticism, he bemoaned the ways in which a narrow-gauge moralism among late Victorians had eroded religious experience. Whereas religion sought to define the ways in which a person relates to fate, destiny, and divinity, morality seeks only to regulate the ways in which people relate to one another. For this reason, Yeats thought of the moral and religious impulses as essentially opposed: "the moral and religious impulses destroy one another in the end." He found in the practice of criticism all the tell-tale signs of a panicky ethics, in which the moralizing instinct grows monstrous after the evacuation of God. The rule-bound bureaucracies of modernity were no substitute for a truly religious life.

Yet such a bureaucracy had been instituted in Ireland as early as the middle decades of the nineteenth century, when a vernacular form of folk Catholicism was forced to make way for a middle-class church. That church resolutely discouraged such "superstitions" as healing wells, the waking of dead bodies, or the saying of prayers to local saints. Its theology became more Victorian with every passing year . . . and more Protestant, as Sir William Wilde noted in an essay. Sir William's famous son, Oscar, would proceed to castigate many of these changes in his fairy tales for children, which lament the increasing importance of pulpits and the decreasing importance of altars in the lives of his characters. In these stories, the letter killeth while the spirit giveth life—especially that form of spirit which manifests itself as a kind of eucharist.

James Joyce was born into an Ireland in the grip of an ecclesiocracy, determined to reduce Irish Catholicism to a set of Victorian rules but all too often devoid of a wider religious vision. Forms of folk Catholicism still survived, albeit precariously, in the practice of some older people and in the writings of a subversive artist such as Wilde. Any close reader of *Ulysses,* or of Joyce's essay on Wilde, will quickly understand how deeply he engaged with the traditional dramas and values of Catholicism—and how deep was the contempt which he felt for the external formalities of the post-Tridentine church. The early prose works—such as the stories of *Dubliners* or key passages of epiphany in *A Portrait of the Artist as a Young Man*—are filled in equal measure with such a double imperative.

Yet, such has been the coruscating power of Joyce's critique of the flawed institutions of late nineteenth-century Catholicism that even some of his subtlest readers have taken him for an arrant secularist. He has been recruited to the banner of a godless modernism by a criticism which fails not only to notice the godly in most modernists but also in Joyce's own project. If Joyce was scathing about the failures of those priests who taught him, that was mainly because he took far more seriously than they the claims of the Catholic Church in which he was raised. While they were enforcing rules, the young Joyce was studying ways in which to love God . . . and feeling the bitter hurt of his own failure to do so.

Of course, the scholarly criticism of Joyce recognizes the ways in which he employed many iterative images and ideas of Catholicism—Epicleti, Epiphany, Eucharist. But this is almost invariably followed by the claim that Joyce annexed these for the more secular purposes of art, in an act of reappropriation. The great virtue of Father Colum Power's study of Joyce is that it starts from an assumption that there is far more at stake in the texts than a reworking of religious images. While other Irish artists might study religion in terms of its social effects, Joyce follows Yeats in using literature for an altogether different purpose—as a mode of spiritual exploration. The result is religious writing—as opposed to a mere writing about religion.

There is no doubt that Joyce felt some jealousy towards priests: near the close of *A Portrait* Stephen Dedalus accuses a girl-friend of flirting with a priest and with a church which is "the scullery-maid of Christendom." Some of that jealousy takes blunt enough form: in "An Encounter" a boy yells "ya yaka yaka yaka!" in a war-game, with the result that "everyone was incredulous when it was reported that he had a vocation for the priesthood." The ability to yell a meaningless chant may be the one necessary qualification to become a rule-enforcer in Victorian Ireland. Yet Joyce will proceed in his writings to describe the artist in distinctly priest-like mode—taking the daily bread of creation and transforming it into the body of an eternal life. Joyce's art is not so much a simulacrum of priesthood as an extra-institutional priesthood by other means: priest-craft, like art, appeals to him for the same reason that it appealed to Yeats—its semblance of reality and at the same time its distance from it.

Joyce was deeply anti-clerical because he disliked the institutional form taken by Catholicism in the Ireland of his youth. But he remained haunted by the essences of the religion he only seemed to flout. Friends recalled how he would stand at the back of churches in Trieste and Paris during the ceremonies of Holy Week, reciting the entire service perfectly from memory. Stanislaus Joyce (just the kind of atheist that most Joyceans want his brother to be) observed rather sardonically of James that "he who has loved God in youth can never love anything that is less than divine." A sister said that "all of Jim's loves were really created in the love of God." Francini Bruni, friend to Joyce in Trieste, wrote that "he only completely admires the unchangeable: the mystery of Christ and the mute drama that surrounds it."

Colum Power, in a study of remarkable patience and rigor, traces Joyce's deep engagement with the more articulate forms which that necessarily mute, often mystical drama has sometimes taken when reduced to the humiliations of language; and he does so in tandem with a cool appraisal of the major modern schools of Joycean criticism. There have been some interesting analyses of Joyce written from an avowedly religious viewpoint in the past—perhaps the finest being those by Hugh Kenner—but they have been largely overwhelmed by the determination of even his greatest admirers to capture him for a purely secular humanism. It is part of Joyce's greatness that he resists such appropriation—with that same steadfastness which caused him to refuse an Easter communion. The young Stephen had said to his imploring mother: "No. Let the Eucharist come to me." This happens in the fullness of time, of course, when a drunken Stephen near the close of *Ulysses* is offered coffee and a bun by a kindly ad-man of Jewish aspect. Whether such a scene can be taken as a parody of communion or as a version of the real presence in an unexpectedly everyday form is an old debate, within Joyce studies and within Christianity itself. But, given the ways in which it is prepared for (by Bloom's ministration of bread to birds; by Stephen's debate with his mother in the prior book), it does seem to carry even more weight than Marcel Proust's screen-memory of the Eucharist in the *madeleine* of *A la recherche du Temps Perdu*. There have been many fake consecrations in earlier scenes of Joyce's masterpiece: but this one seems utterly real. After all, it is the climactic moment of the book.

Even as he works to expand our readings of Joyce to take a fuller account of Christian tradition, Colum Power also presents in a relaxed, authoritative way the lineaments of that tradition as inflected through the mind of Joyce. The result is a book of wisdom and insight, tracking themes from Augustine to Ratzinger and beyond. It also takes its place in a sequence of emergent studies of the religious dimensions in the art of high modernism. Its author has a mind of his own and the eloquence to express it in lucid prose—but it is ultimately a mind too serene for self-assertion, as it was over twenty years ago when I first met Colum Power in a classroom of Joyce's own university. While the tabulated sections of the work may seem to pin down many mysteries, the author knows that the highest art, like the religious experience out of which it comes, cannot be finally explained. The things of God may be intuited in flashes of insight or epiphany, but never all at once in any human language.

Declan Kiberd
Dublin
2016

James Joyce's Catholic Categories

INTRODUCTION

1: Content and Method

1.1: Bipolarity in Joyce Studies

Beyond the confines of specialist Joyce scholarship, Umberto Eco is arguably the world's best-known Joycean. In a recent article on Eco's reading of Joyce, entitled "Great Misinterpretations, Umberto Eco on Joyce and Aquinas," Dominican Thomist Antoine Levy has flatly stated and incisively argued that Eco has misinterpreted both James Joyce and St. Thomas Aquinas:

> Since Joyce's literary revolution was supposed to be used to illustrate Eco's theory on the essence of the Modern, Eco *had* to point to an original Thomistic delusion . . . in order to explain what was to follow. The very doubtful reality of such a conflict leads me therefore to question the coherence of Eco's view on Joyce's literary evolution.[1]

Levy's argument, then, is that ideological bias has blinded Eco to essential aspects of Joyce's art, leading to a distorted and erroneous interpretation.

On the other side, Jeffrey Segall has made a very similar accusation—of blinding ideological bias—against Catholic Joyce readers:

Joyce's humor, Joyce's obscenity, and Joyce's irrepressible irony are too frequently ignored or soft-pedalled by Catholic readers. . . . Catholic critics . . . simply do not take Joyce's anti-Catholic pronouncements seriously. When they appear to do so, they insist that while Stephen may have been guilty of blasphemy, Joyce was not. Joyce's antipathy for the Church was at least as deep-seated as his awe of it, and his protest against its repressiveness, its dogmatism, and its authoritarianism was, in his mind, a reasoned and legitimate one. The darker side of Catholicism that Joyce was so familiar with is often effaced from revisionist readings by Catholic intellectuals.[2]

These two quotations reflect a state of "bipolarity" in Joyce studies.

In 1990, Professor Augustine Martin wrote of "two large categories" in contemporary Joyce criticism: "those which view the novelist against the intellectual world that shaped him, Aristotle, Bruno, the school of old Aquinas; and those who view him through the retrospective apparatus of subsequent literary theory—let old Aquinas be Foucault!"[3] Twenty-five years later, in 2015, the tension between two trends in Joycean criticism, one celebrating rupture and fragmentariness, the other unity and equilibrium, is unresolved. It divides Joyceans, and our understanding of Joyce's art depends on ascertaining his position between these two poles, assuming he has any definable position at all. We must therefore clarify the lines of the debate. This may be done by analyzing the Catholic categories that remained in Joyce's thought and art.

1.2: A Catholic Structure of Mind

One Joyce critic, Harry Levin, has stated that Joyce "may have lost his faith but he did not lose his categories;"[4] hence the title of this book, "James Joyce's Catholic Categories." Joyce scholar and current Director of the James Joyce Centre at Antwerp, Geert Lernout, notes that "quite a few Joyce critics have argued that in one way or another Joyce and his work remain locked in a catholic [*sic*: Lernout prefers lower-case letters for religious terms] frame of reference." This view originated, Lernout informs us, from Joyce's friend Mary Colum, who remarked upon "the catholic structure of Joyce's mind."[5] Mary Colum wrote that she had "never known a mind so fundamentally Catholic in structure as Joyce's own."[6] Lernout argues against this thesis, arguing that Joyce rejected Catholicism and simply became an atheist.

Lernout rejects the concept of a Catholic structure of mind as "impossible to define." It is true that a Catholic structure of mind seems a difficult if not impossible concept to verify. He is not on sure ground, however, when he reduces Catholic categories to two: "If . . . we have to identify something specifically catholic in the structure of Joyce's mind we would have to say that . . . it can only involve the immaculate conception and papal infallibility."[7] Lernout fails to take into account an important difference between a Catholic structure of mind and

Catholic categories. The former notion is a nebulous one, as Lernout rightly affirms, but the latter idea is one that is susceptible to objective investigation and verification.

Harry Levin's assertion that Joyce lost his Catholic faith but not its categories, while at first sight similar to Mary Colum's assertion concerning a Joycean "structure of mind," is not identical to it, and permits a rational debate with evidence *pro* and *contra*. Moreover, the Catholic categories with which Joyce engages are not reducible to two. Joyce's break from Catholicism was not as radical and total as is often assumed. In the course of this study, we will encounter coincidences between the Joycean and the Catholic positions in multiple areas in doctrinal matters, for example, relating to the Eucharist and the workings of grace, and in ethical matters, such as homosexuality and artificial contraception.

1.3: Joyce's Catholic Categories

Two contrasting quotations suffice to introduce our subject, giving an idea of its complexity. First, from the young Joyce in a letter to Nora Barnacle:

> I left the Catholic Church, hating it most fervently. I found it impossible for me to remain in it on account of the impulses of my nature. I made secret war upon it when I was a student and declined to accept the positions it offered me. By doing this I made myself a beggar but I retained my pride. Now I make open war upon it by what I write and say and do.[8]

Next, these observations from his atheist brother's memoir:

> The strange doctrine of actual and sanctifying grace and its relation to original sin, which last was to be the subject of *Finnegans Wake*, had puzzled and fascinated my brother, as he had found it in his reading of Saint Augustine, and even viewed from outside the Church it held his interest. He had, in fact, gone to listen to a sermon on the subject . . . and had come away angry and disgusted at the inadequacy of the exposition.[9]

James Joyce's relationship with Catholicism strangely combined loathing and fascination, reactions usually considered diametrical opposites of the emotional spectrum. This disconcerting combination is reflected to this day in the world of Joyce interpretation. Geert Lernout, for example, writes at the beginning of *Help my Unbelief*, his book on Joyce's religious position, that "I believe, and I intend to demonstrate in this book, that James Joyce was an unbeliever from the start of his life as a writer, that he never returned to the faith."[10] Irish literary critic and cultural analyst Declan Kiberd, in contrast, in his book on Joyce's *Ulysses*, writes that "Joyce's desire was not to destroy religion. He had far too much respect for the wisdom of the ages to want to do that."[11]

Concretely, this tension is played out in three areas upon which I will focus: epiphany, individuation, and the Eucharist.

The first term is that of "epiphany." Literary critic Dominic Manganiello remarks that Joyce "gave the

Christian holy day [of the Epiphany] wide currency as a literary term."[12] The term is central to Joyce's much-debated adoption of Thomist aesthetics in his first novel, *A Portrait of the Artist as a Young Man*. Joyce's aesthetic position is, of course, crucial to discerning whether, philosophically, he is a realist in the tradition of Aristotle and Aquinas or a postmodern relativist. Umberto Eco states that in the matter of aesthetics there is, at most, a superficial connection between Aquinas and Joyce: "[I]t is a purely formal Thomism adopted into the *forma mentis* of the great Irish writer."[13] Fr. Antoine Levy flatly disagrees: "[W]hen Joyce speaks of imagination as a faculty that beholds the content of sensitive perception, he is moving on firm Thomistico-Aristotelian ground."[14] In the first chapter of this book we will see that Joyce is an Aristotelian realist whose work has been dominated by relativist hermeneutics. Later, we will see how Nietzschean emotivist and voluntarist readings have eclipsed Joyce's Aristoteliean individuating teleology, his perception of how human beings become more fully human through openness to the divine.

The second term, individuation, denotes the process by which the individual person matures in his humanity and also the typical characteristics, the end result, so to speak, of that maturation. This is arguably Joyce's single most important theme: what it means to be more fully human and how this comes about. His interest in the doctrine of grace sprang logically from this thematic focus. Polarization is a feature of Joycean scholarship in this area too. Richard Ellmann, for example, maintains that Stephen Dedalus, the chief protagonist of *A*

Portrait of the Artist, has overcome the stifling influence of Catholicism to achieve human and artistic maturity at the end of that novel: "The soul is ready now, it throws off its sense of imprisonment, its melancholy, its no longer tolerable conditions of lower existence, to be born."[15] Hugh Kenner, in contrast, sees Stephen depicted at the end of the same novel as a stunted character: "Stephen does not, as the careless reader may suppose, become an artist by rejecting church and country. Stephen does not become an artist at all."[16]

The third doctrinal area in which Joyce's contradictory reactions to Catholicism are reflected and prolonged in Joycean critical discourse is that of the Incarnation and its prolongation in the Eucharist. Joyce was interested in this doctrine too; the Circe chapter of *Ulysses,* for example, notoriously contains a black Mass. Roy Gottfried maintains in his book on Joyce and religion, published in 2008, that Joyce preferred "the unorthodox reformist position that the elements of the Mass are emblematic rather than actual."[17] Literary critic Frances Restuccia, on the other hand, in an article written in 1986, affirms the very opposite: "[W]hile Joyce toyed with the artistic blasphemy of basing his novel on an erroneous conception of the Eucharist . . . he makes clear finally that he remains faithful—artistically—to the Church's Eucharist."[18]

The purpose of this book is to adjudicate this debate. Joyce is emblematic of a kind of modernist atheism, and our aim is to understand his religious mind. It is necessary to clarify the theological categories under debate, in order to judge the degree to which Joyce understood them, accepted them or rejected them, and the degree to which they remained in his work and his worldview. By combining literary scholarship on Joyce's work with theological categories and historical contexts, we may distinguish between historically contingent aspects of turn of the century Irish Catholicism which Joyce finds distasteful and rejects, and other categories that he retained, thus reaching a better understanding of his tense and complex relationship with Catholicism and his final religious position. Contrary to the prevailing opinion in Joyce studies, there is evidence to suggest that Joyce remained not only a believer but a distinctly *Catholic* kind of believer. Let us look now, briefly, at the general state of Joycean literary criticism.

1.4: The Joycean Critical Landscape

1.4.1: Overall Summary

The level of interest in Joyce and of his continuing influence is manifest in the voluminous and unabating output of books and articles that feature his name and his work, a phenomenon that has given rise, jocosely but justifiably, to the term, "The Joyce Industry." Joyce is a focal point for studies in semiotics, politics, gender ideology, psychology, and feminism, among other fields of study and discourse.

Wikipedia is a useful source for providing a sense of Joyce's contemporary impact. Its entry on James Joyce, under the heading "Legacy," states that, "In 1999, *Time Magazine* named Joyce one of the 100 Most Important People of the 20th century, and stated; 'Joyce

... revolutionised 20th century fiction.'" *Time Magazine* is another reliable indicator of general opinion. The Wikipedia entry continues: "In 1998, the Modern Library ... ranked *Ulysses* No. 1, *A Portrait of the Artist as a Young Man* No. 3 ... on its list of the 100 best English-language novels of the 20th century."[19]

In the same section, Wikipedia quotes Maurice Beebe's assertion that Joyce's *Ulysses* is "a demonstration and summation of the entire [Modernist] movement,"[20] and provides a list of major writers and thinkers who declare discipleship of and indebtedness to James Joyce among whom are named Samuel Beckett, Jorge Luis Borges, Salman Rushdie, John Updike, and David Lodge. To that list I would add such figures as Vladimir Nabokov, Umberto Eco, and Gabriel García Márquez, to mention only a few of innumerable possible examples not included on Wikipedia's list. This provides a sense of Joyce's representativeness for 20th century thinking.

Under the heading "Joyce and religion," Wikipedia provides a selective representation of the contrasting views on the matter of Joyce's religious position, echoing the impression of tension and ambivalence provoked by the two conflicting quotations I have provided above, one from his letter to Nora Barnacle expressing his vehement animosity towards the Catholic Church and the other from his brother Stanislaus recounting his fascination with the Catholic doctrine of grace. In this, Wikipedia is an accurate barometer of prevailing opinion in the microcosm of Joycean literary criticism. However, it is safe to add that the dominant trend of Joycean critical discourse is secularist, and Joyce's post-Catholicism and anti-Catholicism has usually been taken for granted. Religious belief is a minority position among Joyce critics; a situation that is reflected in the ideological positions of leading Joyce critics.

1.4.2: Leading Figures

Joycean criticism of the latter half of the 20th century was dominated by two imposing and opposing figures, namely Richard Ellmann and Hugh Kenner. The opposition between them was not a well-kept secret, as evidenced in these opening sentences of a review by Kenner of a book by Ellmann: "Here's an old-fashioned book, not least so in its rhetoric . . . abristle with parlor paradox. 'After fifty years *Ulysses* still presents itself as the most difficult of entertaining novels, and the most entertaining of difficult ones.' That's less an insight than a device for traversing a sentence."[21]

Ellmann was an American liberal humanist and Kenner a Canadian convert to Catholicism. In his influential biography of Joyce, Ellmann presents the Irish writer as a strictly post-Christian secular humanist.[22] He sees Joyce's Catholicism as skin-deep and reads him as an essentially non-religious or even anti-religious writer. As for Kenner, his Catholicism informs his reading of Joyce, without taking center stage. His discovery of an ironic critical distance between the author, James Joyce, and his aesthetic *alter ego*, Stephen Dedalus, constituted a milestone and landmark in the history of Joyce studies. Kenner's point is that the "as a Young Man" part of the title of Joyce's first novel had too long been overlooked, but the implications of this for Stephen's statements vis-a-vis religion have not been developed: the portentous pronouncements of young men are not usually taken to be mature and definitive beyond possibility of posterior revision, and in this Stephen Dedalus is no exception. Nevertheless, the majority view of Joyce as a secular humanist writer, which Ellmann elegantly presents, persists.

Similarly, in the debate concerning whether Joyce was a realist or a relativist, the relativist camp continues to predominate, although authoritative and persuasive voices are being raised to argue the contrary case, and the legacy of Hugh Kenner remains difficult to dismiss, persistently asserting itself by virtue of his formidable critical intelligence and the textual fidelity of his interpretations.

There are indicators that the tide may be turning. Some contemporary critics are beginning to probe and question Ellmann's legacy. As early as 1965, Jesuit Father and respected Joycean, William Noon, expressed grave reservations concerning the paltriness of Ellmann's treatment of the Catholic influence in Joyce,[23] and prominent contemporary Joyceans like John McCourt have recently repeated those reservations. On the other hand, no less prominent contemporary Joyceans like Umberto Eco, himself an apostate, and Geert Lernout, in recently published books and articles which I will examine at greater length in the course of this study, continue to insist that Joyce is a post-Catholic and often anti-Catholic secularist, humanist writer.

One name deserving of special mention in this context is that of Weldon Thornton. Thornton has been a major voice in the post-Ellmann era of the Joycean debate, making an indelible mark with the publication of his *Allusions in Ulysses* and subsequent works which will feature prominently in the first chapter of this book. His argument that Joyce, far from being a champion of what he calls "the Modernist Syndrome," is an ingenious and prophetic critic of the same, has not yet been fully confronted and assimilated in the Joycean *milieu*. Thornton argues with a combination of impressive scholarship, incisive interpretive skill, and implacable logic, that Joyce remained a realist from first to last.

This book takes Thornton's thesis a step further, arguing that Joyce is a religious writer (open to a transcendental reality) as well as a realist, or at least that his realism is not at all incompatible with religion and, particularly, with Catholicism; that the driving focus of his art is synthesis and not rupture. The implications of this for such eminent relativist writers, thinkers, and social observers as Umberto Eco and Gabriel García Márquez, who have seen in Joyce a source of inspiration and authority, a mentor figure, are, to understate matters, challenging. In fact, the discovery of Joyce as religious and realist would have repercussions for all of the fields of intellectual discourse above mentioned—i.e. semiotics, politics, gender ideology, psychology, and feminism—not to mention the field of literary criticism.

Is Joyce a realist or a relativist? Is he religious or is he a secularist? These are not peripheral questions. Nor may they be numbered as two more issues of equal status with all the others on the interminable Joycean list. Rather, all the other questions and answers would be affected by the answers to these two. If Joyce may be identified as a believer in objective universal truths and in a transcendental principle at work in human affairs, then conclusions may be drawn from this regarding his position on a range of related issues. Moreover, if his position on issues like gender identity, for example, may be identified, conclusions may be drawn from this also regarding whether or not he is a believer in objective universal truths or such a transcendental principle. This latter question is the subject of this study, but the former question is intimately related to it. A clear statement, from the outset, of the parameters and focus of my argument is necessary.

1.5: Terms and Boundaries

1.5.1: Clarification of Terms

The first term requiring clarification is that of relativism. My study begins from the premise that relativism, though at first glance an exaltation and even an absolutization of human freedom, is nonetheless, when taken to its ultimate logical conclusions, a dogmatic and tyrannical absolutization of the human ego. It is therefore inimical both to social harmony and to true personal individuation and is conducive to what Cardinal Joseph Ratzinger has called "the dictatorship of relativism."[24] Realism, on the other hand, attributes a prior and ultimate authority to an entity, be it Being and/or God, other than the human ego. In this it has much in common with religion. If it can be shown that Joyce ascribes authoritative priority to an entity other than the human ego, although the human I may respond to and then participate in this authority, this would establish Joyce as a philosophical realist and favorably introduce the possibility that he is also a religious writer.[25]

In clarifying these positions—the relativist, the realist, and the religious—I will have recourse to Catholic thinkers, like Ratzinger, who are posterior to Joyce, but it will be clear whenever this occurs that such thinkers are responding, with the benefit of greater hindsight, to dilemmas with which Joyce had earlier wrestled, and that their thought is already contained, if sometimes only embryonically, in the Catholic Tradition prior to Joyce. The Catholic intellectual establishment in Ireland and elsewhere underwent what I term a "theological hiatus" that coincided, more or less, with Joyce's lifetime, which was subsequently rectified without disconnecting from the Catholic Tradition. The clarity of Ratzinger's reflections in *Deus Caritas Est*, for example, on the subject of love as a coalescence of *eros* and *agape*, will help us to understand conceptual and emotional dilemmas which Joyce had also struggled to understand and represent in his art.

The term individuation also requires clarification. The title of chapter III is "Joycean Individuation," and the title of chapter IV is "Judeo-Christian Individuation." I do not use this term in a strictly Jungian sense but rather in a general sense indicating the process by which an individual human being, in interaction with others and as a result of life experiences, matures to become the fully human personality that he or she is capable of becoming.

A preliminary clarifying word needs to be given here

also regarding the term "secular" and its multiple derivatives throughout this book. To provide one example of the many that will appear, Geert Lernout, in his book *Help My Unbelief*, speaks of Joyce's offering us, through his adolescent *alter ego* Stephen Dedalus, a "secular" creed: "The closest we get to a secular creed on Stephen's part is . . . just before he is ready to leave Bloom's house."[26] I will discuss this moment in detail in chapter I, but I mention it also here in order to clarify that Lernout uses the term, as do most Joyce critics, in a general and wide-ranging sense, as if it were an antonym of words like transcendental and religious. Thus used, the term "secular" is closely related to others like atheist and agnostic, immanentist or skeptic. Although commonplace, this usage is a semantic oversimplification and distortion.

The one word "secular" denotes critically distinct positions. It has much in common with the biblical word "world," which also has a diverse and confusing semantic content; in English this one word is employed to render several distinct words in Hebrew and in Greek. "World" has three meanings: firstly, the world as cosmos, created by God and therefore "very good" (cf. Gen 1:31); secondly, fallen humanity so loved by God that He sent his Son to save it (cf. Jn 3:16); and, thirdly, the collective atmosphere of evil, fruit of diabolic activity and human moral corruption, which murderously "hates" the Son and his disciples (cf. Jn 15:18).

Similarly, "secularity" is seen, by opponents of Christianity and by some Christians, in terms of outright rejection of religion; whereas others, who would self-identify as Christians, see it in terms of a critical embrace of this-worldly values and dynamics which have their origin in God and are therefore necessarily good. In the case of both terms—*world* and *secularity*—an ample perspective that recognizes the positive as well as the negative aspects of the terms and the realities represented—a position neither of acritical acceptance nor of total rejection—better reflects the Scriptural and the traditional Catholic position. I will argue that the terms secular and religious are not antonyms and that neither Joyce nor the Catholic tradition sees them as such. Although many Joyce critics use the term secularity in the first sense just described, I will use it in this third sense, and provide justification for my preference for this nuance when the occasion arises. It has important implications which will be made evident.

Having clarified the terms relativism, individuation and secularity, a preliminary word is required, too, to clarify the boundaries of my argument, or, some might say, the lack thereof. I will merge categories usually kept strictly separate—especially those of theology and literature—and this also requires justification and explanation.

1.5.2: Clarification of Boundaries

The categories of theology and literature are not mutually exclusive. Declan Kiberd, referring to the writer Samuel Beckett, remarks that he "always wrote out of the conviction that theology was too important to be left to theologians."[27] No theologian worthy of the name would disagree with this conviction, although it does beg the rejoinder that literature is too important to be left to literary critics. Charles Moeller, a pioneer in the field of confronting modern literature with Catholic theology, wrote that:

> My intention . . . is to give a few lessons of theology: theology has a bad name, for which theologians are frequently to blame. However, it seems to me feasible to incarnate some essential Christian truths with the aid of contemporary literary works. It is possible that, by chasing two hares at the same time, that of literary criticism and that of catechism, both of them escape me. I fear that neither the theologians nor the lettered will be satisfied.[28]

I commence this work with intentions similar to those of Moeller and with the same trepidation. Nevertheless, there is common ground between the artist and the theologian, the philosopher and the poet, the historian and literary critic.

Theological dialogue with Joyce is possible and fruitful not only because of the common ground he specifically shares (as we will see) with Catholicism, but also because of an original overlap between the theological and the poetic tasks. In Plato's *Republic* Socrates famously exiled the poets from his ideal city, establishing the "ancient quarrel" between poetry and philosophy, with the human soul as the contested terrain, but in Book X he lets them back in, challenging them to better creative and more constructive behavior; indicating the possibility of cooperation. The *Republic* itself is a work of literature and a work of philosophy. The same may be said of Augustine's *Confessions*. Subsequently there occurred a gradual compartmentalization of disciplines that led to a separation of genres. But a common ground—in subject matter always and in form often—remains. Josef Pieper has written of a "natural connection" between art, religion, and philosophy by virtue of their "common power to disturb and transcend."[29] He invokes the authority of Aquinas in favor of this view: "[A]s for the close connection between philosophy and poetry, we can refer to a little-known statement by Thomas Aquinas . . . the Philosopher is akin to the Poet in this, that both are concerned with the *mirandum*, the 'wondrous,' the astonishing."[30]

The common denominator between mythology, theology, philosophy, and poetry is beauty, with its surprising, epiphanical irruptions in everyday realities. St. Augustine's famous exclamation is addressed, tellingly, to God as Beauty: "Late I came to know you, Beauty ancient yet new. Late I loved you."[31] Hans Urs Von Balthasar lamented the divorce of aesthetics from theology and championed the soteriological role of beauty, intrisically allied to "her two sisters," truth and goodness: "[B]eauty demands for itself at least as much courage and decision as do truth and goodness, and she will not allow herself to be separated and banned from her two sisters without taking them along with herself in an act of mysterious vengeance."[32] Von Balthasar maintains that superciliously to marginalize aesthetics in performing the theological task would exact a high price: "We can be sure that whoever sneers at her name as if she were the ornament of a bourgeois past—whether he admits it or not—can no longer pray and soon will no longer be able to love."³³

In August 2002 Joseph Ratzinger expressed regret that while many "details" of Von Balthasar's grand concept may be found in subsequent theological reflection, "his fundamental approach, in truth the essential element of the whole work, has not been so readily accepted." Ratzinger concurs with Von Balthasar that theology performed without love is mere Gnosticism:

> Being overcome by the beauty of Christ is a more real, more profound knowledge than mere rational deduction. Of course we must not underestimate the importance of theological reflection, of exact and careful theological thought; it is still absolutely necessary. But to despise, on that account, the impact produced by the heart's encounter with beauty, or to reject it as a true form of knowledge, would impoverish us and dry up both faith and theology. We must rediscover this form of knowledge—it is an urgent demand of the present hour.³⁴

Beauty is an essential aspect of God's way of relating to us, of his being good to us, revealing truth to us, saving us. Matter, sensuality, beauty, and manifestations of meaning are intimately interrelated elements of the soteriological *modus operandi*. Ratzinger evokes a Beautiful Truth that defies categorical comprehension and provokes worshipful awe, memorably evoked also by Christian thinker Michael Polanyi: "Christianity sedulously fosters, and in a sense permanently satisfies, man's craving for mental dissatisfaction by offering him the comfort of a crucified God."[35] We will see that Joyce's art critiques forms of beauty that ultimately fail to satisfy and celebrates a mystery that combines *eros* and *agape* and defies categorical definition.

Pieper, in *Enthusiasm and the Divine Madness*, neatly affirms the distinctness between the religious and artistic modes of expression—"Naturally, we will not go so far as to speak bluntly of a *divine* voice speaking through the poet's own"—without denying their relatedness:

"But could we very confidently assert that the power of great poetry to stir the soul has no connection whatsoever with the ultimate, allembracing divine Ground of the universe?"[36] Joyce held a similar belief in the power of poetry and the task of the poet, speaking of the artist as being "like the God of the creation,"[37] and aspiring to become "priest of the eternal imagination."[38]

1.5.3: A Common Ground Explored by Joyce

To venture into the world of Joycean literary criticism is to be surprised at how much is being said there about Catholic orthodoxy and theology with varying degrees of accuracy and often without response. Joyce himself, by his recurring employment of Catholic imagery, has given origin to this vein of speculation. We are about to enter an already-existing dialogue on the subject of James Joyce's religious position in which, according to my perception, orthodox Catholicism has thus far been under-represented. A recurring feature of the Joycean debate, however, according to the reading I will propose, is a tendency to underestimate and over-simplify not only the depth, complexity and richness of the Catholic tradition, but also the depth, complexity and richness of Joyce's engagement with the same.

The first premise of my approach, frankly stated from the outset, is that James Joyce, baptized and educated as a Catholic, became an apostate. The goal is not to re-claim him for Catholicism but to discover what *kind* of an apostate he became, how far his apostasy from Catholicism took him from religious belief. As we have briefly glimpsed, the matter is not as self-evident as it first appears. Joyce is a figure of particular interest, given that he is an early and pre-eminent apostate of the modern age, and therefore emblematic. His case sheds light on the color of post-Catholic secularism and atheism in the 20th century. How far from Catholic beliefs did Joyce's apostasy actually take him? When faith is lost, how does Catholicism survive? How does it manifest its lingering influence? Joyce was confoundingly capable of intense aversion and vehement diatribe towards the Catholic Church, and, almost simultaneously, of a nuanced and favorable disposition towards the historical Catholic contribution.

2: Contours of the Debate

2.1: Catholic Nostalgia

Joyce's brother Stanislaus also wrote of his brother that, "He was habitually a very late riser, but wherever he was, alone in Paris or married in Trieste, he never failed to get up at about five in all weathers to go to the early morning Mass on Holy Thursday and Good Friday."[39] R.J. Schork, in an article published in 1999, mentions this well-known and oft-commented fact that, "Throughout his life Joyce liked to attend Eastertide services, at various ecclesiastical venues." Schork provides several testimonies from friends and family concerning Joyce's continuing devotion to the Easter liturgy, to the point of "secret tears," and then deduces that "The magnet that drew Joyce to these ceremonies was not some residual trace of personal piety, but an abiding appreciation for the music and hymns."[40]

But before thus distinguishing (precipitously) between personal piety and appreciation of the music, Schork quotes a friend of Joyce who in turn quotes Joyce himself on his reasons for attending the liturgies. Joyce stated that he liked to attend the liturgies because they "represented by their symbolic rituals the oldest mysteries of humanity."[41] This suggests that there was more in it for Joyce than the music, and that there was more in the music for Joyce. Music is a vehicle not only of delight but also and more importantly of meaning. The conventional assumption that Joyce's motive for attending these ceremonies was purely and solely aesthetic is an interpretation as reductive of aesthetics as it is of Joyce.

Joyce was notoriously impatient with aestheticism and with sentimentalism. He was also an alert observer of the common ground between myth, literature, and religion. Even his declaration of war on the Catholic Church paradoxically suggests shared and disputed terrain; one does not wage war against irrelevancies. If Joyce's interest in the Easter liturgy had been solely academic or intellectual, one or several attendances would have been sufficient to satisfy that interest; the fact that he returned repeatedly to these ceremonies, when already familiar with them, to the extent of lifelong annual participation, suggests that he was seeking out an experience that was aesthetic or existential or religious or all of these together, as well as intellectual. To repeat his own words, as reported by his friend Mercanton, he may have been seeking to experience again and again "the oldest mysteries of humanity."[42] In short, perhaps something deeper and more complex was going on.

2.2: "Christ-Hauntedness"

Although not in many points an orthodox Catholic approach, the guiding principle of Declan Kiberd's reading of Joyce is more neutral and ample than that of Geert Lernout. Kiberd quotes varying sources that converge on the point of Joyce's ambiguity in relation to religion, beginning on a negative note: "When asked why he chose Odysseus rather than Christ as a model for Bloom, Joyce was curt. Living with a woman was one of the most difficult things a man could do—and Jesus was a bachelor who never did it."[43] To this three possible responses spring to mind: that Homer's epic has little to do with Odysseus living with a woman; that Bloom *is* in fact modeled upon Christ; and that God in Christ married humanity and the Church.

Kiberd continues: "Yet Joyce was haunted by the mystery he flouted. According to Francini Bruni, his friend in

Trieste, 'He only completely admires the unchangeable: the mystery of Christ and the mute drama that surrounds it.'"[44] This is followed by the testimonies of his devout sister: "I think that all of Jim's loves were really created in the love of God,"[45] and of his atheist brother: "[H]e who has loved God in youth can never love anything that is less than divine."[46]

Kiberd's use of the term "haunted" ("by the mystery he flouted") recalls the oft-quoted words of the American Catholic writer Flannery O'Connor: "By and large, the South is not so much Christ-centered as it is Christ-haunted. The southerner who isn't convinced of it is very much afraid that he may have been formed in the image and likeness of God."[47] O'Connor greatly admired and often recommended Joyce's writings, and once, in the context of mentioning modern writers who manifest "a hunger for a Catholic completeness in life," said of him that he "can't get rid of it no matter what he does."[48] In the shift from Christ-centeredness to Christ-hauntedness Joyce may be seen as prophetic and emblematic of the modern age. He is therefore perennially and immensely *relevant*. Apart from the interesting complexity of his relationship with Catholicism, he also offers insights to the complex phenomenon of atheism.

We will see that there are many shades to the phenomenon of atheism in the world of Joyce criticism; and Joyce and Joyceans do not always share the same religious and philosophical positions. Joyce was a passionate believer in the soul, as he himself wrote in a letter to Lady Gregory: "All things are inconstant except the faith in the soul, which changes all things and fills their inconstancy with light. And though I seem to have been driven out of my country here as a misbeliever I have found no man yet with a faith like mine."[49]

There are atheisms that deny the existence of the soul. Joyce was evidently not an atheist of this kind. There are atheisms that deny the existence of transcendental reality. It remains to be seen whether or not Joyce categorically and irrevocably made this denial. He certainly never made it explicitly; whether or not he made it *implicitly* is our subject of analysis. Joyce does not see the human person as capable of individualist self-realization, or even see this as desirable. Man becomes himself in relationship with others and in receptive response to a mysterious agent of individuating dynamism, immanently present and active, inherent to the spirit of man but also extraneous to it, an agent to whom believers might be tempted to refer as the mysterious transcendental Other, though we cannot be sure that Joyce would have done so.

2.3: Trajectory of my Argument

As mentioned above, my research has uncovered three main areas of common ground and/or disputed ground, between Catholic and Joycean fields of discourse: epiphany, individuating dynamics, and the Eucharist. The first and third of these themes—epiphany and the Eucharist—are the primary Catholic "bones of contention" among Joyce critics. The second one, individuation and divine grace, has not been much addressed, in spite of Stanislaus Joyce's testimony that James was fascinated by Augustine's doctrine on grace. Joyce explicitly engages with the theme of epiphany and the teachings of Aquinas in his first novel, *Portrait of the Artist*, and, both in *Portrait* and in *Ulysses*, he makes explicit references to the Eucharist which are central to the development of the narrative. His treatment of the theme of grace and engagement with Augustine are generally implicit rather than explicit, which explains the sparsity of critical commentary thereon. However, in spite of differences in vocabulary, a phenomenon suggestively similar to the workings of grace may be identified in both novels, lending weight to Stanislaus's report.

My methodology will be to follow the Joycean trajectory insofar as it touches these three areas of Catholic teachings. This will enable me to assess the range and depth of Joyce's vestigial Catholicism. I will assess the extent of Joyce's post-apostasy "Catholic categories," much spoken of but not methodically confronted and examined as I propose to do here, with the amplitude and authority afforded by the patrimonial riches of the faith, exercising due economy and discrimination.

In the first chapter, I will examine the first concrete area of overlapping terrain; namely that of epiphany and Joyce's Thomist aesthetic as it is presented in *Portrait*, and the implications thereof regarding his philosophical position as realist or relativist. Chapter II, "*Agape without Eros*," will examine Joyce's short story "Eveline" and his novel *Portrait of the Artist*, both of which contain revealing data concerning late 19th and early 20th century Irish Catholicism and Joyce's view thereof. This chapter constitutes an important contextual curtain-raiser to the more extensive reading of Joyce's work that will follow thereafter. In the third chapter, I will trace the Joycean trajectory of personal individuation as reflected in his writings, with implicit and explicit reference to Catholic teachings on the dynamics of divine grace. The fourth chapter will avail of accumulated information to identify resonances on the subject of personal individuation between Joyce and leading representatives of the Judeo-Christian tradition with whom he engages: Moses, Saints Augustine, Thomas Aquinas, and Ignatius of Loyola. In the fifth and final chapter, I will discuss the treatment of the Eucharist in his writings with the aid of published readings by Joyce scholars.

In all five chapters we will discover real coincidences in the midst of apparent discrepancies. Joyce's complex treatment of Catholicism poses challenges to consider, questions to answer, criticisms to accept, to refute or to qualify, and "alternatives" to Catholic doctrine which on closer inspection prove not to be alternatives at all but rather coincidences with the Catholic intellectual and spiritual tradition. The newness of my contribution is threefold. I will provide a synthesis of the arguments that Joyce is a realist (by Thornton, Levy and others, against the positions of Ellmann, Lernout, Umberto Eco, and others); I will compare the Joycean anthropology of personal individuation with Catholic teachings on the workings of grace; and I will confront the alleged blasphemy in Joyce's writings, especially in relation to the Eucharist.

I will not discuss Joyce's last and most dauntingly complex work, *Finnegans Wake*. As Weldon Thornton has put it, "this book is fundamentally different . . . in the nature of the underlying issues that it addresses and consequently in the aspects of the psyche and of reality that it evokes and represents."[50] Thornton discerns a pedagogical, paradigmatic agenda in Ulysses—"Ulysses is in some degree paradigmatic of how Joyce feels we should respond to our own life crises"—and maintains this is not the case in *Finnegans Wake*: "But this is not to say that *Finnegans Wake* is valueless, any more than to say that our dreams and fantasies are valueless. It is simply to acknowledge that the aim of *Finnegans Wake* is radically different from that of the earlier novels."[51]

This study does not pretend to be an exhaustive theological response to Joyce's oeuvre in its entirety. It will be selective but nonetheless representative of Joyce's thought as interpreted by noted and established Joyce critics. I do not hope to arrive at a conclusion to end all debate. My purpose is to gain a greater understanding of Joyce's relationship with Catholicism and thereby to understand his post-Catholic religious, or atheist, position. To achieve this, I will examine particular themes that Catholic authors, and Joyce, have extensively addressed, entering a dialogue between Catholicism and Joyce (and Joyceans) that already exists.

My primary and recurring focus will be to explore the nature of Joyce's post-apostasy position regarding transcendental reality. The object is to discover, by analyzing Joyce's aesthetic adaptation of Catholic categories, whether or not he opted for a clear and definitive position, be it atheist or religious. This question entails engagement with the many and varied interrogatives he raises. The final summary and conclusion will consider the options presented by the evidence and suggest the nature of Joyce's "atheism." By way of a secondary effect, we will see if Joyce's literary vision can be accommodated within the orthodox Catholic spiritual tradition.

CHAPTER I:

JAMES JOYCE: RELATIVIST OR REALIST?

I.1: Introduction

The purpose of this chapter is to focus our interpretive lenses. There are many competing ways in which our interpretive lenses get focused, and some schools of Joyce criticism have poorly focused lenses. They do not give us a clear picture of Joyce. As explained in my Introduction,[1] relativism is a school of thought that interprets "truth" in terms of subjective projection. Realism, on the other hand, interprets it in terms of an objective given which it is the subject's task actively and creatively to discover, assimilate, and communicate. This distinction is related to the matter of religious belief. If an apostate were subsequently to become a relativist, he would thereby distance himself further from religious belief than if he were to remain a realist.

Relativism and realism are two irreconcilable approaches to reality with diametrically opposed implications in the realms of faith and morals. In his encyclical letter, *Veritatis Splendor,* Pope John Paul II explained the radically diverse implications of the realist and relativist approaches to truth and being in the ambit of morality: "In the case of the correct conscience, it is a question of the *objective truth* received by man; in the case of the erroneous conscience, it is a question of what man, mistakenly, *subjectively* considers to be true" (*VS* 63). If Joyce remained a realist, then he shares this at least in common with the Catholic tradition; philosophical realism is compatible with and even characteristic of religious belief and recognition of objective moral norms. But many Joyce readers see Joyce as a pioneer and champion of relativism.

The positions of the relativist school of Joyce criticism will be presented first, and afterwards we will see an alternative perspective which will help us to understand the distortions of that school and to focus our lenses so we can get a clear look at Joyce the man, his times, and his work. It makes sense to engage in this perusal of the trends of Joycean literary discussion before narrowing our focus on the writer himself and his work. He is often introduced to us, without our realizing it, by experts whose readings are distorted by their own interpretive lenses, perhaps without their realizing it too. A necessary preliminary step, therefore, is to make explicit the possible ways to focus our interpretive camera. The question of the religious mind of Joyce emerges inevitably from this process of focusing the lens, because it is a recurring aspect of the literary criticism which, in turn, emerges from his life and work.

This chapter will present the two major positions with respect to the religious mind of Joyce. The theory of aesthetics expounded by Stephen Dedalus in *Portrait* is a propitious point of entry. This will be followed by an account of recent contributions to the debate on Joyce's aesthetics which will, in turn, be followed by a reflection by Joseph Ratzinger on two hermeneutical approaches to reality and truth. The remainder of the chapter will apply Ratzinger's reflections to the two major currents of Joyce criticism, by the end of which we will be in a better position to discern whether Joyce was a realist in the mold of Aristotle and Aquinas, or a thinker and writer in the postmodern, relativist mould.

I.2: The Aesthetics Debate

I.2.1: Stephen's Thomist Aesthetic in Stephen Hero and in Portrait

The posthumously published *Stephen Hero* draft of *Portrait* clearly states Stephen's indebtedness to Thomist thought for his aesthetic theory: "His Esthetic was in the main applied Aquinas." Stephen aspires to be an artist, and so, he strives intellectually to elaborate a personal philosophy of art. The language used is notably Aristotelian and Thomist in its subject-object coordinates. The artist, as "mediator," is "gifted with twin faculties, a selective faculty and a reproductive faculty."[2] The selective faculty is focused on experience, and the reproductive faculty on artfully recreating in words that which is extracted from experience by the selective faculty.

Stephen articulates his theory in an essay, "Art and Life," which the College President refuses to publish on the grounds that it "would emancipate the poet from all moral laws." Stephen answers, "I have only pushed to its logical conclusion the definition Aquinas has given of the beautiful . . . *Pulcra sunt quae visa placent.*"[3] He rejects the notion that art must elevate and instruct, thus remaining subordinate to moral laws, and invokes the authority of

Aquinas on this point. When Stephen reads his paper at a meeting of the Literary and Historical Society, the College dean and professor of English, Fr. Butt, effectively makes the same critique; grudgingly admitting, though, that Stephen's approach is also legitimate: "Mr Dedalus had chosen to consider beauty intrinsically and to neglect these other considerations. But beauty also has its practical side."[4]

The distinction between the intrinsic and moral considerations of beauty arises also in Stephen's discussions with Fr. Artifoni, from whom he receives lessons in Italian, and with whom he engages in religious and philosophical discussion. For Aquinas, and for Stephen, the true and the beautiful are desirable goods which operate on related but not identical registers, allowing a certain autonomy to the beautiful, to the imagination, and to art. In later reflections, Stephen gives this tribute to the influence of Thomas in the "formulation of his artistic creed": he "found item after item upheld for him in advance by the greatest and most orthodox doctor of the Church."[5]

The concept of epiphany also arose conveniently for Stephen's purposes out of the mass of Catholic theology: "By an epiphany he meant a sudden spiritual manifestation, whether in the vulgarity of speech or of gesture or in a memorable phase of the mind itself." These "most delicate and evanescent of moments" are the focus and fodder of the "man of letters." He must observe and record and reproduce them. The ontological priority of the observed object is recognized as a given and never eclipsed in his thought. It is the starting-point of his whole theory: "Consider the performance of your own mind when confronted with any object, hypothetically beautiful."[6]

For further understanding of the aesthetic dynamic, Stephen turns again to St. Thomas Aquinas: "Aquinas says: The three things requisite for beauty are, integrity, a wholeness, symmetry and radiance." Having briefly defined the first two aspects, he ascribes particular importance to the third (*claritas*; radiance), speaking, whether notionally or literally it is hard to say, of the mind "discovering" these qualities sequentially, not simultaneously, in one intuitive moment. It is when the mind "discovers the third quality" that epiphany happens: "This is the moment which I call epiphany."[7] Here, the emphasis is on the protagonism of the perceiving subject, but the objective reference is not lost.

In *Portrait* itself, the novel of which the surviving parts of the *Stephen Hero* manuscript is a mutilated sketch, several of the above statements have been cut, others remain, as does the gist of the argument, and one extra statement is added. Specifically, Aquinas's definition of beauty—*Pulcra sunt quae visa placent*—remains, as do the references to the truth, as "desired by the intellectual appetite . . . appeased by the most satisfying relations of the intelligible," and to beauty, as "desired by the esthetic appetite . . . appeased by the most satisfying relations of the sensible." The added statement refers precisely to the objective or ontological coordinate of Stephen's theory: "So far as this side of esthetic philosophy extends, Aquinas will carry me all along the line."[8] In *Portrait* as well as in *Stephen Hero*, Stephen clearly *thinks* he is being Thomistic, and it is unlikely that Stephen or Joyce thought Thomas to be a relativist.

In short, Stephen accepts the Thomistic ontological reference as his starting point. His reflections flow therefrom to the subjective operations of the perceiving, conceiving artist: "When we come to the phenomena of artistic conception, artistic gestation, and artistic reproduction I require a new terminology and a new personal experience."[9] The Thomist identification of the three constituent "qualities of universal beauty"—"*integritas, consonantia, claritas* . . . wholeness, harmony, and radiance"[10]—also remain, as do Stephen's elaborations thereon (focusing mostly on the triple, phaseal apprehension of the perceiving subject).

I.2.2: The Convertibility of the Transcendentals

Joyce critics have argued back and forth about whether or not Stephen's "Thomist aesthetic" is truly Thomist. The nature and extent of the "newness" that Joyce adds to the thought of St. Thomas has provoked debate in Joyce circles from the beginning up to the recent present. Some have argued that the element of newness consists of radical departure; others argue that there is radical continuity between Joyce and Aquinas and that the newness consists of development, not departure.

As recently as 2011, Fran O'Rourke, for example, professor of philosophy at Joyce's *alma mater,* University College Dublin, wrote that Stephen's (and Joyce's) adoption of St. Thomas's thought in this area betrays a fundamental misapprehension of his alleged mentor and is anti-Thomist in the name of Thomism: "Joyce apparently is unfamiliar with Aquinas's metaphysics regarding the relations among being, goodness, truth and beauty (the doctrine of transcendentals)."[11] O'Rourke's objection is effectively a repetition of the objection articulated by Umberto Eco in *The Aesthetics of Chaosmos*:

> In the Thomist hierarchy of ends and means, the value of an object is established upon the relationship of means to ends: the entire thing is evaluated in terms of the supernatural ends to which man is oriented. Beauty, Goodness, and Truth are reciprocally implicated. Thus a statue used for obscene or magical ends is intrinsically ugly, reflected in the sinister light of its distorted finality.[12]

In the *Stephen Hero* sketch of *Portrait*, the very same accusation made by O'Rourke and Eco is put to Stephen by the College President, as we have seen above, and by Fr. Butt. Therefore, in *Stephen Hero* Joyce anticipated and rejected the accusation that he was distorting Thomist thought. As we have also seen, the fictional Fr. Artifoni supports Stephen's reading of Aquinas on this point, and the fictional Fr. Butt admits that beauty may be considered intrinsically and independently of its final end. Both Artifoni and Butt admit that the thwarting of that final end would not impact negatively, according to Thomas and contrary to Eco, on the intrinsic beauty of the beautiful object thus misused; it would remain intrinsically beautiful in spite of its extrinsic misuse. This interpretation of Thomas has been supported by a contemporary Thomist scholar.

Dominican Thomist Fr. Antoine Levy makes this very argument against Eco, admitting the legitimacy of Stephen's reading as did Frs. Butt and Artifoni. In an article published in 2010, Levy affirms that art does in fact, according to Aquinas (as claimed by Stephen), enjoy a relative autonomy from the good and the true:

> Aquinas would certainly have considered the case of a religious statue used for obscene ends as an evil thing, since one of the goals of a religious statue is to be used for reverent worship. But the fact that a statue can be improperly handled has nothing to do with the statue's inherent aesthetic claim . . . Beauty, according to Aquinas, has a logic of its own in reference to the adequacy of means and ends . . . The teaching on the convertibility of the transcendentals implies that Beauty points to Goodness and Truth simply by being what it is: beautiful.[13]

Levy arrives at the same conclusion as Stephen regarding the thought of Aquinas: "Aesthetics applies some logic of its own to reality, a logic which is distinct from moral goodness and scientific truth."[14] Thus, Levy shows that there is a way of reconciling art as a conception of something independent while maintaining its connection to the true and the good; as we have seen, Fr. Butt recognized the possibility of considering beauty intrinsically, and Stephen said to Fr. Artifoni that there is no need to contrast the good and the beautiful. This is Levy's point also.

Therefore, Levy affirms, Stephen is right when he claims Aquinas as an authority who legitimizes artistic autonomy: "The fact that aesthetics has a register of its own sets the artist free from having to conform his work of representation to a set of predetermined moral norms."[15] This would imply that Stephen would not *need* to distance himself from Aquinas, would not need to divorce beauty from truth and goodness or intellect from imagination, in the forging of his own aesthetic charter, since for Aquinas beauty already has "a logic of its own." This responds to the objection made by O'Rourke and Eco. Joyce has not divorced beauty from truth. This debate is connected to the Joycean debate about epiphany and ontology, as we will now see.

I.2.3: Epiphany and Ontology

This Joycean debate revolves around Joyce's adaptation of the Catholic term "epiphany," meaning manifestation. The concept is by its nature referential to a reality that is present but customarily hidden. It straddles the transcendental and the immanent, the otherworldly and the this-worldly, remitting the observer to a dimension that is fleetingly manifest in the material. Roy Gottfried offers this explanation: "Epiphany is clearly about something transcendent in the world the artist observes: the real world of people, events, and places engages something spiritual which illuminates them from behind or beyond [I would add: or within], and the artist has a superior role in its revelation."[16] Since by definition epiphany entails ontology—a radiance of truth which it is the artist's role to transmit—the term, adopted from the Catholic liturgy by Stephen Dedalus and central to his aesthetic, is a recurrent issue in Joycean debate. Neither Joyce nor Stephen ever explicitly renounces the ontological dimension of epiphany.

It may be argued that, by omitting in the final version of *Portrait* the earlier ontological references and thus highlighting the subjective side of the phenomenon, Joyce has distanced himself from the earlier portrayal of Stephen and therefore also from Aquinas. This omission seems to tip the scales in favor of the psychological machinations of the perceiving subject and away from Thomistic ontology. However, it was Aquinas who introduced the subjective psychological coordinate to the conversation about beauty, as the Jesuit William T. Noon has explained in his book *Joyce and Aquinas*. Aquinas, true to the holism and equilibrium that characterizes his approach to reality, added to the notion of beauty a subjective, psychological dimension not found in previous thinkers: "Saint Thomas introduced a really new dimension into 'aesthetic' discussion by his insistence that the experience of beauty must be as much considered in its psychological as in its ontological aspects."[17]

This fact obviously favors the argument that there is continuity between Aquinas and Joyce. Umberto Eco argues, however, that Stephen's appropriation of this Thomist contribution exaggerates the subjective dimension amounting to an essential separation from the Thomist inspiration: "Joyce interprets the three criteria, not as objective properties of things, but rather as stages in our aesthetic encounter with them . . . It is clear that to understand Aquinas's term in this fashion is to strip it of its original ontological character."[18] Eco, contradicting Stephen, speaks of radical departure. Joyce has "stripped" his Thomist inspiration of its ontological character.

I.2.4: Eco's Reading and Levy's Critique

Antoine Levy, against Eco, argues that there is an easy harmony between the aesthetic ideas of Stephen Dedalus in *Stephen Hero* and *Portrait* and those of St. Thomas Aquinas, whom Stephen himself claims as the source of their inspiration, and that these ideas continued to shape Joyce's art in *Ulysses*, in spite of the fact that Stephen/Joyce adds an emphasis on the role of the subjective imagination to St. Thomas's statements. According to Levy, this emphasis is already present in Thomist thought (even if it is augmented by Joyce): "[W]hen Joyce speaks of imagination as a faculty that beholds the content of sensitive perception, he is moving on firm Thomistico-Aristotelian ground."[19]

Eco maintains that Joyce outgrew and distanced himself from the Thomist aesthetic, that this departure is already hinted at in Stephen's adaptations, and will be consummated in *Ulysses*. Levy explains as much: "Reading *Opera Aperta* and *Chaosmos* gives one the impression that Joyce was somehow caught up by the fluidity of a notion he had at some point wanted to scholasticise or crystallise in some superficial manner."[20] But Levy points out Eco's mistake, showing that there is no contradiction between existential fluidity and aesthetic perception and expression, and that "what Joyce calls an epiphany, the sudden aesthetic stability of existential fluidity,"[21] achieves this reconciliation.

When Stephen speaks of the truth as beheld by the intellect appeased by the most satisfying relations of the intelligible and beauty beheld by the imagination, which is appeased by the most satisfying relations of the sensible, he is still in Thomist territory, given that the ontological reference is still present: "The *convenientia*—the harmonious distribution of the parts that comprise external entities—somehow 'rings a bell' in the inner structure that constitutes us as perceiving subjects." Levy points out that although St. Thomas never uses the word *imaginatio*, its "precise equivalent, *phantasia*,"[22] performs the operation Joyce describes.

While Umberto Eco sees artistic maturation in the abandonment of the epiphany motif (because of its alleged intrinsic opposition to the fluidity of reality) in favor of an approach that refuses to fix and to impose form on what is fluid and formless, Levy argues that, since the epiphany motif is in fact intrinsically respectful of existential fluidity, the suggestion that Joyce perceived the need to abandon it is itself a groundless supposition and superimposition. Therefore: "[O]ne can only wonder at the reasons that have induced Eco to underestimate Joyce's adhesion to the principles of Aquinas's aesthetics in such a flagrant manner."[23]

The school of interpretation which Umberto Eco represents, in coherence with its philosophy of fragmentation and relativism, maintains that the maturer Joyce abandoned the notion of epiphany. In the final part of his article, Levy addresses this argument with a reinterpretation of the very passage of *Ulysses* in which Eco discovers this abandonment: "I contend that this passage simply cannot be understood in any way other than as suggesting a directly antithetical perspective." Instead of rupture, Levy discovers interdependence: "Its use of the epiphany concept demonstrates that the Modern rests on the Medieval as on its insuperable hermeneutical horizon."[24] Here is Levy's conclusion:

> In this manner, it is clear that far from describing the disintegration of the Aristotelian-Thomistic notion of epiphany, the passage of Joyce is the demonstration of its almost unbounded fecundity. As promised in *A Portrait,* the Aristotelian aesthetics of Aquinas has really 'carried' Joyce 'all along the line,' down to the point where Aquinas's *claritas* becomes able to fuse with Blake's most revolutionary insights regarding the secret power of imagination. As people use the reverberating power concealed in the hollow of seashells to hear the music of the sea, it is now clear that, contrary to Eco's interpretation, Joyce has never ceased to rely on Aquinas aesthetics to transcribe the music of his world—what we call the modern world.[25]

There is no need, then, to contradict Joyce's own declarations through Stephen in *Portrait*, and there is no evidence that he changed his aesthetic philosophy.[26] According to Levy, Stephen, indebted to Aquinas and expressly recognizing that debt, has arrived intellectually at a coherent and workable theory of aesthetics. However, to have a workable theory of aesthetics is one thing, and to be a writer is quite another.

I.2.5: A Strictly Theoretical Breakthrough

In *Stephen Hero*, the subjective coordinate is already greatly emphasized in Stephen's theory (perhaps more than in Thomas but still, as Levy has shown, in harmony with Thomas); and in *Portrait* the objective coordinate is still the starting point of the entire dynamic and the entire theory: "An esthetic image is presented to us either in space or in time."[27] It is not stripped of its ontological character. It is true, however, that the scales are tipped to the side of the perceiving subject. Stephen's aesthetic theory is faithful to its Thomist inspiration and source, as Levy maintains, but there is a tension in it (as opposed to rupture) not found in the Thomist synthesis. Rather than the radical departure postulated by Eco, it is more lopsided than one-sided.

As critics almost universally agree, there is still in Stephen an emphasis on cerebral cogitation over alert receptivity, on the protagonism of the subjective intellect and imagination rather than on artistic attentiveness to reality's fleeting flashes of *claritas*. Declan Kiberd provides a typically incisive diagnosis: "Stephen's weighty selfconsciousness has often intimidated readers, who may not appreciate that the portraiture is largely satiric. Joyce is dramatizing a consciousness suffering the over-effects of a recent university education, and immobilized accordingly."[28] Philosophically convinced and convincing as

Stephen now is, he is not yet equipped appropriately to process the reality he must artistically reproduce in spite of having intellectually achieved the approach which, in theory, would enable that reproduction by providing him with the guidelines he has been seeking.

To put it "in plain words," as Molly Bloom would famously have us do, Stephen is still living inside his own head. Something else has to happen in order for Stephen to be able as artist fittingly and fruitfully to approach the mystery of life. That "something else," according to the reading to be proposed in this book, is the humiliation and "conversion" of the intellect in a process akin to that of the workings of divine grace as experienced and described by the Doctor of Grace, St. Augustine, in his *Confessions*.[29] But Joyce will never abandon his Thomist aesthetic. The terms of indebtedness to Aquinas for his aesthetic philosophy—"Aquinas will carry me all along the line"[30]—and innovativeness when it comes to artistic conception, gestation, and reproduction—"I require a new terminology and a new personal experience"[31]—are expressed on Joyce's behalf by Stephen and there is no need to second-guess the matter.

Later in this chapter and throughout this book we will see abundant collateral evidence in Joyce's work that he did not "outgrow" ontology. Instead of rupture, there is a correction of generally acknowledged shortcomings of scholastic philosophy, as exemplified in the way that Joyce saw the relationship between the Middle Ages and the Renaissance. There is more at stake here than aesthetics. Effectively, what is at issue is whether Joyce was a realist or a relativist.

I.3: Joyce's Views on Scholasticism and the Enlightenment

I.3.1: The Mundane and the Supernatural; Rupture or Synthesis?

When Umberto Eco—medievalist scholar, semiotician, novelist, Joycean, apostate, and skeptic—joked in an interview that his studies of St. Thomas Aquinas in his twenties had "miraculously cured me of faith,"[32] he was alluding to that same dissatisfaction with perfect cerebral systematization, intellectually convincing but hermetically closed and existentially irrelevant (i.e. Thomism misunderstood), which contributed also to the apostasy of James Joyce's fictional character, Stephen Dedalus (as we shall see). Levy explains: "In *Art and Beauty in the Middle Ages,* Eco describes a type of aesthetics perfect in its order, but closed upon itself, with its own maze of symbols and allegories that confidently lead to the one and only Signified."[33] There is evidence that this was also Joyce's impression of the medieval worldview.

Eco represents a school of thought that sees the trajectory of Joyce's work in terms of progressive emancipation from ontology, culminating in *Finnegans Wake,* a feast of life's flux in which the notion of order is relativized and confined to the level of the verbal. The horizons of experimentation have been thrown open by the modernist liberation from the restrictions of ontology. The text becomes an "open work," without definitive authorial authority and unanchored by ponderous ontological reference; hermeneutic opportunity usurps canonical pedantry. In his *The Aesthetics of Chaosmos*, Eco describes a new thematic intranscendentalism and a corresponding stylistic miscellaneity:

> The traditional novel must disregard, for example, the fact that the protagonist blew his nose, unless the act means something from the point of view of the necessity of the plot. The act which does not 'mean' is an insignificant and therefore a 'stupid' one. With Joyce, we have the full acceptance of all the stupid acts of daily life as narrative material. The Aristotelian perspective is radically overturned. Important things no longer happen in the novel, but an assortment of little things, without order, in an incoherent flow—thoughts and gestures, psychic associations as well as behavior automatisms.[34]

It is doubtful that Joyce would agree that important things do not happen in his novels. Eco sees the fact of dealing with the mundane as rupture between the mundane and the supernatural and therefore as radical self-distancing from traditional aesthetics. He does not consider the possibility that Joyce sought to recover the relationship between the mundane and the supernatural. Joyce's aim is to reveal the profound importance of the apparently unimportant. This, in itself, argues in favor of a project that, rather than constituting semantic celebration of the certainty of ambiguity for its own sake, has a clear underlying agendum of significance.

For example, part of the Joycean plot is precisely

the restoration of the dignity of the body. For Joyce, the needs and functions of the body are not stupid or insignificant but participate in and reflect the comic dignity of life itself and of the human person. We know that he stated to his friend Frank Budgen that, "In my book the body lives in and moves through space and is the home of a full human personality. The words I write are adapted to express first one of its functions and then another."[35] Eco's point just cited is that dealing with the mundane is a sign of a turn to immanentist materialism. But Joyce's dealing with the mundane retains a scholastic feel to it, which critiques an intellectualist distortion among some scholastics (an obsession with minutiae and abstractions), while exploring and expanding the relationship between the mundane and the supernatural, which was precisely what good scholastic or realist philosophy does.

Eco's hermeneutic perceives the Joycean employment of the Thomist aesthetic in terms of a kind of literary over-farming which leaves the land barren behind it as it makes off with the spoils: "Thus *Ulysses* appears as the incredible image of a world that supports itself, almost by miracle, on the preserved structures of an old world which are accepted for their formal reliability, but denied in their substantial value."[36] Levy objects that the "old world," which Eco (in the company of Stephen Dedalus, and perhaps of Joyce) perceives as exhaustively ordered and intricate but naïvely circumscribed and bankrupt of potentiality, contains within its own epistemology a principle of infinite openness. There is no inherent incompatibility between the medieval vision and an inexhaustible infinitude of possibilities. Levy makes the ironic point that the Book of Kells, which Joyce used as a model and point of reference for *Finnegans Wake* and which Eco uses to justify his hermeneutic, is in fact a medieval work of art: "Indeed, the aesthetics of such a Middle Ages hardly corresponds to the closed universe that Joyce, according to Eco, is supposed to contest from within and eventually overcome."[37]

I.3.2: The Medieval and the Modern; Rupture or Synthesis?

There is evidence that Joyce's project was one of synthesis, not separation, and of innovation within continuity, rather than radical departure. Levy quotes a passage from an essay entitled, "On the worldwide literary influence of the Renaissance," written by Joyce in 1912 (between the completion of *Portrait* and commencement of *Ulysses*, when he was about thirty years old)—"a text," according to Levy, "utterly neglected by Joyce scholars."[38] Addressing the Renaissance reaction to the Middle Ages that preceded it, Joyce wrote:

> The human mind felt perhaps the attraction of the unknown. It heard the voice of the visual, tangible, inconstant world and leaving the monastic peace in which it used to languish, it embraced the new Gospel. It abandoned its peace, its true home *(la sua vera dimora)* because it had gotten weary of it, as God, being tired (I beg your pardon for these somehow irreverent ways of speaking) of his own perfections, called the world out of nothing; that is,

as a woman who, being bored with the peace and tranquillity in which her heart is slowly consumed, turns her eyes towards life's power of enticement *(la vita tentatrice)*.[39]

In this Joyce concurs with Eco's hermeneutic and with Stephen's. There is a perception of the scholastic vision, not only in its decadence but even at its heights of intellectual achievement, as somehow stifling of (or at best myopically indifferent to) the sentient, the immediate and the emotional; as remote from the principle of vitality itself.

However, as Levy points out, Joyce's position is not one of un-nuanced outright dismissal of the medieval contribution: "Joyce starts by stating that he did not find the idea that culture had to wait for the Renaissance in order to reach adulthood convincing. The former rebel of Belvedere College wrote that he would rather fight these views with drawn sword." Nor is it one of acritical embrace of the Enlightenment: "There ensues a diatribe against the effects of the Renaissance, the indisputable technical achievements of which . . . are said to mask an overall degradation of human spiritual freedom through social and economic pressures that favor the growth of languid mass mentality."[40]

Joyce as defender "with drawn sword" of the pre-Renaissance achievement is an interesting image. Apropos of the Renaissance itself, he wields the sword in a less defensive mode: "'The skin,' writes Joyce, 'has replaced the soul in modern man.' The 'hurricane' of the Renaissance, placing 'journalists on the chair once occupied by monks,' has left us with nothing more than a 'tumult of voices.'" Levy deduces that, "For Joyce, the time has come to reunite the power of Scholasticism to the counterpower of the Renaissance."[41] That is, to reunite skin and soul, matter and spirit, senses and substance.

The Joycean aesthetic restoration of the body constitutes an iconic reintegration of mind, heart, soul and matter of which the Eucharist, as we shall see in chapter V, is the apotheosis. In this reintegration of spirit and matter, intellect and senses, the Medieval and the Modern are harnessed and harmonized, not divided. Levy offers a positive formulation of the Joycean paradox (as opposed to contradiction) which fruitfully unites the past and the present; Ancient and Medieval intellectual achievements are joined with the Modern prioritization of the existential:

> Joyce suggests that the great products of the old western culture do not only witness to their own time; they have the power to tell us something about the essence of the present. The authentic understanding of our modern being arises from the "hermeneutic shock," the dramatic contrast between the great cantors of the past and our present daily life, taken in its concrete and saddening triviality ... Joyce ends his short essay calling for an art that could supersede the works of the Ancients themselves by integrating, with their help, the new existential content discovered by the Renaissance.[42]

Levy recognizes the presence of contrast, but sees this as a means to an end, that end being a remedial synthesis, whereas Umberto Eco's hermeneutic describes a tension, never resolved, between irreconcilable opposites. We will look at Eco's interpretation now, to assess its accuracy and to see if the tension he discovers is really irresolvable.

I.3.3: Resolving Eco's Dilemma

In a recently re-published edition of Eco's book on Joyce's poetics, the indicators are that his understanding of "Thomist categories" (*categorie tomiste*) has not substantially changed. Eco sees the medieval *Summae* as the "most high and complete expression" of a "vision of the Universe . . . as a totality which may receive a unique and incontrovertible definition in which everything finds a place and a reason."[43] Still coinciding with Joyce, Eco sees the modern culture as a reaction against this highly ordered and structured vision, but adds that modernity has never entirely succeeded in breaking free of its impressive and imposing medieval inheritance: "[E]ven in opposing it, it has never been able to subtract itself entirely from . . . the majestic comfort of a module of Order in which everything is justified."[44]

Eco incisively describes that tension between order, security and comfort on the one hand, and vitality, spontaneity, unpredictability on the other, that we will see vividly dramatized in Joyce's *Portrait*. The vital longing for the unpredictable never quite succeeds in escaping the ineluctable necessity and stubborn objectivity of order. On one side there is the medieval man, "nostalgic for a defined world in which he could live finding clear signs of direction," and on the other side there is the contemporary man, "who perceives the exigency to establish a new habitat, but without yet managing to find its statutory rules, much more ambiguous and difficult, with the constant disquiet of nostalgia for a lost infancy." Eco ultimately maintains that in Joyce, "the definitive election is not produced, and his dialectic affords us . . . the development of a continual polarity and of a tension never placated."[45]

Effectively, Eco's position is that Joyce is a post-modern before there was postmodernity. The terms of the debate may be stated as realist versus postmodern; that is, on the one hand there is the Medieval conception of reality as material and spiritual with Being and God as the ultimate point of reference, while on the other hand there is the Modern conception of the individual making himself, independently of being and God, and by making himself, recreating reality independently of being and God. Joyce, according to Eco, establishes aesthetic agreement with some things medieval while at the same time pioneering a divorce from the restrictive categories of ontology.

Eco's analysis enticingly evokes the great drama of postmodern uncertainty, subliminally associating Thomist certainties with suppression of mystery and vitality. It perceives the inherent tendency of order towards life-denying formulas and stagnation, highlighting by contrast the authenticity and attractiveness of uncertainty. But there is a "third way" that overcomes Eco's either/or polarities of staid dogmatism and anarchic experimentalism. Skepticism is not the only possible response to an order that has become stiflingly comfortable; nor dogmatism the only response to unbridled experimentation. Faith combines certainty and risk, peace and excitement, tradition and perfective dynamism; as should theology, and aesthetics.

In *Le poetiche di Joyce* Eco has made his argument in a contemporary context, employing the 1970s and 80s language of postmodernity. It is legitimate to respond then, with the aid of a contemporary philosopher-theologian who helps us to understand the conceptual context of this late 20th century debate. I will attempt to resolve Eco's position of protracted ambiguity with Joseph Ratzinger's response to the challenge of pluralism in theology and his insights on artistic expression in his book *The Spirit of the Liturgy*. This book addresses the themes of rupture and continuity in aesthetics in a liturgical rather than a literary context, and Ratzinger's essay on pluralism addresses theological rather than strictly literary issues, but Joyce's incursions into the realms of philosophy and liturgy bespeak a common ground between literature, philosophy, and theology. Ultimately, the debate is about the relationship between the Modern and the Medieval. Ratzinger's reflections will help us to frame this debate, the better to resolve Eco's dilemma, and, more importantly, to see how Joyce dealt with this same debate.

I.4: Ratzinger on Theology and Aesthetics

I.4.1: Two Ways of Doing Theology

Joseph Cardinal Ratzinger has offered a response to the relativist challenge in the ambit of theology; a response that favors unity, objectivity, and pursuit of absolute truth, without negating pluralism, subjectivity, and even fragmentation. Ratzinger outlines a theological *modus operandi* which justifies a reverent respect for the intricate integrity of Revelation as an inherent principle of sound theological inquiry, without negating the possibility of newness. His analysis provides a way of better understanding the Joycean debate, and of mediating its points of tension. Indeed, Ratzinger's "philosophy of theology" will provide the guidelines for my entire approach to Joyce and to Joycean literary criticism.

Ratzinger identifies the principle underlying objection to the Church's magisterium. He asks, "Are dogma and the Magisterium the sole principle," dominating oppressively, "or is there a breathing space of plurality even here?"[46] In other words, are variety and development possible, or is Catholic doctrine static, monolithic and circular? The harmonization of tradition and newness, multiplicity and unity, structure and dynamism, solidity and fluidity, is the perennial challenge of theology. Ratzinger answers that pluralism and dynamism are compatible with orthodoxy and tradition.

The Church is a "single historical subject" awakened by the preaching of the Apostles. One becomes a believer "by joining this community of tradition, thought and life," this "subject" which "remains one with itself throughout its own transformations."[47] Unity and pluralism are mentioned in the same breath as entirely compatible realities: "[F]ruitful theological pluralism succeeds in bringing the pluriform historical manifestations of faith into unity. Such unity, far from cancelling multiplicity, is the recognition that it is the organic structure of the truth which transcends man."[48]

The harmonization of tradition and transformation, dogma and novelty, is an exciting theological possibility, not always recognized as such: "[T]here is a persistent suspicion today, even among wholly Church-minded theologians, that orthodox theology is hopelessly condemned to repeat magisterial statements of doctrine and traditional formulae."[49] This would not constitute a third way of doing theology; rather, it is a position not really conducive to doing theology at all. With such a view of "fidelity," heresy presents itself as the exciting alternative to a loyal but stubborn and staid orthodoxy: "To become 'creative,' it appears downright indispensable to throw out the old rubbish and to pass boldly even to open contradiction."[50]

The dichotomization of newness and tradition is easy and enticing but ultimately superficial and sterile, whereas the harmonization of creativity with fidelity to tradition is the more challenging and ultimately rewarding task. Theology builds upon already established insights, while opening new ground, as occurs in the natural sciences:

> [T]he more they increase in number, the more possibilities of inquiry are disclosed and the more

concrete space is won for real creativity. I mean the sort of creativity which does not forge ahead into the void but connects the already existing paths in order to open up new ones. It is not otherwise in theology. It is precisely the profusion of the forms of faith in the unity of the Old and New Testaments, of the New Testament and the early Church dogma, of all these elements together and the ongoing life of faith, which increases the excitement and fecundity of inquiry.[51]

Ratzinger recognizes the attraction of a pseudo-creativity emancipated from tradition: "For a long time I shared the impression that the so-called heretics were really more interesting than the theologians of the Church, at least in more recent times," but adds that it soon became clear to him that those who made the more profound and lasting contribution were those whose ultimate point of reference was not change or novelty for its own sake but a higher value. Truth is attractive and always challenging and elusive, not static, oppressive and easily codified: "The truth is never monotonous, nor is it ever exhausted in a single form, because our mind beholds it only in fragments; yet at the same time it is the power which unifies us. And only pluralism in relation to unity is great."[52] The affirmation that our mind beholds the truth "only in fragments" bears emphasizing, joined to the important fact that this does not entail denial of unity.

I.4.2: Fragmentation Within and Without Unity

Two hermeneutics are presented here, both characterized by openness and creativity. But one never loses contact with the center and the whole even as it expands infinitely in multiple directions, whereas the other, without reference to its own source and to a grand incomprehensible totality, disperses into the void. It is important to note that although the first approach presupposes unity, it recognizes that it is capable of apprehending that unity only fragmentarily even as it strives to preserve totality and integrity within the tension of the understanding fragmentarily achieved. It may be seen from this that the term "conservative" fails lamentably to describe Ratzinger's theory of theology. The ultimate incomprehensibility and infinite inexhaustibility of the divine mystery was aphoristically encapsulated by the Lateran Council IV in the year 1215 when it pronounced that "between the Creator and the creature there cannot be a likeness so great that the unlikeness is not greater."[53]

The second approach, although it also features creativity and openness, since it presupposes the absence of unity, lacks a point of reference to guarantee coherence and to preserve itself from arbitrariness and contradiction. Although open, it is an openness that leads to the void—a dead end. Discussing elsewhere this hermeneutic in its ultimate form—atheistic relativism—Ratzinger speaks of it not in terms of openness but of fragile closure: "For the unbeliever faith remains a temptation and a threat to his apparently permanently closed world. In short, there is no escape from the dilemma of being a man."[54] (In this thought Ratzinger has an unlikely ally of "convinced atheist" H. L. Mencken: "In every unbeliever's heart there is an uneasy feeling that, after all, he may awake after death and find himself immortal".)[55]

The fundamental unchanging truths of Catholic doctrine are therefore endlessly capable not only of new, multiple and harmonious explanations but also of new, multiple and harmonious *revelations and discoveries.* This epistemology, condensed by Christ in a sentence when He said of the Paraclete that "he will guide you into all the truth" (Jn 16:13), will characterize my approach not only to Catholic theology but also to Joycean literary criticism. Before proceeding thereto, however, it will be useful to see how Ratzinger's philosophy of theology is reflected in his thinking on aesthetics outlined in his book on the liturgy. This will help further to establish the connection between Ratzinger's thought and Joycean literary criticism.

I.4.3: The Aesthetic Argument; The Spirit of the Liturgy

What is true for theological thought is true also, *mutatis mutandis,* for liturgical expression. Ratzinger's "theory of aesthetics," so to speak, resonates logically with his philosophy of theology. Liturgical "creativity," like theological speculation without regard to tradition, culminates in arbitrariness and banality. In the ambit of theology Ratzinger speaks, as we have just seen, of the challenge to "remain at a standstill" before a reality that has been established and "to make oneself vulnerable to its demands," in order to climb to "the pinnacle" and draw "closer to the truth."⁵⁶ In the ambit of the liturgy something very similar is required: "Humble submission to what goes before us releases authentic freedom and leads us to the true summit of our vocation as human beings."⁵⁷

Just as theological experimentalism is a misguided reaction to dogma, liturgical experimentalism is a misguided reaction to religious rite; a term, he says, that is not currently fashionable: "'Rite' suggests rigidity, a restriction to prescribed forms. It is set in opposition to that creativity and dynamism of inculturation by which, so people say, we get a really living liturgy in which each community can express itself."⁵⁸ There is in our postmodern climate of thought a widespread uneasiness with foundations and traditions: "Modern theories of art think in terms of a nihilistic kind of creativity. Art is not meant to copy anything. Artistic creativity is under the free mastery of man, without being bound by norms or goals and subject to no questions of meaning."⁵⁹ This sounds similar to Umberto Eco's theory of art; it remains to be seen if it describes Joyce's.

And, just as in the case of theology, stubborn dogmatism and random improvisation are not the only alternatives; in the liturgy too there is a third way: "Yes, the liturgy becomes personal, true, and new, not through tomfoolery and banal experiments with the words, but through a courageous entry into the great reality that through the rite is always ahead of us and can never quite be overtaken." The word "conservative" fails lamentably to describe this dynamic too: "Does it still need to be explicitly stated that all this has nothing to do with rigidity?" The solution is a synthesis that is perennially faithful to tradition and open to innovation, developing organically out of its Scriptural and Apostolic origins and harmonious with its later expansion, "without haste or aggressive intervention, like the grain that grows 'of itself,' in the earth (cf. Mk 4:28)."[60]

Ratzinger has helped us to frame the debate. Evidently, James Joyce did not settle for the artistic equivalent of staid dogmatism. That postulate may be summarily dismissed. The matter still to be discerned is whether he opted for the "artistic creativity" described by Ratzinger and apparently championed by Eco—"under the free mastery of man, without being bound by norms or goals"—or whether his project is, as indicated by Stephen Dedalus in *Portrait* when he expresses his position of creative indebtedness to Aquinas, one of dynamic, open and expanding synthesis, as also described by Ratzinger (and claimed by Levy). The debate about Stephen's mind and Joyce's Thomistic aesthetic has been one, first step in the response to this question.

I.4.4: Evidence of Overlapping Terrain

According to Roy Gottfried, Joyce "took on the unitary thinking of its [Catholic orthodoxy's] universal authority to challenge its premises, to redefine its claims ... Joyce is attracted to schisms in the church because, as he rehearses them, they open up for him possibilities of his art." We have seen that Joseph Ratzinger's concept of theology recognizes that its achievement will always and inevitably be a partial grasp of the incomprehensible whole, and that the unity between those fragments partially grasped is a pale (but beautiful and luminous) reflection of the unity of that ever-elusive whole. Gottfried's impression of orthodoxy is that it makes claims to circumscribed completeness, and his impression of Joyce's art is that, heretically emancipated from orthodoxy (and from unity and ontology), it celebrates a multiple and irreconcilable disparity tantamount to marvelous anarchy: "Joyce advanced the powerful argument that truth is not unitary and complete—his true reaction to what he had been taught by the catechism—but rather always partial and fragmented."[61]

Gottfried makes the mistake which Ratzinger described as an early temptation in his work as a theologian: "Orthodoxy is a standard, rigorously upheld; if not arbitrary, by virtue of being derived from a long-running dialectic of challenge and questioning, it is, however, intrinsically circular in the logic of its definition." And again: "Dogma evolves over time, as Joyce well knew and in knowing must have felt that each such development seriously called into question the very nature of revealed truth and authority's ability to pronounce on it."[62] Dogma and development are assumed to be mutually exclusive: "If the Pope cannot proclaim a word of false doctrine *ex cathedra*, then the circularity inherent in orthodoxy—what is true is what is articulated by authority—is made most evident."[63]

For Gottfried, tradition and transformation are incompatible dynamics. His assertions, apart from misunderstanding orthodoxy in the way we have seen diagnosed by Ratzinger, amount to a claim that Joyce was a relativist, not a realist, and bring us conveniently to the two ways of reading Joyce. Joycean literary criticism is at a crossroads akin to the theological one expertly described by Ratzinger. We need to weigh the evidence concerning which option Joyce himself took. That is essential to the subject of this book. Let us turn now to a book by Geert Lernout that presents the foundation of the relativist reading of Joyce, claiming that Joyce was an atheist.[64]

I.5: The Case for Joyce as a Relativist

I.5.1: Geert Lernout on Dogma and Development

Lernout shares Gottfried's view that Catholic orthodoxy is necessarily circular and closed to development, but maintains that throughout its history the Church has repeatedly performed the feat of alteration behind a facade of tradition: "[I]n the course of the nineteenth century the Roman catholic church managed to transform itself radically and [. . .] paradoxically managed to do so in the name of tradition."[65]

The nature of this "transformation" is twofold: "Its philosophy and theology had become Thomistic and its structure much more centralized and hierarchical than it had ever been before."[66] Ironically, the work of Aquinas is seen by the Church as a paradigm of the harmonization of creativity with fidelity to tradition. It has a perennial exemplary relevance because it synthesizes Scripture and previous theology while innovatively integrating Aristotelian thought. The structure of the Church became "more centralized and hierarchical," as Lernout rightly states, because a renewed disciplinary emphasis for the sake of doctrinal clarity and unity in the midst of intensifying secularist dissent and antagonism was a logical response to the increasing precariousness of the Church's political position. Strong and serene acceptance of her political precariousness would soon be reflected in ecclesiastical language, and there is no evidence of rupture from doctrinal tradition.

Lernout presents no concrete example in Joyce's writings of exposure of disguised rupture from tradition in the Church's teachings. He does, however, present his own allegation of rupture in one doctrinal area. In the closing pages of his book Lernout alleges that in Vatican Council II the Catholic Church has again performed the feat of intellectual gymnastics that introduces dramatic change behind a façade of fidelity to tradition. He quotes a letter of Julian Cardinal Herranz on behalf of Pope Benedict XVI dated 13 March 2006 addressed to the presidents of all episcopal conferences: "It remains clear, in any event, that the sacramental bond of belonging to the Body of Christ that is the Church, conferred by the baptismal character, is an ontological and permanent bond which is not lost by reason of any act or fact of defection," and offers this as a concrete example of doctrinal change: "[A]ccording to the most recent canon law, it is simply impossible to stop being a catholic. But of course that is only true according to a new kind of catholicism that did not exist when James Joyce died."[67]

Perhaps the context of Herranz's letter led Lernout to interpret it outside of its historical context. Herranz is a canon lawyer interpreting an updated code of Canon

Law. And so, he did not gesture to historical realities about the doctrine of the indelible character imprinted upon the soul in Baptism, which was dogmatically defined by the Council of Trent and is a feature of Catholic doctrine traceable to St. Augustine (who defended it in his battle against the Donatists regarding their requirement of re-baptism for the *lapsi*) and St. Paul.[68] Joyce knew this teaching. Lernout's book ends with a repetition of this error and a reaffirmation of its main argument: "According to the rules of the church he was baptized in, James Joyce lived and died as an apostate, as somebody who had placed himself knowingly and willingly outside of that church. It would be a great injustice (if not a mortal sin) to drag him back in."[69]

Lernout begins his book with three affirmations: one, that Joyce was an atheist; two, that he himself is an atheist; three, that his subjective experience has no impact on his reading of Joyce.[70] This last is a bold, perhaps an impossible, claim. Awareness of personal subjectivity is a necessary factor in relativizing it, but the pretension to eliminate it is utopian. Scholarly debate is enriched, not inhibited, by the freedom openly to declare and argue one's personal reading experience, whilst being aware of the rich subjectivity, conscious and unconscious, that inevitably accompanies that experience. This is valid for religious and for relativist readers. To anathematize the religious hermeneutic would surely impoverish the field of discourse. Evidently, this does not legitimize arbitrary projection of a subjective ideological agenda on Joyce's texts, be this by the Catholic or by an anti-Catholic school; there must be a rigorous concern for objective validation.

This hermeneutical rule applies as much to secularist as to religious readers. It is by critically assimilating opposing viewpoints that we approximate the interpretation most faithful to the original text. Lernout is correct in many ways about Joyce's views on Catholicism, but he misses crucial nuances. His incisive exposition of Irish Catholicism in Joyce's time is a case in point.

I.5.2: The Irish Context

Lernout informs us that Irish scholar Eamonn Hughes, in an essay published in 1992, maintained that Joyce's religious position oscillates always between Stephen's "I will not serve" in *Portrait* and his resignation in *Ulysses* to being "servant of two masters" (one English—political imperialism; one Italian—religious imperialism). Hughes condemns the prevalence in Joyce criticism of a negative oversimplification of Catholicism itself and of Joyce's relationship to it in the service of a secularist agenda which has "turned Joyce's work into: [a] mirror to the various vanities of a secular criticism which elevates his works to the level of sacred texts to endorse those vanities." He perceives an ideological blindness in the secularist refusal to consider Stephen's contrary affirmation: "That Stephen also says 'I am a servant' is a contradiction with which most critics choose not to cope preferring to ignore Stephen's and Joyce's testament to the power of Catholicism."[71] According to Hughes, Joyce was ahead of Catholic doctrine by a century.[72]

Lernout understandably displays little patience with this reading: "If this essay is not a hoax, it must be listed among the more perverse readings of Joyce. In almost every instant it manages to misrepresent what Joyce actually thought and what he made his characters say and do . . . Hughes willfully distorts the evidence."[73] Hughes's reading does at times seem to demand something akin to suspension of disbelief. Stephen's self-identification as "servant of two masters" is indeed a recognition of the power of Catholicism but his tone is wry, weary, and bitterly resentful (the same tone, incidentally, which accompanies the words, "'You behold in me,' Stephen said with grim displeasure, 'a horrible example of free thought'"[74]). But it is also true that the secularist reading is often a distortion and an oversimplification.

Contrary to Lernout's position and in agreement with that of Hughes, I will contend, in the course of sequentially analyzing the Catholic categories which remain in Joyce's thought even after apostasy, that there is in fact a sense of the sacred and the supernatural in Joyce's writings; contrary to Hughes's position and in agreement with that of Lernout, I will also contend that Irish Catholicism, far from being championed by Joyce as a positive alternative to ultramontane Roman Catholicism, is scathingly critiqued by him as anti-human. I will show progressively throughout this study that the explanation for Joyce's increasingly nuanced attitude towards Catholicism and the confusion arising therefrom in Joycean criticism, is to be found in his gradual discovery not only that the Irish Catholicism he knew was an aberration, but also that Catholic doctrine in fact coincided in many ways with his own insights and aims. Not that this is the chief purpose of this study. The chief purpose of this study is to analyze Joyce's "Catholic categories" and to discover his philosophical position, and his religious position, if any. But the clarification just described is an important subtheme of this main task. Familiarity with Joyce's Irish context is crucial for understanding his relationship with Catholicism and his religious mind.

In his conclusion to this chapter, entitled "Anticlericalism," Lernout provides interesting statistics: "In the half-century after the Famine . . . the number of priests, nuns and other religious rose from 5,000 to 14,000, while in the same period the number of inhabitants in Ireland dropped by a third."[75] A book published in 1908 describes Ireland as "the sole exception to the process of secularization in Europe."[76] The subject of this chapter is to ascertain whether Joyce was a realist or a relativist, but this is connected to the matter of his rejection of Catholicism in particular and of religion in general. My contention is that he did not reject realism or religion; that he rejected only a very specific historical manifestation of Catholicism. Lernout rightly states that this historical manifestation of Catholicism is different to contemporary Catholicism, without profoundly analyzing the differences. This subject requires further treatment than it receives in Lernout's book. I will return to it in greater detail in the next chapter. Meanwhile, let us continue to focus on Joyce's philosophical realism.

I.5.3: Joyce and the Principle of Causality

I.5.3.1: Causality in the Eumaeus Conversation

The principle of causality is essential to Aristotelian realism, enabling the Greek philosopher to infer the existence of an unmoved mover or first cause, identifiable with God. This subject arises in a conversation between Leopold Bloom and Stephen Dedalus in the Eumaeus episode of Joyce's *Ulysses*. Bloom brings up the subject of the human soul and Stephen responds: "They tell me on the best authority it is a simple substance and therefore incorruptible. It would be immortal, I understand, but for the possibility of its annihilation by its First Cause, Who, from all I can hear, is quite capable of adding that to the number of his other practical jokes." Bloom, comically out of his intellectual league, admits that "you do knock across a simple soul once in a blue moon," but begs to differ on the point of the existence of a First Cause: "but it's a horse of quite another colour to say you believe in the existence of a supernatural God."[77] Stephen's patience, exhausted after a long and eventful day, runs out: "O, that, Stephen expostulated, has been proved conclusively by several of the best known passages in Holy Writ, apart from circumstantial evidence."[78]

Lernout identifies a tone of facetiousness in Stephen's exasperated response: "It is evident that Stephen is being facetious, because of course he knows that the existence of god cannot be proved conclusively, neither by Holy Writ, nor by circumstantial evidence."[79] Lernout is only partly right in this interpretation, as a quick consultation of the Catechism reveals. Admittedly, the Catechism is a recent document, but it quotes sources—Aquinas and Vatican Council I—with which we know Joyce was familiar. Number 36 of the Catechism, for example, quotes the declaration of *Dei filius* which Joyce studied at the Biblioteca Vittorio Emanuele[80] in the course of research for his short story "Grace": "Our holy mother, the Church, holds and teaches that God, the first principle and last end of all things, can be known with certainty from the created world by the natural light of human reason."[81]

The Church's position on this point is nuanced: the existence of God can be rationally proved (as Aristotle shows), though not empirically demonstrated. The content of Stephen's statement does therefore withstand intellectual analysis. Its tone is another matter. Stephen's tone is facetious, as Lernout says. He is tired and easily exasperated. However, his statement is readable not as outright sarcasm but as begrudging assent; as irritated and reluctant recognition of fact. On an earlier occasion in the novel he discovers to his annoyance the coincidence of his own thoughts with Catholic (and Platonic and Aristotelian) thinking on the subject of how the imperfect goodness of immanent realities refers suggestively to an incorruptible reality, and he expostulates: "Ah, curse you! That's saint Augustine."[82] Encapsulated here in a typical Augustinian aphorism is the rational process described by Aquinas and the Catechism; that of re-tracing steps from effect to cause. The existence of God can indeed be known via the principle of causality, and "Holy Writ" (along with Greek philosophy) argues this very point in at least two "well known passages."

Those two passages affirm that insightful scrutiny of the physical induces inevitably to the metaphysical. The first passage is in the *Book of Wisdom*: "For from the greatness and beauty of created things comes a corresponding perception of their Creator" (Wis 13:5). The second is in St. Paul's *Letter to the Romans*: "Ever since the creation of the world his invisible nature, namely, his eternal power and deity, has been clearly perceived in the things that have been made" (Rom 1:20). The doctrine common to these passages entails that the dichotomy between secularity and the transcendental is artificial, regardless of whether that dichotomy is championed by materialists, idealists, or Catholics. Epiphany, therefore, is not divorceable from theophany.

That Joyce did not see epiphany as separable from theophany is revealed in an essay he wrote on Giordano Bruno, in which he describes the Italian philosopher (whom we know he greatly admired) as a "god-intoxicated man": "Inwards from the material universe, which . . . did not seem to him, as to the Neoplatonists the kingdom of the soul's malady, or as to the Christians a place of probation, but rather his opportunity for spiritual activity, he passes, and from heroic enthusiasm to enthusiasm to unite himself with God."[83] This is a Christian doctrine. It is true, as Joyce affirms here in passing, that Christianity sees the material universe as a "place of probation," a "vale of tears." But it is also true (although this doctrine was perhaps not as prominent in Joyce's time and place as it is in ours) that it is valued as a sacramental opportunity for intimacy with God, through whom, as the Creed proclaims, "all things are made." In this the Catholic Creed and Joyce's creed, implied in his admiring remarks on Bruno, coincide.

I.5.3.2: Causality and Stephen's "Secular Creed"

G. Lernout maintains that the closest Stephen Dedalus comes to the utterance of a secularist creed which would divorce epiphany from theophany, secularity from the transcendental, occurs in the Ithaca chapter of *Ulysses*, just before parting from Bloom: "He affirmed his significance as a conscious rational animal proceeding from the known to the unknown and a conscious rational reagent between a micro and a macrocosm ineluctably constructed upon the incertitude of the void." Lernout adds: "This could function as a cumbrous but adequate description of a freethinker's philosophy."[84] This may be so, but it is not conclusive. Stephen uses the term "ineluctably constructed," which would seem to refer to a necessary causal agent. He does not say "the certitude of the void," he says the *incertitude* of the void." Negotiating one's way "between a micro and macrocosm . . . upon the incertitude of the void" may also be interpreted as a good description of the risk factor in the journey of faith.

With or without faith, the void is always a threat in the human experience; a fact not denied by Catholicism. There is nothing definitively anti-Catholic or anti-religious in this "creed." Whatever about its content, there is a pomposity to the statement that is satirized by Joyce and perhaps also by Stephen himself. We cannot unerringly deduce from Stephen's first statement a creed of unequivocal faith or from his later statement a freethinker's creed of convinced atheism. Facetiousness is the tone of both statements.

Lernout dubiously discovers a "secular creed" in the Eumaeus exchange between Bloom and Stephen, but Stephen's throwaway reference to "circumstantial evidence"[85] provides the closest that Joyce comes not to a secular but to a transcendental creed. It is in fact the "circumstantial evidence" of a divine agent, that is, those mysterious epiphanical irruptions of the sublime in the secular (flashes of *claritas*), which provide the raw material and the focal points of the experiential and aesthetic adventure upon which Stephen, after leaving Bloom at the end of *Ulysses*, will embark. Stephen's choice (also Joyce's) would marginalize him from what he considered the institutional Church, but not from the idea of a supernatural force actively involved in human experience.

The discovery of this divine agency occurs in the climactic scene of *Portrait*, at the end of the fourth chapter. Stephen's "apostasy" and aesthetic quest culminate in the scene when he beholds a girl paddling in the waters at Sandymount strand: "'Heavenly God', cried Stephen's soul, in an outburst of profane joy."[86] Always a precise user of words, Joyce knew that the word "profane" in its Greek roots means outside of the temple. Joyce's focus is on an elusive humanizing principle ever at work in the human experience *and* in the human heart *outside* of the visible realm of the Church—an "ontological and psychological reality," as Pope John Paul II put it (*Dominum et vivificantem* 54), referring to God. This choice is alluded to again in the Nestor chapter of *Ulysses* when Stephen, in reply to Mr. Deasy, gestures to God's presence in the "shout in the street," referring to the noise of schoolboys playing outside: "'All history moves towards one great goal, the manifestation of God.' Stephen jerked his thumb towards the window, saying 'That is God . . . A shout in the street.'"[87] This theistic stance is repeated by Molly Bloom in the final chapter of *Ulysses*.

I.5.3.3: Causality in the Penelope Soliloquy

Joyce's interest in the principle of causality and his option in favor of God "in the street" come together in Molly Bloom's robust dismissal of atheism and atheists in the final chapter of *Ulysses*:

> nature it is as for them saying theres no God I wouldnt give a snap of my two fingers for all their learning why dont they go and create something I often asked him atheists or whatever they call themselves . . . I know them well who was the first person in the universe before there was anybody that made it all who ah that they dont know neither do I so there you are they might as well try to stop the sun from rising tomorrow.[88]

Richard Ellmann reads Molly's dismissal of atheism as evidence of agnosticism: "She quickly resolves the questions of belief and incertitude which have dogged Stephen and western philosophy, and with which Bloom has bothered her, by finding them not worth asking;"[89] but Molly's words surely express the unquestioning conviction of intuitive faith rather than the unquestioning doubt of ideological agnosticism.

Lernout maintains that Joyce wishes to portray the susceptibility of women to religious propaganda: "With Molly's reaction to her husband's freethinking at the close of the book, it is clear that Joyce distinguishes the ideological choices of his two male heroes . . . from the women in the book, not just Molly, but also Stephen's mother."[90] By thus pairing the "liberated" Molly and Stephen's mother, Lernout goes against the grain of the almost universal consensus of Joyce criticism. Lernout holds that, "Women are portrayed as victims of a religion that oppresses them and that inflicts physical and psychological damage."[91]

Here we must choose between the learnedness of Lernout and the bluntness of Molly Bloom; there is no middle ground. However, Molly's argument enjoys in its favor the rational principle of causality (to which we shall often return, because Joyce does so), whereas Lernout's is strictly and solely *ad hominem* (or *ad mulierem* and *ad Ecclesiam*; all three amounting in this instance to the same thing). In direct opposition to this perspective, Joyce's intent is to show not how much women can learn from men but how much men need to learn from women, on the subject of religion among others.

In the *Stephen Hero* fragment, Joyce wrote that, "The general attitude of women towards religion puzzled and often maddened Stephen . . . It did not strike him that the attitude of women towards holy things really implied a more genuine emancipation than his own."[92] Joyce has a similar intent to show how much the learned have to learn from the unlearned. There is evidence that he was a believer in "common sense" and in the *sensum fidelium*, exemplified by Molly Bloom; in which case Joyce goes against the grain of consensus of contemporary secularists. We will look at that position now.

I.5.4: The Standard Secularist Reading

I.5.4.1: Ellmann's Joyce

Joyce's final and lasting post-Catholic position, having committed to apostasy, is summarized somewhat glibly by Richard Ellmann as follows: "He was no longer Christian himself; but he converted the temple to new uses instead of trying to knock it down, regarding it as a superior kind of human folly and one which, interpreted by a secular artist, contained obscured bits of truth." Joyce, according to Ellmann, had to "conquer his Catholicism" in order to become a writer, and a mature human being. Thus, literature itself becomes the "liturgy" of a secularist worldview artfully and happily "emancipated" from religion. In terms suggestive of Jungian individuation, Ellmann goes on to describe the Joycean project in *Portrait* and *Ulysses* as one of artistic self-recreation. The great ambition, Ellmann claims, is "to overcome his mother's conventionality and his father's rancor, to mother and father himself, to become, by the superhuman effort of the creative process, no one but James Joyce."[93]

In his book *Ulysses and Us*, Declan Kiberd has given a recent reexpression of Richard Ellmann's secularist reading of Joyce in a way that helps to elucidate further the philosophical and religious issues at stake in the Joyce debate. Kiberd presents Joyce as high priest and prophet of post-Christian humanist secularism. He compares the relationship between the Old and New Testaments with the relationship between Joyce and the Christian tradition: "Then it [the Old Testament] was free to disappear into the new narrative [the New Testament], much as Homer, the Bible, Dante, and Shakespeare are intended by Joyce to vaporize into *Ulysses*."[94] This reading, reminiscent of Umberto Eco's as well as Ellmann's, is suggestive more of scavengery than symbiosis: "[T]he new form evolved by the evangelists implies the abolition of the Old Testament, except as a source for the New."[95] It leads to the following startling claim: "But latent in the prophetic method was also a warning: if Jesus really was someone who surpassed Moses and Elijah, then some day the Christian gospels might themselves be superseded."[96] Kiberd speaks then in terms of subordinating and superseding the Judeo-Christian tradition.

The dynamic we have seen described by Ratzinger is one of crossfertilization and continual unfolding towards fullness; Kiberd's is one of "ransacking" and rupture, abolishing and displacing. To this assertion of abolition, any spokesperson for the Christian position would have to reply that Christ spoke of not abolishing the old but of bringing it to fulfillment and these words are faithfully recorded and implemented in the New Testament (cf. Mt 5:17). The Old Testament certainly becomes a source for the New, but the New Testament is also a source for the Old. As we have seen, Ratzinger's theory of the theological task considers a dynamic of continuity, harmony, and mutual fecundation not found in Kiberd's.

We know from Stephen Dedalus that Joyce aspired to be "priest of the eternal imagination."[97] What we don't know is whether the Joycean project is one of supplantation and substitution or one of seamless "postcreation,"[98] to use another of Stephen's own terms. The idea of art as superhuman in its capacities and solipsistically individualist in its ambitions sounds more like the juvenile Stephen Dedalus than the mature James Joyce. The question that inevitably arises is whether Joyce saw himself as an improvement not only on all preceding art but also on Christianity itself, and whether his approach to all that preceded him is defined by continuity or by discontinuity. Other, related questions arise too; such as, how complex and nuanced was Joyce's relationship with the Catholic tradition? How nuanced and how accurate is the secularist reading of Catholicism and of James Joyce?

I.5.4.2: Critiques of the Secularist Reading

It was Joyce's compatriot, W.B. Yeats, who stated, "We make out of the quarrel with others, rhetoric, but of the quarrel with ourselves, poetry;"[99] some readers seem inclined to reduce Joyce's work to rhetoric. Joyce did not make the secularist mistake of knee-jerk rejection of religion. His struggle with Catholicism was also a quarrel with himself—as evinced by the diverse attitudes to religion exemplified in Molly, Bloom, and Stephen—and that quarrel was enormously fruitful for his art because it was fierce, profound, and longlasting. Distinguishing between Joyce and Stephen is one challenge of the

Joycean reading experience; distinguishing between the subjective projections of Joyce readers and the thematic intentions of Joyce himself is another.

In the world of Joyce criticism it is increasingly noted that Ellmann's biography presents the difficulty of distinguishing between the mind of the biographer and the mind of his subject, i.e., between Ellmann and Joyce. The over-simplification that characterizes Ellmann's long unquestioned reading is now being noted. Contemporary Joyce scholar John McCourt, for example, has identified a move in the Joyce community towards a "post-Ellmann phase." McCourt quotes a comment by Ellmann which reveals the highly subjective slant in Ellmann's approach to the biography writing enterprise: "Now," says McCourt, "Ellmann's *Joyce* can be read in the light of Ellmann's own comment that 'My notion of biography is that it should be a portrait of the writer [biographer] as well as the subject.'"[100] Ellmann wrote his biography of Joyce for a reader "much like himself, an American liberal humanist."[101]

So, liberalism has been a distorting lens in the reading of Joyce, and the distortion requires correction: Joyce's "relationship with the Catholic Church remains to be explored further—and this will be another of the vital *lacunae* in Ellmann's portrait which will be addressed in the coming years."[102] The disproportion between the sparsity of reference to Catholicism in Ellmann's voluminous and otherwise encyclopedic biography of Joyce and the density of reference to Catholicism in Joyce's own writings is itself an indicator of the gap between the biographer and his subject. The absence of Catholicism from Ellmann's hermeneutic is not merely a *lacuna*; rather, it denotes an ideology among Joyce readers that projects upon Joyce certain positions regarding realism and religion which Joyce may not be presumed to have held. Joyce was nothing if not nuanced, but this may not always be said about his critics, and the secularist over-simplification leads to important distortions of Joyce's work.

Fr. Bruce Bradley, Joyce scholar and Jesuit, in a critique of a book which applies to Joyce's work the secularist hermeneutic, intelligently articulates a skeptical response to a tendency in Joycean criticism to confer upon the Irish writer a Christ-like or cultic status: "I feel that I am dealing not only with the author's lack of sensitivity to the religious traditions invoked but also with a kind of obsessiveness about Joyce and an overestimation of his importance that leads to a loss of perspective." Bradley, author of *James Joyce's Schooldays*, laments the absence of religious sensibility and theological *nous* in Joyce scholarship. Joyce's employment of Catholic doctrine and liturgy in the service of his aesthetic project lends itself to a curious secularist sacralization of the author and his work among readers of a humanist persuasion, but Bradley maintains that Joyce's own position is not so simple or self-aggrandizing: "Joyce's work does not represent the rigorous deconstruction of religious meaning . . . And Joyce's own attitude was a good deal more complex than this book[103] suggests."

Bradley finally expresses his own view and suggests an approach to Joyce which might succeed: it is necessary to "investigate the genesis of his religious sensibility," with "a sufficiently sympathetic understanding of the faith that Joyce considered he had lost and some degree of critical detachment from his proclamations of having done so."[104] It would be hard to conceive of a better outline of what this study proposes to do. Bradley's critique of Lang echoes McCourt's of Ellmann: they fail to grapple with the nuanced richness of Joyce's treatment of Catholicism. It is not an easy task. In order to understand the bigger picture, we must tackle the thorny question of the tone of Joyce's irony. It has confounded critics on both sides. Understanding the nature, tone, and targets of Joyce's irony is a key factor in discerning whether he is a realist or a relativist. Misunderstanding it has given rise to much confusion in Joyce studies. One Catholic reader, Hugh Kenner, has suggested a way out of the impasse.

I.5.4.3: *Joycean Irony and Stephen's Apostasy*

Kenner stands out as an important Catholic contributor to Joycean criticism whose readings retain authority. His discovery of Joyce's ironic self-distancing from Stephen Dedalus has left an indelible mark on Joyce criticism. Kenner crystallized the ironic intent in Joyce's portrayal of Stephen Dedalus. This applies also to his religiosity: "[H]is reaching out after orthodox salvation is . . . presented in terms that judge it."[105] In other words, the very terms with which Joyce depicts Stephen's religiosity are intended to expose its falsity. Kenner offers a way out of the morass of contradictory interpretations of Stephen's apostasy and Joyce's views on religion.

Lernout ably charts Stephen's route to "apostasy" from his early religiosity, exhaustively cataloguing its critical moments and manifestations both in *Portrait* and in *Ulysses*. Kenner would dispute few if any of the points he makes in this regard. Rather, his response to this would be that it does not prove Joyce to be an atheist and that there is evidence that Joyce is aware that what Stephen rejects is, to quote the words employed by Vatican Council II, "a fallacious idea of God" (*GS* 19). Stephen's ecstatic apostasy is depicted in the fourth chapter of *Portrait*, but that position is thereafter shown to be insufficient in the remainder of that novel and in *Ulysses*; Lernout and secularist Joyceans in general, fail to deal with the implications of this fact.[106]

Lernout is partially right about Joyce's position regarding religion and about the blinkered readings of some Catholic critics. It cannot be proven that Joyce recovered his Catholic faith, but neither can he be catalogued as a convinced atheist. Joyce severely critiqued what he perceived as "Catholic" deformities, but he did not acritically embrace atheism. To establish his spiritual position, we would have to know what values he condemns and what values he endorses. If he endorsed objective and universal human values, this in itself would be an additional argument in favor of the case for Joyce as a realist and not a relativist, and would bring us closer to discovering his religious position. Weldon Thornton, developing Kenner's critique, will help us to discover the intentionality of Joycean irony and the values that Joyce believed in.[107]

I.6: The Case for Joyce as a Realist

Ellmann was looking at Joyce (as Lernout would later do) from the standpoint of Joyce's religio-historical context as well as from the standpoint of the modern religio-historical context of Joycean interpretation. Kenner's reading of Joyce aspires to discover neither a religious nor an atheistic-humanist agendum. With Kenner, and later with Thornton, the argument shifts to the texts themselves and to the mind of Joyce as an artist who is creating something. What is implied by the very act of creating? And then, what is implied by the act of creating of a 19th century man influenced by the Enlightenment? That is Thornton's perspective. His argument is that Joyce is not creating as a 19th century post-Enlightenment man. He is creating as a perennial artist would create; employing, to use Joyce's own terms, the artistic selective and reproductive faculties to recapture the essence of the human experience. He is as interested in portraying the negative effects of Modernism as he is in portraying the affirmative effects of tradition, and vice versa of course.

Ellmann sees Joyce's portrayal of Stephen as emphatically affirmative; Thornton's view, like Kenner's, is that Joyce's portrayal of Stephen is critical, with some positive elements and some negative ones. He maintains that Stephen's "modernism," for example, is critiqued by Joyce. To be modern and antimodernist are not, according to Thornton, antithetical positions. Enough volumes have been written on irony in Joyce's portrayal of Stephen Dedalus to justify speaking of this as an established trend in Joycean literary criticism, of which the following from

Thornton is a good example: "Young Stephen Dedalus, very much a creature of his time, has a conception of reality and of his own psyche that is deeply influenced by the Modernist Syndrome. In this novel [*Portrait*] Joyce reveals to us the shallowness and insufficiency of Stephen's views."[108]

Thornton finds Stephen's Thomistic theory of aesthetics "not only coherent but very close to what Joyce himself believed,"[109] thus placing himself firmly on the side of those who see continuity between Joyce and the medieval worldview. Thornton's bias in favor of ontology is evident; his project is to prove that Joyce had the same bias. Commenting upon the general climate of literary criticism, he observes that it too has its biases and restrictive taboos: "Admittedly, to say that literature presents the meaning of an event or the spirit of a milieu, or even that it interprets reality, involves ontological assumptions that are difficult to defend in our present climate of opinion."[110]

Thorton helps us contextualize the environment of modern Joycean literary criticism, an era that itself has its own biases. By critiquing this climate, he helps us not only to understand better how to interpret Joyce; he takes us closer to the way in which Joyce's mind worked in relation to his own epoch. He helps us to recover aspects of Joyce's mind that many contemporary interpreters de-emphasize due to the limitations inherent in the 21st century environment of literary criticism; such as its skepticism that anyone can rise above cultural prejudices, its unreasoned disbelief in the possibility of omniscience, its tendency to interpret multiple literary devices as a sign of relativism, its misunderstanding denial of ontology and its reactionary rejection of religion.

While not always dealing specifically with religious issues, Thornton asserts nonetheless that he sees Joyce "as having a very substantial religious sensibility."[111] When asked to confirm this, he commented that, "this is a topic that I continue to find of great interest and importance."[112] In these statements there is an implicit recognition of the connection between ontology and religion. This is not a majority position in Joyce studies or indeed in literary criticism in general: "[L]inguistic and ethical relativism has such authority in the modernist critical milieu that ... the burden of proof falls on those of us who would argue for a continuity in Joyce's 'normative' attitudes."[113] Thornton confronts that burden of proof and presents the fruits of his endeavors. Now that we have seen the deficiencies of Lernout's pro-Enlightenment and anti-Catholic lens for understanding the mind of Joyce and interpreting his works, let us turn our attention to a scholar who draws us closer to a better understanding of these realities.

I.6.1: Thornton on Joyce's Portrait of the Artist as a Young Man

I.6.1.1: Joyce's Critique of Modernism

The boldness of the title of Thornton's book on Joyce's first novel—*The Antimodernism of Joyce's* Portrait of the Artist as a Young Man—arises from the fact of Joyce's reputation as pioneer and paradigm of literary modernism. Thornton outlines what he understands to be the defining characteristics of literary modernism, thereby to show Joyce's opposition to it in *Portrait*: "The modernist idea . . . that the individual is self-contained and self-determining—is undoubtedly a central theme of that novel." Many critics of a humanist persuasion have perceived as much, but presuppose an identity of intention and vision between James Joyce and Stephen Dedalus which endorses the theme of self-creation. Thornton disagrees: "Joyce's purpose in the novel is not to celebrate such individualism; on the contrary, it is to show how superficial and insufficient this understanding of the individual psyche is."[114]

Thornton sees Joyce's cultural context, and our own, as burdened by a harmful subject-object, mind-nature, and inner-outer dichotomization inherited from Galileo and Descartes—"expressing itself in literary terms mainly in symbolism vs. naturalism"—and argues that Joyce perceived its distortive effects: "Joyce saw the essential falseness and pernicious effects of this dichotomization, and prepared himself to effect a synthesis of these two perspectives."[115] Thornton then, like Levy, sees the Joycean project in terms of remedial synthesis rather than celebratory emancipation from ontology. *Portrait*, he says, is a revelation of the superficiality and artificiality of the modernist anthropology. It involves a "profound criticism of the modernist view of the self."[116]

Among the defining characteristics of modernism as described by Thornton is the exaggeration of subjectivity and individuality to the point of the elimination of the unifying concept of human nature; the concept of humanity as a vast community sharing certain irrefutable values and perspectives. The rejection of religion is at the root of this relativism and individualism: "We are told that the purported abandonment of traditional omniscient point of view by modernist novelists reflects their recognition that there simply is no 'omniscient' perspective." Thornton dismisses as "shaky and imprecise" the analogy between the omniscient narrator and the omniscient-omnipotent Victorian God whose supposed death modernist narrative techniques seek to reflect, "for it is doubtful that the traditional omniscient point of view ever 'stood for' or represented the mind of God."[117] Although self-evident, this truism needs to be restated, due to the tendency to interpret Joyce's mind as that of an atheist individualist whose aim it is to overthrow the concept of an omniscient and omnipotent God.

Thornton points out with matter-of-fact simplicity that by the very act of setting out to write something, the author declares a commitment to something he thinks has value. It is impossible for a writer to write without committing himself to some valuational vision. Writers write because they have something to say. The "value laden words" in their novels are not always attributable solely to their characters but evoke "some qualitative perspective other than that of an individual character, and we should ask ourselves what we think these words represent."[118]

According to Thornton, the modernist emancipation from authority and celebration of individuality is, in fact, critiqued by many writers who are taken to be modernist. Joyce's writings, for example, exemplify modernist Enlightenment ideals, but ironically and critically. Thornton's argument is that this is Joyce's intention in his portrayal of Stephen Dedalus. As we have seen in Levy's article and Joyce's own essay on the Renaissance,[119] the impression emerges that he was anything but an acritical child of the Enlightenment and therefore cannot be readily catalogued as a modernist writer. Thornton argues his case by confronting ancient, medieval and modern cultural categories with Joyce's texts.

I.6.1.2: Joyce's Ontological Categories

Of the "leading ideas" that provided guidelines for Joyce's art, Thornton singles out three: one, that of the unity of mind and matter as opposed to Cartesian dualism; two,—this idea is of surpassing importance for the purposes of our study—"the idea of potentiality, which sees life in terms of unfolding processes through which persons and societies realize (or fail to realize) in the future certain potentialities inherent in their past and present"; and thirdly, the idea that when we perceive, we perceive "qualities and natures and meanings."[120] Thornton holds that Stephen's Aristotelian-Thomistic aesthetic outlined in *Portrait* was and remained Joyce's aesthetic also. To terms like ontology and epiphany, he adds the term potentiality; in the Aristotelian sense of the dynamic process by which potency becomes actuality, reaching its end, its *telos*, as described in the second "leading idea" just outlined above.

On the subject of this second leading idea, Thornton

quotes what he calls Hugh Kenner's "most perspicacious statement" about Joyce's "mind and work" and "belief in potentiality": "[T]he sharpest exegetical instrument we can bring to the work of Joyce is Aristotle's great conception of potency and act."[121] The possibility of growth and the frustration thereof is arguably the primary driving passion of Joyce's art. The term "potentiality" entails other terms like dynamism, process and plenitude, means and ends, growth and goals, which will be crucial to our study of Joyce in the light of Catholic doctrine, and to the attempt to understand his anthropological and theological positions after apostasy.

Human potentiality becomes act in response to life experiences; these, in turn, occasionally coalesce in the form of epiphanical moments, opportunities of insight, readjustment and growth. Thornton usefully summarizes the Joycean aesthetic in which the hermeneutic surrounding the word epiphany, although the term itself doesn't explicitly appear, is described in a way that resonates with Stephen's aesthetic as described in *Stephen Hero* and *Portrait*. Joyce seeks to penetrate to "the dimension of meaning that lies within every experience and which the artist is always attempting to get at in any character, any scene, any series of events."[122]

The ontological aesthetic described here, with its clear Thomistic resonances of subjective striving to "get at" objective meaning, is the one that Eco claims Joyce abandoned, and that Levy argues remained a source of boundless fecundity.[123] Joyce's understanding of ontology does not falsely preclude the possibility of change—in the form of growth or regression—within a permanent substratum of personal identity. Personality may evolve or regress while remaining identical. Identity and change are not irreconcilable opposites, and neither are individuality and universality. The individual wishing fully and truly to become himself, may only do so in relationship with others.

I.6.1.3: Identity, Evolvement, and Universality

In his book, Thornton discusses the evolution of the personality of Stephen in *Portrait*. The first thing to note is that there is unity in dynamism; it is identifiably the same "I" who grows throughout the four phases presented in the first four chapters of the novel, in which there is also an alternating inner-outer pattern: social (outer), sensuous (inner), religious (outer),[124] aesthetic (inner). In the fifth and final chapter there is no clear breakthrough along the lines of the previous four chapters because, Thornton argues (following Kenner), Stephen is deliberately portrayed as having arrived at an impasse yet to be overcome. The "innerness" of his aesthetic stance, with its lopsided emphasis on the intellectual and imaginative subjectivity of the artist, continues to frustrate the potentiality of growth that is possible only by means of receptive engagement with external reality.

The reconciliation of the inner-outer and subject-object dichotomies and resolution of Stephen's inner imbalance will occur in *Ulysses*, through the suffering he undergoes at his mother's death and through the selfless and salvific intervention of Leopold Bloom. The "innerness" of Stephen's aesthetic is as important for my purposes as the "outerness" of his religiosity. Religion reduced to externals is no less an aberration than art as solely or primarily subjective. Stephen must emerge from his splendid intellectual isolation, must engage with entities and with others in order to grow and bear fruit as a man and as an artist. This emergence and immersion will happen in *Ulysses* not by his initiative but by Leopold Bloom's.

The self, of itself, is insufficient; the initiative proceeds from another. Contrary to the modernist notion of autonomy, Stephen cannot "fix" himself. Thornton perceives Joyce's anti-modernism in his rejection of the Enlightenment notion of fulfilled individuality as total self-awareness and total self-determination, as though man were capable of autonomously understanding and programming himself. Stephen is shown to be a frustrated proponent of this ideal, continually confounded by his own complexity.

"Interrelatedness" and "intersubjectivity"[25] are key terms in Thornton's reading of Joyce. Joyce is a believer in the existence of "human nature"; not as a permanently static mechanism, but as an incalculably rich, enormously complex and universally shared experience. Since Thornton's reading is not overtly religious, he gives no explicit treatment to an elusive mysterious principle propitious to growth and unity that is operative in the Joycean simulacrum of the human struggle. This belief is given fuller artistic expression in *Ulysses*. Whether this elusive principle is Joyce himself as artist and "god" of his creation or God or a cooperation of both is difficult to discern. It is the subject of this book. Thornton helps us to realize that Joyce is a highly nuanced and complex thinker not easily categorized because he rejects the temptation to superimpose facile categories on the human experience. One such categorization is the Cartesian dichotomization of individuality into the strictly distinct entities of mind and body; a categorical superimposition which Joyce, according to Thornton, exposes as false.[126]

I.6.1.4: Mind and Matter

Professor Augustine Martin wrote of Joyce's endeavour to overcome Cartesian dichotomies, one of which is the dualism of mind and matter: *res cogitans* and *res extensa*. Joyce, he claims, worked towards "unity of vision," and sought the means "of harmonising the great antinomies that divided modern consciousness."[127] Thornton shares this opinion. He maintains that Joyce's Stephen must get beyond "the dualism that now holds him in thrall . . . coming to understand that matter is not the enemy of the spirit, but is the indispensable means of its manifestation."[128]

The challenge to overcome Cartesian mind-body, spirit-matter dualism is related to the theme of complexity of the self. In *Portrait*, especially but not exclusively in the final chapter, there is evidence of a dawning discovery on Stephen's part that he remains a mystery to himself in spite of the sense of arrival and self-discovery depicted in the fourth chapter: "Stephen's psyche has a vitality and richness of which he is not even aware."[129] This is a liberating discovery but one that disconcerts the modernist individualist optimism. Influences apparently alien to himself intrude uninvited upon his interior monologue:

observing this, he asks, "Could his mind then not trust itself?"[130] The sense of consciousness that pervades in *Ulysses*, as no less a mystery than the unconscious, as a psychic field of unpredictable and uncontrollable influences, is already present in *Portrait*: "That his mind has 'a life of its own' is shown repeatedly by its associations, by its responsiveness to bodily sensations, to associations triggered by scenes, odors, etc."[131]

In the soul-body synthesis being presented here, Thornton, consciously or otherwise it is impossible to say (and not crucial to know), is describing Stephen's discovery of an entirely Catholic anthropology: "Man is not the soul alone,"[132] and, "The soul does not possess the perfection of its own nature except in union with the body."[133] The discovery of Stephen comes very close to the description articulated many years later and in a different context by Josef Pieper, who, although not of course a Joyce scholar, is a fellow 20th century Neo-Platonist, Aristotelian, and Thomist who can help us to understand the subtlety of Joyce's mind. (For this reason, I will have recourse to Pieper's incisive erudition more than once in the course of my study.) In his book *Death and Immortality*, Pieper welcomes the fact that modern empirical sciences "not only testify that there is in fact nothing 'purely spiritual' in man, nothing that is thought alone, exclusively intellectual product; rather, there are always accompanying operations of the senses and functions of the organs."[134] This is a confirmation of the "ancient proposition of the *anima forma corporis*" which was declared obligatory dogma of the Church at the Council of Vienne in 1311-12.

By an inscrutable perversity of fate this quintessentially Catholic doctrine of the soul as form of the body came to be seen as a liberation from Catholicism: "It is hard to understand how this proposition . . . should have fallen so entirely into oblivion . . . that modern philosophical anthropology has had to rediscover the idea anew as something supposedly contradictory to the Christian view of man's physicality." We will see in the next chapter that this perversity of fate is not entirely inscrutable: it had much to do with the confusion of Catholicism with Puritanism. Pieper completes his clarification with the point that the Catholic anthropology of man as a soul-body unity in duality precludes materialism no less than spiritualism: "[T]here is nothing in the human realm which could be called 'purely material,' purely physical, purely biological."[135] It is well known that a part of the human body is symbolically ascribed to each chapter of Joyce's *Ulysses*, as part of the writer's aim to assert the dignity of the body. This is not the only theme that the later novel shares with *Portrait*, as Thornton shows.

I.6.2: Weldon Thornton on Joyce's Ulysses

I.6.2.1: Reconciling Multiplicity and Unity

As a kind of first premise for approaching Joyce's work, Thornton distinguishes between Joyce the man and Joyce the writer. Recognizing that this may seem an arbitrary distinction more likely to confuse than to clarify, he explains: "How such a difference can exist is not easy to understand, but it is undeniable that writers can project saner values into their works than they manifest in their lives."¹³⁶ He cites the example of F. Scott Fitzgerald whose writings expose with profundity and precision the hollowness of the very ideals that he himself pursued to sad effect in his own life, and quotes Joyce's letter to his brother Stanislaus referring to himself as "the foolish author of a wise book"¹³⁷ as an indicator that Joyce himself was conscious of the distinction. This distinction relativizes the importance of biographical information about Joyce the man, and prioritizes his writings as the final site of arbitration when it comes to discerning the thematic concerns and worldview of Joyce the author.

Now, the way is opened up to access the convictions of Joyce the author of *Ulysses*. The discovery of authorial intention is an ongoing bone of contention in Joyce studies. In *Portrait*, Stephen likens the role of the artist in relation to his art to that of the deist God of creation: "the artist, like the God of the creation, remains within or behind or beyond or above his handiwork, invisible, refined out of existence, indifferent, paring his fingernails."¹³⁸ Thornton quotes Joyce scholar Sheldon Brivic, who "astutely points out that Stephen's statement doesn't preclude the author's going *into* his work."¹³⁹ So, Joyce's worldview is discernible *in* his work. Thornton claims to have discovered *the* authoritative narrative voice of Joyce's novel.

With the aid of Brivic's insight, Thornton presents the daring theory that there is a single unifying perspective, incalculably ample and multifaceted, encompassing and governing the bewildering multiplicity of narrative voices, perspectives, and styles of *Ulysses*. Therefore, far from celebrating the horizons of anarchic opportunity opened by fragmentariness, Joyce's vision is one that champions unity and harmony and exposes the harmful reductionism of dichotomization and relativism. If Thorton's theory about the unity of Joyce's work and his truth-oriented commitment is correct, then it would help us understand more fully what James Joyce believed in. To prove that it is correct, he would have to provide evidence of one identifiable authorial voice with an identifiable thematic and technical agendum in the dizzying carnival of themes and styles, voices and values that is *Ulysses*.

Just as *Portrait of the Artist* is commonly assumed to be a novel in the modernist mould, *Ulysses* is commonly assumed to have surpassed the notion of one narrative voice whose authority aspires to preside over all other voices and perspectives in the novel. Declan Kiberd, for example, has stated that *Ulysses* is "a text without any final authority."[140] Thornton argues that Joyce has not in fact done away with the conventional so-called "omniscient" narrator. He notes this goes against the grain of current scholarship and laments a certain taboo in literary criticism, rooted in "contemporary biases against authority generally."[141] So, the absence of authorial authority is a construct of their, the interpreters', historical time, not of Joyce and his time. Thornton maintains that Joyce is very much an author with serious and challenging pretensions to authority.

In short, *Ulysses* "does not involve linguistic or moral relativism."[142] Thornton describes the trajectory of Joycean individuation from *Dubliners* through *Portrait* to

Ulysses, not from a religious perspective but simply from a realist perspective. Joyce's concern as artist, he argues, is to expose and critique "modes of discourse" that "frustrate the potential" of human beings: "Joyce devoted so much time and energy to developing this array of styles in *Ulysses* not because he was a relativist, but in order to expose for his readers certain modes of language and received ideas and attitudes that would inhibit their lives."[143] As well as being a watermark contribution to Joycean criticism, to demonstrate the presence of narrative "omniscience" in *Ulysses*, no matter how skillfully effaced, along with a consistent and coherent authorial thematic intent, would be a major aid to understanding the nature of Joyce's "atheism."

I.6.2.2: The Thematic Agendum of Joyce's Techniques

Zooming in on the intentions of the hidden Joycean author, Thornton's second claim is that the "initial style" of the first six chapters of *Ulysses*, which blends narrative devices with consummate unobtrusive skill, represents the "collective cultural psyche," which is the ultimate authoritative voice of the novel. The convictions of that voice are the convictions of Joyce the writer. Its mode of expression is established in the first six chapters, and the remaining twelve chapters, each of which is written in a different style or an array of different styles, should be referred back to this original style. It is hard not to notice the absence of a clear explanation, in Thornton's exposition, of what is meant by the expression "collective psychic milieu" and its close synonyms "cultural psyche" and "communal mind." It seems to signify something as simple as "common sense," i.e., an instinct for the authentic shared by the human community.

All of the subsequent narrative voices, styles and perspectives, regardless of their scientific or rhetorical persuasiveness, and/ or lack thereof, will be measured against this initial voice and found wanting. Often, Joyce wishes to make it clear that the style or styles being employed fail woefully to correspond to the content they contain. This in itself is an anti-relativistic strategy. Thornton argues that Joyce as an artist navigated his way between the naïve naturalism (or materialism) and ersatz symbolism (a form of idealism) that were fashionable in his time, exposing their shortcomings; that he is no symbolist and that his undeniable realism is not empiricist.

Joyce, in an admiring lecture on William Blake, argued: "If we must accuse of madness every great genius who does not believe in the hurried materialism now in vogue with the happy fatuousness of a recent college graduate in the exact sciences, little remains for art and universal philosophy."[144] Joyce's close friend Frank Budgen is a useful ally in Thornton's endeavor, since his approach is the same: "Budgen's point—and my own—is that the realism of *Ulysses* captures the very spirit of the place"[145] (i.e. of turn of the century Dublin).

By speaking in ontological terms of "realism" that "captures the very spirit of the place," Thornton is clearly thinking of Joyce's artistic endeavour in a way that corresponds with the Thomist aesthetic described by Stephen in *Portrait*. Joycean criticism generally views Joyce as a convinced and able champion of a liberating relativism, interpreting Joyce's virtuoso mastery of a diverse plethora of literary styles as a way of proving, and celebrating, the impossibility of accessing objective truth. Thornton believes that in *Ulysses* style is subordinate to substance and technique is subordinate to theme; that the novel ultimately presents in its own uniquely original and surprising way something so "conventional" as "norms and values."

In a relativist climate the onus of proof is on the side of those who hold the minority position, and Thornton accepts the challenge to argue his case. This he does by exposing the prejudices of the age of the contemporary critic and by presenting evidence and arguments that enable us to access Joyce's authorial convictions. One such argument is that in the act of deciding what characters to draw and what events to narrate an author is already establishing a clear thematic purpose. Such an argument may be received as so self-evident as not to merit mention, or it may be received as a refreshing breath of common sense that it is imperative to make in an environment in which even the obvious is subjected to interminable methodical doubt. It is the first block of Thornton's argument in favor of Joyce's "continuous agency" in *Ulysses*: "I believe that Joyce [chose] . . . to ground his novel in narrative devices and techniques and in values that manifest his own artistic purposes and values."[146]

I.6.2.3: Joyce's Valuational Stands

What are those purposes and values? Religious and secularist readers often coincide in answers to this question. Thornton mentions Marilyn French in support of his case. She approaches Joyce from a secularist and feminist perspective and yet finds in Joyce the same values found by a religious reading:

> Among the values that the novel sanctions are the sincerity and commitment and intellectual courage behind Stephen's struggles to find a viable worldview, and the openness to experience and concern for others that are such deep features of Bloom's personality (in Marilyn French's terms, his *caritas*). Among the qualities that the novel criticizes are the materialism, mockery, and cynicism exemplified in Mulligan, the presumptuous and insular 'wisdom' of Deasy, and the purblind chauvinism of the citizen.[147]

To champion some qualities and critique others is itself a proof of commitment to objective values, but the admiration of Stephen's "struggles to find a viable worldview" is also an important element of the Joycean aesthetic, because it indicates dynamism and the possibility of growth or regression, paralysis or progress.

In his book on antimodernism in *Portrait*, Thornton had already made the claim that Joyce's concern is with Aristotelian potentiality, that anything which paralyzes human growth is exposed with surgical honesty and anything which facilitates it is artfully epiphanized. In his book on *Ulysses* that idea surfaces again: "Through this narrative perspective we come to regard Stephen and Bloom with profound sympathy"—the infectious authorial tone of "profound sympathy" is another important point we will return to and should be mentally noted—"but we also recognize their foibles and failings ... and as a result we hope that they will confront their fears and become what they are capable of becoming."[148]

The teleological resonances of this hermeneutic are loud and clear; the human experience is about growth and goals; the opportunity to advance towards universal, objective values, and the danger of failure. This is what is at stake in the great human drama. By this I refer to a mystery that is beyond words which it is the task of the word somehow to transmit. Words at their artful best have the power to come wonderfully close. By showing how some styles fall horribly short and others come breathtakingly close, Joyce pays homage to this mystery. In parody as well as in poetry Joyce is mediating that mystery. We are now better positioned to return to the point of discerning the tone and targets of Joyce's irony.

I.6.2.4: Understanding Joycean Irony

Joyce's irony is not mere cynicism. Some of the values in favor of which he takes a stand are unmistakably Christian: "for in the book he reveals his preference for *caritas* over selfishness or chauvinism, for responsiveness and engagement over solipsism and self-centeredness, for honest self-assessment over sentimental self-indulgence."[149] With regard to the tone of Joyce the author towards the characters he depicts, Thornton makes and repeats an observation that will be important in my own reading of Joyce's works: "It requires special care for an author to remain present but effaced, and especially to do so in a way that maintains an overall tone of sympathy toward his fictive creation—as Joyce does." A rare achievement, Thornton notes: "Most authors' attempts at effacement result in distinct irony toward their characters."[150]

Joyce's sympathetic stance is compatible with irony, as when he uses irony to show how some styles fail to measure up to the richness of the human experience. The conventional interpretation of the Wandering Rocks chapter, for example, is that it critiques the mechanizing and fragmenting impact of urbanization like Eliot's "The Waste Land," but this reading is confounded by the "many acts of charity and kindness, large and small, that run through the episode."[151] The episode's clinical and cynical tone fails to do justice, *and fails to do injustice*—because the underlying truth triumphs—to the caliber of the endearingly all too human characters. The imperfection of their motives is more poignant than pathetic; their actions retain a stubborn dignity. By thus exposing the shortcomings of the "scientific" sociological survey, the perspective of the implied author prevails over that of the treacherously factual narrator.

The gentleness of Joycean irony and the benevolent disposition towards struggling humanity is general throughout the novel. Thornton gives a chapter by chapter analysis in his book. His reading of the Circe chapter, in which Stephen and Bloom must confront their inner psychological demons,[152] is of particular interest, since it contains the climax of the novel. He shows how Joyce critiques Freudianism, another literary lens through which many Joyce interpreters distort Joyce, unearthing several biographical proofs of Joyce's derisive attitude towards Freudian theory and its dichotomization of conscious and unconscious. Joyce parodies Freudian theory in the Circe episode, along with the expressionist style used to dramatize it, but Freudian critics did not get the joke. This error is gradually being overcome in recent criticism: "[R]ecent critics have expressed misgivings about how well the agenda of the episode aligns with Joyce's own thinking."[153]

Marshall Needleton Armintor condemns Thornton's book on *Ulysses* as an attempt to "browbeat" readers into sharing his "absolutist bent." Needleton sweepingly rejects Thornton's argument—along with a welter of textual and extra-textual evidence, plus the testimony of a plethora of other recent Joyce scholars—that Joyce parodies Freudian psychoanalytical theory in the Circe chapter of *Ulysses*, and that generations of Freudians failed to get the joke. Needleton is on unsure ground in his overly sure rejection. If Joyce's "when they were young and easily freudened" in *Finnegans Wake* is not sufficient to show his comic irreverence towards Freudian theory, there is also the fact that he, Joyce, called psychoanalysis "neither more nor less than blackmail" and stated, "I have nothing to do with psychoanalysis."[154] Needleton is an expert in the history of Jewish comics and in Freudian psychoanalysis (and Jacques Lacan, Catholic apostate). This might go some way towards explaining his position: "Joyce's work always has and still continues to invite widely varied critical approaches, which give his oeuvre plenty of room to breathe, withstand any analysis, and leave open the possibility of other readings;"[155] open, that is, to any reading but one informed, like Thornton's, by Aristotelian realism. Only relativism is allowed to be absolutist.

Again, the tone and targets of Joycean irony, and the intentionality of his literary techniques, are subordinate to his thematic aims. His thematic aims help us to discover the tone and targets of his irony and technical intentionality, and vice versa. With Joyce, the right explanation is often the simplest one. In the case of the Circe episode, the plain historical facts are that Stephen is drunk and is rescued by Bloom from a brothel. It is this act of kindness that leads him out of his depression and prompts a turning point in his heart and in his art: "Again Frank Budgen shows great insight about this episode: 'It is steeped in the atmosphere and governed by the logic of hallucinations, but its dominant theme is the fatherly love and care of Bloom for Stephen Dedalus.'"[156] Stephen emerges unscathed from the Circe crisis, thanks not to cathartic Freudian hallucinations, but to Bloom's discreet and charitable intervention.

I.6.2.5: Religion in the Oxen of the Sun Episode

So, Thornton confronts the prejudices of modern literary criticism and offers a way out of the morass of conflicting opinions to discover the grand Joycean literary plan. Let us turn now, briefly, to the more directly religious elements in the mind of Joyce. Thornton's analysis of the Oxen of the Sun chapter of *Ulysses* is of particular interest to us because of its religious theme. Thornton provides a long list of epithets for God in this chapter, and finds in them three categories or, as he puts it, three "faces" of God: "(1) God as creator—as the source of everything that exists, physical and spiritual; (2) God as prohibitor, curser, and punisher; and (3) God as reconciler and redeemer."[157]

Regarding God as creator, Thornton displays an awareness of the positive implications of creational doctrine in favor of the material (as sourced in God) not always present in Joycean criticism. It has important philosophical implications; "for unless we understand that God is the source of the *prima materia* underlying both matter and spirit, we fall into a dualism that denigrates one or the other"—a dualism which has often been preached heretically in the name of Christianity—"and thus we fail to see the inextricable unity of matter and spirit, of nature and imagination, that forms one of Joyce's main themes in *Ulysses*."[158]

The "faces" of God as creator and as punisher feature strongly in *Portrait*, as we shall see; God as reconciler and redeemer features little in Stephen's formation, or in *Dubliners*. God the creator and God the punisher feature much more prominently. Thornton identifies a shift in the Oxen of the Sun episode from God the punisher and prohibitor to God the reconciler and redeemer, a "more beneficent visage." The "beneficent visage" is the face of God the redeemer and reconciler. There follows an affirmation of an intent to recuperate religious *eros*—denoting attraction, joy, ecstatic union with the divine—in the Joycean aesthetic. Thornton provides this evidence from the Oxen in the Sun chapter: Stephen alludes to Christ as "our Agenbuyer," and refers to a "postcreation" phase initiated in God's assumption of human flesh in the womb of Mary to become the Incarnate Word in Christ: "As Stephen puts it, 'In woman's womb word is made flesh but in the spirit of the maker all flesh that passes becomes the word that shall not pass away. This is the postcreation' (U, 14.292)."[159]

Stephen likens his own role as artist—"priest of the eternal imagination"[160] who aspires to unite spirit and flesh, history and eternity—to that of Mary: "[M]ankind, made in the image of God, is an agent of God's continuing creation." Therefore, like Mary, we are called to co-creation or post-creation: "Nature is not . . . static and sacrosanct, but is an array of potentialities to be given still undiscovered forms . . . [W]e are obligated . . . to participate in the continuing creation." The primacy given to woman, represented by Mary, is unique to Christianity in world religions, and more so to Catholicism than to other Christian denominations. That doctrine has a profound theological and anthropological richness recognized by Thornton and, he argues, by Stephen: "God's willingness to turn to a second woman, Mary—herself a part of the natural creation—as the vehicle of his redeemer aspect, is a sign of his wish to reconcile himself with his creation and to invite mankind to join its extension."[161]

The discovery in Stephen's words of a call to dynamism and co-creativity—"postcreation"—is insightful, as is the identification of a shift from God as creator and punisher to God as redeemer and reconciler. By itself, however, this passage would be thin evidence of a religious sensibility. Further evidence will have to be furnished.

I.7: Conclusion

We have seen that there is a current of Joyce studies—represented by figures like Eco, Ellmann, and Lernout—which holds that Joyce outgrew and abandoned the Thomist categories of his early intellectual formation and that the overcoming of Catholicism was pre-requisite to his artistic fecundity, which is mostly about rejoicing in the freedom of uncertainty. Antoine Levy and Weldon Thornton have strongly argued that there is another way of reading Joyce. Freedom is not about moving the mountain or throwing away the map, and an approach to Joyce's work unconditioned by the dogma of deconstructionism discovers a different dynamic at work. It is true that Joyce wishes to celebrate life's definition-defying unpredictability along with the wonder of the mundane, the material, the quotidian as the usual domain of the human experience and therefore of art; but it is no less true that he perceives that domain as invested with a transcendent luminosity and vehemently defends its light from the forces that besiege it from the outside and betray it from the inside.

The presence of disorder in *Ulysses*, linguistic and existential, is undeniable. But the disorder is never complete. Chaos is ever-present and omni-threatening, but it does not engulf meaning, which can neither be engulfed nor exhausted. The light is never extinguished by the winds of mere wordplay, and nor is it ever quite captured by the incalculable potency of metaphor, but it is always *there*. Joyce will often depict "order" as darkness luminously camouflaged, and "chaos" as simplicity in wonderful disguise. *Ulysses* celebrates the failure of language at its worst to obscure and at its best to reflect the light that makes life worthwhile. Hence Joyce's pained response to the news of his favorite aunt's rejection of the novel: "If *Ulysses* isn't fit to read, life isn't fit to live."[162] It is the converse of a Pyrrhic victory—a glorious defeat. In the course of that defeat, patterns reductive of humanity are exposed with unflinching surgical precision, and "redemption" is implied, implored, and even offered.

What is at stake here is whether Joyce was a realist or a relativist. As a relativist, he would be a convinced sceptic about the existence of objective and universal truth; as a realist, he would be a convinced believer in the existence of objective and universal truth. Relativism often labors under important misconceptions about the pretensions of realism to understand the divine and human mysteries. Ratzinger has corrected these misconceptions and clarified the pretensions of realism. Realism and religiosity are so connected that the presence of one strongly corroborates the simultaneous presence of the other. Levy and Thornton, by proving Joyce's realistic bent, have provided grounds for hope of finding clarity regarding Joyce's enduring position on the subject of religion, and proofs of religious belief in Joyce's writings will reinforce the argument that he remained a realist.

This chapter has been a kind of "pre-religious preamble" to our study of Joyce's religious mind. Reading Joyce with the Catholic doctrine of divine grace as a hermeneutical reference, in chapter III, will enable us to take Weldon Thornton's theory a step further. In order to provide an important preliminary context of Joyce's writings, however, we must first examine one of the major *obstacles* to grace, mercy and human dignity in the Joycean *oeuvre*, namely 19th century Irish Catholicism.

Chapter II: *Agape* without *Eros*

II.1: Introduction

The purpose of this chapter is to identify what it is about Catholicism that Joyce unequivocally rejects; that is, to confront what Jeffrey Segall calls the "darker side of Catholicism that Joyce was so familiar with."[1] Similarly to Segall, Lernout maintains that Joyce's critique of crippling guilt in *Portrait* necessarily entails rejection not only of Catholicism but of religion: "We all know that religion and the loss of religion is a major theme in *A Portrait of the Artist as a Young Man*."[2] Joyce scholar Roy Gottfried cites authoritarianism and repressiveness as causes of Joyce's rejection of Catholicism:

> If Joyce found the Catholic Church unattractive precisely for its monolithic authority and rigidity, he most particularly resisted the church's obtuse silence about issues of real life: its unwillingness to acknowledge the forces within human beings and the forces in the surrounding culture that spoke to their drives and needs... He consistently demanded frankness, resisting the church's way of idealizing, even etherealizing human drives.[3]

Gottfried quotes from one of Joyce's letters: "I am nauseated about [the church's] lying drivel about pure men and pure women ... lying in the face of truth."

Gottfried inserts "the church's," but in fact, Joyce was referring in this letter to Irish patriots as much as to Irish priests.[4] This is very important to know. It means that whatever it was about the Church in Ireland that provoked Joyce's wrath was present also in the Irish nationalist movement and in Irish society at large. The Church, sometimes for better and sometimes for worse, does not and cannot exist in a society as a spiritual and intellectual islet. It influences the society where it is present, and is inevitably influenced by that society. Knowledge of historical and sociological context is therefore helpful in understanding the Church, and in understanding James Joyce.

In order to help the literary critic better understand what it is about Catholicism that Joyce robustly and definitively rejects in his apostasy, it is necessary to provide a realistic picture of the 19th century Irish society from which he emerges. The main task of this chapter is to show that Joyce does not reject religion *per se* but a distorted religiosity; a secondary task is to establish what it is that he retains, if anything.

In short, I will argue that what Joyce rejects is *agape* without *eros*, but that he does not respond to this distortion with a Nietzschean anti-*agape* advocation of Dionysian frenzy; rather, he desires to retain a nebulous, ill-defined idea of religious *eros*.[5] For present purposes, *eros* may be understood as that aspect of love that desires union of the self with the other, and *agape* as that aspect of love that disposes the self towards sacrifice for the other. To understand these dynamics which Joyce himself wished to understand and artistically represent, it is essential to know the historical background out of which the Irish author emerged. The short story "Eveline" is an optimal point of entry in the endeavour to decipher Joyce's nuanced response to his Irish Catholic inheritance.

"Eveline" will serve as the "antechamber" of my interpretation of Joyce's Catholicism in his other works. I will first present the findings of contemporary literary criticism in relation to the story. Then I will present a summary of the historical context out of which the story arises, with the aid of remarks made by Joyce himself and by his brother Stanislaus, and with the analyses of contemporary Irish cultural commentators. Having seen the historical context, we will be in a position better to understand the story; accepting, but completing, the findings of Joyce's literary critics. Thereafter, with the historical background established, I will trace Joyce's route to apostasy as it is fictionally represented in *A Portrait of the Artist as a Young Man.* By the end of the chapter we will be better positioned to understand the negative and positive aspects of Joyce's disposition towards the religious realities.

II.2: "Eveline" and Irish Catholicism

II.2.1: "Eveline" and Critical Interpretation

In "Eveline" Joyce presents to us, with a minimum of deft strokes, a young Dublin woman who is trapped by a sense of loyalty to her family, having promised her dying mother that she would look after her alcoholic father, which ultimately impedes her from embarking on a boat with her suitor Frank, a sailor, to a new life in Buenos Aires. The first and strongest impression even of the alert reader, in spite of nagging doubts, is that this is a story of absurdly missed opportunity, and the emotional reaction is one of sorrow and anger at the forces that conspire to frustrate Eveline's destiny and at her lack of personality in allowing them to do so.

This reaction has been ably articulated by Joanna Luft in an article in which she argues that Eveline "is arguably subject to the most severe inculcation by catholic / colonialist . . . and patriarchal . . . authority, making her representative of the paralysis in *Dubliners*."[6] It is not fear of Frank or "emigration anxiety," as other scholars have said, that holds Eveline back. Luft incisively summarizes Eveline's situation with the aid of Warren Beck:

> At the root of Eveline's paralysis is the evisceration of self that results from being colonised by feelings of obligation. Her concern for her father springs from a burden of obligation which equals the other burdens of obligation that she feels. In fact, as Beck points out, her entire inner life consists of feelings of obligation, to her family and then to Frank: "For Eveline, the possibility of 'life, perhaps love, too' has been eroded by an exacting sense of obligation," the consequence of which is a loss of "the sense of self"[7] and a life that boils down to "a stark dilemma of duties." Even her feelings about Frank are based on obligation—not surprising since this seems to be all she knows of human relationships. On the verge of leaving with him, "what she thinks

of is not love, even for him, but of something owed here too—'Could she still draw back after all he had done for her.'"[8] The question of what she wants to do never crosses Eveline's mind. Rather, she wonders if she is being wise, and in her anxiety at the docks prays to God "to show her what was her duty."[9] Torn between feeling obligated to her family and feeling obligated to Frank, and having no other basis for making decisions but feelings of obligation, she is overwhelmed absolutely.[10]

This is the standard reading: that Eveline has lost the opportunity of a lifetime by not boarding the boat with her suitor. Luft, without naming the terms, provides a succinct explanation of *agape* without *eros* (self-sacrifice without self-fulfillment). However, Joyce was an artist, not an anti-Catholic propagandist, and, as is usually the case in his writings, there is more to the story than first meets the eye.

Hugh Kenner enriched the fatalist reading of the story by observing the shady aspects of the ironically named Frank, a suitor too good to be true, arguing that if she had boarded the boat Eveline might well have set herself up for a life of exploitation and degradation. Kenner perceives Frank as "a bounder with a glib line" who is trying to "pick himself up a piece of skirt" with "the patter of an experienced seducer."[11] Kenner shares the opinion of Eveline's father, who, though no angel himself, is unimpressed by Eveline's consort: "I know these sailor chaps,"[12] he says, forbidding the affair. Eveline is ill-equipped to see through the wily charms of this devious Frank, who can hardly be said to represent Catholicism in any way. This makes the story even more fatalistic and more tragic: Eveline is trapped in a lose-lose situation. If she allows herself to be carried away by romantic emotions (*eros*) in search of self-fulfillment, she sets herself up for a life of misery; if she acts according to her sense of duty (*agape*), she condemns herself to a wretched existence too. If she is to find fulfillment, Joyce is suggesting, it must be by some mysterious, not-yet-identified "third way."

Joyce's story "Eveline" is undoubtedly a critique of *agape* without *eros*, but it also contains an incipient intimation that *eros* without *agape* is no solution to this distortion. This intimation will be developed more profoundly in Joyce's later work. The pertinent task at present is to clarify that *agape* without *eros* is not a Catholic doctrine. Luft errs when she describes Eveline's frustration as the fruit of Catholic "inculcation." According to Catholic teachings, donation without reciprocity does not occur in the divine interpersonal relationships and is not preached or prescribed in the divine-human relationship or in inter-human relationships. Except in the circumstance of an extraordinary grace—of which there is no evidence in the story—Catholic spiritual theology would not require or recommend Eveline's anti-natural decision to forsake the opportunity of a dignified life with her suitor in order to remain with her abusive alcoholic father in obedience to the wishes of her dying mother.

Nonetheless, in fairness to Luft, there is a suggestion in the story that the necessity of temporal misery, the denial of personal happiness in this life, is preached in the name of Catholicism as prerequisite to eternal bliss, contrary to Christ's promise of a hundredfold *in the here and now* and eternal life in the hereafter (cf. Mt 19:29). Eveline's decision is presented as one that is entirely consonant with, and socially engineered by, Catholic doctrine and Catholic spirituality. This very point is made by Geert Lernout, who unfolds the suggestiveness of the Sacred Heart image that presides over Eveline's room, and the Twelve Promises to St. Margaret Mary Alacoque: "Since we know that Eveline's violent and drunken father is hardly likely to allow his 'hardened heart' to be touched, we can imagine the life that awaits her when she decides to stay home . . . and that in no way will live up to the promises."[13]

Thus, the pressures imposed upon Eveline to remain in self-annihilating domestic servitude are associated with depersonalizing Catholic teachings. Lernout makes two assumptions here, one correct, and the other mistaken. It is correct to assume that a disordered *agape*-without-*eros* relationship with the divine will have negative repercussions, of self-annihilating *agape* without *eros*, in interhuman relationships. However, Lernout makes the same error as Luft when he assumes that *agape* without *eros* is a Catholic doctrine. The Catholic response to this charge must be that these are not Catholic teachings; they are heretical deformations of Catholic doctrine. Catholicism does not preach the *agape* without *eros* doctrine (unrequited self-sacrifice) that pressurizes and depersonalizes Eveline. This is a Puritan doctrine. H. L. Mencken famously wrote of Puritanism as characterized by the haunting fear that someone, somewhere, might be happy.[14] The distinction being drawn here between the Puritan and Catholic positions is founded upon demonstrable doctrinal and historical evidence. Most significantly for the purposes of my argument, it is a distinction that was perceived by Joyce himself. This, too, is demonstrable, with evidence from his writings and with biographical evidence.

II.2.2: "In Ireland Catholicism is black magic"

That Joyce made the discovery that the Catholicism he had encountered in Ireland was at least "different" is related in Ellmann's biography, in an account of Joyce's conversation with his French Catholic friend Maria Jolas, during which he so vehemently "attacked Catholic methods" of education that she responded, "You make me sad, since I'm bringing up my children as Catholics." Joyce replied: "Ah, it's different in France. In Ireland Catholicism is black magic."[15] Lernout deduces that, "Joyce's attitude did not change: in the final year of his life he was still attacking catholic education to Maria Jolas, who was bringing up her children in the faith (*JJ* 743), and there is no indication that at any point of his life he changed his mind."[16] This reading bypasses an important point. It would be uncharacteristic of Joyce to backpedal and be polite at the expense of a deeply felt personal conviction, and there is a superabundance of textual and circumstantial evidence that he meant what he said before and after Maria Jolas's pained reaction to his vehemence.

To underestimate the distinction between "Irish Catholicism" and Catholicism *per se* is to overlook an important hermeneutical key to the Joycean experience. Joyce's brother Stanislaus speaks of the "Irish blend" of Catholicism in terms of "ignorant obedience mixed with Puritanism,"[17] and a "hybrid . . . of Catholicism under the inevitable influence of English Puritanism . . . the vigilant and ruthless enemy of free thought and the joy of living."[18] There are indicators that Joyce discovered that the "Catholicism" he encountered in Ireland did not entirely coincide, and in many points clashed, with Catholic doctrine. In *Portrait*, in conversation with the College dean, who is English, Stephen muses inwardly that his psyche, language, and spirituality, even his "Christianity," have been colonized: "How different are the words home, Christ, ale, master, on his lips and on mine! I cannot speak or write these words without unrest of spirit . . . My soul frets in the shadow of his language."[19] This introduces us seamlessly to a clarification of Ireland's social and political circumstances in Joyce's time, and an analysis of the peculiarities, not to say perversities, of Victorian Irish Catholicism.

II.3: The Irish Context

II.3.1: Irish Catholicism in the 19th Century

A "devotional revolution," as historian Emmet Larkin defined it, took place in Ireland between the years 1850 and 1875, under the ecclesiastical leadership of Cardinal Paul Cullen.[20] On the threshold of that time period, the Irish suffered the Potato Famine, in which they lost a sizeable portion of the population to death and emigration.

They also suffered the loss of the Gaelic language and culture, leading to a national identity crisis. Cullen's response to the ensuing void was to implement the remedial formula of the Council of Trent, which emphasized effective organization of Church structures and the use of devotions to respond to spiritual destitution.[21] Statistical records show that his campaign enjoyed phenomenal success. As Larkin puts it, under Cullen, "the Irish were transformed as a people—men and women alike—into practicing Catholics."[22]

However, Cullen's determination to keep religion separate from politics did not outlive him. Although Catholicism was one of the factors enlisted by the nationalist movement to differentiate Ireland from Britain, it did not retain a pristine purity unaffected by Victorian Protestantism in its occupied situation, just as nationalism itself did not retain an identity uninfluenced by the imperial model from which it sought to be free. Catholic Ireland was emerging from the dominance of Protestant British Imperialism but the impact of that dominance in every ambit, including the religious, was profound, and the emergence from it would be a slow and complex process.

The 1916 Easter Rising was only a moment in that process. The Irish Catholic revolutionary, Padraig Pearse, strategically organized the insurrection to coincide with the Easter Triduum, to maximize the religious symbolism of the sacrificial spilling of blood for the resurrection of the nation. Fr. Vincent Twomey identifies a common denominator between Puritan Protestantism and Irish Catholicism which is also to be found in Joyce's writings, namely, "a common Gnostic (or Puritanical) tendency that . . . tends to collapse religion into politics or, vice versa, transforms politics into religion, 'the cause' on whose altar men sacrifice both themselves and the innocent."[23]

Those willing to sacrifice themselves and the innocent were, however, notoriously in the minority. It was only when the defeated and captured insurgents were coldly executed that Pearse's prophetic blood-and-resurrection rhetoric was fulfilled. Before then, the social mainstream scenario did not conform to the classic pre-revolutionary pattern. Afterwards, it settled into a conformist materialism. Twomey describes the rise of "a new breed" in the aftermath of the great famine and the massive abandonment of the Irish language in favor of the English language that offered better prospects of prosperity. The trauma of the great famine provoked a reaction understandably motivated by the instinct for survival; adapt or perish: "The tradition was neither Irish nor Catholic, but an Anglo-Saxon puritanical culture which had come to pervade not only English society, but that of America and indeed of the entire English-speaking world."[24]

The socio-historical situation in which James Joyce grew up is a complex scenario of intense cultural confusion in which, while still suffering the effects of post-famine trauma, pragmatic materialism, nationalist idealism, and religious fervor vied for predominance. Two poems by the Irish poet W. B. Yeats, one called "September 1913," composed before the Easter Rising and the other written after the Rising and called "Easter 1916," reflect the trajectory just outlined. The first identifies an alliance of middle-class materialism and piety in the Ireland of his time (also Joyce's time): "What need you, being come to sense / But fumble in a greasy till / And add the halfpence to the pence / And prayer to shivering prayer."[25] After the 1916 uprising, Yeats would write with a mixture of dread and hope, "All changed, changed utterly: A terrible beauty is born,"[26] but that "terrible beauty" turned out to have much to do with the merging of Irish patriotism with middle-class materialism and Puritan piety.

II.3.2: 20th Century Testimonies of Irish Puritanism

In 1954, thirteen years after Joyce's death, *The Furrow* published a conference by Fr. Donnchadh Ó Floinn in which he spoke of the Irish Catholic Church as one bearing the scars of discontinuity: "[O]ur Irish Faith has been living amongst us for more than a century as a kind of separated form, wrenched apart from its connatural body." Fr. Ó Floinn attributed this lack of initiative and energy to a failure (in many ways understandable and perhaps inevitable) of the newly re-established Irish Church, after the Catholic Relief Act of 1829, to reconnect creatively with its own tradition: "She had grown used to obscurity . . . So, since she had to perform her worship publicly once more . . . she made common cause with her sister church in England."[27]

Certainly the Irish had absorbed a Puritan ethos; as a sign that this was so, the Irish in the United States and elsewhere manifested the same tendencies. Ó Floinn's analysis calls to mind a corresponding analysis by a contemporary American commentator on the influence of

Irish Catholicism in that continent. John Rao observes that Irish Catholics in the United States lived a Puritan spirit in the same way that James Joyce was critical of the Irish experience in Ireland, describing an impossible burden of obligation that drives those who live under it towards atheism in a way that seems uncannily applicable to the Irish Catholicism apparently experienced by Joyce:

> Secularization was promoted by Puritan Protestantism in three ways. One was by having supported tenets so inhuman as to drive men away from God in horror. A second was through establishing such a stark dichotomy between God and man as to throw into doubt the rationality of Christ's whole mission, to deny the reality of the Incarnation and to retire the divine beyond man's reach. The last was by so disdaining the world and ridiculing the possibility of its transformation as to liberate nature entirely from God's direction.[28]

Other commentators have argued that the harshness of Irish Catholicism proceeded from Jansenism and preceded Cullen, since many of its priests, during the times of persecution, were formed in France, and, later on, several of the professors of Maynooth had received a French formation: "The sharp insistence of the Irish priest on sexual conformity is sometimes attributed to a puritanical, Jansenist, strain brought to Maynooth by its original professoriate in 1795."[29] Patrick Corish found records of two priests ordained at Maynooth in the 1820s who lamented the "excessive rigorism introduced into the national seminaries by French professors and their disciples."[30]

Whatever the source, or sources, it is safe to say that a Jansenistic spirituality found a propitious climate in a post-Famine Ireland without culture, religious or otherwise, easily persuaded that it had just suffered the horrors of God's wrath rather than of big business and Malthusian eugenics. In the prevailing circumstances of extreme poverty, sexual sin was a form of Irish roulette: extramarital pregnancies could thrust an entire family back into life-threatening destitution. Memories of the real threat of extinction were raw, and the dread of a recurrence intensified the stigma of sexual sin and the determination to repress it.

In short and in summary, Irish Catholicism was deeply marked either by English Puritanism or by French Jansenism or both. When Joyce creates puzzles out of contradictory dilemmas, as he does in "Eveline," these puzzles come out of the historical experience in which he lived: the puritanical, post-Colonial Ireland of the late 19th Century. In some ways, there were signs of great success in that environment, like the phenomenal number of priests and nuns. But there were also deficiencies. Perhaps the numerical success created a blindness to those deficiencies among the members of the Church. Joyce saw the deficiencies and complexities. His response to a complex situation is itself rich, profound, and complex.

II.3.3: The Dynamics of Decolonization

The political philosopher Frantz Fanon wrote of political independence as only one level of a process that requires a subsequent phaseal decolonization of the mind. Declan Kiberd applies Fanon's theory to the Irish situation and Irish art, "which corresponds very neatly with Frantz Fanon's dialectic of decolonization, from occupation, through nationalism, to liberation."[31] The mutilations of masculinity described by Fanon as integral to the colonial experience left their mark on Irish nationalism, on Irish Catholicism and on Joyce's writings. Joyce grew up precisely in the period before 1916 in which, as Kiberd puts it, men were "hardening themselves into hyper-masculinity, in preparation for an uprising"; but nationalism, Kiberd says, following Fanon, "is not liberation, since it still persists in defining itself in categories imposed by the colonizer." It is only by "breaking out of the binaries, through to a third point of transcendence, that freedom may be won."[32]

The call to sacrifice oneself on the altar of patriotism—*agape* without *eros* for the nation—is one that Joyce, through Stephen, rejects: "My ancestors threw off their language and took another . . . They allowed a handful of foreigners to subject them. Do you fancy I am going to pay in my own life and person debts they made? What for?"[33] Stephen effectively puts to his nationalist friend Davin the same question that Simon Peter put to Christ: "Lo, we have left everything and followed you. What then shall we have?" (Mt 19:27). Christ responds with a promise of a hundredfold in the here and now and eternal life in the hereafter. Davin has no such answer, and Stephen rejects the *agape* without *eros* of political messianism. Joyce will seek a different solution.

Ireland's situation was further compounded by the recent trauma of the Potato Famine and the subsequent loss of the Irish language. In the aftermath of the Black Plague, which devastated the population of Europe in the 14th century, there was an upsurge of religiosity, healthy and unhealthy. Overemphasis of a good can cause its contamination; as, for example, in the case of clericalism. Something similar happened in the aftermath of the Famine which devastated the population of Ireland. In the midst of positive fruits like the vocations boom and the flourishing of initiatives of corporal and spiritual charity, there was a current of excessive otherworldliness, which feeds into a purist separation of temple and workplace, a demarcation of boundaries that artificially dichotomizes religion and ordinary life.

In this dichotomizing tendency Liberalism and Puritanism have something in common: the former scorns religion as other-worldly, the latter scorns secularity as this-worldly. The liberalist ideology promotes the strict separation of Church and State, of religion from politics and ordinary life. The exaggerated otherworldly religiosity of Puritanism does it also, with different motivations but with the same end result. It leads to the living of a double life, not perhaps in the name of a conscious secularizing ideology but by unreflecting prejudice towards the profane realities which translates in praxis into a Godless and/or inhuman existence. Evidence indicates that this happened in Ireland. "Eveline" is best understood against this background: it depicts the tragic failure of an excessively otherworldly religiosity to enable its adherents to live an authentically human life in this world. This, for Joyce, is the Irish religious situation.

The overriding impression gleaned from an analysis of the Irish situation is of a cluster of diverse negative pressures converging implosively in one time and place. This is by no means tangential to our topic. Joyce explores this mystery of repression, confusion, and mistaken options in a serious way. His is not a juvenile knee-jerk reaction. Overcoming an initial reactionary impulse violently to rebel and reject all religious authority, in maturity he strives to see if and how the divine can operate in messy human situations. This is an apt description of postcolonial Ireland. The problem was postcolonial and Irish, not Catholic, but the Church was the principal if not the only authority that was respected by the majority of the people. In times of revolution it is extra-difficult for entities of authority and leadership to avoid being overly rigid or overly indulgent, to strike that elusive balance between firmness and flexibility. Perhaps the Church exercised its authority excessively. Perhaps it too was infected to some degree by hyper-masculinity, succumbing to an authoritarian exaggeration of its royal *munus*. It is difficult to imagine how it could have remained entirely unaffected by the surrounding ethos and atmosphere.

In the midst of the maelstrom of destructive pressures the challenge was how to create or develop or reconnect with a genuine, living, humanizing Irish culture. This was Joyce's focus, "to forge in the smithy of my soul the uncreated conscience of my race."[34] The problem was not religion in itself or even Catholicism *per se*. The Church was operating in the same dynamic with the same difficulties, seeking its place. It was an Irish cultural problem not related to the essence of Catholicism, though dealing with the problem did, of course, fall under the Church's responsibility. The challenge was not doctrinal; it was one of statesmanship and governance and discernment, and there were failures in the Church and in the society at large. There were also successes.

II.3.4: The Broader Picture and Joyce's Personal Motivations

It would be simplistic to allow Joyce the last word on Irish Catholicism. As is usually if not always the case, the true Faith was present alongside the distortion. Speaking of the "divine spark" in Irish Catholicism, Twomey points out that it "frequently flared up into heroic virtue at home and abroad, that in turn enkindled numerous fires of divine faith, hope, and love in many parts of the world."[35] In his book *James Joyce's Schooldays*, Fr. Bruce Bradley, with the aid of testimonies from Joyce's contemporaries and access to school records, shows that Joyce's education was not as draconian as it is depicted in *Portrait* and that Joyce's peers knew him as a happier and more outgoing boy and youth than Stephen Dedalus.[36] Stanislaus shares this impression: [I]n boyhood and youth [he] was of such a cheerful and amiable disposition that in the family circle he was given the nickname . . . of 'Sunny Jim.'"[37]

Richard Ellmann informs us that the young Joyce's

sexual appetites played a major part, by his own admission, in his abandonment of the faith: "[H]e declared flatly some time afterwards to a friend, that sexual continence was impossible for him."[38] He wrote this to Nora Barnacle too: "I found it impossible for me to remain in it [the Catholic Church] on account of the impulses of my nature."[39] It would therefore have seemed to serve Joyce's short term interests to perceive and portray Irish Catholicism as puritanical and repressive, and this may well have led not to outright invention but to exaggeration, at least initially. Ultimately, the Joycean aesthetic, rather than simply (and simplistically) rejecting religion, is committed to the recuperation of religious *eros*. We have seen in the case of the short story "Eveline" that it is committed to a critique of *agape* without *eros* and that religion is depicted as a contributory factor in this dehumanizing dynamic.

"Eveline" is a dramatization of the depersonalizing effects of *agape* without *eros*, i.e., of obligation and self-immolation without mutuality and personal enrichment. But we have seen in "Eveline" a hint that unmitigated *eros* may not be the Joycean solution. Joyce rightly saw also that disordered religiosity was part of the problem, not religion itself. The task of the next section is to demonstrate further with evidence from Joyce's first novel that this is his position. The first step in this task is to present the dominant opinion in the intellectual climate of Joyce's time concerning Christianity's position regarding *eros*, followed by a clarification of the *true* Catholic position vis-a-vis *eros*, past and present, recently expounded by Pope Benedict XVI.

II.4: The Eros Controversy

II.4.1: An Introductory Summary

Joyce was familiar with Christianity's reputation for being anti*eros*. Nietzsche wrote in 1886 (Joyce was born in 1882) that Christianity had robbed humanity of joy and the capacity for greatness, making of man a "sublime abortion."[40] Concretely, "Christianity gave *Eros* poison to drink; he did not die of it, certainly, but degenerated to Vice."[41] Nietzsche railed against Christian *agape*-love—"The Christian conception of God . . . is one of the most corrupt concepts that has ever been set up in the world . . . Yea! In him war is declared on life, nature, on the will to live! . . . In him, nothingness is deified, the will to nothingness is made holy!"[42]—and responded to the perceived Christian indoctrination of *agape* without *eros* by championing Dionysian erotic frenzy. We know that the young Joyce had a brief Nietzschean phase when he was approximately twenty-one years old. Ellmann tells us so in his biography: "[I]t was probably upon Nietzsche that Joyce drew when he expounded to his friends a neo-paganism that glorified selfishness, licentiousness, and pitilessness."[43]

Around this time Joyce wrote to his brother along these same lines, as Stanislaus later testified: "He has ceased to believe in Catholicism for many years . . . Jim wants to live. Life is his creed. He boasts of his power to live . . . He demands an absolute freedom to do as he pleases;" (adding, curiously, that, "Catholicism he has appreciated, rejected and opposed, and liked again when it has lost its power over him").[44] Joyce subscribed for a time to the Nietzschean opposition of Christianity and vitality, but we will see presently that the maturer Joyce, even in *Portrait*, did not maintain an *eros* without *agape* position. Ellmann rightly observes that this line of thought did not take a deep hold: "At heart Joyce can scarcely have been a Nietzschean . . . his interest was in the ordinary."[45] Joyce's Leopold Bloom and his "will to laugh" could not be much further from Nietzsche's Ubermensch and the will to power.

Pope Benedict XVI observes that Nietzsche's accusation against the Church was not new, that it has been a "widely-held" view: "[D]oesn't the Church, with all her commandments and prohibitions, turn to bitterness the most precious thing in life?" (*DCE* no. 3). Benedict then provides a brief historical summary of the concept, showing that *eros* had a poisonous aspect, and a positive aspect, long before Christianity arrived on the historical stage. On the positive side, the ancient Greeks and other cultures thought of *eros* as "a kind of intoxication, the overpowering of reason by a 'divine madness' which tears man away from his finite existence and enables him, in the very process of being overwhelmed by divine power, to experience supreme happiness" (*DCE* 4). But, on the negative side, *eros* also led to fertility cults and ritual prostitution which exploited and dehumanized the participants: "The Old Testament . . . in no way rejected *eros* as such; rather, it declared war on a warped and destructive form of it, because this counterfeit divinization of *eros* actually strips it of its dignity and dehumanizes it" (*DCE* 4).

Eros without *agape* ends in *thanatos* (death), as does *agape* without *eros*; *eros* and *agape* together produce love and life. Benedict goes on to describe the synthesis of *eros* and *agape* which constitutes the perfection of love in which both aspects are harmonized and mutually perfected. *Eros* is an aspect of the relationship with the Divine, a foretaste and promise of eternal ecstasy, but left to itself it is a poisoned chalice; it requires medicinal measures of purification and maturity and renunciation to protect it from itself: "Far from rejecting or "poisoning" *eros*, they [i.e., purification, maturity, renunciation] heal it and restore its true grandeur" (*DCE* 5). Purification, maturation, and renunciation are aspects of the *agape* dimension of love.

Joyce has in common with Nietzsche a vigorous rejection of unilateral other-worldliness, of a religiosity of *agape* without *eros*, and a determined re-focus on the this-worldly. But Joyce's endeavour to recover and celebrate the experience of ecstasy is more nuanced than the German philosopher's. In *Portrait of the Artist* we will observe evidence of a Joycean concern not only to critique *agape* without *eros*, as incipiently in "Eveline," but also positively to epiphanize *unpoisoned eros*.

II.4.2: A Portrait of the Artist as a Young Man

Geert Lernout affirms after briefly discussing a few stories from *Dubliners* that "none of the heroes in these stories is genuinely religious in the way that Stephen is in parts of *A Portrait of the Artist as a Young Man*."[46] This assertion mistakenly assumes that the religiosity depicted in *Portrait* is "genuinely religious." In fact, Joyce's *conscious* concern in that novel is to demonstrate that Stephen's early piety and so-called "conversion" cannot be described as "*genuinely religious*" and to expose and reject an infirm religiosity. Joyce scholar Coilm Owens writes that, "To a young man of Joyce's intellectuality, sensibility, and knowledge of the world, his Dedalean representation of his short-lived spiritual arousal has a bemusedly sardonic edge."[47]

Weldon Thornton makes the same distinction between genuine and distorted religiosity, but in Catholic versus Protestant terms. He crystallizes a typical misconception about Catholicism, or perhaps a correct conception of a misconstrued Catholicism, when he says of Stephen's Catholic experience that "we are dealing here not with a Protestant fundamentalist or 'inner light' tradition in which religious experience is construed as inherently personal, but with Irish Roman Catholicism." The innerness of the Protestant religiosity is contrasted with the outerness of the Catholic, "in which the institutional element is very strong."[48] It is true that when Catholicism allows the necessary institutional aspect of its identity to outweigh and eclipse its charismatic aspect, it loses vitality, but again, the concern of Catholic doctrine is to avoid this.[49] Stephen's religiosity is formal and external, not interior and vital.

In other words, Stephen's religiosity is one of *agape* without *eros*; there is no heartfelt rapturous connection with the divine, no sense of joyful self-enrichment. As Hugh Kenner put it, Stephen's "reaching out after orthodox salvation is . . . presented in terms that judge it."[50] By this Kenner means that the very language that portrays Stephen's relationship with religion contains signs of the Joycean ironic intent, "a bemusedly sardonic edge," as Owens so well puts it. It is evidently not meant to be taken seriously except as a juvenile distortion. Only those who measure Christianity through the lens of the Victorian distortion could take these as "genuinely religious" manifestations of Christian faith. In order to expose that distortion, let us trace Stephen's route to apostasy from childhood onwards.

II.4.2.1: Stephen's Childhood Formation

From the beginning Stephen's formation is marked by the inculcation of "repentance" under threat: "His mother said: 'O, Stephen will apologize'. Dante [a pious aunt] said: 'O, if not, the eagles will come and pull out his eyes.'"[51] ("Dante" is a contraction of "the auntie," also evoking the threat of infernal punishment). All of this for having expressed the childish desire to marry a girl of a neighboring Protestant family;[52] virulent sectarian anti-Protestantism was one aspect of the politicization of religion we have seen described by Twomey. And in the boarding school run by the Jesuits, going to bed at night: "His fingers trembled as he undressed himself in the dormitory. He told his fingers to hurry up. He had to undress and then kneel and say his own prayers and be in bed before the gas was lowered so that he might not go to hell when he died."[53] The unjust beating received from Fr. Dolan for not bringing his glasses to class brutally confirms the legitimacy of his fears.[54]

In the later years of childhood there are already signs that Stephen has distanced himself from this form of religion. He accompanies his uncle Charles in his frequent visits to the chapel: "While he prayed he knelt on his red handkerchief and read above his breath from a thumb blackened prayer book wherein catchwords were printed at the foot of every page. Stephen knelt at his side respecting, though he did not share, his piety."[55] Joyce does not intend us to take this as representative of a healthy manifestation of the religious sensibility.

Competing with this mechanical, superstitious piety is the call—the *eros*—of the "real" world: "The hour when he too would take part in the life of that world seemed drawing near and in secret he began to make ready for the great part which he felt awaited him the nature of which he only dimly apprehended."[56] There begins to arise in his worldview an irreconcilable opposition between a cold and sterile religiosity and a world that is ample and rich, filled with vitality and possibilities (as we have seen described by Umberto Eco in his analysis of the clash between the Medieval and the Modern worldviews and Joyce's response thereto). The "real world" is immediate, its call urgent and pressing; God is remote, his call increasingly vague and insubstantial.

II.4.2.2: Stephen in Early Youth

The adolescent Stephen begins to associate the sexual experience with the initiation into this mysterious "real" world that beckons him: "Weakness and timidity and inexperience would fall from him in that magic moment."[57]

In an essay for class in this period, speaking of the relation between the soul and its Creator, Stephen writes: "without the possibility of ever approaching nearer."[58] A normative indoctrination strongly marked by threat and authoritarianism fails to prepare Stephen for the crisis of adolescence. He abandons himself to the inner tide of sensuality. The second chapter of the novel ends with his first encounter with a prostitute at sixteen years of age. Coincidentally, St. Augustine in his *Confessions* laments his surrender to sensuality at the same age: "Where was I, and in exile how remote, from the joys of your home, in that sixteenth year of my flesh when, in the mad rage of unbridled lust . . . I accepted its dominion over me, and to it made a full surrender."[59]

In Stephen's clinical self-diagnosis of his "relationship" with God, the categories of Scholastic theology are apparent:

> He had sinned mortally not once but many times and he knew that, while he stood in danger of eternal damnation for the first sin alone, by every succeeding sin he multiplied his guilt and his punishment. His days and works and thoughts could make no atonement for him, the fountains of sanctifying grace having ceased to refresh his soul. At most, by an alms given to a beggar whose blessing he fled from, he might hope wearily to win for himself some measure of actual grace.[60]

It is a mechanistic vision of Christianity with clear, albeit uncontextualized, Scholastic resonances: "His pride in his own sin, his loveless awe of God, told him that his offence was too grievous to be atoned for in whole or in part by a false homage to the All-seeing and All-knowing."[61] God is the Primary Cause, omniscient and omnipotent, the Unmoved Mover. All of which is true, of course, but incomplete. The Good Shepherd who comes in search of the lost sheep seems somehow, somewhere, to have gotten lost.

Bearing in mind Stephen's conception of God, it is hardly surprising that it is the figure of the Virgin Mary who most stirs him towards repentance: "If ever he was impelled to cast sin from him and to repent the impulse that moved him was the wish to be her knight."[62] Mary is Stephen's only glimpse of feminine warmth in a religiosity dominated by hyper-masculine harshness. His "conversion" is provoked by a three-day retreat centered on the final realities of death, Judgment, and Hell (no mention is made of Heaven or of the "hundredfold" temporal rewards of faith; cf. Mt 19:29). The account of it lasts some 28 pages (of a total of about 245) in which the references to Jesus Christ and his Redemption are scarce, brief, and sad. This third chapter ends with Stephen's confession, moved more by terror than by love, and thereafter Stephen simply returns to the religiosity of his earlier childhood: "His daily life was laid out in devotional areas. By means of ejaculations and prayers he stored up ungrudgingly for the souls in purgatory centuries of days and quarantines and years."[63]

There is a form of "piety" that if left uncorrected will lead inevitably, in a person of minimal intelligence and sensitivity, either to nervous collapse or to weariness, irritation, and apostasy. Stephen's "conversion" ends in—one may even say leads to—the latter eventuality. His piety in this phase of life is cerebral and surreal. The excitement factor of Christian faith, the "divine madness" of religious *eros*, is notably absent, begging the question if this piety can be called Christian at all; the God incarnate in Christ seems utterly absent. There is biographical evidence that Joyce as a youth lamented the eclipse of Christ's humanity in Irish Catholicism. In an article written in 1899 (at the age of 17; i.e., around Stephen's age during the time of his "conversion") on a painting of the *Ecce Homo* scene by the Hungarian Mihaly Munkacsy, the teenage Joyce lauds the humanity of the portrayal and implicitly critiques a pseudospirituality that would make Christ so "divine" as to withdraw him beyond human reach.

The 17-year-old Joyce enjoys the realism of Munkacsy's portrayal of Mary's humanity and of Christ's. At no point in the essay does Joyce explicitly declare disbelief in Christ's divinity, but his abhorrence of a "divinization" that would etherealize Christ's humanity is clear: "[N]o matter how you view Christ, there is no trace of that in his aspect. There is nothing divine in his look, there is nothing superhuman." His conclusion regarding the painter's position hints also at his own: "This is no defect of hand on the part of the artist, his skill would have accomplished anything. It was his voluntary position." Admiration for the figure of Christ remains, in spite of apparent apostasy: "The whole face is of an ascetic, inspired, wholesouled, wonderfully passionate man. It is Christ, as the Man of Sorrows . . . It is literally Behold the Man."⁶⁴ Joyce is clearly reacting here and in *Portrait* against a Deistic deformation of Christianity that is literally dehumanizing.

II.4.2.3: Is this Christianity or Deism?

Deism is the belief in God as Architect. Christianity proclaims a multi-faceted God: Creator, Lover, Bridegroom. The discovery of God as Architect would for Christianity be true, but insufficient for the human spirit, and ultimately disappointing. Stephen's liberating "apostasy" in favor of the daily bread of mundane experience is preceded by an enthralling "conversion" to a divine abstraction: "Gradually, as his soul was enriched with spiritual knowledge, he saw the whole world, forming one vast symmetrical expression of God's power and love . . . he could scarcely understand why it was in any way necessary that he should continue to live."⁶⁵ This is a strangely impersonal God, so symmetrical as to negate the very will to live. The tension felt here between discovering a "divine meaning" and losing a rationale for continued existence is pure Gnosticism. Small wonder that this line of spirituality culminates in affirmations like the following concerning the figure of Jesus Christ: "He is more like a son of God than a son of Mary."⁶⁶

That Stephen's religiosity is not truly Christian is evident again when he likens the artist to the God of creation. Whatever about the role of the artist, "indifferent, paring his fingernails," is not a Christian image of God. In its formal perfectionism Stephen's spirituality at this point is reminiscent of Platonic Idealism, and in its behavorial perfectionism it is evocative of Pelagianism. There is no sense of joyful, ecstatic *eros* at having connected with the Divine Lover, only surreal satisfaction at having discovered that everything fits symmetrically into its place. Aquinas makes a distinction that is applicable here: "Between ordinary science-knowledge and faith-knowledge there is this difference. The first shines only on the mind, showing that God is the cause of everything, that he is one and wise and so forth." The knowledge of God experienced by Stephen Dedalus in his religious phase does not get beyond what Aquinas calls science-knowledge to reach what he calls faith-knowledge: "whereas the second enlightens the mind and warms the heart, telling us that God is also saviour, redeemer, lover, made flesh for us."[67]

In faith-knowledge there is a different sweetness; intimacy, *eros*. For St. Thomas, union with God is volitional as well as intellective, affective as well as cognitive: "The more the intellect is participating in the light of glory the more perfectly will it see God. But it will participate more in the light of glory the more it has charity since where charity is greater there is greater desire." Intellect is essential but insufficient; there must be desire, active affectivity: "and desire somehow makes the one desiring more apt and ready to receive what is desired. Hence the more anyone will have of charity, the more perfectly will he see God and the more blessed will he be."[68] Stephen's piety remains on the level of science-knowledge; it lacks energy, joy, enthusiasm. The unpredictable *eros* of "divine madness" is sadly absent. Understandably enough, he quickly tires of it.

II.4.2.4: Stephen's "Vocation"

But even though he has interiorly tired of this mode of being religious, Stephen does not yet outwardly abandon his pious practices, and his apparent piety draws the attention of his teachers: "He listened now to the priest's appeal and through the words he heard even more distinctly a voice bidding him approach, offering him secret knowledge and secret power." The precise nature of that secret knowledge and secret power is exemplified in two sins: "He would know then what was the sin of Simon Magus and what the sin against the Holy Ghost for which there was no forgiveness."[69] This thought that crosses Stephen's mind, about the sin of Simon Magus and the sin against the Holy Spirit, is a curious one; it demands, and rewards, scrutiny.

Knowledge of the sin of Simon Magus—simony, the subordination of sacred things to financial opportunism—and of the sin against the Holy Spirit—final impenitence, definitive closure to God's mercy—is the common patrimony of all Christians. It is available even to curious or interested non-Christians. Simon Magus was a sorcerer who sought to purchase from the apostles the power of the Spirit: "Now when Simon saw that the Spirit was given through the laying on of the apostles' hands, he offered them money, saying, 'Give me also this power, that any one on whom I lay my hands may receive the Holy Spirit,'" to which Peter emphatically answers, "Your silver perish with you, because you thought you could obtain the gift of God with money! You have neither part nor lot in this matter, for your heart is not right before God" (Acts 8:18-22). On hearing Peter's words, Simon expresses repentance.

The second sin mentioned, the sin against the Holy Spirit, is about hardness of heart to the point of refusal to repent. The scribes and Pharisees, seeing their authority and social position threatened by Christ, accuse him of casting out demons with the power of the prince of demons, thus calling evil good and good evil (cf. Is 5:20) and doing the work of the devil themselves. This position is symptomatic of a hardness of heart and refusal to convert that leads Christ to speak of the unforgiveable sin against the Holy Spirit: "Truly, I say to you, all sins will be forgiven the sons of men . . . but whoever blasphemes against the Holy Spirit never has forgiveness" (Mk 3:28). The implication is clear. By putting these two sins together in the context of the call to the priesthood, Joyce is hinting that this is what has become of the Catholic priesthood, at least as it is presented to Stephen: hardened, institutionalized, unrepenting simony.

Joyce is not saying that there is no difference between Simon the Magus as presented in Acts and Peter or one of the Apostles. Joyce as an artist is aware of the Bible at least as literature, and he knows these scenes. He knows that Christ, for example, in the passage referred to, was not accusing the Apostles of commiting a sin against the Holy Spirit. Thus, from both examples, we can conclude that Joyce is describing what he sees as a distortion of an original reality, and he is scandalized into apostasy because he sees the successors of the Apostles falling into the sins that Christ warned them against and that their predecessors condemn.

From his knowledge of the Gospel and of Aquinas,[70] Joyce would have known that what Stephen rejects here is a distorted form of the priesthood. Aquinas reduces the multiple manifestations of idolatry to four broad categories: wealth, honor, power, and pleasure.[71] Two of these—honor and power—are blatantly offered to Stephen as enticement to the priestly vocation. The other two—wealth and pleasure—are offered, albeit not so blatantly, in the form of financial security and comfort. The priesthood of Christ, characterized by free and joyful renunciation of human securities for a life of donation, sacrifice and service, is notably absent. Joyce was aware of the true Catholic doctrine on the priesthood, and he is presenting a critique of a corruption of Catholicism and not Catholicism *per se*, a distinction that Joyce scholars have largely missed.

Joyce is also critiquing Stephen's perception of the priesthood, warped as it is by prideful ambition, in a clear case of Joycean irony at Stephen's expense. Rather than rejecting God, Joyce is rejecting manipulation of the divine for love of money. He chooses integrity and interior freedom over personal compromise for the sake of financial security. This is Stephen's choice too.

II.4.2.5: *Stephen's Surrender to Eros*

For Stephen, the Church is a decaying and oppressive institution that threatens his freedom and seeks to frustrate his destiny. In his encounter with the dean, the irreconcilable opposition presents itself again, between the "real world" filled with vital possibilities and adventure, and the old and sterile world of the Church. An instinctual vitality stirs Stephen away from the latter: "It was a grave and ordered and passionless life that awaited him."[72] Instinct, subtle and quick, is juxtaposed with order, cold and passionless: "Some instinct, waking at these memories, stronger than education or piety, quickened within him at every near approach to that life, an instinct subtle and hostile, and armed him against acquiescence. The chill and order of the life repelled him."[73]

The dean invites Stephen into a priestly aristocracy, reminiscent of the priesthood of the Sadducees in the time of Christ, anachronistic and repellent to an idealistic mind and heart; an esoteric and elitist priesthood with Gnostic overtones. In orthodox Christian terms, therefore, Stephen's rejection of the dean's invitation is comprehensible and admissible as an action of grace, even if Stephen twice calls it "instinct." In contrast to the call of the priesthood, the voice of the "real world" promises him unsuspected joys and adventures: "His throat ached with a desire to cry aloud, the cry of a hawk or eagle on high . . . This was the call of life to his soul not the dull gross voice of the world of duties and despair."[74]

In these climactic moments of the novel the language of liberation and discovery of mission is ecstatic and even religious. Impelled onwards by the restless joyfulness of his mood, his walk takes him toward the sea. There he beholds a girl paddling near the shore. The word *ecstasy* is employed twice in this climactic passage:

> 'Heavenly God', cried Stephen's soul, in an outburst of profane joy . . . Her image had passed

into his soul forever and no word had broken the holy silence of his ecstasy . . . A wild angel had appeared to him . . . to throw open before him in an instant of ecstasy the gates of all the ways of error and glory."[75]

For this onward and upward flight to be able to happen, a preliminary fall will be necessary: "The snares of the world were its ways of sin. He would fall. He had not yet fallen but he would fall . . . Not to fall was too hard, too hard."[76] Religious *agape* without *eros* is anti-natural and humanly impossible.

Joyce's "Eveline" and parts of *Portrait of the Artist* depict a harsh, dehumanizing religiosity: sacrificial, dutiful, self-immolating, bereft of emotional compensation or intimate mutual attraction and possession. Against this background, Stephen's experience on the beach is about the liberating recovery of religious attraction and vitality—of *eros*. That his "ecstasy" is not entirely unrelated to the supernatural is evident in the exclamation, "'Heavenly God' . . . in an outburst of profane joy."[77] This paradoxical combination of "Heavenly God" and "profane joy" in one climactic exclamation is a key moment in the entire Joycean opus, and I will return to it in the next chapter. The main concern at this point is to clarify that while a religiosity of *agape* without *eros* is undoubtedly depicted and critiqued in his writings, it cannot be said that Joyce wholly rejects religion itself. In *Stephen Hero* and in the final chapter of *Portrait* there are already hints of a positive religious alternative. We will turn to these now.

II.4.3: Eros and Agape: "Bat-like Soul" and "Red-rimmed Eyes"

We may discount the idea that Stephen's epiphany on the beach is for him and for Joyce no more than a joyful relapse into the poisoned *eros* to which he had surrendered in early adolescence. The wretchedness of that state is well enough documented in the early chapters, which tell of Stephen's torment by "the wasting fires of lust"[78] before his first encounter of many with prostitutes and "the swamp of spiritual and bodily sloth in which his whole being had sunk"[79] after it. If Stephen, after seeing the girl on the beach, hurried to the nearest brothel, it would surely be a grossly insufficient response to his epiphany. Stephen may well have done precisely this, but, as we shall see later, the gross insufficiency of such a response is exposed in the climactic Circe chapter of *Ulysses*, which occurs in a brothel. *Portrait* is only part of Stephen's story. The novel ends on a note of unfinished business. In fact, as early as the *Stephen Hero* draft of *Portrait* there are signs that Joyce is intent on epiphanizing not poisoned but unpoisoned *eros*.

II.4.3.1: The Bat-like Soul: Repressed Femininity

We are familiar with the conversation about beauty and aesthetics between Stephen and Fr. Artifoni in the *Stephen Hero* manuscript.[80] Artifoni admits to Stephen that his interpretation of Aquinas is justifiable and that beauty may be considered intrinsically, independently of its relation to goodness and truth. The conversation arose out of a discussion of an Italian novel: "A priest in the house had read the novel and condemned it to the dinner-table. It was bad, he said." In response to this judgment Stephen distinguishes between the book's moral value and its aesthetic value: "Stephen urged that it had given him at least esthetic pleasure and that, for that reason, it could be said to be good." Artifoni's response is initially non-committal—"Father Byrne does not think so"—and Stephen insists, "But God?" Artifoni's answer is hesitant but affirmative: "For God it might be . . . good," and Stephen's response to this, in turn, is unhesitant and satisfied: "Then I prefer to side against Father Byrne." The narrator, who is much less effaced in this version than in the completed novel, presents the moment as a victory for Stephen: "Father Artifoni had to admit . . . to Stephen that the most reprehensible moment of human delight in as much as it had given pleasure to a human being was good in the sight of God."[81]

Interesting as it might be to discuss the theological reliability of Fr. Artifoni's answer, this would be a distraction from the core issue. Of more pressing interest for my purposes is to note that Stephen is groping to get at the inner "delightful" dimension of the *eros* experience which is unpoisoned, pure joy: not displeasing to God. The term *eros* does not explicitly appear in this conversation but it is implicit almost to the point of being obvious.

The *eros* theme is implicit again in the fifth chapter of *Portrait*. Stephen's friend Davin, a personification of patriotic rural Irish simplicity, narrates an encounter he had with a woman while hiking home to Killmallock from Buttevant having missed the train following a hurling match. Around nightfall he knocks at the door of a cottage to ask for a drink of water and the woman of the house who answers attempts to lure him inside: "She asked me was I tired and would I like to stop the night there. She said she was all alone in the house . . . she took my hand to draw me in over the threshold." Davin did not succumb: "I didn't go in, Stevie. I thanked her and went on my way again, all in a fever. At the first bend of the road I looked back and she was standing at the door." This episode would lodge itself in Stephen's imagination. He deeply identifies with this woman: "The last words of Davin's story sang in his memory and the figure of the woman in the story stood forth . . . as a type of her race and of his own, a bat-like soul waking to the consciousness of itself in darkness and secrecy and loneliness."[82]

The motif of the bat-like soul representing repressed womanhood recurs twice in this last chapter of the novel: "He had told himself bitterly . . . that she was a figure of the womanhood of her country, a bat-like soul waking to the consciousness of itself in darkness and secrecy and loneliness,"[83] and again: "And under the deepened dusk he felt the thoughts and desires of the race to which he belonged flitting like bats across the dark country lanes . . . A woman had waited in the doorway as Davin had passed by at night and . . . had all but wooed him to her bed."[84] For Stephen this woman is a kindred spirit. It would be reductive to think of his obsession with her in terms solely of vicariously rueing Davin's missed opportunity of easy sex. There may be that to it, but there is more to it too. He identifies with her, sees himself in her. She is "a type of her race and of his own"; she is "of the race to which he belonged." She represents womanhood but she also represents Stephen and Ireland itself.

Stephen's artistic imagination sees the "bat-like" woman as a personification of repressed *eros*: unsatisfied, alluring desire. She calls to mind the girl that Stephen saw on the beach, but she also calls to mind another figure we have come across. It requires no stretch of the imagination to believe that Joyce had her in mind when in his essay on the Renaissance he wrote of the human spirit in terms of "a woman who, being bored with the peace and tranquillity in which her heart is slowly consumed, turns her eyes towards life's power of enticement (*la vita tentatrice*)."[85]

II.4.3.2: The Red-rimmed Eyes: Repressive Masculinity

Nor does it require a stretch of the imagination to discover this repressed Irish woman's repressive Irish "husband" in a later image in the final pages of *Portrait*. Stephen has attended a conference by a Gaelic scholar named John Alphonsus Mulrennan who has returned from his folklore research in the west of Ireland. We are privy to an entry on the conference in Stephen's diary: "He told us he met an old man there in a mountain cabin. Old man had red eyes and short pipe. Old man spoke Irish. Mulrennan spoke Irish. Then old man and Mulrennan spoke English." The beleaguered confusion of the Irish identity, suspended forlornly between two languages, is deftly evoked in these short, staccato lines.

Mulrennan witnesses to the old man about a larger world, eliciting an uncouth reaction: "Mulrennan spoke to him about universe and stars. Old man sat, listened, smoked, spat. Then said: 'Ah, there must be terrible queer creatures at the latter end of the world.'" Mulrennan presumably related the exchange as a humorous incident of quaint Hiberno-English colloquialism, but its impact on Stephen's imagination is much more profound: "I fear him. I fear his red-rimmed horny eyes. It is with him I must struggle all through this night till day come, till he or I lie dead, gripping him by the sinewy throat till . . . Till what? Till he yield to me? No. I mean no harm."[86]

The old man, like the young woman, represents Ireland and therefore part of Stephen himself. The implied allusion to Jacob wrestling with a "man" who represents God (cf. Gen 32:23-32) adds a religious dimension to the image, prompting thoughts not just of Ireland but concretely of Catholic, or puritanical, Ireland. Stephen tempers his initial, fear-driven impulse to fight with him "till he or I lie dead," expressing willingness to reach some kind of amicable settlement: "Till he yield to me? No. I mean no harm." The biblical passage alluded to is composed of approximately the same number of sentences as the number used in Stephen's account of Mulrennan's meeting with the old man. More importantly, the word "man" appears five times in the biblical passage, and Joyce uses that same word the same number of times. These are indicators of a puzzle in Joyce that can only fully be resolved with reference to *eros* and *agape*. In Joyce's imagination *agape* without *eros* is associated with hyper-masculinity and *eros* without *agape* with hyper-femininity.

The association is an artistic motif, not a mathematical equation, and is therefore neither exact nor exhaustive, but we will see in the next chapter that the Joycean reconciliation of *eros* and *agape* is closely related to the reconciliation of femininity and masculinity, of *anima* and *animus*, in the self. The association of woman with *eros* is not original or unique to Joyce; the German psychoanalyst Carl Jung made the same woman-*Eros* association before the publication of *Portrait*,[87] though Jung associated man not with *agape* but with *Logos*: "Woman's psychology is founded on the principle of *Eros* . . . whereas from ancient times the ruling principle ascribed to man is *Logos*. The concept of *Eros* could be expressed in modern terms as psychic relatedness, and that of *Logos* as objective interest."[88] This association may be explained in terms of emotion that seeks inter-subjective union, and reason that seeks objective understanding. Joyce sees the dehumanizing dangers of exclusively overemphasizing either of these tendencies and seeks somehow to reconcile them.

Joyce associates both *Logos* and *Agape*, and their attendant distortions of intellectualism and self-immolation without affective compensation, with the masculine psychology, or *animus*; the male is more predisposed to immolate self for an idea or a cause (and the female for union with another). Aquinas trained his mind on this same challenge, seeing it in terms of ordering and harmonizing the activities of the intellect and the will, knowledge, and desire. The French Neo-Thomist Jacques Maritain has summarized Thomas' thought in terms that help us to understand the issues that Joyce is wrestling with. This point merits attention, in order better to understand the dynamics at work, the seriousness of Joyce's dilemma, and the merits of his response.

II.4.3.3: The Intellect and the Will

The dynamics at work are those of the intellect and the will. Maritain, explicating Part I, question 82, article 3 of the *Summa*, says that "St. Thomas shows us two complementary but essentially different activities in every spirit, each as exacting and voracious as the other." The first of these is the intelligence, which is "an activity wholly turned towards the being of the object, towards what is 'other' as it is 'other,' and of itself only concerned with that, living only for it."[89] Without explicitly using the same terms, this description elaborates upon Jung's explanation of the *Logos* principle, and justifies associating it with the dynamics of *agape*. Maritain's subsequent deliberations reinforce the association: "If humanity is purely and exclusively intellectual, it scorns its eternal interests; and what does its own being matter to it? It gets intoxicated with the hows, it becomes a kind of monster as metaphysician or aesthete."[90] Although not a commentary on Joyce, these words describe a major Joycean concern: intellectualism.

The contrary danger—of sensualism—is also a major Joycean concern. The other major activity of the spirit is the will. The will, Maritain explains, unfolding Thomas, is "an activity wholly occupied with the good of the subject or of the things with which the subject is united, which of itself is concerned only with this good, living only for it."[91] Simply put, the intellect is object-centered, seeking understanding, and the will subject-centered, seeking self-enrichment. This latter dynamic, left to its own devices, is no less dangerous than the former one: "Woe to humanity if one monopolizes all the nourishment at the expense of the other! If humanity is purely and exclusively volitional, it contemns truth and beauty."[92]

Sensualism, poisoned *eros*, entails the death of noble and ennobling aspirations to beauty and truth. It leads, paradoxically, to a self-destructive selfishness and the sterilization of sensuality. Any philosophy that is "based on the absolute superiority of will or feeling, that is, of a faculty occupied essentially and exclusively with what affects the subject," will degenerate inevitably into subjectivism and sensualism: "it will cause will to fall from its own order and will pass inevitably into the service of the lower affective powers and the instinct."[93] If sensualism and intellectualism are to be avoided, then will and intelligence, desire and knowledge, *eros* and *agape*, *anima* and *animus*, must be harmonized. This challenge is at the core of the Joycean aesthetic; hence the importance of capturing the imaginative repercussions of the bat-like soul of Davin's temptress and the primitive coarseness of Mulrennan's old man.

Of course, on the basis of the little we know of him, Mulrennan's old man could scarcely be accused of intellectualism or of being self-sacrificial (unless we associate him with Mulrennan himself and nationalistic idealism), but he does embody the harshness that Joyce associates with Irish hyper-masculinity. In any event, if it seems forced at this point to interpret the images of the bat-like soul of the young woman and the old man with red-rimmed eyes as evocative, respectively, of *eros* and *agape/logos*, it would be sufficient for now to accept them simply as images of sensuality and harshness; of thwarted and distorted femininity and masculinity. Mulrennan's old man will reappear in many guises in Joyce's prose (even in the guise of a woman in the short story entitled "Mother," with heavy irony), and the bat-like woman too; one of her guises will be Molly Bloom, whose erotically repressed husband Leopold has refused to have sex with her for ten years. Joyce's *Ulysses* takes up where his *Portrait of the Artist* unsatisfactorily ends.

II.4.3.4: Portraits Unfinished Business

Stephen is not portrayed at the end of *Portrait*, or indeed in *Ulysses*, as a "finished product." He has turned away from a formal, ritualistic priesthood to embrace his destiny as priest of the eternal imagination, but he has written nothing of value. Hugh Kenner wrote that "the last chapter makes the book a peculiarly difficult one for the reader to focus, because Joyce had to close it on a suspended cord."[94] For all his euphoria and sense of mission, Stephen is depicted at the end of the novel as a solitary figure and remains so, now more dejected, when we next encounter him in *Ulysses*.

Stephen, having had his epiphanical breakthrough, has reached a dead end: "This problem Joyce didn't wholly solve; there remains a moral ambiguity (how seriously are we to take Stephen?) which makes the last forty pages painful reading."[95] In the closing line of the novel—"Old father, old artificer, stand me now and ever in good stead"[96]—Stephen invokes his namesake Daedalus, father of Icarus and artificer of waxen wings. With this invocation Joyce achieves two effects. One is to hint that Stephen is flying too close to the sun and is headed for a fall; in the opening chapters of *Ulysses* he is depicted by the sea, notably bereft of the soaring optimism at the end of *Portrait*. The other effect Joyce achieves with the invocation "Old father, old artificer" is to gesture towards *Ulysses*, the main theme of which will be fatherhood. Stephen's combination of ingenuous optimism and arrested development is not untypical of early adulthood and may not therefore reflect negatively on the virtue of the novel as a portrait of a young man. A traumatic life experience—his mother's death—will paradoxically rescue him from the rut of arrested development. The rut is naïve optimism: he has renounced *agape* without *eros*, but is *eros* a sufficient replacement?

There are enough clues in Joyce's writings hinting in the direction of *eros* to require, for the sake of good literary criticism, a fully-fledged theological treatment of *agape* and *eros*. Such a discussion is a need that arises naturally out of reading his works. It is a discussion that Joyce wanted those who read his works to have, either to resolve puzzles that Joyce himself never resolved, or simply to see the puzzle as Joyce saw it. At the very least the discussion is needed to articulate problems that literary critics encounter when they read Joyce, preventing them from perceiving a puzzle that Joyce wrestled with. I believe, in fact, that Joyce understood the *agape-eros* puzzle, even if he did not present it expressly in these terms—he is an artist, not a philosopher or a theologian—and that the solution to it that he eventually presents in his works coincides with Catholic orthodoxy. The final proof of this will come in *Ulysses*.

For now, it will suffice to establish that what Joyce rejects in "Eveline" and in *Portrait* is not religion *per se* but disordered *agape*. In this, not only did he coincide with the Catholic tradition; he knew this to be the case. The Christian doctrine of *eros* may have been eclipsed for a time by Puritanism but it was never erased, as a second glance at its historical vicissitudes quickly reveals. Now that we have seen that Joyce had these categories in his mind, at least implicitly, we may proceed to a fuller explication.

II.4.4: The Condemnation and Defence of Eros

Nietzsche was not the only contributor to the *eros* controversy. On the opposite side to Nietzsche, Swedish Lutheran theologian Anders Nygren, and later Karl Barth, argue *in favor* of the radical separation of *eros* and *agape*.[97] According to Nygren, it was Luther who restored the purity of Christian love by asserting not only faith without works but, correspondingly, *agape* without *eros*, *agape* referring to the divine love which is pure, gratuitous, selfless, sacrificial, and *eros* referring to a human love which is motivated by attraction, desire, possessiveness, and the seeking of self-enrichment. *Agape* without *eros* may be Lutheran, as Nygren argued, it may be Puritan or Kantian, but it is not Catholic. This is a crucial clarification.

Even St. Augustine's "You made us for You, Lord,

and our hearts are restless until they rest in You" comes under Nygren's critical focus, as evidence that Augustine was negatively influenced by the Platonic doctrine of *eros* which is contrary to the true and pure Christian *agape* love. Similarly, the mystical writings of St. John of the Cross and St. Teresa of Avila typify for Nygren the Catholic covert pseudo-spiritualization of mere sensualism. Nygren first published his thoughts on *eros* and *agape* in 1930, but they crystallize an uneasiness with the term *eros* ever latent in certain strands of the Christian tradition.

Defending this tradition, Pope Benedict XVI, when still Joseph Cardinal Ratzinger, reflected on this subject: "The first thing needed here is to ward off a tendency that would separate *eros* and religious love as if they were two quite distinct realities."[98] Such a separation, he argues, would lead to the deformation of both. The solution is to be found not in separation but in synthesis. Ratzinger acknowledges his indebtedness on this point to Josef Pieper's "masterly treatise" on love.[99] Pieper, in turn, in a section entitled "*Eros* and *Agape*" of the chapter on love in his book on the three theological virtues,[100] cites C.S. Lewis, who, putting pen to paper to write his *The Four Loves*, was ready to speak negatively of mere "Need-love" (*eros*) and positively of "Gift-love" (*agape*), but realized on reflection that the matter was more complex than it first appeared. Pieper speaks of the "denigration" and "defamation" of *eros* which has entered the general consciousness to the point of appearing natural.

Fr. Raniero Cantalamessa, in a book entitled *Eros e Ágape* which builds upon Ratzinger's argument, explains that the general uneasiness with *eros* originates in the ambiguity of the word even in the original Greek. On the one hand, there existed the sense of *eros* as sexual attraction, natural and passionate and good, but with an inherent egotistical and destructive tendency. Plato had also spoken of *eros* as the energy which is awakened by the contemplation of beauty and impels us towards unity, in terms that recognized the nobility of the mutual attraction and desire for possession that is also present in human love. The early Church was reluctant to use the word while this confusion was present and preferred the term *agape* until the distinction was sufficiently clear to be able to say, as St. John Climacus did in the seventh century, that the chaste man is the one "who drives out *eros* with *Eros*"[101]—not with *agape*, as we might have expected, but with *Eros*. (At the risk of quibbling at the expense of a good aphorism, it might have been better to speak not of driving out *eros* with *Eros* but of regulating inordinate *eros* with *Eros*).

The separation of *eros* from *agape* leads on the one hand to a profanation and secularization of *eros*, and on the other hand to a purist dehumanization of *agape*. Cantalamessa describes the ensuing dichotomization: "If worldly love is a body without a soul, religious love practiced that way [*agape* without *eros*] is a soul without a body." It is an obvious but often overlooked fact that "The human being is not an angel, that is, a pure spirit; he is soul and body substantially united: everything he does, including loving, must reflect this structure."[102] If there is disordered *agape* or disordered *eros* in our relationship with God, this disorder will overflow into our human relationships. Interestingly, James Joyce was familiar enough with the Catholic tradition to be able to distinguish between orthodox Catholic spirituality and unhealthy deformations thereof.

II.4.5: Eros in the Catholic Tradition

James Joyce was *not* unaware of *eros* as an aspect of Catholic doctrine. Stanislaus Joyce admits to bewilderment at the indiscriminate breadth of his brother's reading interests, which included, "certain mystical writers . . . the anti-Jesuit Miguel de Molinos, St. John of the Cross, St. Teresa, St. Catherine of Siena, Thomas à Kempis. A cursory dip into these writers was enough to convince me that I could not work up any interest in them." James Joyce's "atheism" was not as plain and simple an affair as that of his brother, Stanislaus. Nor was his interest in the mystical phenomenon one of mere metaphorical opportunism as has been suggested; rather, he was drawn to it as an artful form of expression of what he perceived as a real psychological experience: "'Why are you pottering about with the misty mystics?'. . . 'They interest me . . . In my opinion, they are writing about a very real spiritual experience you can't appreciate . . . with a subtlety that I don't find in many so-called psychological novels.'"[103] From these writers if nowhere else, Joyce would have learned of the doctrine of mystical *eros* and the "divine madness" in the Catholic tradition.

Since this aspect of the Catholic religious relationship is fundamental to my discussion of Catholicism and of Joyce, I quote here some famous and energetic expressions of it by St. Augustine in his *Confessions*:

> How joyous it suddenly became to me to forgo the varied sweetness of trifles I feared to lose, and now was glad to fling aside. For you, true, supreme sweetness, cast them out of me, and in their place came into me, sweeter than all pleasure . . . , brighter than all light, deeper than all depths, higher than all honour . . . And I babbled like a babe to you, my fame, my wealth and health, my Lord God; Late I came to know you, Beauty ancient yet new.
>
> Late I loved you . . . You cried and called aloud, and broke my deafness. You flashed, shone and shattered my blindness. You breathed fragrance, I drew in my breath, and I pant for you. I tasted, I hunger and thirst. You touched me, and I burned for your peace. When I shall with my whole being hold fast to you, sorrow and toil will have no more part in me. My life will be alive, wholly full of you.[104]

St. Teresa of Avila describes her ecstatic experiences in similar terms. The poetry of St. John of the Cross is rich with religious *eros*. Such tastes in faith of the divine Lover are available to all, albeit not always so intensely. The relevance of Augustine's expressions in terms of tone (urgent, passionate, emotive) and content (personal, intimate, nuptial) will be general and implicit throughout our discussion, but we will return to them particularly and explicitly when we examine in greater depth the climactic ecstatic experience of Stephen Dedalus in *Portrait*.

We will see that Stephen's spiritual itinerary and Augustine's are strikingly similar. For Augustine, there are "two hands," so to speak, of divine grace: *admonitio* and *delectatio*: admonition and delight. Augustine spoke of a "*disciplina Dei* or *Domini* to which corresponds a *correptio Domini*." God's discipline is "a sign of his mercy because a person, within the time of his earthly existence, still has the possibility of reform (= *correctio*)."[105] Augustine believes in a divine dynamic of discipline, "in the first place by the words of Scripture," but God disciplines also "by some afflictions, like famine, sickness, or the death of people around us."[106] Stephen suffers this process.

For Augustine, the divine, parental, gracious *modus operandi* is not exclusively about admonition and discipline; instead, the divine pursuer combines and alternates coercion and seduction, sanction and enticement, in pursuit of the wilful soul. St. Augustine called this latter strategy—that of seduction—*gratia delectans*: "Grace then is a blessing of sweetness that produces delight in us and makes us desire or love that which has been mandated."[107] It is closely related to, if not synonymous with, religious *eros*. Here is one of many descriptions to be found in Augustine's writings: "I say it is not enough to be drawn by the will; you are drawn even by delight . . . Give me one that longs, one that hungers, one that is travelling in this wilderness, and thirsting and panting after the fountain of his eternal home . . . he knows what I say.[108]

Joyce was familiar with the Catholic doctrine of

religious *eros*: dynamic attraction and ecstatic delight. He defended that doctrine against his brother's derision as a "very real spiritual experience," written of in the Catholic tradition with a subtlety that he didn't find elsewhere. But there is evidence that this aspect of Catholic doctrine was somewhat silenced in Joyce's time. By presenting the thought of Augustine and the great mystics of the Catholic Tradition as we have just done, and the thought of modern representatives of Catholic spirituality like Ratzinger, Pieper, and Maritain, as we have also just done, we may consider Joyce in the context of Catholic intellectual history, having thus highlighted the theological hiatus to which he is responding.

II.5: A Theological Hiatus

Pope Benedict XVI, in the second volume of *Jesus of Nazareth*, speaks of a nineteenth-century distortion of the Catholic faith: "Nineteenth-century piety brought back a one-sided notion of purity by reducing it to the sexual sphere, thereby burdening it once again with suspicion of material things, of the body."[109] Also condemning spiritualist distortions, Pope John Paul II wrote of Gnosticism as a heretical "shadow" that has dogged Christianity from the beginning: "Gnosticism . . . has always existed side by side with Christianity . . . assuming the characteristics of a religion or a para-religion in distinct, if not declared, conflict with all that is essentially Christian."[110] Manichaeism, itself a form of Gnosticism, is another heterodox traveling companion of Christianity, but it is not Christianity.[111]

So, the dichotomization of flesh and spirit, of the earthly and the heavenly, of *eros* and *agape*, is not attributable to Catholicism, be it Irish or otherwise. T. S. Eliot, in his essay "The Metaphysical Poets,"[112] laments the "dissociation of sensibility" as a grave problem—not solely aesthetic—of our time, diagnosing a lamentable separation, originating in the late 17th century, of emotion from thought; an exaltation of the rational and spiritual at the expense of the corporal and affective which leads to a passionless intellectuality; an eclipse of *eros*. It may be argued that this movement originated with Cartesian dualism and culminated in Jean Paul Sartre's Catharist contempt for matter and consequent atheism as related in *Nausea*.

By dating the origins of the distorting "dissociation of sensibility" in the late 17th century, Eliot implicitly attributes this dichotomization to Descartes. Jacques Maritain does so explicitly. Descartes, Maritain writes, "is an obstinate divider and he has not only separated modern and ancient, but he has set all things against each other—faith and reason, metaphysics and sciences, knowledge and love." For Maritain, the Cartesian revolution constituted a rupture of the Thomist synthesis and an impoverishment of thought by separating it from love, or, perhaps more precisely, from religious *eros*: "The world sighs for deliverance; it sighs for wisdom, for the wisdom, I say, from which the spirit of Descartes has led us astray, for the wisdom which reconciles man with himself and, crowned with a divine life, fulfills knowledge in charity."[113]

C. S. Lewis wrote in the first pages of his book on

love that "I was looking forward to writing some fairly easy panegyrics on the first sort of love [Gift-love; *agape*] and disparagements on the second [Need-love; *eros*];" on reflection, the task turned out not to be so simple: "I cannot now deny the name *love* to Need-love . . . Every time I have tried to think the thing out along those lines, I have ended in puzzles and contradictions. The reality is more complicated than I supposed."[114] If in 1960, having set himself the task of writing about love, Lewis found himself negatively conditioned towards "Need-love" (*eros*), and other major twentieth century thinkers like Pieper and Ratzinger (and, implicitly, Eliot and Maritain) have felt the need to train their minds on this problem, it was because this aspect of love had been eclipsed in Christian teaching and anti-Christian thinkers had falsely responded to the void.

Joyce was caught in a theological hiatus in which the Catholic doctrine of mystical *eros* seems not to have been much proclaimed. It is not a new doctrine, although it has recently undergone new penetration and development. There is evidence of penetration into this mystery in the writings of James Joyce too. The prevailing opinion is that Joyce may be numbered among those anti-Christian thinkers who championed *eros* against the baleful influence of Christianity, but this opinion does not survive a close analysis. Ultimately we will see that, in the Joycean pilgrimage of ongoing self-critique, *eros*, whether poisoned or unpoisoned, is shown to be insufficient. But now we will briefly recapitulate what has been established thus far.

II.6: Conclusion

Joyce's historical context has helped us to see that Jeffrey Segall and Geert Lernout are partially right about "the darker side of Catholicism" with which they say Joyce was familiar. However, they do not address the socio-political context out of which Joyce emerged. It would be difficult to overestimate the impact of the Great Famine on the Irish people, along with the subsequent almost nationwide abandonment of the Irish language within just one generation, from the 1850s to the 1880s. James Joyce was born in 1882. As Kiberd puts it, "What had happened in Ireland was what would happen across the world in the later 19th and early 20th century: traditional patterns of living had been gravely disrupted . . . The people were suffering from that most modern of ailments: a homeless mind."[115]

After the trauma comes the void. In the jostling of ideologies that sought to fill that void, Joyce, with a prophet's eye for the authentic and the spurious, navigates the waters to negotiate his own identity and that of his people. He responds to a Catholicism that has been partially mutilated by distorting pressures. Antoine Levy, due to his knowledge of the intricacies of Catholicism, introduces an important distinction into our reading of Joyce. In the course of his article Levy asks this question: "During his school years, did not Joyce precisely discover a way of turning Aquinas's ideas against the teaching of his Jesuit masters?"[116] Levy is referring here to Joyce's Thomist aesthetic, but St. Thomas's ideas about aesthetics were not the only aspect of orthodox Catholic doctrine that Joyce employed to subvert the "Catholicism" that he was taught. He uses Catholic doctrines on grace too, and on the Eucharist. He is cognizant of the experience of religious *eros* in the teachings of the great Catholic mystics and doctors.

He is cognizant also of Nietzsche's attacks on Christianity and takes a more nuanced stand. In early adulthood he had a Nietzschean phase, and this is reflected in the depiction of Stephen Dedalus, but it is not his final position. Like Nietzsche, Joyce vigorously rejects a religiosity of *agape* without *eros*, but, unlike Nietzsche, Joyce gives no proof that he rejected religion itself or that his response to this distortion was a reactionary polar-opposite philosophy of Dionysian ecstasy without *agape*. We will see in the next chapter that Joyce did not see this as a way to human plenitude.

In the first chapter it has been established that, although Joyce rejected a form of ontology that seeks to codify and catalogue the divine and human mysteries, he did not react by crossing over to absolutist relativism. He remained a realist. In this second chapter it has been established that, although Joyce rejected a religiosity that empties the human experience of *eros* in the human-divine and interhuman relationships, his final word is not one of outright dismissal of the supernatural. He remains open. Stephen Dedalus is not a "finished product," and does not represent Joyce's final position. Joyce's prose epiphanizes the activity of a mysterious principle conducting Stephen (and Bloom), instinctually and circumstantially, towards human fulfillment. This is compatible with a realist and religious anthropology. In the remaining chapters we will see ever-deepening similarities of means and ends between Joycean individuating dynamism, epiphanized in his writings, and the Judeo-Christian journey.

Chapter III: Joycean Individuation

III.1: Introduction

We have seen that Joyce remained a realist and therefore a believer in universal objective values. We have also seen that Joyce rejected a distorted version of *agape* as it existed in nineteenth century Ireland. It is clear that errors occur when *agape* is collapsed into sexual *eros* or when *eros* is eliminated and *agape* asserted. Twentieth century philosophers and theologians like Pieper and Ratzinger strove to understand this mystery and to synthesize *eros* and *agape*. Now, we will compare the Joycean paradigm of personhood and the Christian one, and their respective processes (dynamism and grace) by which human potentiality becomes act, and reaches fulfillment. Joyce praised the Renaissance for "creating in us and in our art a sense of mercy for all creatures who live, die, and yield to their illusions."[1] The supreme value ultimately affirmed by Joyce is Christian *charity*, and the climate in which human beings flourish is for Joyce that of Christian *mercy*.

The "sense of mercy" in Joyce's art, and the struggle to acquire and epiphanize it, will be the recurring central point of reference in this chapter. It seems from Joyce's words that the Renaissance, by showing us the ancient world, highlights aspects of the Christian religion that are not present in the ancient world, aspects which humanity now possesses as a result of Christianity, one of those realities being mercy. The Renaissance was also, as I read Joyce's statement, an anthropocentric movement that in focusing on the human figure, human events, etc., shows the presence or the possibility of mercy, and the urgent need for it, in ordinary everyday experience. It represents a development, at least in the mind of Joyce, and so, it enriches the human experience in a way that was not possible before. Little or nothing has been said about the sense of mercy in Joyce's art, an oversight I hope to correct.

It is not possible to speak of the sense of mercy in Joyce's art without speaking also of the challenge of reconciling *agape* and *eros* and the theme of sexual identity. In Joyce's imagination the challenge to reconcile *eros* and *agape* is connected with the challenge to reconcile the feminine, or *anima*, and the masculine, or *animus*, in the self, and both challenges are connected to the theme of mercy, since mercy requires the harmonization of exigency and tenderness, discipline and nurture. Declan Kiberd writes as follows of Joyce's experience with male friends: "He was left to conclude that at the root of many men's inability to live in serenity with a woman was a prior inability to harmonize male and female elements in themselves."[2] For Joyce, when men and women are overly masculinized, *agape* dominates; when they are overly feminized, *eros* dominates. Extending and specifying the association further, for Joyce, two symptoms of hyper-masculinity are intellectualism and emotional ineptitude, while symptoms of hyper-femininity include sensualism and ineffectuality.

Extremes on both sides of the spectrum, i.e., hyper-masculinity and hyper-femininity, are found both in men and in women. Ultimately, in *Ulysses* it becomes apparent that transvestite sadomasochism is for Joyce the sexual expression of failure to reconcile *agape* and *eros*, *animus* and *anima*, sacrifice and sensuality. When that failure happens, pain is confused with pleasure, and femininity with masculinity. Success in the reconciliation of these binaries—sacrifice and sensuality, *agape* and *eros*, *animus* and *anima*—is manifested in strong and serene sexual identity: honest masculinity and honest femininity. Although Joyce did not explicitly express the male-female dialectic in terms of *agape* and *eros*, and the association has not been made by Joyce critics, there is a more than sufficient textual basis to meet the onus of proof that the challenge of reconciling *eros* and *agape* is a major theme for Joyce, and that it is connected with the themes of sexual identity and mercy. This will become apparent as we identify the dynamics of personal individuation epiphanized in Joyce's writings.

As we trace the trajectory of Joycean individuation as manifested in his writings, we will discern the influence of a mysterious and *merciful* God-like principle at work in human affairs to provoke change, epiphanized in Joyce's prose. Catholic orthodoxy does not envisage anthropology as being separable from theology or the religious as separable from the secular, and neither did Joyce. We will see that Joyce's views on sexual identity are compatible with Catholic anthropology; we will see that the *eros-agape* synthesis Joyce eventually achieves is harmonious with the Catholic theology of Christian love expounded by Pope Benedict XVI in his encyclical *Deus Caritas Est*; and finally, we will see that the Joycean anthropology of sexual identity and his *eros-agape* equilibrium are bound up with the Christian concept of divine mercy.

The *Dubliners* short stories are initial explorations of the *eros-agape, anima-animus* theme; *Portrait* is a continuation and gradual elucidation of the tensions that need to be resolved; the resolution occurs in *Ulysses*, in the form of reconciliation of *animus* and *anima*, *agape* and *eros*. This happens in the climactic "consecration" scene of the black Mass in the Circe episode, as we are about to see. Three of the *Dubliners* stories in particular—"The Sisters," "A Painful Case," and "The Dead"—are early manifestations, and crucial locations, of the Joycean anthropology, and are helpful introductions to the thematic trajectory that concerns us.

III.2: Dubliners

III.2.1: "The Sisters"

III.2.1.1: Clerical Distortions

"The Sisters" is the very first story of *Dubliners*.[3] It introduces us conveniently to the Joycean exploration of male and female identity and the relatedness of this theme to the ruinous effects of distorted *agape*, effects that include excessive rigidity, guilt-complex, and scrupulosity. The story is about a young boy (who is also the narrator) and his friendship with an elderly priest who has just died. The priest, Father Flynn, is an embodiment of frustrated masculinity evocative of the old man with red-rimmed eyes in *Portrait*. The boy has a lively inquiring mind and enjoyed the priest's vast knowledge in matters of faith and morals. A cloud of suspicion hovers strangely over the priest and the relationship, and the boy labors psychologically and emotionally under an obscure, unresolved tension. He mysteriously achieves a kind of interior resolution when he overhears the dead priest's two sisters discussing their brother over evening tea after his death, remarking that he had suffered a breakdown and was never the same again after dropping and breaking a chalice.[4]

An unbeliever would easily underestimate or even fail entirely to imagine the deep dread present in the heart of a priest of profound faith of one day knocking over in a clumsy moment during the celebration of the Eucharist the chalice containing the Blood of Christ; hence the tendency of many to ascribe to Father Flynn sinister aberrations ranging from pedophilia to sexual promiscuity, schism and syphilis, to mention but a few. There is no hint in the text that Father Flynn is in any way sexually enticing, or that the boy found him so or that he found the boy so. The word "queer," used by old Cotter referring to Father Flynn, did not have the predominant connotation of homosexuality that it has today, as some contemporary critics have mistakenly assumed. It simply meant odd, in a slightly disturbing kind of way, as when the priest's sister Eliza describes his final deterioration: "I noticed there was something queer coming over him latterly." The boy is odd too, but his oddness is not sexual, it's intellectual. This is not your typical teenager. He has a voracious hunger for knowledge. Hence his attraction to Father Flynn.

Undoubtedly, old Cotter suggests something ugly

about the priest, and about his relationship with the boy: "'I have my own theory about it,' he said. 'I think it was one of those . . . peculiar cases . . . But it's hard to say . . . ' / He began to puff again at his pipe without giving us his theory.'" Cotter fixes his "little beady black eyes" on the boy and pronounces his verdict on the strange friendship: "'I wouldn't like children of mine,' he said, 'to have too much to say to a man like that.'" Whatever he suspects, old Cotter finds it so "hard to say" that he doesn't bring himself to say it. We are left in suspense. Significantly, so is the boy: "It was late when I fell asleep. Though I was angry with old Cotter for alluding to me as a child, I puzzled my head to extract meaning from his unfinished sentences." Old Cotter's suspicion may well have been that the old man liked young boys too much, but surely, if old Cotter correctly suspected something as glaringly perverse as pedophilia, the boy would have had no need to puzzle his head "to extract meaning from his unfinished sentences;" it would have been immediately obvious to him. If anything, Joyce seems to suggest that, whatever old Cotter suspected, he was wrong.

The sisters allude to the episode of the chalice obliquely because of its deeply disturbing nature for the faith-filled sensibility. Father Flynn's obsession with casuistry as revealed in his conversations with the boy is a typical symptom of the sickness of advanced scrupulosity. His unhinged laughter while alone in the church confessional late at night is another. And scrupulosity would also explain why his facial expression is twice described as "truculent" in death.[5] The boy is instinctively repelled by the physically and spiritually paralyzed priest, even though he finds in him an encyclopedically erudite and intellectually stimulating companion, a brilliant and broken man. The night after Father Flynn's death, the boy has a disturbing dream in which the dead man's ghost seeks pardon and reconciliation. At first, there seems to be a disproportion between the guilt of the dead man's ghost and the innocence of the friendship. The "heavy grey face" of Flynn that comes to the boy in his dream is strangely seductive and repulsive: "It began to confess to me in a murmuring voice and I wondered why it smiled continually and why the lips were so moist with spittle." The face is described again later in the story: "When he smiled he used to uncover his big discoloured teeth and let his tongue lie upon his lower lip," and again towards the end: "Whenever I'd bring in his soup to him there I'd find him with his breviary fallen to the floor, lying back in the chair and his mouth open."

Joyce critic Florence Walzl has identified a sinister factor that accounts for the negativity that darkens the relationship. There is a hint of simoniacal male ambition—which is for Joyce the great clerical sin—in Flynn's implicit invitation to the boy to enter an elite and esoteric cult of "secret knowledge and power";[6] these are the words Joyce would use later in *Portrait* to describe Stephen's priestly calling. Walzl quotes Stephen's words in *Stephen Hero*—"Don't you think they're trying to buy me?"[7]—and draws attention to the similarities between the priestly calling as represented in *Stephen Hero* and *Portrait* and the boy's relationship with Father Flynn in "The Sisters": "The vocation in both these works is a call to power and pride, not service and humility, and

Joyce sees it as simony. Father Flynn's appeal to the boy is similar."[8] "The Sisters" is a critique of encyclopedic "know-all" erudition, associated with the male, and a celebration of simple intuitive wisdom, associated with the female.

III.2.1.2: Male Authority and Feminine Wisdom

It would be a mistake, however, to take the critique of the male authority figure too far, as Roy Gottfried does. Gottfried interprets "The Sisters" as follows: "The death of all fathers . . . would mean a break with orthodoxy; would mean freedom from the need to subordinate; would deny authority once and for all. It would be fully schismatic."[9] He quotes the description of the boy's sense of liberation in support of this argument, and deduces that this freedom has to do with heresy and schism. Again, we are confronted with the important and often overlooked distinction between religion itself and an infirm religiosity and between authority and authoritarianism. The boy is liberated not from authority in itself, much less from fatherhood, but from an aberrant and abusive authority which has lost the authority to call itself authority at all.

In their analysis of the Irish situation, Lernout, Twomey, and Kiberd have helped us to understand that in Joyce's time the Catholic priesthood sometimes bore an authoritarian (as opposed to authoritative) power that is difficult for the contemporary mindset to conceive of; a power and prestige that conjoined the mystical, the social, and the political. In *Portrait* the dean warns Stephen of the terrible danger of entering the priesthood for the wrong reasons. In *Portrait* and in "The Sisters," the impression created is not only that in both cases these priests have done precisely this but also that they are inviting the boy to do the same. Collusion in simony is suggested too by the fact that when the empty chalice fell and broke, both priest and boy were somehow involved (the boy perhaps as acolyte). For a man of acute intelligence and scrupulous conscience to take upon himself the sacerdotal power without a sincere vocation would be an implosive combination. This seems to be the case of Father Flynn, another of many manifestations of mutilated masculinity in the Joycean *ouevre*.

Father Flynn's two sisters have similarly been seen by critics as manifestations of mutilated femininity. Until quite recently, it was conventional to interpret the sisters as emblems of withered sterility stifled by Catholicism and bereft of insight. Florence Walzl speaks of the sisters' "pious platitudes" and "obvious hypocrisy"—at least one obtuse reader (myself) sees no sign of hypocrisy, obvious or otherwise—and notes that the boy refuses to partake of the sherry and crackers, but then notes also that, having listened to their conversation concerning Father Flynn's priesthood, life, and death, "He immediately crosses the room and sips the sherry."[10] Initially the boy refuses to partake of the snack in the parlor, but then does so, leading critics to speak of a "secular communion."[11] Before meeting with the sisters the boy is confused and frightened; afterwards he is contented and at peace. Walzl's analysis fails to account for this enigmatic change of attitude. It is through the sisters' conversation that the boy mysteriously passes from "before" to "after" in his reaction to the priest's death. Why does the boy suddenly "enter communion" with the sisters?

This story is entitled "The Sisters" because it is in them (and not in the male authority figures) that the young boy, struggling to assimilate, finds the appropriate response, marked by delicacy and profound pity, combining truthfulness, toughness, and tenderness: "He was too scrupulous always . . . The duties of the priesthood was too much for him. And then his life was, you might say, crossed." In their humane response to this man's life and death he finds resolution and release from his own pseudo-vocation. Father Flynn's psychological hold on him is broken by the simple but superior wisdom of the two women.

III.2.1.3: Emancipating Faith and Unsatisfying Apostasy

This is an opportune moment to recall the words about women and religion in *Stephen Hero* which hint that "feminine" faith may be a superior wisdom to "masculine" apostasy: "The general attitude of women towards religion puzzled and often maddened Stephen . . . It did not strike him that the attitude of women towards holy things really implied a more genuine emancipation than his own."[12] At this juncture it may be tentatively deduced from this authorial aside that, for Joyce, there is an unhealthy harshness in Stephen's rejection of an unhealthy and harsh religiosity. In contrast, the "general attitude of women towards religion," characterized by kindness and mercy, is a "more genuine emancipation." Father Flynn's religiosity is unhealthy and harsh; that of his sisters is healthy and humane.

Highlighting the virtues of the sisters, Vicki Mahaffey notes the differences between their faith and that of their brother: "[I]t is simpler, more loving, more tiring, and less rewarding and mysterious. It expresses itself through actions, not words." Mahaffey ends with a pointed question: "What kind of faith is closer to the teachings that the priest claims to understand and represent?"[13] This interpretation takes into account the facts as presented in the story and harmonizes with the Joycean presentation of Catholicism in *Portrait*. It also features the dehumanizing effect of intellectualism, simoniacal male ambition, and the suppression of the feminine which is a recurring theme in *Dubliners* itself and in the other works.

Father Flynn's exhausted face represents the gaping abyss of a sick religiosity, enough to put anyone off, as it did Joyce. In the normal course of things, the repulsive aspect of the friendship between the boy and the priest is not so clear, but in the dream, as sometimes happens in dreams, the dangerousness of its seductiveness becomes startlingly obvious. In fact, in the dream, Flynn's sin is overtly stated: "I felt that I too was smiling feebly as if to absolve the simoniac of his sin." Old Cotter certainly had a point, but the boy does not connect with his verdict on Flynn and the friendship. Moreover, the boy finds Cotter bothersome, more bothersome than Flynn, twice calling him tiresome: "Tiresome old fool . . . Tiresome old red-nosed imbecile!" The boy does, however, connect with the sisters.

Joyce will not compromise with the cold hard nuances. The nuances are all present in the text. But his project is not about the ambidextrous manufacture of a perpetual stalemate, the preferred terrain of postmodernism. Joyce's purpose is epiphany. He wants the reader to wrestle with the story again and again, but the conditions are present for the reader to participate in the boy's breakthrough. Joyce has something to say. Loud and clear does not describe how he wants to say it. Quiet and complex would be a closer description, but this does not entail that the impact is weakened. On the contrary, once discovered, the truth of the matter is experienced as irrefutable. The flash of *claritas* is not blinding, it's eye-opening.

Joyce presents competing visions of the Church. One is the nationalistic, rigid, puritanical, prideful Church that we have seen in the last chapter, which Joyce clearly rejects. He shows his rejection further in "The Sisters" by honing in on rigid scrupulosity, having the boy reject it, and then rejoicing in the simple faith and gentle generosity of the sisters. The sisters represent a kind of common-sense Christian faith-wisdom which can remain faithful or loyal while seeing the deficiencies. But, at the same time, they do not give Joyce what he is looking for, an articulated philosophy or theology of the humanizing dynamics he seeks to understand. They represent faith without intellectual understanding.

In conclusion then, the story helps us further to understand what it is that Joyce critiques, confirming what we have seen in the analysis of "Eveline" and *Portrait* in chapter II, and it points us in a direction of finding a positive theology to epiphanize the puzzle and its solution. The sisters cannot express this in an intellectual form, which Joyce, the artist, strives after. When the *agape* aspect of love is overemphasized—the duty to sacrifice oneself for the other—the fruits of its impossible demands are moral and intellectual perfectionism, scrupulosity, and dread of punishment. When the *eros* aspect of faith is restored—God's desire for loving union with his children and their desire for loving union with Him—then there is confidence in mercy and true humanization. Once again, in Joyce's imagination these diverse tendencies are associated, respectively, with the masculine and the feminine. The next story I will look at further exposes the unsatisfactoriness of atheistic apostasy and dramatizes the challenge to reconcile male and female, *agape* and *eros*, intellect and emotion.

III.2.2: "A Painful Case"

III.2.2.1: A Heartbreaking Story

Joyce's interest in the suppression of the feminine in the male is present also in the heartbreaking story, "A Painful Case." "Heartbreaking" is the story's purpose and its only note of hope, expressed in the final line: "He felt that he was alone."[14] The weight of the story hinges crucially and cryptically on one word in the final line: *felt*. Mr. Duffy *is* alone, has been alone, unbeknownst to himself, from the beginning and, unless something drastically changes, will remain so until his death. The intended reader response is surely this: "At last—thank God!—Mr. Duffy *felt* that he was alone!"

Mr. Duffy is a middle-aged bank cashier, an intellectual, an atheist and a determined bachelor. At a music concert one evening he strikes up an acquaintance with Mrs. Emily Sinico, who is married with one daughter. Mr. Sinico is neglectful towards his wife Emily (another embodiment of the "bat-like soul" of *Portrait*). She and Mr. Duffy spend time together in innocent, intellectual conversation until one evening, in an impulsive, emotional moment, Mrs. Sinico takes Mr. Duffy's hand and presses it to her cheek. Mr. Duffy, discovering that the relationship has passed the boundaries of platonic friendship, recoils in horror and terminates their meetings. Four years later he reads a newspaper article entitled "A Painful Case" which relates the death of a drunken Mrs. Sinico under a train, hinting at suicide. Her husband is quoted as saying she began to drink uncontrollably two years before her death. Mr. Duffy's reaction is at first one of horror, contempt, and self-justification, followed by a sense of personal responsibility and profound loneliness. He discovers that he is an "outcast from life's feast."[15]

The story is of particular interest to the present investigation given that it constitutes a critique of convinced atheism as penetrating as any critique Joyce wrote on Catholicism if not more so. The scantiness of Geert Lernout's engagement with it—just a few lines culminating in, "Duffy, although a freethinker, is just as dead spiritually as all the other Dubliners"[16]—is an indicator of the difficulties it presents to his thesis. Misogyny, intellectualism, and arrogance—traits that notoriously describe Mr. Duffy's skeptical mentors, Schopenhauer and Nietzsche—are symptoms of inner imbalance. Duffy is modeled largely on Joyce's brother Stanislaus, who was an avid reader of Schopenhauer.[17] The aphorisms he likes to coin and record in his personal notebook are unmistakably Schopenhauerian. And Nietzsche's *Thus Spake Zarathustra* and *The Gay Science* enjoy pride of place on Duffy's shelves. In fact, Nietzsche is the only philosopher who receives explicit mention in the entire collection of short stories that compose *Dubliners*.

Although he vaunted Dionysian frenzy and vituperated against Christian *agape*, Nietzsche steered clear of exalting *eros* because *eros*, properly understood, is at odds with his philosophy of heroic egotism and self-realization; *eros* is about union with the other and therefore implies the impossibility of autonomous self-realization.[18] Hence, in one of his sublime conversations with Mrs. Sinico, Mr. Duffy, bewitched by his own rhetoric, hears himself say, "We cannot give ourselves . . . we are our own."[19] With tragic irony, Mrs. Sinico interprets Duffy's Nietzschean exaltations of magnificent solitude as poignant confessions of desolate loneliness and responds in kind, to Mr. Duffy's horror, provoking his termination of the affair. The misunderstanding exposes the failure of the Nietzschean ideology to comprehend the human heart, male or female, and its inhuman lovelessness.

Schopenhauer, Duffy's other mentor, was as skeptical about love as he was about God, man, and woman, and interpreted all manifestations of romantic love as mere disguises of the sexual instinct for the "composition of the next generation."[20] Both philosophers were notoriously unsuccessful in love. The aloof Mr. Duffy is a faithful disciple of his two mentors, and in Mr. Duffy Joyce is saying that Schopenhauerian and Nietzschean atheisms are hyper-masculine, misogynistic, and repressive ideologies. Duffy's initial attempt intellectually to process Mrs. Sinico's death symptomizes his own impoverished humanity: "Evidently she had been unfit to live, without any strength of purpose, an easy prey to habits, one of the wrecks on which civilisation has been reared."[21] "A Painful Case" is Joyce's ironic observation that in their effects on the human personality, particularly the male, there is little to distinguish atheism from Puritanism. For Joyce misogyny is as damaging to men as to women, as are intellectualism and arrogance. Add robotic imperviousness to the list and we have a good description of Duffy himself. There is the slightest hint of hope at the end of the story—"He *felt* that he was alone" (italics added)—that Mrs. Sinico's death may have therapeutically shocked Mr. Duffy out of his cerebral stupor and put him in contact with his own heart, i.e., with emotion.

Mr. Duffy is Joyce's statement that celibate atheism is not a happy result of rejecting distorted *agape*, but the undiscriminating and escapist *eros* that we see in Mrs. Sinico is not the remedy either. Mrs. Sinico, another victim of unfulfilled *eros* reminiscent of the bat-like soul in *Portrait*, has "a temperament of great sensibility,"[22] and her husband "had dismissed his wife so sincerely from his gallery of pleasures that he did not suspect that anyone else would take an interest in her."[23] Investing her hopes for happiness in Mr. Duffy, she is cruelly disappointed by his termination of their emotional affair—"she began to tremble so violently that, fearing another collapse on her part, he bade her good-bye quickly and left her"[24]— resorting eventually to alcohol and ending her own life.

We are surely intended to experience the tragic emotions of pity and terror at her plight, but we are also intended to understand that, as we have seen in the case of "Eveline," *eros* alone was never going to be the solution to her situation.

III.2.2.2: Eros Alone is Not the Answer

Joyce scholar Dr. Coilm Owens has written an analysis that unpacks many of the rich implications of "A Painful Case." The first premise of Owens's interpretation is that, "The hypothesis upon which he [Joyce] constructs 'A Painful Case' is Mr. Duffy's inability to transcend his childhood faith."[25] Duffy is still emotionally bound by his Catholic indoctrination, in spite of his conscious intellectual rejection of the same and subsequent Schopenhauerian skepticism: "Despite these efforts at disengagement from the past, he is still haunted by the guilt of having rejected the grace to ascend to the altar and become the instrument of God's love for mankind. In short, he is a spoiled priest."[26] According to Owens, Joyce creates out of this tension between intellectual skepticism and residual scrupulosity "a painful case" of moral casuistry. Mr. Duffy's failure to overcome the legacy of guilt at his own rejection of the priestly vocation and apostasy leads him with tragic inevitability towards a self-repressive relationship with Mrs. Sinico which is doomed from the outset to frustration.

Owens reads Mrs. Sinico's reaching out to Mr. Duffy as an opportunity of grace to which the emotionally arrested Mr. Duffy has been rendered incapable of responding:

> From a Christian perspective... when Mr. Duffy's moment of potential grace arrives, he is unable to recognize and assimilate it. His impulsive rejection of Mrs. Sinico's proferred touch (at first justified as a decorous shrinking from sin) and his termination of their relationship (rationalized after a week's reflection as his removal of 'an occasion of sin') amounts to a considered rejection of divine grace. Mrs. Sinico is Christ in female form, her sensual gesture, paradoxically, unveils the face of God... Still possessed of a univocal sense of evil, he refused the opportunity to respond to her with largesse of spirit.[27]

However, the terms "shrinking from sin" and "occasion of sin" do not appear in the Joyce text. Nor is there any mention of a childhood flirtation with a priestly vocation. I agree with Owens that "A Painful Case" dramatizes with typical Joycean economy and ingenuity a tension between what would be morally correct and what would be conducive to human growth, but I disagree that the "solution" suggested—of responding in kind to Mrs. Sinico's touch—would be a Christian response to divine grace, or even a Joycean hint at an opportunity for happiness.

For Mr. Duffy to enter an adulterous relationship with Mrs. Sinico is the obvious soap opera solution, with all the fragile guarantees of success that provide soap operas with repetitive dramatic opportunities. The *true* Christian response to this painful case (as distinct from a back-of-the-book answer in the kind of "Jesuitical" manual of moral theology typical of Joyce's era) would admit that it does not have a moral solution, because it is not at root a moral problem but a religious one. For Mr. Duffy to recognize the mind-boggling emotional obtuseness of his role in the affair would be a partial solution, of little avail to the now deceased Mrs. Sinico.

The situation has no horizontal solution because the underlying problem is vertical. Until such time as this is perceived, the Mr. Duffys and Mrs. Sinicos of the world will perpetually provide subject matter for romantic tragedies and soap operas. To use Joyce's own ingenious expression, "A Painful Case" comes too close to replacing the soul with the skin. Owens' interpretation pays too little heed to the implications of Duffy's discipleship of Nietzsche and Schopenhauer. Also, it is shortsighted towards Joyce's critique of Mrs. Sinico's pinning all her hopes on unmitigated *eros*. Finally, it lacks familiarity with a crucial element of Catholic teachings about religious *eros*.

III.2.2.3: Celibacy and Eros

Owens' description of the priestly vocation and priestly celibacy helps us to identify this missing element: "Celibacy . . . serves as a screening device: since the observance of sexual continence is beyond the capacity of the average man, it helps ensure that only those of strong character and high principle would enter the priesthood."[28] In the emphasis here on strong character and high principle there is more than a hint of Pelagianism.

Christ described celibacy not as an achievement of character but as a divine charism or gift: "Not all men can receive this saying, but only those to whom it is given" (Mt 19:11). It is primarily a gift and a mystery of faith, offered as often to the weak as to the strong of character. Moreover, it is humanly impossible even for the strongest of characters.

Owens continues: "On a practical and psychological level, it allows the priest to give his undivided attention to the faithful, while also on a spiritual level, it is a sign of the priest's dedication to the life of the eternal spirit."[29] In this and the following lines Owens presents a description of the Catholic priesthood that is correct but incomplete because it omits or at best understates the most important aspect of all, that of mystical *eros*, the dynamism of mutual attraction, without which *both* the Christian vocation in general *and* the Catholic priesthood are anti-natural, incomprehensible, and humanly impossible. While rightly ascribing importance to the secondary, functional aspect of priestly celibacy ("undivided attention to the faithful"), and to the theological aspect ("dedication to the life of the eternal spirit"), Owens neglects to mention the primordial aspect of the divine initiative in the form of seduction and donation, and the sweet surrender and ecstatic receptivity of the soul (so well described by St. Augustine). It does not take into account the reality of the priestly (and Christian) vocation as a kind of "erotic love affair."

Recent magisterial statements point to this prevalent error: "It is not sufficient to understand priestly celibacy in purely functional terms," and insist on the prioritization of the nuptial dimension: "Celibacy ... has first and foremost a nuptial meaning; it is a profound identification with the heart of Christ the Bridegroom who gives his life for his Bride" (*Sacramentum Caritatis*, 24). Religious *eros* provides the key to priestly celibacy, because it is the sublimation (as opposed to repression or even control) of sexuality within this love affair that capacitates the person chosen for this gift—priest, religious or any other called to lifelong chastity—freely and joyfully to relativize them other options. The priest is bride insofar as he is a baptized member of the Church, and bridegroom insofar as he is sacramentally configured to Christ by Holy Orders. In him the harmonization of masculine and feminine is sacramentally paradigmatic. But *all* Christians, lay and consecrated, male and female, by virtue of their baptism, are sacramentally destined to a nuptial relationship with Christ the Bridegroom.[30]

When human beings enjoy *eros* and its "divine madness" in their relationship with the divine—i.e., with Christ, who is called Savior and Spouse—there is a strong and serene wisdom, fruit of grace, in the management of their thoughts, words, gestures, and sentiments, which spares them the trauma of tragic emotional disappointment. They become capable of regulating inordinate destructive *eros* with *Eros*. Christianity thus integrates mysticism and morality, religion and ethics. Hence Augustine's famous, "*Dilige et quod vis fac.*"[31] Recently, some Joyce scholars have begun to grasp, partially, that Joyce and Jesus might have similar purposes.

III.2.2.4: Parables and Provocation to Change

The similarity of genre between Joyce's short stories and Jesus's parables has been noted, albeit nervously, in a recent book of commentaries entitled *Collaborative Dubliners: Joyce in Dialogue.* In their introduction to the collection, Vicki Mahaffey and Jill Shashaty recognize this similarity: "At this point, our argument takes a controversial turn, as we widen the frame of analogues to Joyce's *Dubliners* to include the parables of Jesus of Nazareth." This affirmation is hastily followed by an apologetic disclaimer: "We want to make it clear at the outset that we are examining these parables not in a religious context but in a literary and political one. Our approach to the topic of historical Christianity is not doctrinal, but secular."[32]

Having thus attempted to distance themselves from a religious hermeneutic, Mahaffey and Shashaty go on to speak almost immediately of Joyce's stories (like Jesus's parables) in terms not in fact reducible to the literary and the political, employing the term "spiritual teaching." The stories are remarkable for their "capacity to prompt individuals to reexamine their foundational assumptions about their relation to the world, a reevaluation that may generate a desire to change their circumstances through action."[33]

Pope Benedict XVI's description of the challenging impact of Christ's parables is not without relevance here: "At this point . . . the parable that seemed to be just a story about the past crosses over into the situation of the audience. History suddenly enters the present . . . I'm talking about *you* and about *me*."³⁴ The final effect of many of the *Dubliners* stories may be described in similar terms, "A Painful Case" included. For Joyce (and for Jesus), the politicization of religion is an aberration; his stories (like the parables) promote personal maturation: "[T]he stories 'teach' in much the same way [as the parables of Jesus], that is, by presenting narrative 'problems' designed not to indoctrinate, but to awaken critical acumen and to promote new self-awareness.³⁵

This is a well-stated truism, but, ironically, it misses the fact that one of the forms of awareness that Joyce wishes to promote is that neurotic mutually exclusive compartmentalization of religion and secularity is neither Christian nor Joycean and is doomed to failure because the Joycean agendum as priest of the eternal imagination is to explore and expose their interrelatedness. We have seen that Joyce was *not* unaware of the tradition of mystical *eros* in the Christian relationship with the divine, but he saw that this crucial aspect of the life of faith had fallen into disuse. "A Painful Case" dramatizes once again the *eros-agape* puzzle that Joyce strives to resolve by a process of trial and error and elimination, and exposes the inadequacy of secularist interpretive lenses that are not as alert and open to the vertical, or religious, dimension of the human experience as Joyce was.

Declan Kiberd says of Joyce's writings in general that, "He understood that religion had by his time shrunk for many people to a matter of mere morality—that the relationship of humanity to destiny and eternity had ceased to be as urgent to people as the regulation of their relations to one another."³⁶ Kiberd's assertion here of a Joycean artistic intent to recuperate the religious reference constitutes a flat contradiction to Geert Lernout's insistence on Joyce's atheism. It also opens the way to a discussion of the relationship between religion and morality. The dichotomization of religion and morality is alien, even antagonistic, to Christianity: "If anyone says, 'I love God,' and hates his brother, he is a liar" (1 Jn 4:20); "[A]s you did it to one of the least of these my brethren, you did it to me" (Mt 25:40). For Christianity—and, I will argue, for Joyce—there is a "third way" of both/and that reconciles and transcends the either/or polarities within which critics are often unconsciously confined.

III.2.2.5: Both Mysticism and Morality

The either/or polarities I allude to end in dichotomizations by one side or the other with the same end result. By some accounts, for example, Irish Catholicism dichotomized religion and morality, exalting the latter by championing a robust masculine and Pelagianist Christianity, and relegating, or even eliminating, the humanizing influence of the religious reference; namely the mystical relationship, with the living, breathing, speaking God, which is primordial.

A typical error is to respond to one dichotomization with another: to favor religion, eclipsing morality, by way of reaction against the insistence on morality to the point of eclipsing religion. If Joyce may be shown to have avoided dichotomization in both of these forms, he would have to be considered a religious as well as a moral writer, open to transcendental reality. Kiberd is correct about

Joyce's concern with recuperating the vertical, religious reference, so that religion is not reduced to "mere morality," as Kiberd puts it. But this does not entail denial of the moral dimension; rather, it entails hierarchical and organic harmonization of religion and morality.

The main purpose of this chapter is to demonstrate coincidences between the Joycean and Catholic anthropologies on the horizontal or moral level, but in the course of doing so we will also see coincidences in the religious dimension. In "Eveline," "The Sisters," and "A Painful Case," we have seen Joyce portray Dublin citizens trapped in loveless lives, the ecstasy of *eros* unknown to them. Even when there is a faint promise of ecstasy, as in the case of Eveline's prospects with Frank the sailor and Mrs. Sinico's with Mr. Duffy, that promise is hopelessly dashed and there seems to be no way out.

In "The Dead," however, the last story of the *Dubliners* collection, the parade of Dublin's living dead goes on, but we will see Joyce achieving in the end a perspective of the human experience that may be described as religious, intimating a way out of the dynamics of paralysis and death. The perspective achieved at the end of this story is the one from which all of Joyce's work should be read, and it is the perspective that will ultimately resolve the *anima-animus* and *eros-agape* puzzles. Let us look at that story now. Its ending is notoriously impenetrable, but the hermeneutic of *eros* and *agape* offers the key to unlock the enigma.

III.2.3: "The Dead"

III.2.3.1: A Story about Breakthrough, or Stalemate?

The much-debated last words of "The Dead" are these: "His soul swooned slowly as he heard the snow falling faintly through the universe and faintly falling, like the descent of their last end, upon all the living and the dead."[37] In her article "Gabriel and Michael: the Conclusion of 'The Dead,'" Florence Walzl called this ending "one of the most remarkable ambiguities in literature, a conclusion that offers almost opposite meanings, each of which can be logically argued."[38] Walzl explicates the antithetical connotations of the story's symbolism: the archangelical names Gabriel (Conroy) and Michael (Furey) respectively representing peace and annunciation, war and judgment; the coordinate of west representing rural simplicity but also sunset and death, and east representing urban sophistication but also sunrise and life; and finally the snow, deathly cold and slushy underfoot but also pure-white, bespeaking renewal and life. There is an interpretation of the ending with textual and extra-textual evidence which resolves the critical dilemma and offers not only a way out of the interpretive impasse but a key to understanding all of Joyce's work.

The story's title seems at first to refer to the participants in the evening party who live nostalgically in the past, indulging in a romanticizing escapist sentimentalism. Gabriel Conroy is a sophisticated Dubliner, at least in his own eyes, and his wife Gretta is a simple Galwegian from the rural West of Ireland. After an evening of pleasant conviviality and reminiscing, at once mellow and morbid, Gabriel is transfixed by the sight of Gretta in rapt attention on the stairway as a fellow guest, Mr. D'Arcy the tenor, sings *The Lass of Aughrim* upstairs. Gabriel's attraction towards his wife is rekindled and later, in their hotel room, he asks what she remembered in that moment, imagining that her interior thoughts are related to himself, only to learn that the song reminded her of an old flame, Michael Furey, who left his sickbed in the pouring rain to go and say goodbye to her when he learned she had to leave Galway for Dublin. He died a week later. This revelation is an epiphany for Gabriel, a painful learning experience. The story ends with his musings on the mysteries of life, death, and love as he looks out the hotel room window on the snow falling on the living and the dead.

In a recent essay called "Dead Again," Vincent Pecora confronts with intellectual honesty and acuity the interpretive dilemma of the story's ending, which has divided critical opinion for generations. Pecora proposes that this "awfully good story" encapsulates the contradictoriness and "perplexity" of Joyce's own position: "Joyce was finally so troubled and frustrated by the impossible morass of personal and political claims that Ireland made on him that he could not decide whether he should reconcile with it or turn his back on it." Therefore, "deep and irresolvable ambivalence" is the final note of the story.[39] This reading has the virtue of overcoming an either/or approach to the text that determinedly ignores inconvenient contrary evidence; it attempts to reconcile the cryptic and conflicting intimations undeniably present in the text. But the idea that the underlying Joycean intention is to epiphanize his own failure to resolve satisfactorily the dilemma he represents is itself unsatisfactory.

Margot Norris, co-author with Pecora of their collaborative commentary, reads the story not, as Pecora does, through the lens of Joyce's relationship with Ireland but through the lens of romantic love. She argues very persuasively that the sentimental power of Michael and Gretta's story derives from the remarkable absence of sentimentalism in the living of it and in the telling of it. It is profoundly moving because it is not remotely sentimentalist: "[O]ne might hazard the possibility that Michael Furey offered Gretta something that her husband does not: namely, love without palaver." Norris correctly identifies a critique of sentimentalism, but fails to grasp the full nature of the puzzle Joyce presents. She tells us that Gabriel "has no response to such a world of sincere feeling except an initial imitation, followed by a blizzard of palaver."[40]

To call the ending of "The Dead" mere palaver is to fail to grasp the subtlety and richness of Joyce's teaching. There is a way of reading the story, consonant with the Joycean project as we know it in general, which surpasses an either/or approach in favor of a both/and one—Pecora speaks expressively of a "binocular, rather than monocular, perspective"[41]—and satisfies without satiating, provokes and disconcerts without frustrating. Pecora's reading remains within the ambit of nationality and Norris's within the ambit of romance, but the ending of "The Dead" is not confined to these categories of discourse. A hermeneutic that is open to the possibility of the religious reference enables us to discover Joyce's position vis-a-vis the mysteries of God and man. Such a hermeneutic must, evidently, adhere strictly to the wording of the story itself, and to statements that Joyce himself made. A close scrutiny of the text is necessary, and a detailed rendering of the hermeneutic that arises from it.

III.2.3.2: Gabriel's Epiphany

With a typical minimum of deft strokes Joyce characterizes Gabriel Conroy as a curious mix of superiority and inferiority complexes. He is a teacher who likes to consider himself a man of culture. The evening gets off to a bad start when he playfully engages with Lilly the maid about her marriage prospects only to receive a retort "with great bitterness" to his condescending small talk: "The men that is now is only all palaver and what they can get out of you."[42] Gabriel writes book reviews for a newspaper called *The Daily Express* under the pseudonym G. C. When Miss Ivors, a one-time University classmate and friend, now a political activist, rebukes him for writing for a newspaper of the ruling British establishment, calling him a West Briton, Gabriel becomes flustered and defensive. Mischievously, she reassures him that she is only teasing and invites him on a month-long trip to the Aran Islands: "It would be splendid for Gretta too if she'd come. She's from Connacht, isn't she?" Gabriel's reply reveals his lingering discomfiture and his classist embarrassment at his wife's origins: "'Her people are,' said Gabriel shortly."[43]

His mood alternates between nervousness at the

prospect of the after-dinner speech that he has been charged to give and peevishness at the cultural inferiority of the company: "He was undecided about the lines from Robert Browning, for he feared they would be above the heads of his hearers . . . their grade of culture differed from his." This combination of snobbery and insecurity make him a nervous wreck: "They would think that he was airing his superior education . . . His whole speech was a mistake from first to last, an utter failure."[44] In the end, the speech is rapturously received and Gabriel's mood changes to contentment. By the end of the evening he is jovial and well-disposed towards one and all until he catches sight of Gretta standing transfixed by D'Arcy's rendition of *The Lass of Aughrim*.

Now, Gabriel's approach to Gretta turns effetely lyrical; Lilly the maid would call it palaver: "If he were a painter he would paint her in that attitude."[45] In the terms that Gabriel represents his mood to himself, it is passionately romantic: "Like the tender fire of stars moments of their life together . . . broke upon and illumined his memory."[46] Later, as the hotel porter leads them to their room, his mood turns passionately sensual: "He could have flung his arms about her hips and held her still, for his arms were trembling with desire to seize her and only the stress of his nails against the palms of his hands held the wild impulse of his body in check."[47] But in the hotel room something happens that suddenly transmutes his mood into one of profound reflection, without the intervening cathartic occurrence of sexual intercourse. This change is too dramatic to depict anything other than a moment of surprising epiphanical understanding.

Gretta explains why the song had so deeply affected her, recounting the story of her relationship with Michael Furey. Gabriel's romantic and sensual feelings are cruelly dashed, his image of himself shattered: "He saw himself as a ludicrous figure, acting as a pennyboy for his aunts, a nervous, well-meaning sentimentalist, orating to vulgarians and idealising his own clownish lusts." As Gretta innocently and inexorably pursues her story, each word, each new detail turns the knife of humiliation in Gabriel's heart. When he asks how the boy died, Gretta answers, "I think he died for me," and Gabriel experiences a sensation of a nameless force bearing down relentlessly upon him: "A vague terror seized Gabriel at this answer, as if, at that hour when he had hoped to triumph, some impalpable and vindictive being was coming against him, gathering forces against him in its vague world."[48]

Gabriel's ego instinctively recoils from the imminent impact. He feels that somehow he has been "set up." But then, strangely, the unceremonious frustration of his romantic imaginings and sensual desires and the undeniable humiliation of his ego produce positive fruits. As Gretta continues her painful story, Gabriel's comportment is marked by delicacy and discretion: "He did not question her again, for he felt that she would tell him of herself. Her hand was warm and moist: it did not respond to his touch, but he continued to caress it just as he had caressed her first letter to him." The situation brings the best out of him. When Gretta, "overcome with emotion," finally exclaims, "O, the day I heard that, that he was dead!" his reaction in apparent defeat is gracious: "Gabriel held her hand for a moment longer, irresolutely, and then, shy of intruding on her grief, let it fall gently and walked quietly to the window."[49]

Gabriel's self-protective veneer of mild snobbery is a strategy to arm with an artificial sense of security a deeply insecure and complex-ridden postcolonial man entrapped in classist, chauvinist, and intellectualist categories. That veneer is cracked open by a complex coincidence of circumstances and emotions, and his heart is humbled and re-awakened to life and to his wife. He contemplates her "unresentfully" and with "pity" as she sleeps: "Gabriel . . . looked for a few moments unresentfully on her tangled hair and half-open mouth . . . His curious eyes rested long upon her face and . . . a strange, friendly pity for her entered his soul."[50] He muses reflectively on the events of the evening, anticipating the imminent death of his aunt: "Poor Aunt Julia! . . . He had caught that haggard look upon her face for a moment when she was singing . . . Yes, yes: that would happen very soon . . . One by one, they were all becoming shades." His thoughts turn to the boy who did not wish to live without the woman he married, and: "Generous tears filled Gabriel's eyes."[51]

In the friendship between Michael Furey and Gretta—"I think he died for me"—there is a "fureyous" fire with Christ-like resonances reinforced by the detail of his standing in the garden "where there was a tree" and by the allusion to the "crooked crosses . . . the spears . . . the barren thorns" which the urbane Gabriel has never known and in which his soul glimpses a hope of redemption from a passionless life: "He had never felt like that himself towards any woman, but he knew that such a feeling must be love." This association of true love with willingness to die for the beloved is unmistakably Christ-like: "Greater love has no man than this, that a man lay down his life for his friends" (Jn 15:13). Gabriel's "riot" of romantic emotions and desires for union with Gretta was all *eros*; Michael Furey's love for Gretta is a superior coalescence of *eros* and *agape*. Gabriel's mood expands to give new meaning to the story's title, which had seemed a damning verdict on its protagonists: "The tears gathered more thickly in his eyes and in the partial darkness he imagined he saw the form of a young man standing under a dripping tree. Other forms were near. His soul had approached that region where dwell the vast hosts of the dead."[52]

As the story fades to its denouement, Gabriel experiences a compassionate empathy with all humanity. Redemption in some form is proffered to him from the west of Ireland which produced Michael and Gretta and which he as a sophisticated Dubliner had heretofore spurned as primitive: "The time had come for him to set out on his journey westward."[53] As he falls asleep beside Gretta, Gabriel muses that the snow which the weather forecast had said would be "general all over Ireland" would surely be falling also on Michael Furey's grave and all the living and the dead: "His soul swooned slowly as he heard the snow falling faintly through the universe and faintly falling, like the descent of their last end, upon all the living and the dead."[54]

III.2.3.3: Mercy and an Ariel-like Being

"The Dead" was written in the year 1907, when Joyce was twenty-five years old. Five years later he wrote the essay on the effects of the Renaissance, praising it for "creating in us and in our art a sense of mercy for all creatures who live, die, and yield to their illusions."[55] The clear verbal resonance between this sentence and the final sentence of "The Dead" is a crucial clue indicating a positive epiphany. Linking the two statements about the living and the dead, we discover in the now humbled and more "generous" Gabriel at the end of the story a newly gained perspective of the human condition that may be described as *merciful*; Joyce's own words in his essay confirm that the closing words of "The Dead" describe a global, gentle embrace of a struggling humanity that earlier that same night Gabriel had contemplated with embarrassment.

The passage immediately following Gabriel's humiliation is filled with terms of gentle humaneness: "caress," "held her hand," "shy of intruding," "let it fall gently," "walked quietly," "looked . . . unresentfully," with a "strange, friendly pity" and "generous tears." Unlike Nietzsche, Joyce held the humbler virtues like gentleness and pity in high esteem. Gabriel's soul expands to embrace Aunt Julia and all the living and the dead. It bears repeating that this occurs precisely after Gabriel experiences a deep, obscure dread as humiliation bears down upon him: "A vague terror seized Gabriel . . . as if, at that hour when he had hoped to triumph, some impalpable and vindictive being was coming against him, gathering forces against him in its vague world."[56] These words, like those about the living and the dead, echo other words pronounced by Joyce in a different context in a way that sheds light on their meaning.

A matter of weeks before his eighteenth birthday, Joyce delivered a conference entitled "Drama and Life" to the Literary and Historical Society of University College, Dublin, in which he enthused about an elusive vital principle:

> It might be said fantastically that as soon as men and women began life in the world there was above them and about them, a spirit, of which they were dimly conscious, which they would have had sojourn in their midst in deeper intimacy and for whose truth they became seekers in after times, longing to lay hands upon it. For this spirit is as the roaming air, little susceptible of change, and never left their vision, shall never leave it, till the firmament is as a scroll rolled away. At times it would seem that the spirit had taken up his abode in this or that form—but on a sudden he is misused, he is gone and the abode is left idle. He is, one might guess, somewhat of an elfish nature, a nixie, a very Ariel.[57]

It may be surmised that by the time he wrote *Portrait of the Artist as a Young Man* and *Ulysses*, and even *Dubliners*, Joyce had reached a maturer understanding of this "elfish" being, and had come to see mercy as one of its attributes. Ariel is the originator of the storm in Shakespeare's

The Tempest, shipwrecking the King of Naples and his crew but then keeping them from harm and ensuring that they land safely. He is at once protector and inflicter of pain. No doubt, Joyce would also have been drawn by his "aerial" elusiveness and his matchmaking prowess (in bringing Ferdinand and Miranda together), since Joyce too aspires to unite the sexes.

A little over one year after writing the article that mentions Ariel, in March 1901, a nineteen-year-old James Joyce wrote a letter to Henrik Ibsen that included the remark that "we always keep the dearest things to ourselves."[58] In "The Dead," Joyce "reveals" what is for him "the dearest thing." It is *not* romantic love or nation or art for its own sake. If we link the description of the Ariel-like spirit with the description of the spirit that Gabriel felt bearing in on him in that awful, humiliating moment, we discover the *modus operandi* and aims of a mysterious principle epiphanized again and again in Joyce's prose. Gabriel is on the receiving end of a stinging and valuable lesson, masterfully orchestrated by an unseen hand, about himself, about love and life. Despite the pain he undergoes, the fruits of his encounter with this spirit are sublimely positive.

The intervention may be called *merciful* because, although painful, it produces in Gabriel a compassionate empathy with others, enriching his humanity. The sense of a concatenation of circumstances and emotions orchestrated with ineffable firmness and finesse to effect moments of individuating opportunity is a recurring Joycean effect, pointing not to the individual soul as font of its own personal development—although it must of course play its part—but to an ontological reality external to the soul and at the same time intimately interior to it. In theological terms it would be called an actual grace. Joyce's art is about epiphanizing the actuations of an elusive spirit piloting such moments in favor of human individuation, which for Joyce is largely about harmonization of the masculine and feminine virtues. This is what happens not only in "The Dead," but also in several other *Dubliners* stories and in the later works.

III.2.3.4: Admonitio and Delectatio

In the portrayal of Gabriel there is a suggestion, which we will later see developed in the portrayal of Stephen Dedalus, that concepts and words may sometimes have the effect of removing us from reality rather than of enabling us to access it. Here we find again the theme of the masculine (associated with the analytical intellect) and the feminine (associated with unitive emotion). Before his encounter with the "vindictive being," Gabriel, like Fr. Flynn, Mr. Duffy, and Stephen Dedalus, was slightly removed from those around him by an irritable intellectual snobbery, rigidity, and aloofness. He is all analysis and no empathy. After it, he is all gentleness and magnanimity, and admiringly rediscovers Gretta's simplicity and naturalness. He is cut to the core, but he is also set free. The work of the elfish Ariel-like spirit is alternately to soften and to strengthen, to humble and enrich; to purify *agape* and *logos* of dehumanizing harshness, and *eros* of sensualist escapism. This it will achieve with the caress and the correction, recalling St. Augustine's description of the divine *modus operandi* and what I have called the "two hands" of divine grace: *admonitio* and *delectatio*; admonition and delight.

Other stories of *Dubliners* also present the challenge to an inner equilibrium that reconciles *anima* and *animus*. Qualities like mercy and gentleness are usually more readily associated with femininity, as in "The Sisters," but the story called "A Mother" deals with the suppression of the feminine in woman, as bitter fruit of frustrated social ambition and escapist romantic idealism. Conversely, Little Chandler of the "A Little Cloud" story is an example of overdevelopment of the *anima*– the female principle—in the male, leading to an effete ineffectuality (prefiguring Leopold Bloom). Like Mr. Duffy, Chandler's tragedy is not so much that he has to live in Dublin as that he *refuses to live* in Dublin: given to the kind of melancholic pseudo-mystical daydreaming idealized by the Celtic Twilight movement which Joyce despised as effeminate and escapist, he fails to realize that real art is to be created out of the raw material of real life that is right under his nose. The story ends with the familiar effect of therapeutic shock, and the denouement is not clearly declared because to do so would provide the reader, for whom the therapeutic shock is most urgently intended, with facile resolution instead of energizing provocation.

The recalcitrant inconclusiveness of Joyce's "endings" testifies to his recognition of the essential *endlessness* of temporal dynamism. Joyce understood that the human experience at its best is ineluctably processual and that no epiphany may be considered exhaustive and definitive, immune to subsequent revision and re-elaboration. No matter how penetrating and illuminating and transformative the epiphany has been, there always remains more to discover, even if only in the form of new nuances to temper, deepen, correct, and perfect previous hard-won insights. Resurrectional epiphanies of the kind experienced by Gabriel are purchased not infrequently at the price of pain and death. Humiliation is integral to apprenticeship.

These dynamics will recur in the later works. Stephen Dedalus, like Mr. Duffy, groans under the burden of inner imbalance and its triple symptoms of misogyny, intellectualism, and arrogance. We have seen that Stephen rejects *agape* without *eros*, be it for nation, for neighbor, or for God. Having now seen this rejection articulated more clearly by Joyce in the short stories, we are better placed to return to Stephen's epiphany on the beach to discern the nature of his ecstatic experience of *eros* on Dollymount Strand, to compare it thereafter to Catholic teachings. Concerning Stephen's rapturous breakthrough, three questions arise that need to be separated notionally for the sake of argument even though they are essentially related.

The first question is this: does Joyce declare a radical disassociation of the profane and the divine, of the natural and the supernatural, implying that Stephen embraces atheism like Mr. Duffy? To put the same question in different terms, is Stephen simply swearing gratuitously when his soul cries "Heavenly God!" in profane joy, or is there an element of prayer in his cry, at once ironic and sincere? The answer to the second question depends on the answer to the first one. How are we to interpret the *eros* celebrated by Stephen? Is it self-centered and "poisoned" *eros* or is it other-centered and pure? Is it sensual, or spiritual, or both? Finally, the answer to the third question depends on the answers to the first two. Is there a place for *agape* in Joyce's vision of love? More concretely, are there grounds for seeing in Michael Furey's love for Gretta a Christ-like coalescence of *eros* and *agape*, which is as paradigmatic for Joyce as it is for Gabriel? Joyce scholars have trained their minds on the first two of these three questions, with interesting results.

III.3: A Portrait of the Artist as a Young Man

III.3.1: Disassociation of the Profane from the Divine?

III.3.1.1: Heavenly Beauty and Earthly Beauty

In an article comparing the works of Joyce and Evelyn Waugh, literary critic Dominic Manganiello quotes a remark made by Waugh in 1945 on the suitability of the feast day of the Epiphany as the special feast day of art and artists, and surmises that Waugh owed the insight to Joyce, "who gave the Christian holy day wide currency as a literary term," thereafter offering this definition of Joyce's adaptation of the term: "an aesthetic equivalent to the mysterious action of grace."[59] This definition already suggests a separation of realms—i.e., of the religious and the aesthetic, the supernatural and the natural—which Manganiello returns to and develops in the course of his reflections. In fact, the term epiphany effectively respects and reflects the distinction as well as the mutuality of the this-worldly and the other-worldly, the immanent and the transcendental. Manganiello argues, however, that Stephen's epiphany on the strand entails a departure from this meaning of the term, and a radical disassociation of the profane from the divine, of secular realities from the sacred and supernatural.

The purpose of Manganiello's article is to compare and contrast the "radically different trajectory" of the protagonist of Evelyn Waugh's novel, *Brideshead Revisited*, with that of Stephen Dedalus in Joyce's *A Portrait of the Artist as a Young Man.* He will focus "on the progress of Charles Ryder, who, like his Irish predecessor, initially sets out to create beauty for himself, but whose 'aesthetic education' at Brideshead estate leads him to the first Author of beauty."[60] This first premise of Manganiello's argument does not take into account that Stephen speaks not of creating beauty but of *recreating* it—"to recreate life out of life!"[61]—having first discovered, not created, it.

David Jones, poet and critic, points out that the first principle of Stephen's argument is that "'an esthetic image is presented to us' (*Portrait* 212)," from which he deduces with irrefutable logic that, "The verb 'presented' should preclude the possibility of interpreting the subject, esthetic image, as a result of the creative imagination of the artist."[62] The final sentence of Jones's article, replete with quotations from Stephen himself and from Joyce, is worth quoting in full:

> Joyce emphasized the value of vivisective observation: cutting through the veil of illusion; trying to

pierce 'to the significant heart of everything' (*SH* 33); disentangling 'the subtle soul of the image from its mesh of defining circumstances' (*SH* 78); discovering the 'everlasting hopes, desires and hates of humanity' (*CW* 32); contemplating 'the truth of the being of the visible world' (*SH* 80); the artist goes beyond present things 'to their meaning which is still unuttered.' (*SH* 78).[63]

This is not the subjectivist, relativist project of a skeptic. With Joyce there is always the risk of successfully refuting a straw man, due to his elusive complexity. Manganiello offers a very useful description of the dichotomization of religious and secular forms of beauty in Stephen's adolescence. On the one hand there is heavenly beauty, on the other earthly beauty: "Later, as an adolescent, he learns to associate . . . floral hues with opposing types of beauty—one conducive to eternal salvation, the other detrimental to it." Manganiello quotes Stephen's ruminations on sin, which confirm the bifurcation of beauty into two categories, the earthly (dangerous) and the heavenly (luminous): "'Their error had offended deeply God's majesty . . . but it had not offended her whose beauty is not like earthly beauty, dangerous to look upon, but like the morning star, which is its emblem, bright and musical' (*AP,* 116)."[64] But, significantly, Joyce does not self-identify with the adolescent Stephen's dualistic outlook.

III.3.1.2: Divisive Contradiction or Unitive Paradox?

The adolescent Stephen labors under a dichotomization of beauty, ideal versus incarnate, which the maturer (not yet mature) Stephen in the penultimate chapter of *Portrait* will reject. Significantly, Catholicism rejects it too. Neither Joyce nor Catholicism is as easily pigeonholed as critics on both sides of the debate sometimes unconsciously assume. Manganiello correctly states that, later on in *Portrait*, "Stephen locates 'the essence of beauty' (*AP*, 176) not in some ethereal setting governed by a transcendent idea or principle but in the realm of the immanent where sense perception prevails." But this statement seems to operate upon the underlying assumption that the transcendental and the immanent are polar opposites, as held by the antithetical philosophies of idealism and materialism and by their aesthetic cousins, symbolism and naturalism; both of which Joyce rejects. It prepares the way for this assessment by Manganiello of Stephen's climactic cry: "'Heavenly God! . . . in an outburst of profane joy' (*AP*, 171). With this contradictory cry Stephen subverts a long-standing Christian, as well as Platonic, tradition of aesthetics."[65]

In Manganiello's analysis of Stephen's decisive apostasy scene, no consideration is given to the possibility that his cry is not contradictory and divisive but paradoxical, Aristotelian, Incarnational, and unitive. Does Manganiello here take the side of "heavenly beauty" as opposed to "earthly beauty," thereby entrenching himself in the very dichotomization that Joyce seeks to subvert and surpass, not by antithesis but by synthesis?

For Joyce, "earthly beauty," profane beauty, is not at all incompatible with the divine. In this he is being perfectly orthodox, and from his familiarity with Aquinas he would have known as much. In a much different context, St. Josemaria Escriva made the same observation: "Speaking with theological precision . . . one cannot say that there are realities—good, noble, or even indifferent—which are exclusively profane."[66] Joyce's position, therefore, thus interpreted, is not a subversion of the Christian one (or indeed of the Platonic position, as we will see explained very shortly by Josef Pieper).

Manganiello, pursuing the assumption of a radical Joycean disassociation of the profane from the divine, maintains that "Joyce's godlike artist begets a new, self-referential word before which he bows down on the altar of his imagination." For Joyce, the godlike artist, art itself is god: "The failure to distinguish between means and end, between perishable food and the bread of life, makes art the object rather than the vehicle of worship."[67] This reading imputes to Joyce a position of hermetically sealed immanentism. In fact, Stephen himself, while still more readily identifiable with Icarus than with Daedalus, shows signs of having outgrown aestheticism—his focus is on life, not art for its own sake—and naïve immanentism, as does Joyce himself in the *Dubliners* stories, like "A Little Cloud" and "A Painful Case." In these stories, and in "The Dead," there is evidence that Joyce does not consider the secular and the supernatural as entirely separate realms.

Manganiello believes that Joyce believed otherwise. In an early endnote in the course of his comparison of

Joyce and Waugh, he invites us to consider "an astute observation" by Jeffrey Heath, who argues that while Joyce's Stephen Dedalus "rejects religion on his way to artisthood," the trajectory of Waugh's chief character takes the very opposite direction: "Charles's successful maturation as an artist depends upon his religious awakening, an awakening that comes about through his repudiation of secular art and action."[68] In fact, Heath's observation is not really so astute. It contains three highly debatable assumptions: one, that Joyce and Stephen Dedalus are identical; two, that Joyce rejects religion *per se* (as opposed to a distorted religiosity), seeing artisthood as the ultimate end in itself to which he will consecrate his life and soul (in fact, Joyce abhorred aestheticism); and thirdly that, in truth, though Joyce fails to realize it, "religious awakening" and "secular art and action" are somehow essentially opposed. This final assumption is the least astute—or most obtuse—of the three, and there is strong evidence that Joyce's life's work was largely devoted to refuting it.

Some Joyce critics have argued that the Joycean project is *not* about the disassociation of the profane and the religious; that it is precisely about the connectedness and *mutuality* of these realms. We will look at their findings now.

III.3.2: Poisoned Eros or Pure?

III.3.2.1: The Sacred Assimilated to the Profane

In 1980, Erwin Steinberg read the beach scene in terms of a sacramental rediscovery of the sacred in the secular: "[T]here is general agreement, in Tindall's words, that 'The wading girl . . . who embodies mortal beauty, unites all previous suggestions.'"[69] Those "previous suggestions" are summarized as follows: "Chapter II ends with a profane encounter with a prostitute, Chapter III with a sacred encounter with a priest, both of which merge in Stephen's response to the vision of the bird-girl: 'Heavenly God! cried Stephen's soul, in an outburst of profane joy.'"[70] In other words, Stephen's encounter with the prostitute at the end of the second chapter was an occasion of sensualistic, poisoned *eros*, and his receiving of Communion at the end of the third chapter was an expression of purist, pseudo-mystical *eros*.

Against this background of two contrasting extremes, the synthetizing encounter with the girl at the end of the fourth chapter is sensual, not sensualist, and pure, not purist. While the sense of the sacred is not absent, Steinberg observes a marked inclination towards the secular: "Despite the fact that, as Epstein puts it, 'The sacred and the profane here join,' Stephen's commitment at the end of Chapter IV is more strongly to the profane than to the sacred."[71] Certainly, it would be a distortion of the textual evidence to etherealize the girl that Stephen sees wading in the water, and his ecstatic discovery of *eros* is undoubtedly an emancipated celebration of the sensual.

Nevertheless, the dichotomization of the sacred and the sensual is precisely what Joyce wishes to challenge. Steinberg concludes with an illuminating observation regarding the markedly religious language used to express Stephen's aesthetic vocation, particularly the language of Annunciation and Incarnation of the Word:

> At the conclusion of Chapter IV the sacred is assimilated to the worldly and becomes a metaphor of dedication, a "consecration" to the necessarily worldly life of the artist: "To live, to err, to fall, to triumph, to recreate life out of life!" (*P* 172). Moreover, it is the same metaphor employed in Stephen's now widely quoted statement about the artist: "The artist, like the God of the creation, remains within or behind or beyond or above his handiwork, invisible, refined out of existence, indifferent, paring his fingernails" (*P* 215). The artist is like God. Here, again, a worldly function is described by means of religious imagery, as it is in the statement that "In the virgin womb of the imagination the word was made flesh" (*P* 217) . . . The sentence "Gabriel the seraph had come to the virgin's chamber" (*P* 217) is an extension of such images as "God would enter his purified body" (*P* 146), "He felt some dark presence . . . ; its subtle streams penetrated his being" (*P* 100), and "Her image had passed into his soul" (*P* 172).[72]

One school of Joyce criticism perceives the employment of religious language noted in the above passage as a form of linguistic "hijacking" which subverts the semantic content of the terms used by emptying them of their original content and press-ganging them into service of a new, solely secular cause. But it is more likely that the author's intention is to harness the religious language, and then to harmonize it with the secular reality he wishes to celebrate. Joyce's rejection of *agape* without *eros* does not impel him unthinkingly by the law of the pendulum to embrace Godless *eros* without *agape* or Dionysian frenzy. If the religious reference is retained, even though the main focus is on the profane, then the sacred and the profane are united, and *eros* too retains a religious connection with the divine.

III.3.2.2: A Religious Experience

Stephen's experience on the strand is not intrinsically anti-religious. Nor is it solely an account, contrary to the reductive claim of many critics, of the discovery of his artistic vocation. Rather, it is an ecstatic discovery of the principle of vitality itself and its call to dynamism and fullness in and through everything that is ordinary and immanent. This is entirely compatible with a religious approach to reality, as Joyce knew from his reading of the Catholic mystics in whose writings he found reflected a "very real spiritual experience,"[73] and in his praise for Giordano Bruno as one who "from the material universe . . . passes . . . from heroic enthusiasm to enthusiasm to unite himself with God."[74]

As of the moment of his enthusiastic discovery of *eros* on the beach, love of life will be the love of Stephen's life. His artistic vocation will be to celebrate and communicate this principle, "recreating life out of life," as "priest of the eternal imagination"; as artistic mediator between . . . God and man? Christ said, "I came that they may have life, and have it abundantly" (Jn 10:10). As St. Irenaeus famously put it, "The glory of God is man fully alive."[75] Stephen's grand epiphany shares much in common, as Robert Klawitter has argued,[76] with the process philosophy, intuitionism, and vitalism of Henri Bergson, which in turn shares much in common with the Judeo-Christian anthropology. The artificiality and insufficiency of Stephen's earlier "religious" experience is best exposed in the light of this later experience.

The "in-between" world of temporal human existence is precisely where life is debated between extinction and eternity. Cartesian intellectualism led to the reductive perception of reason and rational knowledge in terms of the collection of scientifically controllable data, whereas the classical perception of reason's role in the quest for understanding was more ample and vibrant. The classical quest begins from temporal and material realities, and remains always referenced to these, but without being confined or conformed to them. It aspires to transcend the gravitational pull of the here and now to penetrate the realms of the eternal, to contemplate the unfathomable without anxiousness to control it and without scorning immediate realities.

Joyce's aesthetic project as "a priest of eternal imagination, transmuting the daily bread of experience into the radiant body of everliving life,"[77] expresses this same aspiration. It will take the form of artful re-actualization of the quotidian, the ordinary, the material, the middle and mundane range of human experience: "The faint sour stink of rotted cabbages came towards him . . . He smiled to think that it was this disorder, the misrule and confusion of his father's house and the stagnation of vegetable life, which was to win the day in his soul."[78] The ironic allusion to the parable of the prodigal son is clever and suggestive. Stephen will gladly feed on "the pods that the swine ate" (Lk 15:16) in his life-art enterprise. He determines as artist to discover and celebrate beauty as a transcendental or omnipresent species of the good. It is questionable whether it is really "the Father's House" that Stephen rejects in favor of "his father's house," or a spiritualized and intellectualized caricature of the same.

For present purposes, suffice it to note the content of his discovery and the tone of complacent optimism that accompanies it. Joyce certainly reclaims the experiential context of the human struggle, comically, joyfully, and often beautifully. But the experiential context has never been denied by the Catholic tradition. The passions, the earthly, the experiential, have always formed part of the Catholic worldview. An experientialism that abhors superimposed systematization in favor of the spontaneous exuberance of the life force and the "erotic" attraction of profane beauty is to be welcomed. This is, in fact, the Catholic position, as Josef Pieper reminds us.

III.3.2.3: Pieper: A Catholic Defence of Eros

The repression of *eros* and sensuality is no stranger to the Christian tradition, but Catholic orthodoxy has always considered it heretical. Josef Pieper, once again, provides a helpful clarification concerning the origins and evolution of this heresy, which is often falsely preached in the name of Catholicism, *and* falsely preached, he also maintains, in the name of Platonism: "Strangely enough . . . a spiritualized negation of the body is always being called 'Platonism.'" That Plato advocated a body-soul dualism according to which the spiritual is incarcerated in the corporal, is tantamount to "common knowledge," and yet it is an error, attributable to Plotinus: "Plotinus was one of those who are ashamed to be in the body—an attitude, incidentally, which has always accompanied Christianity as a Manichaean undercurrent."[79]

Elsewhere, Pieper repeats his defence of the true Platonic position, with a text from Plato on human immortality: "'We think,' he says, 'of a living being, spiritual and physical at once, but both, soul and body, united for all time.'"[80] From this Pieper concludes, not without strong evidence, that "Plato seems to be suggesting: If ever immortality is conferred upon us, not just the soul but the entire physical human being will in some inconceivable manner participate in the life of the gods."[81]

In *Enthusiasm and the Divine Madness*, Pieper goes on to elucidate the duality, as opposed to dualism, of body and soul, *eros* and *agape*, sensuality and self-sacrifice, which is to be found in both the Platonic and Christian traditions: "Thomas Aquinas would undoubtedly say that *dilectio* and *caritas* can regulate, purify, and heal the *passio amoris*." In other words, *eros* needs *agape*, but, perhaps more surprisingly, *agape* also needs *eros*: "Thomas, like Plato, holds an opinion which a 'Christian mind' infected by Manichaeism and spiritualism would find hard to accept: the opinion that *caritas* as a human act can neither be kindled nor kept alive if it is separated from the vital foundation of *passio amoris*."[82]

To put the matter bluntly, sacrificial self-immolation is neither sufficient nor healthy nor humanly possible without passionate need, attraction, and union. This thesis "of Eros being rooted in the sensual realm—the same Eros which seeks to carry us with the wings of birds to the abode of the gods" enjoys overwhelming empirical evidence and "is corroborated existentially in the experiences of treatment of depth psychology."[83] The findings of modern psychology confirm the negative neurotic consequences of unnaturally repressing *eros* (as often portrayed in Joyce's writings).

III.3.2.4: The Perils of Repressing Eros

Pieper, availing of the evidence provided by modern psychology, provides a description of the distortions and sicknesses that ensue from self-repression which is startlingly evocative of many of the characters of Joyce's fiction: "For this modern branch of the art of healing demonstrates that any harsh repression of the capacity for erotic emotion which is rooted in the realm of the senses makes love altogether impossible. Both intellectual and spiritual love are smothered." The warning issued by Raniero Cantalamessa about repressing *eros* in the name of pure *agape*, quoted earlier, has already been given by Pieper (and by Joyce): "It shows, further, that the intolerance, harshness, and rigidity frequently found in men who seek to lead a 'spiritual' life may well be caused by unnatural repression of the *passio amoris*. Man is a physical being, even to the point of the sublimest spirituality."[84]

This very point is made by St. Teresa of Avila when she insists, in opposition to Gnostic currents of spirituality that prospered in her time, on the perennial centrality of the *physical humanity* of Christ in the Christian, mystical relationship: "But that we should painfully and laboriously accustom ourselves to give up trying with all our strength to keep always before us . . . this most sacred Humanity; this, I insist, seems to me wrong." St. Teresa's common sense and natural humanity rebel against so ethereal a spirituality: "It leaves the soul, as they say, in the air; it has no support . . . no matter how full it may think itself of God." Hers, like Thomas' (and like Christ's), is a "down-to-earth" spirituality: "While we live as human beings, it is very important for us to keep Christ's Humanity before us."[85] So, the Catholic tradition did not have to wait for Pieper or for modern psychology to discover this truth.

Pieper makes the same point as St. Teresa in different terms. The denial of *eros* and of physicality is anti-natural and anti-human. Man's physicality, "which compels him to be a man or a woman even in the most spiritual expression of vitality, is . . . the overflowing vital source of all human activity. Thomas Aquinas and Plato agree on this point."[86] Here, Pieper is making profound observations not only about the relationship between man and wife or the relationship between priest and God but about the relationship between each and every individual and the God-Man Christ, a relationship which encompasses every aspect of the human personal experience, including *eros* and *agape*, body and spirit.

Pieper speculates, with good reason, that the defamation of *eros* in the name of Christianity has greatly contributed to the defamation of Christianity itself as anti-natural and anti-human. He describes the categorization of Platonic Eros as self-love or "egotistical seeking for enrichment and fulfillment" and Christian *caritas* or *agape* as "renunciatory, unselfish, giving love" as a "dreadful simplification" of Christianity. Christian *eros* tends towards rapturous *agape*, and Christian *agape* culminates in rapturous *eros*. The Christian juxtaposition of self-denial and self-fulfillment is a paradox, not a contradiction. *Agape* and *eros* are fused in the ecstasy of mutual donation. The longing for happiness is natural to man, and the denial of it an aberration. The final end of the Christian dynamic is, unapologetically, happiness, also called bliss, which is "the final quenching of the deepest thirst. Man is by nature a thirsting and needy being . . . It is not in our power to be so 'unselfish' that we can renounce the ultimate quenching of our thirst, bliss. We *cannot* want not to be blissful."[87] This teaching about *eros*, always present in the Catholic tradition, has been formally incorporated into the Catholic Magisterium by Pope Benedict XVI.

III.3.2.5: The Catholic Magisterium on Eros

In his encyclical letter *Deus Caritas Est*, Pope Benedict XVI, refuting Nietzsche, reaffirms the Greek concept of *eros* as integral to the Christian tradition, harmonizing it with *agape* as essential not only to interpersonal human relationships but also to the relationship with God. We may speak of a mystical *eros* which, with the Incarnation of Christ, becomes corporal as well as spiritual: "Christian faith . . . has always considered man a unity in duality, a reality in which spirit and matter compenetrate, and in which each is brought to a new nobility" (*DCE* 5). Referring to the Christian synthesis of *eros* and *agape*, Benedict writes, "True, *eros* tends to rise 'in ecstasy' towards the Divine, to lead us beyond ourselves; yet for this very reason it calls for a path of ascent, renunciation, purification, and healing" (*DCE* 5).

As physical and sexuated beings, men and women are destined to enjoy beatific contemplation in a way which is beyond our capacity to conceptualize, but which cannot negate any dimension of human personhood. Rather, there is nuptial synthesis of the natural and supernatural, of the corporal and the spiritual, of donation and possession. This applies to human relationships *and* to the human-divine relationship: "[B]iblical faith does not set up a parallel universe, or one opposed to that primordial human phenomenon which is love, but rather accepts the whole man" (*DCE* 8).

Eros and *agape* are united in the source itself of love which is God: "God loves," continues the text of the encyclical, "and his love may certainly be called *eros*, yet it is also totally *agape*" (*DCE* 9). The biblical revelation of God does not envisage his metaphysical otherness as irreconcilable with passionate nearness and intimacy: "God is the absolute and ultimate source of all being; but this universal principle of creation—the *Logos*, primordial reason—is at the same time a lover with all the passion of a true love" (*DCE* 10). The aspect of what Pope Benedict XVI calls "God's *eros* for man," his "passionate love" for humanity (*DCE* 10), i.e., of irresistible "erotic" seduction on the part of the divine Protagonist and of ecstatic surrender on the part of the human respondent (cf. *DCE* 6), is notably absent from Joycean criticism. This is an unfortunate oversight, since it is the humanizing factor that invests the relationship with vitality, intimacy, and joyful urgency. Benedict's point, and Joyce's, is that repression of the faith-reality of *eros* renders the religious relationship unnatural and incomprehensible.

Joyce evidently abhorred as inhuman the idea of unrequited love, but so does Christianity. *Agape* without *eros* entails the emptying of the self *in order to remain empty*, which is an aberration. It would end in the obliteration rather than the ecstatic fulfillment of the person.

Love without a subject is a self-contradictory impossibility. According to Catholic doctrine, then, *eros* is essential to love, but so is *agape*. This is supremely exemplified in the life and death of Christ, and in the response to the same by the saints. We know that Joyce rejects *agape* without *eros* and embraces *eros*, but the question now is: does he reject *agape, per se*, and embrace *eros, per se*?

Put another way: is Stephen's ecstatic discovery of the erotic power of profane beauty Joyce's last word on the subjects of beauty, love, life, and joy? Certainly, the beach scene should not be interpreted simply and solely in terms of Stephen's joyful reversion to sin. We are given to understand that Stephen has outgrown the enslavement to vice depicted in the second and third chapters of *Portrait*. At the end of chapter IV he "falls" in love not with sin *per se* but with the profane. *However*, this later experience of Stephen is *also* subjected to revision in the Joycean dynamic of ongoing self-critique.

III.3.3: Room for Agape in Joyce's Vision of Love?

III.3.3.1: The Unfinished Ending of Portrait

To describe *Portrait* as a "loveless" book may not in fact be far from Joyce's final intention. Ultimately, Stephen is no paradigm of communication and relationship skills. Quite explicitly, in an encounter with a troop of Christian brothers on a bridge just before his experience on the beach (still, therefore, in chapter IV of the novel), Stephen is confronted with his lovelessness and "a faint stain of personal shame and commiseration rose to his own face" as he reflects that "their humble and contrite hearts, it might be, paid a far richer tribute of devotion than his had ever been."[88]

In an article entitled "Joyce Among the Brothers," John Mahon focuses unerringly on the Joycean (and Dedalan) preoccupation with love:

> This reflection-encounter-reflection [in the encounter with the community of Christian brothers on the bridge] portrays a person who, despite his pride, willfulness, and egotism, can appreciate—even envy—the values represented by these young Brothers exercising together 'two by two': simple piety, generosity toward the neediest,

hospitality, and obedience to the commandment of love . . . These young men may not be the 'shock troops' or intellectual elite of the Church, as the Jesuits were thought to be, but they model the law of love. Their total lack of pride and their simple piety reflect the qualities usually associated with a commitment to the religious life . . . Stephen recognizes that he completely lacks these qualities.[89]

The capacity to sacrifice self for another—*agape*—is the quality of love that Stephen lacks. The "law of love" that the Brothers model is, "love one another; even as I have loved you" (Jn 13:34). The matter does not end here. Later, as Mahon explains, Stephen in his diary records his mother's prayer that he "may learn in my own life and away from home and friends what the heart is and what it feels."[90] Stephen records his mother's words in his diary and adds his own words of prayerful assent: "Amen. So be it."[91] We overlook the words of Stephen's mother at the peril of overlooking the great unifying theme of *Portrait* and of *Ulysses*. They are among the very last words of *Portrait*. Would it be a "theological superimposition" to interpret them as Love's *admonitio* seeking to break through, as Augustine saw it to be in the case of God's voice in his mother Monica?[92] Is it a reductive ideological superimposition on Richard Ellmann's part to dismiss Joyce's mother's faith-wisdom as mere "conventionality" that he must overcome in the "superhuman effort" of becoming himself?

For Ellmann the Joycean grand plan is "to mother and father himself, to become, by the superhuman effort of the creative process, no one but James Joyce,"[93] but as Hugh Kenner succinctly puts it, in *Portrait*, "Each chapter closes with a synthesis of triumph which the next destroys," but May Murray (Stephen's mother) survives the process: at the end of *Portrait*, "The mother remains."[94] What is Joyce's purpose in citing her words among the closing words of *Portrait* and in giving them Stephen's Amen? In fact, the "synthesis of triumph" (in Kenner's expression) that Stephen achieves in the fourth chapter of *Portrait* is already shown to be insufficient in the last chapter of *Portrait*, and will be "destroyed" between *Portrait* and *Ulysses*.

The striking contrast between Stephen's mood at the end of *Portrait* and his mood at the beginning of *Ulysses* has much to do with his mother's intervening death. He is haunted by her death, by her memory, by her love. Stephen's crisis involves not only assimilating the shock of his mother's death and his refusal to kneel and pray by her bedside; it extends to his relationship with women in general and with the feminine in himself. The Stephen of the end of *Portrait* is arrogant and over-sensitive, humorless and over-intellectual. But as Weldon Thornton has persuasively argued, he is not without redeeming features and hopeful signs. Thornton focuses on the final entries to Stephen's diary in the closing chapter, which treat of Stephen's conversations with Emma, the girl with whom he has been infatuated since childhood, and with his mother.

III.3.3.2: Stephen's Relationships

In Stephen's diary entries about Emma he registers surprise that their relationship has passed from *eros* to *philia* and *storge*, from romantic attraction to simple friendship and affection. Stephen regrets having been rude to Emma during a chance meeting with her that day, "But most important is his statement . . . which suggests that this liking—not passion, not adoration, but *liking* ['I liked her today . . . I liked her and it seems a new feeling to me']—might be the doorway to fuller and more meaningful personal relationships."[95]

Thornton's reading suggests a slight and hopeful move on Stephen's part away from a self-defensive frigid haughtiness, which he shares, *mutatis mutandis*, with Mr. Duffy, Fr. Flynn, and Gabriel Conroy, towards a healthy acceptance of the "likeable" ordinariness of others that will be celebrated in *Ulysses*. Thornton finds a similar softening in Stephen's farewell exchanges with his mother, reflecting in his diary entries: "Stephen . . . seems to take a softer attitude toward his mother, acknowledging her love and sympathy for him, and sensing that her love may well be—as Cranly has told him (pp. 241-242)—the most real thing in life." This softening of attitude and attraction toward the feminine and maternal will be developed in *Ulysses*, as we will see, but at the end of *Portrait* Stephen "cannot pause now to consider that—he is about to set out to create the conscience of his race."[96]

Once again in Joyce's treatment of Stephen (and in Thornton's reading of the same), there is a note of gentle and sympathetic irony; Stephen may be without humor, but his creator is not. Leopold Bloom in *Ulysses* will comically and imperfectly but sufficiently embody and import into Stephen's life the harmonization of masculine and feminine that constitutes the true fatherhood he needs to enable him to emerge from the ivory tower of self. Once we have seen (in the next section) the benefits that accrue to both of them from their meeting, we will have a fuller picture of Joycean individuation and will be in a better position to compare the same to the Judeo-Christian journey.

But some similarities between the Joycean and Judeo-Christan journeys may already be observed. Stephen will be "prepared" for his encounter with Bloom, like Gabriel Conroy was "prepared" for his humiliating epiphany, by the trauma of his mother's death. Her death will have a deep impact on Stephen, ultimately altering his worldview in a dynamic closely related to St. Augustine's concepts of *gratia delectans* and *admonitio*, just as Joyce's own mother's death altered his worldview and constituted for him a lifelong source of heartache. In personal correspondence he wrote of his own "cynical frankness of conduct" as a contributing factor in his mother's death.[97] Stephen's "breakthrough" on the beach is an intense emotional experience, an epiphanical revelation of nature as sacrament and a discovery of his artistic vocation in celebration thereof, but it is not enough; *eros*, whether poisoned or pure, turns out to be woefully insufficient when Stephen has to cope with the trauma of his mother's death.

III.3.3.3: Stephen between Portrait *and* Ulysses

Stephen's mother dies, so to speak, between the completion of *Portrait* and the beginning of *Ulysses*. In contrast to the end of *Portrait*, the beginning of *Ulysses* presents Stephen as a dejected and forlorn figure. Like Icarus, son of Daedalus, his flight has taken him too close to the sun, his waxen wings have been burned, and he finds himself cast into the ocean, so to speak: "The snotgreen sea. The scrotumtightening sea."[98] This same sea was the scene of his earlier rapturous discovery. The profane, wonderful as it may be, is grotesquely inadequate when it comes to coping with the trauma of bereavement. According to the modern critical consensus, the beginning of *Ulysses* presents a Stephen who, far from having taken flight, is in fact stuck in a rut. Joyce himself reported to his friend Budgen in the course of writing *Ulysses* that the character of Stephen had come to interest him less than Bloom because Stephen "has a shape that can't be changed."[99] Kenner notes that Stephen is more aesthete than artist: "Stephen does not, as the careless reader may suppose, become an artist by rejecting church and country. Stephen does not become an artist at all."[100]

Noon observes Stephen's despair at finding beauty in the commonplace: "However hard Joyce himself may have tried in the Pola days to work with beauty as a 'transcendental concept,' *Ulysses* shows that he has given up this effort . . . 'Houses of decay, mine, his and all . . . Come out of them, Stephen. Beauty is not there.'"[101] The cited thought from Stephen's interior monologue—"Come out of them, Stephen. Beauty is not there"—is in direct contrast to his commitment in *Portrait* to the "faint sour stink of rotted cabbages" and the "disorder, the misrule and confusion of his father's house and the stagnation of vegetable life"[102] as the raw material of his artistic ministry.

Would Manganiello perceive this renunciation of the pursuit of beauty in the profane as maturation? Stephen is depicted as depressed and tempted to despair. Noon assumes, mistakenly, I believe, that Joyce shares Stephen's despair at finding beauty in the profane and mundane. Kiberd argues that his deeply engrained intellectualist idealism is a sign of arrested adolescence, and that his renunciation of beauty as the fodder of art ubiquitously present in the ordinary and the quotidian—i.e., a transcendental or species of the good—is *not* borne out by *Ulysses* and is therefore not Joyce's final position: "Stephen's rejection of the quotidian ('Houses of decay . . .') is most unJoycean, and will not be ratified by Bloom."[103]

Stephen's intellect, his very manner of reasoning, like Fr. Flynn's, Mr. Duffy's, and Gabriel Conroy's, needs to be humbled and humanized. His mother perceives this, and prays that he will learn what the heart is and what it feels. Joyce perceives it too, and intends us to as well. A "conversion" of the mind is required, an intellectual conversion not of necessity explicitly to Christ, to Church, or to Christianity. It requires primarily a new relationship with Reason itself which can best be described as religious; not in the sense of deifying Reason but rather in the sense of allowing Reason its proper role in the human approach to reality.[104]

The ending of "A Painful Case" suggests that a breaking of mind and heart, or, to put it more technically, a failure of rational categories, a humiliation of intellect through emotional disappointment, is sometimes necessary and therapeutic. The tragic price of Mr. Duffy's entelechial opportunity is Mrs. Sinico's death; for Stephen it is the death of his mother. His mother's death has thrown Stephen into a "heartbreaking" crisis similar to Mr. Duffy's. It is this breaking of the heart that will finally enable Joyce to achieve and express, in *Ulysses*, his resolution of the *agape-eros* puzzle hinted at in "The Dead," in an *agape-eros* "synthesis of triumph," to avail again of Kenner's evocative expression. Stephen's faith in the ordinary, his alertness to epiphany, and his artistic ambition to recreate life out of life will be restored, but first something else needs to happen. That "something else" is his encounter with Leopold Bloom, Joyce's paradigm of the humane, of healthy sexual identity, and of fatherhood.

III.3.3.4: Sexual Identity and Androgyny

Before resuming our task of tracing the course of Joycean individuation, however, a preliminary clarification of terms is necessary. There is early evidence that sexual identity is a major theme in Joyce's mind in his admiring description of Henrik Ibsen in a review of Ibsen's work that Joyce wrote at the age of eighteen: "Indeed, if one may say so of an eminently virile man, there is a curious admixture of the woman in his nature. His marvellous accuracy, his faint traces of femininity, his delicacy of swift touch, are perhaps attributable to this admixture."[105] Joyce's concern with the complexities of sexual identity recurs throughout his writings, as we are seeing, culminating in his novel *Ulysses*. Marilyn French has written of *Ulysses* that "All told, allusions to feminacy in men are rife throughout *Ulysses* and the Notesheets: that it is a major theme is not debatable."[106]

Specific evidence of Joyce's interest in human sexuality would include three moments from the Circe chapter of *Ulysses*: the crossdressing of Leopold Bloom, the presentation of Bloom as "a finished example of the new womanly man,"[107] and the highly theatricalized revelation of his sadomasochistic fantasies. Throughout the novel Bloom is repeatedly shown as empathizing with women in their difficult circumstances, and his unconsummated epistolary affair under the pseudonym of Henry Flower with one Martha Clifford reveals an effeminate and mildly sadomasochistic bent (which is later exaggerated out of all proportion in the Circe episode). But Bloom's weak masculinity is not given the last word, as we will soon see in greater detail.

The Joycean theme of human sexuality has given rise in Joyce scholarship to a concept apparently alien to the Catholic tradition: *androgyny*. The word has immediate connotations more of ambiguity and confusion than of identity and synthesis, although the anthropology of the complete person envisaged by Declan Kiberd is persuasive:

> Apologists for androgyny do not see it thus as a featureless unisex philosophy nor as an obliteration

of the categories "male" and "female", but as a fusion of both. June Singer has written: "The new androgyne is not in confusion about his or her sexual identity. Androgynous men express a natural, unforced and uninhibited male sexuality, while androgynous women can be totally female in their own sexuality. Yet neither tends to extremes: men do not need to exude machismo, or women to pretend to a naïve and dependent character."[108]

Given the confusing nature of the term "androgyny," however, I prefer to speak in terms of Joyce's concern with the discovery of sexual identity using the traditional terms "masculinity" and "femininity," but bearing in mind the above-described legitimate concern to purge such terms of distorting connotations of machismo and effeminacy.

Joyce was certainly interested in correcting polarized caricatures of masculinity and femininity and in harmonizing the masculine and the feminine. He believed that both men and women can be hyper-masculinized or hyper-feminized. His response to these distortions is synthesis, not confusion—not ambiguous androgyny but honest masculinity and femininity. Honesty was an enormously important value to Joyce. The search for identity—national, personal, sexual—is a major Joycean theme. In the discovery of identity there is peace and homecoming, strength, gentleness, and serenity; all of which Stephen Dedalus is lacking, until his father-and-son encounter with Bloom.

III.4: Ulysses

III.4.1: The Theme of Fatherhood

In a chapter entitled "Fathers and Sons" in his book *Inventing Ireland*, Declan Kiberd, inspired by the post-colonialist thinker Frantz Fanon, author of *The Wretched of the Earth*, describes the social context of *Portrait* and *Ulysses*: "In societies on the brink of revolution, the relation between fathers and sons is reversed. The Irish *risorgimento* was, among other things, a revolt by angry sons against discredited fathers." Stephen's father (and Joyce's) fits the description that follows: "The fathers had lost face, either because they had compromised with the occupying English in return for safe positions as policemen or petty clerks, or because they had retreated into the demeaning cycle of alcoholism and unemployment."[109]

Rebellion for its own sake is insufficient for Stephen (and for Joyce). He must find a meaningful alternative to the spurious options he rightly rejects. Mere orphanhood is not an appetizing alternative to patriarchalism. In *Ulysses*, as Noon has observed, Stephen's musings on Sabellianism are symptomatic of his sense of orphanhood and his angry longing for something to fill the void:

> If, as Stephen says, all fatherhood is a necessarily evil, is not Stephen's hopeless characterization of this age quite valid: 'It is an age of exhausted whoredom groping for its god'? 'Paternity may be a legal fiction. Who is the father of any son that any son should love him or he any son?' That is Stephen's question.[110]

Joyce realizes that the so-called "death of God" is not a matter of mere tangential debate between theologians but one of burning relevance for man's understanding of himself and the human drama in which he is unavoidably a protagonist.

The crisis of paternity is indisputably present, but this does not mean that Joyce agrees with Stephen about paternity being a legal fiction. His war was against a distorted and distortive patriarchal authoritarianism and not against paternal authority. Joyce is concerned with paternity as a possible spiritual reality. Fatherhood is more a personal task than a biological function. Faithful to its suggestive Homeric analogue, Joyce's *Ulysses* is about the search for fatherhood. In this ever-present theme his uncanny prophetic perspicacity is focused upon our modern situation. The critical consensus is that in Bloom Stephen finds the father figure his spirit needs. About Bloom himself, however, and his relationship with his wife Molly, critical opinion is divided. The ending of *Ulysses*, not untypically of Joycean endings, has been a lightning rod for critical commentary, producing diametrically opposed interpretations.

III.4.2: Leopold Bloom

III.4.2.1: Breakfast in Bed

Ulysses is a novel that evolves between two instances of breakfast in bed. Bloom first appears in the novel serving Molly breakfast in bed, and receiving scant respect and gratitude for it, in the classic scenario of the frustrated wife and the put-upon husband: "'Hurry up with that tea' . . . Nudging the door open with his knee he carried the tray in and set it on the chair by the bedhead. 'What a time you were,' she said."[111] Indications are that this has been the daily ritual in this household for a long time. Later on, when Bloom arrives home at the end of what has been a long day, before falling asleep he asks Molly to bring him breakfast in bed the following morning, reversing roles and breaking a longstanding tradition. Molly's surprise at this sign of assertive change in her husband is expressed in the first line of her soliloquy in the final chapter: "Yes because he never did a thing like that before as ask to get his breakfast in bed with a couple of eggs."[112] Is this a telltale detail, or a trivial one?

Edmund Wilson maintains it is a vital clue: "Bloom's encounter with Stephen is to affect both Stephen's life and the relations between the Blooms. To have rescued and talked with Stephen has somehow restored Bloom's self-confidence . . . This amazes and disconcerts Mrs. Bloom."[113] Richard Ellmann, on the other hand, ridicules Wilson's reading as "an uncharacteristic burst of optimism,"[114] arguing (in an uncharacteristic burst of pessimism) that Bloom's request for breakfast in bed is simply "an expression of fatigue after a late night which is most unusual for him." Ellmann admits that Wilson's hypothesis is "harder to reject" (than another by William Empson postulating a future affair between Molly and Stephen), but rejects it anyway on the grounds that the "conjugal future at 7 Eccles Street no longer interests him [Joyce]"[115] and should not therefore interest us as readers.

Ellmann's argument does not ring true: Joycean endings are generally crafted to stimulate intelligent reflection and speculation. Bloom specifies that he wants breakfast in bed "with a couple of eggs," which seems to tilt the moment more towards requirement than request, suggesting decisiveness rather than fatigue. Kiberd writes that *Ulysses* is "a book of utopian epiphanies, hinting at a golden future which might be made over in terms of those utopian moments."[116] The task that presents itself then is to discover those utopian moments and discern what that golden future might consist of, who might bring it about and how.

That task is related to the theme of the novel, which is the search for the father, but the theme of search for the father is intimately connected to the recurrent themes we have been discussing in Joyce's writings, namely the themes of sexual identity, reconciliation of man and woman, of *animus* and *anima*, and of *agape* and *eros*. All of these themes are intricately interconnected and dovetail in the final chapters of *Ulysses*. Contrary to Lenin's quip about breaking eggs to make an omelette (a symbol of communist revolution and the overthrowal of corrupt patriarchal authority, only to install another one in its place), Joyce's book revolves around spouses cooking eggs for breakfast for one another.

Ulysses is typical of Joyce's writings in that its ending is notoriously difficult to decipher, but there is an interpretation of the ending of the novel with strong evidence in its favor which is *not* negative or even noncommittal, but positive and hopeful. The *Dubliners* stories and *Portrait* have established the foundations for that interpretation.

All that remains is to gather the evidence that arises out of Bloom's one-day odyssey as it unfolds between his serving Molly breakfast in bed in the morning and his request that night that she return the favor the following day. Despite Molly's low opinion of him—judging by the evidence of her matutinal comportment—we know that Bloom is Joyce's idea of a "good man" because he said as much to Frank Budgen: "[H]e is a complete man . . . a good man. At any rate, that is what I intend he shall be."[117] Let us examine Bloom's credentials as a "good man" and father (the better to compare them thereafter with Catholic virtues), as these are presented to us in the course of the novel.

III.4.2.2: Bloom's Virtues

Gentleness is arguably Bloom's outstanding virtue. Kiberd rightly describes Bloom as Joyce's corrective response to a mythic heroic pseudo-masculinity, citing Stephen's fear of "the big words which make us so unhappy,"[118] a sane and humane reservation which Joyce shared: "In this book, the very ordinariness of the modern Ulysses, Leopold Bloom, becomes a standing reproach to the myth of ancient military heroism. Man's littleness is seen, finally, to be the condition of his greatness."[119] This being said, it is also true that there is heroism in Bloom's behavior: he is non-conformist and courageous in his own strong, gentle, and unassuming way.

Ulysses is peppered with Bloom's acts of empathy and kindness and gentle virtue. In the Hades chapter, he imagines to himself the impact of Dignam's death on his widow and later tries to procure insurance money for her.[120] In Lestrygonians, he helps a blind man across a street, imagining as he does so what it must be like to be blind.[121] In his one-day odyssey on the streets of Dublin, Bloom must navigate his way homeward besieged by forces of darkness, internal and external, which militate against human dignity and personal integrity. In Sirens, Bloom, like Odysseus navigating his way past the hypnotic allure of sensual song, retains his wits and his wit while all around him are bewitched by the audiovisual seductions of the Ormond bar. Although momentarily swayed, his innate good sense ultimately prevails and he makes a successful getaway from the barmaids' coquetry and the maudlin music, while his fellow Dublin men languish behind in the bar under the two women's spell.

Later, in the Cyclops chapter, Bloom goes against the general tide in Barney Kiernan's pub by voicing aloud his sympathy for the long-suffering wife of the mentally unstable Denis Breen whom all around him ridicule.[122] Thornton has written of his "amazing naïveté in speaking out in a pub for the value of Christian love,"[123] but there is endearing boldness in this act too, as Budgen admiringly articulates: "[F]or all his prudence, there is in Bloom an impulsive simplicity . . . that would probably lead him to speak up just when he ought for his own good to lie low. He did it in Barney Kiernan's saloon and might do it again in still more dangerous circumstances."[124]

Bloom empathizes with Mrs. Breen in Barney Kiernan's bar in the Cyclops episode, and he empathizes with Mrs. Purefoy in the hospital in the Oxen of the Sun episode. While the conversation of the inebriated medical students turns coarser by the minute at the expense of Mina Purefoy, who labors nearby to give birth to her ninth child, Bloom "felt with wonder women's woe in the travail that they have of motherhood."[125] In the same chapter he inwardly laments alcoholic excess in a culture that sees drinking as a mark of manhood: "so grieved he also in no less measure for young Stephen for that he lived riotously with those wastrels."[126] He stands out as the only one with the sensitivity to ask Nurse Callan to pass on his kind wishes to Mrs. Purefoy after she has given birth.[127] Before returning to Bloom's virtues in greater detail, we should look first at his defects and ambiguities.

III.4.2.3: Bloom's Defects

On the negative side, in the Lestrygonians chapter we learn that Bloom and Molly have not had sex in over ten years because he "could never like it again after Rudy."[128] This fact is repeated in Oxen of the Sun: "he still had pity of the terrorcausing shrieking of shrill women in their labour and as he was minded of his good lady Marion that had borne him an only manchild which on his eleventh day on live had died and no man of art could save so dark is destiny."[129] That sexual intercourse turned difficult for Bloom in the aftermath of his son's death evinces an understandable, even admirable, sensitivity; but after ten years an understandable difficulty begins to look like a neurotic, hyper-sensitive pathology. His spirit has been scandalized into sterility by suffering and death. He will not risk a repeat occurrence even if it means not having sexual relations with his wife or conceiving more children.

Bloom's repressed sexuality symptomizes in a plethora of petty manias. In the Sirens episode, like Odysseus who wanted to hear the song of the Sirens while tied to a mast, Bloom flirts with sensual danger in composing, in the Ormond bar, his epistolary response to Martha, his suggestively sadomasochistic pen pal. He escapes the snares of the Sirens, and bravely stands up for Mrs. Breen in the Cyclops episode, but then, in the Nausicaa episode, he succumbs to voyeuristic masturbation as he beholds Gerty McDowell on the beach. Ellmann's interpretation of his masturbation—"For the first time in literature masturbation becomes heroic"[130]—is compromised by Bloom himself who sees nothing heroic in it: "What a brute he had been! At it again? . . . An utter cad he had been."[131] Bloom does not share Ellmann's high opinion of his actions.

In a clear case of ideological projection, Suzette Henke holds a high opinion of Bloom's relationship with Molly: "James Joyce, for the first time in the history of English literature, has given us a portrait of an 'open marriage' that works. No longer dependent on sexual union, the conjugal bond has shed its erotic compulsion."[132] This reading presupposes as ideal and desirable a state of emotional and sexual indifference (*agape* without *eros*?) that can best be described as inhuman: "Molly and Bloom have escaped the limits of sexual obsession and are free to relate as full, self-actualizing human beings. Despite masturbatory and adulterous activities, they remain faithful to one another in their fashion."[133]

Joyce is strangely susceptible to misinterpretations that seem oblivious to textual evidence and authorial intention: throughout *Ulysses* Bloom is repeatedly shown to be tormented by his knowledge of Molly's adultery, even as he passively connives in it by way of compensation for his own failure to fulfill his conjugal responsibilities. Bloom knows that Molly has arranged matters to seek satisfaction this very day and the thought crosses his mind that her suitor, Blazes Boylan, may be infected with a venereal disease: "Some chap with a dose burning him. If he . . . O! Eh? No . . . No. No, no. I don't believe it. He wouldn't surely? No, no. Mr. Bloom moved forward raising his troubled eyes. Think no more about that."[134] Bloom lives in dread of Molly's affair.

Bloom's dread is shown again in the Sirens chapter: when Boylan gets up to leave the Ormond Hotel and head towards Bloom's home for his tryst with Molly (she is a singer and he is her agent), a "light sob of breath" involuntarily escapes Bloom.[135] He understands that he has failed Molly as her husband but at the same time cannot help being tormented by her betrayal and is wracked with anxiety at the thought of the affair. After masturbating in Nausicaa, he reflects miserably that Boylan "gets the plums and I the plumstones."[136] And his anxiety is magnified a thousandfold in his masochistic fantasy in Circe. In it, Boylan, about to have sex with Molly, treats Bloom contemptuously, sadistically, as his lackey, telling him: "You can apply your eye to the keyhole and play with yourself while I just go through her a few times."[137] To interpret this situation as paradigmatic is to misconstrue Joyce, and human nature.

III.4.2.4: Bloom's Ambiguous Sexuality

Bloom is not univocally paradigmatic, sexually or otherwise. Softened by sensualism, he is afraid to suffer. Molly is the neglected spouse of a repressed husband whom she does not consider exemplary; neither would her psychologist if she had one, or her social peers. Something is lacking in Bloom's relationship with Molly, and missed in him by her. Of Bloom we may ask, as Kenner does of Stephen, how seriously are we meant to take him? It is clear that Stephen is a "work in progress," but this is no less true of Bloom. The household of 7 Eccles Street is not presented to us as paradigmatic. Marital crisis is one of the most traumatic ordeals that the common man has to undergo, and Bloom's marriage is in serious crisis. Something is radically wrong. This ugly and painful fact is present throughout the entire novel, often harrowingly so. Joyce does not make light of it, any more than he makes light of Stephen's acute interior pain. He does not call human brokenness by any other name.

Without questioning Bloom's undeniable "likeability" we may inquire of the text what it is he seems to be lacking. By all accounts and appearances Molly is an attractive personality. The breakdown in relations is not only sexual, and there are strong indicators that Molly, although she has adulterously betrayed Bloom with Boylan this very day, is not exclusively responsible for the crisis. In Penelope, Molly laments Bloom's lack of affection toward her: "its a wonder Im not an old shriveled hag before my time living with him so cold never embracing me."[138] Bloom's failure to communicate with

Molly indicates that he has unresolved issues of his own. He is fatherless and sonless, his father having died by suicide and his son in early infancy. He is no less an orphan than Stephen. His ineffectuality is not always endorsed. On the contrary, there is a sense in Bloom's case too of lamentable inadequacy.

Kiberd sees Bloom as Joyce's paradigm of the man who has harmonized male and female elements in himself: "In *Ulysses*, the mature artist set forth Leopold Bloom as the androgynous man of the future."[139] Certainly, Bloom has qualities that "disqualify" him from typical forms of male society. There is an effeminacy about him—femininity might be a better way of putting it—that makes his hyper-masculine contemporaries nervous. That nervousness is manifest in Mulligan's verdict on Bloom as "Greeker than the Greeks,"[140] and in many such examples of what Kiberd calls Bloom's "imperfect androgyny" and other men's reactions to it. However, although he is repeatedly humiliated and excluded by their dismissive treatment, Bloom always emerges comparatively well from his encounters with his male peers. There is a gentle dignity about him that their boorishness lacerates but fails to overwhelm; moreover, that dignity is highlighted by contrast with coarseness and hostility.

Some claims in favor of Bloom and of androgyny itself seem exaggerated, however, and rather than elicit admiration for Bloom, elicit sympathy for Molly: "Male and female elements have become so balanced in Bloom that sexual desire is slowly ebbing away."[141] At thirty-eight years of age this seems a premature maturation, hardly meritorious of congratulation; all the more so considering it commenced ten years earlier. We must look elsewhere for the key to unlock Bloom's ambiguity. This entails confronting the issues of homosexuality, masturbation, and contraception because Joyce considered them to be obstacles to genuine human development.

III.4.3 Joyce on Homosexuality and Contraception

III.4.3.1: Joyce's Views on Homosexuality

We know that Joyce commented to Budgen, "You see an undercurrent of homosexuality in Bloom . . . and no doubt you are right."[142] Bloom is depicted as being perilously close to abdication from the exigencies and responsibilities of masculinity and paternity. When Joyce uses Homeric parallels in his imaginative creation of Leopold Bloom, it is true that he wishes to critique certain mythological ideas of male heroism and their dehumanizing consequences, but he also critiques modern manifestations of paralysis, effeminacy, and timidity. We have seen that Joyce values the Renaissance's contribution to culture while at the same time deploring its degenerative tendency towards sensualism. Levy's commentary on Joyce's Renaissance essay offers another helpful insight: "It is . . . the task of the Medieval to free us from the languid slavery to the immanent that is the product of the Modern."[143]

Joyce is certainly committed to the correction of what he perceived to be a spiritualist and intellectualist transcendentalism and to the restoration of the sacramental richness of the temporal and the immanent, but, as Levy rightly maintains, he is also committed to the correction of an emasculating immanentism that is no less a truncation of human potentiality. Bloom and Stephen must navigate their way through both perils: intellectualism and sensualism. Given his understanding of the modern situation in the terms expressed in his essay on the Renaissance and his fascination with human sexuality in all its expressions, it is only logical that Joyce should confront the issue of homosexuality. He does so, principally, in the figure of Leopold Bloom. Bloom's "androgyny" borders, as Budgen saw, on homosexuality.

In a curiously contradictory article on homosexuality in Joyce's works, David Norris expertly accumulates the abundant evidence—in *Dubliners* and episodes of *Portrait* and *Ulysses*—that Joyce saw homosexuality as a "threat" to personal individuation. Norris uses the word four times in this sense, only thereafter to conclude, mystifyingly, that, "Joyce was neither sympathetic nor unsympathetic to the matter,"[144] and that "homosexuality was a subject that scarcely engaged Joyce's attention at all and of which he had little real knowledge. It is consistently presented in his works as an external threat, not fully understood but troubling."[145]

Postmodernist literary critical discourse sometimes shows scant regard for the fundamental philosophical principle of noncontradiction, paying a high price in terms of intellectual rigor. Norris's article is microscopic in its premises and myopic in its conclusion. On the basis of the evidence presented in it by Norris himself (who describes himself in the opening line as "an openly gay man"), it is clear that Sheldon Brivic's assertion, contrary to that of Norris, that Joyce was a "doctrinaire heterosexual,"[146] enjoys more textual validation. In the closing comments of his article, Norris provides what might be a clue to comprehend its contradictoriness: "If one is gay one learns very early on the art of transposing the emotions of mainstream literature, so that they may be more easily identified with."[147] Uncontested.

In an article about Joyce and homophobia, Frances Devlin-Glass examines Joyce's short essay on Oscar Wilde. The existence of this essay is significant in itself: Joyce's custom was to write essays and give conferences only on matters that personally interested him. Devlin-Glass quotes expressions employed by Joyce in the essay: "In Joyce's mind, in this essay, Wilde's behavior . . . embodied an hereditary pathology: his was a 'strange problem' . . . a malady, an unhappy 'mania,'" and her conclusion, at least on this occasion, concurs with her premises: Joyce "implies that it was an illness and the product of a social system, the 'logical and inescapable product of the Anglo-Saxon college and university system.'"[148] Joyce was not homophobic, but he was neither ignorant of nor indifferent to the subject of homosexuality.

The point at issue here is not inconsequential. To miss it or to misinterpret it, willfully or unwittingly, is to misconstrue the Joycean anthropology, which sees the human endeavour as one of navigating the waters of life, after the example of Odysseus, avoiding the rocks of distortion to achieve a humane equilibrium and integrity. This is depicted in Leopold Bloom's comic-epic one-day itinerary through the streets of Dublin. We have seen Levy's argument concerning Joyce's project to achieve a synthesis that avoids the polar extremes of late Scholastic intellectualism, which arguably conduces to a harsh hyper-masculinity, and post-Renaissance modernist sensualism which arguably conduces to an effete effeminacy. On the basis of the evidence presented by Norris, it is clear that Joyce viewed homosexuality as another "rock" of sensualist distortion. This subject greatly interested Joyce, to the point of constituting a recurring central theme of his writings. Curiously, as well as homosexuality, Joyce also saw birth control and masturbation as facilitators of sensualism which debilitate man and threaten his individuation.

III.4.3.2: Masturbation and Contraception

On the subject of masturbation, Joyce has Stephen say, "[W]hat of those Godpossibled souls that we nightly impossibilise, which is the sin against the Holy Ghost, Very God, Lord and Giver of Life? For, sirs, he said, our lust is brief. We are means to those small creatures within us and nature has other ends than we."[149] And Bloom inwardly muses that "A habit reprehensible at puberty is second nature and an opprobrium in middle life."[150] Stephen's convictions are pro-life and anti-contraceptive, albeit in contrast with his own moral habits. Kiberd describes this challenge to critical interpretation: "Both [Stephen and Bloom] practice the very forms of birth control which they denounce."[151] Kiberd adds that "Joyce told Frank Budgen that the crime against the ancient gods was the sterilization of the act of coition. One form of this sin, as Stephen freely admits, is the nightly act of masturbation."[152]

Pursuing even further his pro-life position, Stephen, in the debate at the hospital maternity ward concerning the dilemma of difficult births, "asserts the primacy of the child."[153] As the conversation under the influence of alcohol degenerates into crudity, "Stephen and Bloom, alone among the inebriated students, refuse to join in the nervous mockery, for they understand that the deed of the Purefoys [procreation] seems dignified and purposeful in comparison."[154] Joyce's pro-life position in the Oxen of the Sun chapter, at least intellectual and vocal if not practical, has provoked debate.

Marilyn French, for example, makes this contribution to the debate: "Religious groups have been maintaining for some years that if God ordered increase, contraception is sin, and that is the premise of this chapter [i.e., Oxen of the Sun]. However, this premise is handled ironically and comically as well as seriously."[155] This is a reductive and ambiguous evasion of the challenge presented by Joyce's text, and by the teaching of "religious groups," to the pro-contraceptive position. Catholicism, presumably one of these religious groups, does not base its anti-contraceptive stance solely or simplistically on the order to increase. Nor does it advocate the unreflecting serial childbearing apparently exemplified in Joyce's creation, Mina Purefoy.[156]

Mina happens in any event to be Protestant; her surname literally means "pure faith," which suggests a critique of fideism rather than of Catholicism. Mina reappears in the climactic consecration scene of the black Mass in the Circe chapter of *Ulysses*, where she is referred to as the "goddess of unreason." Her childbearing body is the "altar" upon which this anti-ceremony is performed: *"On the altarstone Mrs. Mina Purefoy, goddess of unreason, lies naked, fettered, a chalice resting on her swollen belly."*[157] The vitriolic expression of British soldier Private Carr's violent designs on Stephen's windpipe—"I'll wring the bastard fucker's bleeding blasted fucking windpipe!"— occurs just as Mulligan raises the host in the black Mass, with the English intellectual Haines as acolyte: "THE REVEREND MR HAINES LOVE: (*Raises high behind the celebrant's petticoats, revealing his grey bare hairy buttocks between which a carrot was stuck*) My body."[158] We shall return to this scene in detail in chapter V; for now, it is sufficient to note that it dramatizes a clash between scientism and "pure faith."

In the light of his essay on the effects of the Renaissance—in which he critiques both Medieval intellectualism and Modern sensualism—and the reading of his work that I have made thus far, it may be deduced that Joyce foresaw the future of Europe in these terms: scientism and sensualism represented by Mulligan complete with carrot and his sidekick Haines, offering fideism represented by the unreasoning Mrs. Mina (goddess of unreason, pure-faith) Purefoy in sacrifice to the devil, with art, reason, and religion crucified in the process. The divorce of reason and faith culminates in the degeneration of the former into empiricism and of the latter into fideism, each scorning the other. Evidently, Stephen is not identified with either of these positions, and neither is Joyce, but Joyce critics who falsely ascribe "pure-faith" motives alone to the Catholic position on artificial contraception play an unwitting part in the fulfillment of

Joyce's prophecy. Joyce was eminently familiar with, and respectful of, the Catholic intellectual tradition.

That Joyce was cognizant of the intellectual implications of denominational difference—a cognizance not always found in his critics—is evident as early as *Stephen Hero*: "He could not accept wholeheartedly the offers of Protestant belief: he knew that the liberty it boasted of was often only the liberty to be slovenly in thought." This is followed by grudging admission of Catholic rationality: "No one, not the most rabid enemy of the Church, could accuse it of being slovenly in thought: the subtlety of its disquisitions had become a byword with demagogues."[159] Joyce was obviously as indifferent to the niceties of ecumenism as he was well-versed in the intellectual intricacies of Catholicism. Leaving this aside, the point here is that the motive of Stephen's (and Joyce's) resistance to Catholicism is not slovenliness of thought. Unlike some Joyce experts, Joyce himself was aware that God's order to increase is not the only justification of the Catholic Church's condemnation of contraception.

III.4.3.3: Attempts at Understanding Joyce's Position

Suzette Henke asserts that Joyce's condemnation of contraception should be understood emotionally and spiritually, not literally: "In this episode . . . Joyce satirically decries the sins of onanism and contraception." The word "satirically" implies that Joyce does not in fact "decry" the sins at all. But then, describing the attitude of the medical students towards the sexual act, Henke suggests a motivation for the condemnation of these sins which seems convincing and not at all satirical: "Locked in the prison of male egotism, they deny themselves the possibility of human warmth, affection, or compassion."[160]

The argument, then, is that contraception facilitates the reduction of the sexual act to mere masturbation, the sexual consummation of egotism. The sensitive (admittedly over-sensitive) Stephen, who theoretically if not practically rejects onanism and contraception, is an outcast from this desensitized hyper-masculine mob, and so is Bloom: "Bloom is glaringly out of place in this boisterous crowd, and his alienation from the younger men further serves to define his androgynous sensibility."[161] Henke attempts to resolve the contradictoriness of Joyce's position (and perhaps her own) with a most unJoycean body-soul dichotomization: the episode, she maintains, "is chiefly concerned with emotional, rather than with physical, prophylaxis."[162]

The most serious attempt to tackle the Joycean pro-life conundrum has been undertaken by Dr. Mary Lowe-Evans. Joyce knew, Lowe-Evans claims, that the liberalization ostensibly proffered by the contraceptive movement masked a Malthusian agenda which had inflicted devastation upon his own people: "Joyce seems to have been acutely aware of the crimes Western civilization has committed against the physical, artistic, and spiritual fecundity of its citizens by attempting to modify their demographic behavior for ideological ends." He understood that artificial contraception would be a useful tool in the hands of those very eugenicist powers that dispassionately observed the drastic population reduction that occurred in Ireland just one generation before his birth: "These attempts take form, for example, in the rhetoric of a political economy that would justify the Famine of mid-nineteenth century Ireland as a way of reducing the surplus population."[163]

Lowe-Evans' formulation of the issue is succinct and incisive: "By 1920, the birth control movement, social Darwinism and the eugenics controversy had gained international notoriety and influence. Counterforces such as the Catholic Church and the populationists responded." However, like Marilyn French, Lowe-Evans errs by over-simplifying the Catholic position: "The world became an arena where neo-Malthusianists and the cultural mandate of Genesis ('increase and multiply') vied for dominance."[164] In his otherwise positive review of her book, Dominic Manganiello deftly registers this lacuna: Lowe-Evans, he writes, is "especially illuminating on Joyce's conflicting attitudes on the question of birth control. She documents the impact of Margaret Sanger's movement on Joyce's consciousness as well as the Catholic Church's position on the subject (the latter needs to be more fully explained)," and adds a curious Joycean tidbit: "Joyce apparently told Sylvia Beach that he regretted not having ten children and generally held fatherhood in great esteem."[165]

Both of the points made by Lowe-Evans have been made also by Pope Paul VI in *Humanae Vitae*. Pope Paul VI was aware of the political implications of the contraceptive issue, warning that legitimization of birth control would "give into the hands of public authorities the power to intervene in the most personal and intimate responsibility of husband and wife" (*HV* 9). The other main Catholic argument is that the procreative and unitive aspects of the sexual act (i.e., the giving of life and the giving of love) are so intimately interlinked that artificial interference with the former aspect impacts clumsily upon the latter one; sterilization of the procreative aspect entails sterilization also of the unitive aspect, facilitating egotistical manipulation principally of the woman by the man: "[A] man who grows accustomed to the use of contraceptive methods may forget the reverence due to a woman, and . . . reduce her to being a mere instrument for the satisfaction of his own desires" (*HV* 17).

In conclusion, Joyce's line of thought reflects what one finds in a fuller presentation of Catholic thought on sexual morality in relation to contraception: that contraception is a dangerous tool in the hands of corrupt powers, and that contraception is an impediment not only to life but also to love, because it facilitates egocentric abdication from commitment and responsibility, contradicting the humanizing logic of ecstatic mutual care and donation inherent to the sexual act. One may never be sure that this was and remained Joyce's position. With Joyce the last word is often a resounding maybe. However, it seems safe to say he was not a categorical apologist of birth control. He certainly was not an admirer of sterility. This much is important to know. Of course, we must still confront the unresolved contrast between the intellectual and vocal stances of Bloom and Stephen on these issues, and their personal habits.

III.4.3.4: The Moral Stands of Bloom and Stephen

How then are we to interpret the many moral imperfections of Bloom and Stephen? How are we to interpret the blatant discrepancy between their stated positions on, for example, onanism and contraception, and their equally blatant failure to live according to those declared positions? How may Joyce's ambivalence on this point and others be reconciled with the fact that these are two characters who Joyce seems to desire that we admire as *authentic*? In the face of such a contradiction, some critics justifiably assume that Joyce is satirizing Bloom and Stephen, or he is satirizing the moral order they verbally uphold, or both. This solution, however, has against it that it replaces one contradiction with another. There is another explanation.

The blatant incoherency of Bloom and Stephen (and Joyce) in the matters of contraception and masturbation could either be seen as cynical hypocrisy or as intellectual sincerity in the midst of human weakness. Stephen and Bloom may be sensualists in praxis but they have not taken the next step of erecting an ideology out of their sins (the innuendo is not gratuitous). We are intended neither to applaud nor to despise them for their occasional, or even habitual, incoherencies. Nor are we intended to despise the moral order which they support in theory and contradict in practice. We are intended to respect the objective truth of that moral order and to be *merciful* towards those who believe it but fail to live it. That at least is the position of the author.

That Joyce never renounced the moral order is evident in his famously disconcerting response to Robert

McAlmon's proposal of a toast to sin: "I won't drink to that."[166] There is no evidence in Joyce's writing that the remedy for human brokenness involves abandonment of moral norms. Joyce's human beings are works in progress, and their failures and inconsistencies should not be construed as their definitive position, or Joyce's. Reading Joyce, the reader intuits an overall authorial presider, paradoxically present and absent, intimate and unfathomable, whose all-encompassing perspective contemplates struggling, failing, defective creatures with an affection describable as fatherly and divine, desiring and facilitating their individuation. Joyce the author epiphanizes this Godlike activity in his writings, albeit in a subtle, almost ordinary way. Humanity flowers in an environment at once hostile and propitious by way of selective response to external and internal stimuli.

This work-in-progress dynamic returns us to the main thread of this discussion. We have now seen that homosexuality, masturbation, and artificial contraception are perceived by Joyce as forms of sensualism that threaten personal individuation. We have also seen that atheism, at least in the form practiced by Mr. Duffy in "A Painful Case," is not for Joyce a humanizing ideology; it, too, is an obstacle to genuine human development. We will look briefly now at Joyce's position vis-a-vis Leopold Bloom's self-declared atheism.

III.4.3.5: Bloom's Atheism

Geert Lernout quotes in support of his presentation of Bloom's healthy and connatural agnosticism—or atheism—his heavily ironic interior reaction to the expressions of faith by his fellow-mourners at Paddy Dignam's funeral in the Hades episode: "The resurrection and the life. Once you are dead you are dead."[167] Lernout describes Bloom as "entirely beyond religion," claiming that "nothing that we learn about him allows us to believe that he is at all religious in any sense of the word." And he is the ultimate paradigmatic personality of *Ulysses*: "[I]t is this completely post-religious Bloom who takes over the novel."[168] This is an over-simplification of Bloom, of *Ulysses*, of Joyce, and of religion. It is true that Bloom is a theological ignoramus. Time after time he demonstrates his almost total lack of formal culture in this department. But, rather than being anti-religious, Joyce is depicting the natural religiosity of the uncultured everyman.

It is also true, however, that Bloom's enthusiasm for life has been dealt a severe blow by the deaths of his father by suicide and of his son, Rudy, in childhood. Lernout's reading fails to consider that Bloom is deeply shaken by and still unreconciled to the loss of Rudy and of his father. So shaken has he been by loss that during the ten years since Rudy's death he has been unable to have conjugal relations with his wife; he is no less in need of resurrection than Stephen. We are not dealing here with merry agnosticism but with the lingering bitterness of unresolved grief. Bloom's faith in life, his evident natural responsiveness to the ever-surprising newness of experience, has been profoundly shaken by the trauma of bereavement which unites him with Stephen.

Unlike Stephen in many ways, Bloom is like him in many others. One experiences a sensation of regret at the spectacle of so much potential, untapped for lack of initiative to win a prize worth pursuing. At the same time, there are luminous signs throughout *Ulysses* that Bloom has learned and lives with natural grace the lesson of service as human and humanizing, a lesson that Stephen has yet to learn. Their encounter will have reaffirming effects on both, as we will now see.

III.4.4 : Resolution of the Agape-Eros Puzzle

III.4.4.1: Bloom's Victory

In Circe, the episode in which Bloom follows Stephen into a brothel with charitable intentions, Bloom's so-called fantasies are just as likely to be his worst fears. The general atmosphere of the episode would lead one to believe they are a hellish combination of both. In rescuing Stephen, Bloom has to confront his fantasies as though they were his demons. He is surreally punished for his little acts of lust throughout the day. Dressed in woman's clothing, he suffers brutal humiliation at the hands of Bella Cohen the brothel madam—whose name changes to Bello—in a hyperbolic enactment of his titillating epistolary affair with Martha Clifford; the first syllable of Martha's surname may be a Joycean hint that Bloom is playing suicidal brinkmanship with sadomasochistic sensualism.

Although the affair with Martha, to which we are introduced in the Lotus-Eaters chapter, does tend towards the sadomasochistic, it has not been consummated. This being said, in Circe it is "consummated" beyond his wildest dreams/nightmares. In the course of a burlesque masochistic court scene, he is introduced by Dr. Dixon as a "finished example of the new womanly man," who is "about to have a baby"; to which Bloom responds, "O, I so want to be a mother."[169] He gives birth to eight children. The scene is an overblown mix of shrill slapstick pantomime and mordant satire, but some degree of truth underlies the bloated surface, concerning Bloom's womanly ways.

On the subject of Bloom's ambiguous sexuality, Joyce scholar Thomas Balazs notes a hermeneutical change of direction in Joyce studies: "Over the past few decades, literary critics have returned to the subject of Joyce and masochism over and over again to try and unpack the complicated discourses of gender, politics, history, and the psyche that intertwine themselves around issues of sexual submission in *Ulysses*." The proponents of this change of direction would presumably view Frank Budgen's reading as outdated and unenlightened: "While early Joyce critics such as Frank Budgen viewed Bloom's masochism as a pathological feminizing condition that he successfully overcomes, a number of modern critics have interpreted Bloom's masochism as a subversive rebellion against patriarchal authority."[170]

Budgen (self-described as an "orthodox agnostic"[171]) had the obvious advantage of being a close friend of Joyce, who discussed his thought and work with him, consulting him and invoking his collaboration, but even apart from this his reading of *Ulysses* has three factors in its favor: it harmonizes thematically with the parallel scene in Homer's epic (Circe being a minor goddess of magic who turned Odysseus' men into pigs); it harmonizes with the Joycean approach to sexual identity discernible in his other writings, creative and critical (as we have just seen); and it harmonizes with Joyce's own words on his work, quoted by Budgen: "In my case the thought is always simple."[172] Balazs's article may be consulted for a summary of alternative readings which seem contrived and convoluted in comparison to Budgen's.[173]

That Joyce wishes to overthrow patriarchal authoritarianism is undeniable, but he also rejects degenerate sensualism as an impediment to individuation. Budgen's interpretation is that Bloom, in the Circe chapter, must confront the effeminate fantasies that threaten to undermine his manliness: "All the sins of Bloom's past rise to complete his degradation."[174] But Bloom ultimately makes "a successful defense of his manhood."[175] Bloom's "successful defense of his manhood" occurs in a crisis situation when his more noble protective instincts towards Stephen, on whose behalf he confronts Bella, overcome his baser and perverse inclinations.

It is in the moment that he confronts Bella that "the best of Bloom, the responsibilities of his social fatherhood," prevails: "Like his Homeric seagoing forebear, he rushes upon the enchantress with drawn sword and death-denouncing looks. After that . . . the spells of the enchantress are broken."[176] This is the moment in which *agape*-love triumphs over poisoned *eros* in Bloom and manliness over effeminate sensualism, as we have seen outlined in Pope Benedict XVI's synthesis in which *agape*-love saves *eros*-love from self-destruction: "Far from rejecting or 'poisoning' *eros*, they [that is, the purification, maturity and self-renunciation of *agape*-love] heal it and restore its true grandeur" (*DCE* 5).[177] Paradoxically, in the moment when *agape*-love triumphs in Bloom over poisoned *eros*, he regains the capacity to have an erotic relationship with his wife; *agape* saves *eros*.

Bloom's intervention, as well as saving Stephen, saves Bloom himself and will save his marriage. When Stephen, tormented by his own demons (we will focus on this in Chapter V), smashes the brothel chandelier in a fit of drunken anguish, Bella demands all of his money—ten shillings—and Bloom gives her just one shilling, enough to pay for the smashed chandelier and no more. Manliness is not machismo. He asserts himself without losing his gentleness and yields without losing his vigor. Again, the Joycean project is about synthesis and equilibrium, not rupture, fragmentation, and anarchy. Later, in the much milder Ithaca chapter, when Bloom arrives at his home with Stephen, he fumbles in the darkness to insert his key in the keyhole and we are given a curiously detailed description of "his firm full masculine feminine passive active hand."[178] In the end Bloom's masculinity, now gentle and strong instead of effete and ineffectual, is exemplary. Bloom is depicted as having lived on the verge of transvestite sadomasochistic failure, but he is rescued by his rescue of Stephen, and his marriage is rescued too.

III.4.4.2: The End

There is a cumulative weight of evidence in Joyce's writings, from the *Dubliners* stories through *Portrait* to *Ulysses*, that Bloom's request for breakfast in bed represents the resolution of a conundrum with which Joyce has wrestled from the beginning—how to reconcile *eros* and *agape, anima* and *animus*—and is suggestive of a profound inner transformation in Bloom that will help to resurrect his marriage. Molly's surprised reaction to her husband's request is a sign that she senses a significant change. Joyce readers of a liberal secularist persuasion are more comfortable with Bloom's effeminate masochistic fantasies than with his unfashionable breakfast-in-bed masculine assertiveness at the end of the novel, but it is hard to explain away the facts of Bloom's newfound confidence and Molly's surprised response to the same, and it cannot be discounted that Joyce might be more politically incorrect than some of his adepts. To be sure, this should not be read as an assertion that wives should always provide breakfast in bed for their husbands, or that Joyce believed so. We should neither make too much of the matter nor too little of it.

But it does not make too much of the matter to say that Bloom's request for breakfast in bed is a Joycean hint of important change. Perhaps he hinted at this too when, having said to Budgen that he considered Bloom a good and complete man, he added, "At any rate, that is what I intend he shall be."[179] This remark was made while *Ulysses* was still *in the process* of being written. *Ulysses* shows Bloom *becoming* a complete man. That *Ulysses* celebrates an ordinary day in the lives of three ordinary people is tantamount to an axiom in the world of Joycean criticism. Stephen Dedalus and Leopold and Molly Bloom may be ordinary people if such can be said to exist, but the 16th of June 1904 has not been for them an ordinary day, unless depression, homelessness, drunkenness, prostitution, flying biscuit tins, smashing chandeliers, brawling, and adultery may be considered daily events. They may be "ordinary" but they are not typical; they are dramatic; and we may intelligently surmise—*must* surmise, in defiance of Ellmann's assertions to the contrary—that they will have significant consequences in the psychologies and lives of the protagonists.

Ellmann and others may reasonably object that it is overly optimistic to attribute too much weight to a trifle like breakfast in bed and to what is, in the final analysis, no more than a fleeting encounter between Bloom and Stephen. After all, Stephen does not accept Bloom's invitation to stay the night and the two men go their separate ways: "Was the proposal of asylum accepted? Promptly, inexplicably, with amicability, gratefully it was declined."[180] Stephen's departure is another proof of Joyce's realistic bent: it is the likeliest thing that a young man would do. Joyce wished to avoid sentimentalism at all costs. Also, however, "Stephen" went on to write a monumental book about the encounter.

It is true, of course, that Stephen is not Joyce, but it is also true that the encounter between Bloom and Stephen is recognizably based upon a real-life encounter that took place between the young Joyce himself on the streets of Dublin and a middle-aged man named Alfred Hunter who gratuitously came to his aid in a time of need, and who "was rumored to be Jewish and to have an unfaithful wife." Ellmann informs us that Joyce was "only distantly acquainted" with Hunter, "having (according to Stanislaus Joyce) met him only once or twice."[181] The encounter clearly had a profound impact on Joyce, despite the lack of contact with his rescuer before and after the event.

Further, it is entirely consonant with Joyce's fascination with the evanescence and potency of moments of epiphany that he should commit himself to such a monumental tribute as *Ulysses* is to the life-transforming power of a fleeting encounter.

Life, for Joyce, is neither a matter of fixed, unchanging essences nor of random flux; he is a believer in identity, potentiality, and teleology. Weldon Thornton, against the general (relativist) trend of Joycean criticism, holds that Joyce's writings ultimately affirm universal and objective values: "[T]he greatness of Joyce and of his *Ulysses* resides not in sophisticated modernist relativism, but in his willingness to take a stand on an array of linguistic and human issues, just as the great writers he emulated—Virgil, Dante, Milton—have always done."[182] Joyce takes a stand on the side of gentleness and strength. Bloom is Joyce's response to the nationalist and "Catholic" hyper-masculinity and patriarchalism of *Portrait*. Paternity without tenderness is a paternity without authority. It is the discovery of this combination in Leopold Bloom that restores Stephen's faith in fatherhood.

But paternity must have vigor and authority too. Paternity is one aspect of a man's humanity, his capacity to fulfill his role as spouse (not only or primarily sexually) is another, and the two are intimately connected. If Wilson's reading is right, then Bloom has recovered that vigor and authority through his encounter with Stephen, which augurs well for his marriage. In Bloom the themes of masculinity, paternity, and mercy meet; *eros* and *agape*, *animus* and *anima*, are finally harmonized to produce the good and complete man. Molly realizes as much in the course of her reminiscences and reflections and repeats her yes to him before she falls asleep; and, thanks to the "sense of mercy" in Joyce's art, the reader has reason to feel included in her affirmative mood.

III.4.4.3: Mercy

We have seen that in his essay on the Renaissance, Joyce expresses indebtedness to the Renaissance, in spite of its deficiencies, for "creating in us and in our art a sense of mercy for all creatures who live, die and yield to their illusions. In this at least we are greater than the Ancients. In this, a vulgar journalist is greater than a theologian."[183] This remark allows us to approach the Joycean *oeuvre* with the concept of *mercy* as an authoritative hermeneutical key. Significantly, when Stephen in *Ulysses* makes his oft-quoted statement, "I fear those big words . . . which make us so unhappy," it is by way of response to Mr. Deasy, who has just spoken of justice: "We are a generous people but we must also be just."[184] No less significantly, Joyce sees the quality of mercy as the preserve of vulgar journalists more than theologians. Joyce's art seeks to redress a perceived absence of mercy.

We have seen in the previous chapters and in sections of this chapter Joyce's subtle presentation of the qualities he was looking for in God and how humans relate to the Divine Being. Now, we see how mercy best characterizes the way in which, according to Joyce, the Divine Being acts towards humans. Joyce sees himself as the artistic priest-mediator in this relationship. He has shown, in "Eveline" and *Portrait*, for example, the ways in which other priests, by adhering to theological distortions of sacrificial love, fail to apply mercy. But he does not want to destroy mercy; he wants rather to convey what he calls a "sense of mercy" in his art. He longs for the Father who shows mercy to his children. Without this mercy, full humanization is not possible.

It may be said at the end of our analysis that *tonally*, *technically*, and *thematically* Joyce's art contrives with consummate skill, unflinching incisive truthfulness, and unremitting mercy and magnanimity to recreate the climate—sometimes favorable, sometimes antagonistic—in which the human spirit best prospers, inviting and provoking reader participation: "tonally," because the tone is of loving enjoyment of human folly and foibles; "technically," because technique is employed to expose the treachery of forces that conspire to thwart human dynamism and dignity; and "thematically" because deep affection and admiration for the subversive charm and unassuming *caritas* embodied by the aptly named "Bloom" is the final and lasting impression of the Joycean reading experience. Joyce's art exposes the forces of stagnation, and champions human development.

Joyce's fiction veritably teems with stunted souls, whose "community" is one of paralysis and shared, quiet despair. Arrested development is the price paid by all of those who refuse to embark upon the Joycean adventure and, let it now be said, the Christian one. To prefer self and stagnation over relatedness and dynamism, moral perfectionism over merciful relationship, is to condemn oneself to a petty existence. But these beleaguered souls are never looked upon harshly. It is here that the two camps of Joycean criticism most coincide.[185]

The final, overriding Joycean effect, recognized by skeptics and believers alike, is not one of bland tolerance and indiscriminate, indulgent kindness; rather, there is a clear call, by turns gentle and vigorous, to pilgrimage and change, communication and growth. The ultimate impression created by the Joycean testament is of an immensely attractive great-heartedness, in which the reader is tempted, appealed, and challenged to participate. Mercy, which combines caress and correction, gratuity and exigency, is the climate in which identity is best achieved. The overlap between this and Christianity is self-evident, and rendered explicit in Stephen's reference to Bloom as *Christus*.[186]

A spirit of mercy and grace reigns throughout *Ulysses*, and *Ulysses* in this way builds upon earlier images and emotions in the Joyce corpus. In the ending of "The Dead" there is a sense of a paternal embrace of "all the living and the dead" who "live, die and yield to their illusions," a disposition of mercy and grace—unmerited favor—towards all human flesh. It is likely that this is what Noon wished to express when he said: "In order to be perfectly a human being, or perfectly a humanist, Joyce is saying . . . that every man and every nation need some supernatural, otherworldly, transcendent image, an image not of nature but of grace."[187] With this the Joycean anthropology would pass undoubtedly from the natural to the supernatural, but it is not at all clear that

Joyce wished to keep these spheres strictly divided. His interest in the Catholic concepts of epiphany and grace arose out of the recognition that they would aid him in his endeavour to acquire and to actualize in art a Godlike view of the human experience.

III.4.4.4: *Joyce the Godlike Artist*

Weldon Thornton questions the relativist resistance to the omniscient narrator as if this convention were symptomatic of the bygone age, now surpassed, of an omniscient God. This position is untenable because "it is doubtful that the traditional omniscient point of view ever 'stood for' or represented the mind of God."[188] Ironically, however, the *milieu* of Joyce criticism is strangely prone to claiming for Joyce a quasi-divine status. We are now in a position to examine this claim. Sheldon Brivic is the Joycean critic who has most probed the reaches of Stephen's priest-artist analogy. He makes the startling claim with impressive evidence that Joyce's ambition as "priest of the eternal imagination"[189] is to approximate with unprecedented nearness the divine omniscience, i.e., to write from and with the mind of God: "Joyce's violations of established styles, his coincidences, his external references and his sudden changes of rules are actually spiritual manifestations, positive acts Joyce performs as God."[190]

Brivic succinctly describes the Joycean authorial activity in overtly religious terms, discovering a dynamic akin to the activity that believers attribute to Divine Providence: "Joyce manifests himself as an invisible constituent of the life of his world in the form of what C. G. Jung called synchronicities." Synchronicities are "meaningful coincidences, psychic events and other violations of probability that indicate the operation of a psychic or spiritual principle." We should think of those startling little "accidents" of life that alert us to the activity of an unseen power. The phenonomen recurs throughout *Ulysses*: "Synchronicity operates in all of the literary references in the book, such as the Homeric parallels, and in all other external references, such as those to Joyce's biography."[191]

A sense of the enormity of Joyce's aesthetic ambition, and the accompanying peril of hubris, will accompany us as we follow Brivic's argument: "Joyce can represent the inner causes of his objects in language only by claiming not only omniscience, but omnipotence." Brivic conveys a sense of the complex vastness of Joyce's artistic plan, and of the virtuosic skill required for its orchestration, but suggests that this points to an infinitely greater vastness and complexity that no amount of authorial or orchestral skill can hope to master: "He must take it upon himself to change the rules of perception and being, epistemology and ontology, constantly in order to represent the dynamic presence of the unknown in life."[192]

That Joyce's purpose is to "represent the dynamic presence of the unknown in life" is a wonderful insight felicitously expressed. But to say that this requires changing the rules of ontology would entail, recalling Ratzinger's clarification, passing from one theological camp to another (i.e., from realism to relativism and/or from orthodoxy to heresy), and passing from one way of reading Joyce, the one that finds unity (albeit fragmentarily), to the dogmatic relativist and skeptical reading. This crossover is not necessary; Joyce understood that ontology, properly understood, admits the reality of mystery and respects the ultimate ever-surprising unknowability of experience.

Brivic articulates the Godlike role of the artist insofar as God and artist are organizing principles, a causal presence, in Aristotelian terms: "Aristotle, in expanding human consciousness by delineating his last two causes, was constructing the idea of God." I draw attention to Brivic's use of words like "cause" and "idea" and "system" and "definition": "His system is the backbone of the definition of God drawn up by Aquinas fifteen hundred years later."[193] The God of Christianity is more than a causal presence and organizing principle; and Joyce, like Aquinas, is more than an Aristotelian. Aristotle did not envisage loving mercy as an attribute of his Primary Cause. Joyce distances himself from a religiosity that is merely noetic. Brivic's analysis overlooks the Joycean critique of a religiosity that is primarily if not solely cerebral, systematic, and architectural. The "God" who reigns in Joyce's fiction is not the God of Aristotle or of Deism. This version of God, which discovers just some of the divine attributes—mainly those of power and intelligence—is presented as insufficient in *Portrait*.[194] In *Ulysses*, he reveals a different face—that of Father as well as Creator and Organizer.

To really understand what is happening with Divinity in *Ulysses*, we need to see it in light of the development of Joyce's thought in the works that precede it. Brivic's allusion to the Jungian term synchronicities is also helpful for reading Joyce. In *Ulysses,* as in *Dubliners* and *Portrait* before it, there is a sense of a mysterious principle at work exposing human fallibility and masterminding circumstances to facilitate, sometimes *almost* to force, human dynamism. In *Portrait* Stephen says the artist is "like" the God of creation and assumes for himself not the role of God but that of priest. The priest (excepting Christ) is not God. He is mediator between God and man by participation in the unique mediation of Christ. The artist who sees himself as priest of the eternal imagination therefore strives to represent the mind and heart of God in order to "affirm the eternal spirit of man." This would not entail supplanting or "surpassing" God.

Brivic's reading is valid and penetrating in many respects, but it imputes a prideful motivation to Joyce's creative mind: "[T]he rapidity with which he changes the rules in his later work, suggests that he was trying to surpass God."[195] In fact, Joyce's writings repeatedly expose the treachery of intellectual pride—in Fr. Flynn, Mr. Duffy, Gabriel Conroy, Stephen Dedalus—and exalt the humbler virtues. His paradigms of humaneness are rounded and gentle people. His God is the God not only of omnipotence and omniscience but, most importantly, of mercy. Of course, the fact that Joyce reveals acute awareness of the perils of intellectual pride in his fictional characters does not necessarily entail that he himself avoided it, but Brivic's hermeneutic must nonetheless be considered incomplete insofar as it neglects to account for the "sense of mercy" in Joyce's art. On the basis of this sense of mercy, it would be more accurate to say that

Joyce aspired to write not only from the omniscient and omnipotent mind of God, but also from God's merciful heart. We should recapitulate briefly the evidence supporting this, at first sight unthinkable, hypothesis.

III.4.4.5: Joyce and Fatherhood

The Joycean concern with sexual identity as reconciliation of the masculine and feminine in the self is not unrelated to the question of mercy. In fact, the discussions we have had thus far on the themes of reconciling *eros* and *agape*, *anima* and *animus*, have been important preparations for understanding mercy. Evidently mercifulness is opposed to harshness, but it is not reducible to mere indulgence or tolerance; it is a quality that combines tenderness and exigency in its desire to see the children it loves develop along lines of authentic humanization. The term "mercy" presupposes objective wrongs that require not only forgiveness but rectification. When "mercy" errs on the side of over-indulgent tolerance, out of fear perhaps of alienating the other (impelled solely by *eros*-love), it militates unwittingly against maturation, stifling growth with ill-judged kindness and tenderness; when it errs on the side of exigency (imposing or requiring *agape*-love), it is also oppressive. True mercy does not do this; harmonizing tenderness and exigency, it facilitates human maturation. Ultimately, Joyce's art strives to reunite mercy with fatherhood.

Fatherhood, biologically, and symbolically, describes the source of being, the origin of identity. If God is the source of being, apostasy entails orphanhood, deicide entails patricide, and atheism entails nomadic bastardization. This is the modern situation. In Stephen's expression it is "an age of exhausted whoredom groping for its god."[196] Joyce is presenting not only a young man without a father (Stephen) or even a nation without a leader (postcolonial Ireland); he is presenting the twentieth century crisis of a fatherless humanity. Paternity and homecoming are major Joycean themes, along with their counterparts, orphanhood, and exile. Joyce is not anti-paternity or anti-authority.

Kiberd maintains that Joyce "offered a text without any final authority."[197] But, to be anti-authoritarianism is not the same as being anti-authority. Joyce himself is the author and an author very much with something to say, especially about authorship and authority. If Joyce is a rebel, he is not a rebel without a cause. Rebelliousness for its own sake, as an endless end in itself, does not do justice to the seriousness of his artistic project. The Joycean treatment of the theme of paternity offers disconcerting questions and answers to modernity and to modernism. *Ulysses* is a prodigious meditation on the matter that goes to the very heart of the great contemporary debate: the question, and the questioning, of authority. The novel is not so much a celebration of the death of fatherhood as an exposure of false paternity and a celebration of true fatherhood.

That Joyce may be considered "father" of Stephen Dedalus, and of Leopold Bloom, is an uncontroversial truism. That he aspires aesthetically to fatherhood of all humanity is a claim with evidence in its favor, as is the claim that he set out to write with, in, and from the heart of divine mercy. We are led by the logic of the Joycean aesthetic to wonder if he aspired to fatherhood with a small "f" or a capital one. It seems improbable and inconsistent that Joyce would have aspired to attribute that fatherhood *absolutely* to himself. On the balance of probabilities, it is more likely that Joyce's war against "Catholicism" took the form of revealing to it and to the world, as Christ the only Priest did, the true face of the Father.

Joyce was not the first to defend true fatherhood, or the first to address the danger of usurpation and of reducing paternity to a legal fiction:

> The scribes and the Pharisees sit on Moses' seat . . . and they love the place of honor at feasts and the best seats in the synagogues, and salutations in the market places, and being called rabbi by men. But you are not to be called rabbi, for you have one teacher, and you are all brethern. And call no man your father on earth, for you have one Father, who is in heaven. Neither be called masters, for you have one master, the Christ. He who is greatest among you shall be your servant.[198]

If paternity (in the married or priestly life) fails to reflect its divine model and source, it remains on the level of mere biology and legal fiction, a travesty of true fatherhood. Joyce's vision may be at odds with some currents of so-called Christian spirituality, but it is not essentially alien to orthodox Catholic theology and anthropology.

III.5: Conclusion

In the course of discerning the Joycean anthropology, we have seen that there is a lot of ideological and selective reading in the ambit of Joyce studies. Joyce's depiction of human sexual behavior does include many transgressive elements, but his treatment of these is ultimately resolved in deeply conventional gender roles; i.e., in views of men, women, and human nature that conform to what popular wisdom has traditionally seen as instinctual norms. As an intelligent student of human nature Joyce, in the final analysis, does not challenge the ground rules; on the contrary, he gives them his assent.

Joyce takes positions that provide a strong index to his views on love and human nature. We have seen thought-provoking similarities between his positions and Catholic teachings in areas like homosexuality and birth control, but there are more important coincidences in the themes of paternity and mercy, the achievement of identity through relationship, and the agency of an elusive, cultivating presence. There are similarities between the divine and Joycean modes of orchestrating human individuation—*admonitio* and *delectatio,* correction and enticement—to provoke personal growth.

A complex combination of secondary circumstances and the impulses of his own soul move Bloom to go out of his way to go to Stephen's aid. This action will be decisive not only for Stephen but also for Bloom himself, for his marriage and future life. His action is a distinctly Christian initiative. Pope Benedict XVI reaffirms a perennial Catholic truth when he says that "Love is indeed 'ecstasy', not in the sense of a moment of intoxication, but rather as a journey, an ongoing exodus out of the closed inward-looking self towards its liberation through self-giving, and thus towards authentic selfdiscovery and indeed the discovery of God" (*DCE* 6). This is what Stephen learns from Bloom. In Bloom, Joyce ultimately affirms "the ordinary ecstatic." He gratuitously "goes out of himself" to help Stephen, thereby augmenting his own humanity.

Ulysses is a humanist novel in the best sense. It reflects life itself. In life too, the "alert reader" enjoys occasional epiphanical glimpses of a hidden, omnipresent Author intent on human illumination and maturation. *Ulysses* constitutes an imaginative re-enactment of the Christian notion of Divine Providence, a long-established reality succinctly expounded in the Catholic Catechism: "The witness of Scripture is unanimous that the solicitude of divine providence is concrete and immediate; God cares for all, from the least things to the great events of the world and its history" (*CCC*, no. 302). The concern of that concrete and immediate solicitude is human growth and fecundity; "life . . . abundantly" (Jn 10:10). The "sense of mercy" in Joyce's art shares common cause with this catechetical declaration about divine solicitude. Its end is authentic humanization in a climate of love that harmonizes *animus* and *anima*, *agape* and *eros*, and its *modus operandi* is reminiscent of the machinations of grace.

In addition to providing us glimpses of the providential Creator, Joyce has given us insights into the heart of the merciful Father. These realities in the writings of Joyce lead us to consider how the reality of grace is present in his writings. Grace is God's way of reaching us to make us more human and more Godlike. Joycean individuation helps us understand the way in which the merciful Father offers his mercy to heal wounded humanity. I will now focus on this common ground between the Joycean and Catholic visions, not as heretofore from the perspective of Joyce's writings and Joycean literary criticism, but from the perspective of representatives of the Catholic tradition with whom Joyce engages in his writings; namely Moses, Augustine, Aquinas, and Ignatius of Loyola. A fuller exposition of Catholic theology on grace will enable the reader better to see the common ground that actually exists between the Joycean and Catholic visions.

Chapter IV:
Judeo-Christian Individuation

IV.1: Introduction

IV.1.1: Anthropologies of Individuation

In chapter I we have seen that, philosophically, Joyce remained a realist, which would entail the possibility of ongoing contact with the Catholic tradition. In chapters II and III we have seen arguments that Joyce remains in contact with Catholicism in concrete doctrinal areas: morally, for example, in matters like homosexuality and artificial contraception; and spiritually, in matters pertaining to virtue and humaneness and the actuation of a humanizing principle in human affairs. With all of this now in the background, in this short chapter we will examine the thought of important voices of the Catholic tradition to see if there is common ground between their thinking and Joyce's on the matter of how human persons become more human. In short, we will compare and contrast the Joycean and Judeo-Christian trajectories of individuation.

In the course of delineating the distinguishing hallmarks of Joycean individuation thus far, chiefly two accusations have surfaced against Catholicism: rigidity and intellectualism. Carl Jung, as we have seen, spoke of the *logos* principle and its focus on objective understanding—associated with the male spirit—and the *eros* principle—associated with the female—with its connotations of emotional empathy and union.¹ The harsh tendencies of self-immolation without reciprocity—distorted *agape*—and intellectualism—distorted *logos*—are linked to the male in Joyce's imagination, and the Joycean worldview exalts flexibility, mercy, and dynamism against rigid moralism; and emotion, sensuality, and instinct against rigid intellectualism.

The task of this chapter is to demonstrate with reference to representatives of the Judeo-Christian tradition with whom Joyce himself engages—Moses, Augustine, Aquinas, and Ignatius—that the very characteristics which Joyce and Joyce scholarship associate with Catholicism—rigidity and intellectualism—are not to be found in these figures, and that, in fact, the dynamism and divine madness of *eros* are recurrent features in the lives and thought of these same figures. In order further to establish the Catholic and Joycean coincidence of aspiration and operation in the dynamic of human maturation, we will look at that dynamic from the Catholic perspective, as exemplified in the personalities in the Judeo-Christian tradition with whom Joyce chose to engage.

If it proves to be the case that *eros* and dynamism are present in these personalities, then Joyce's thought is closer to the Judeo-Christian tradition than the Catholicism he rejects, and the following words of praise that the twenty-one-year-old Joyce wrote of Giordano Bruno are in fact applicable also to Moses, Augustine, Aquinas, and Ignatius of Loyola: "Inwards from the material universe, which . . . did not seem to him . . . as to the Christians a place of probation, but rather his opportunity for spiritual activity, he passes, and from heroic enthusiasm to enthusiasm to unite himself with God."² Joyce's understanding seems to have been that Christianity sees the material universe solely or predominantly as a place of probation, but in fact Christianity also sees the material universe as a sacramental vehicle of grace and as an opportunity for spiritual activity and union with God.

In order to establish that the Joycean and Catholic anthropologies share a common ground, we would have to prove that there are processual and teleological affinities, i.e., similarities of means and ends. The end of Catholic anthropology is holiness, which is related to wholeness. It has three dimensions: union with God, union with neighbor, and union within the self. It is therefore religious, social and personal, and is impossible without relationship. The primary means of reaching this end is grace: "Finding himself in the midst of the battlefield man has to struggle to do what is right, and it is at great cost to himself, and aided by God's grace, that he succeeds in achieving his own inner integrity" (*GS* 37.2).

IV.1.2: The Workings of Grace

Stanislaus Joyce informs us of his brother's lifelong interest in the doctrine of grace. "The strange doctrine of actual and sanctifying grace . . . puzzled and fascinated my brother, as he had found it in his reading of St. Augustine, and even viewed from outside the Church it held his interest."³ Joyce's fascination with this particular point of Catholic doctrine, which is so closely related to the concepts of epiphany and dynamism and to the entire economy of divine intervention, rewards investigation. Joyce was interested in and understood Augustine's teaching on God's transformative action from without and from within the soul. This has important implications for understanding his literary imagination and religious position. This fact has not gone entirely unobserved in the world of Joyce scholarship.

Joyce scholar Dr. Mary Lowe-Evans, analyzing Joyce's relationship with Catholicism, observes that "on balance . . . his forays into his Catholic past, as often as not, enable rather than dismantle the institutional church, inviting an entanglement in rather than liberation from the labyrinthine ways of Catholic theological exposition."[4] Specifically, Lowe-Evans has noted the orthodoxy of Joyce's treatment of the doctrine of grace in the short story entitled "Grace" in *Dubliners*: Joyce "encourages us to consider the apparent abuses and misrepresentations of grace . . . At the same time, he conveys a thoroughly orthodox interpretation of the concept."[5] In "Grace," Mr. Kernan, an alcoholic Protestant nominally converted to Catholicism, is persuaded by his Catholic peers to attend a retreat for his conversion; the story ends with the beginning of the retreat master's sermon. Referring to himself as their "spiritual accountant," the priest invites each retreatant to "open his books, the books of his spiritual life," to be "straight and manly before God," and, if his accounts didn't tally, to say, "Well, I have looked into my accounts. I find this wrong and this wrong. But, with God's grace, I will rectify this and this. I will set right my accounts."[6]

"Grace" ends with this invitation to rectify accounts. Its title is heavily ironic. The entire story is a buildup to a fraudulent climax; a mercenary solicitation for financial contributions thinly disguised as a form of reparation for sin. Paradoxically, then, "Grace" is not a good source, except negatively, for an investigation of the influence of the doctrine of grace in Joyce's thought, because, rather than dramatizing the dynamics of grace, this particular story epiphanizes the simoniacal manipulation of the Gospel to make money, and castigates the Church with prophetic scorn for not being faithful to its own doctrine and to Christ. We have seen in other stories and in the novels, however, a dynamic that is similar to that of "Grace," and in this chapter we will see further evidence of similarity.

In fact, in the *Stephen Hero* draft of *Portrait* Joyce depicts Stephen wrestling with the temptation to realize his aesthetic "revolution"' within the Catholic tradition: "A revolution such as you desire is not brought about by violence but gradually: and, within the Church you have an opportunity of beginning your revolution in a rational manner."[7] Neither Stephen nor Joyce provides a clear answer to this temptation. In the penultimate section of this chapter, I will comment briefly on the spirituality of St. Josemaria Escriva de Balaguer. Escriva is a voice of Catholic orthodoxy and a contemporary of Joyce with whom the Irish writer does not engage, but Escriva's call to refocus on temporal, material, and quotidian realities invites suggestive comparisons (as opposed to exact parallelisms) with the Joycean project, highlighting the legitimacy of Stephen's suspicion that his apostasy may not have been necessary.

Escriva's emphasis on God's this-worldly presence and activity articulates and actualizes an aspect of Catholic teachings that seems to have been forgotten in sectors of Joyce's Irish environment and its Catholic interpretive community. Escriva's thinking on the Eucharist will also serve as a logical link from this chapter to the next and final chapter of this work, the subject of which is Joyce's treatment of the Eucharist. We will look first, though, at those figures of the Judeo-Christian tradition known to Joyce and with whom he clearly engages in his writings, beginning with Moses. Though he obviously precedes Christ, Moses is still one of the great prototypes of the biblical anthropology, a luminous point of reference for all that follows. He is prototype also—as indicated in *Ulysses*—of Leopold Bloom. That Joyce was interested in the figure of Moses is easy to demonstrate.

IV.2: Joyce's Interest in Moses

IV.2.1: Joyce's Dialogue with Ireland

Joyce leads us to consider Moses as a literary type in the Aeolus chapter of *Ulysses*. In that chapter, John F. Taylor's performance of high oratory evokes in the service of the patriotic call to insurrection and liberation clear parallels between the situation of the Israelites in Egypt and that of occupied Ireland under Britain: "[H]ad the youthful Moses . . . bowed his head and bowed his will and bowed his spirit . . . he would never have brought the chosen people out of their house of bondage . . . nor ever have come down . . . bearing in his arms the tablets of the law, graven in the language of the outlaw."[8] To "bear in his arms the tablets of the law, graven in the language of the outlaw" is a mission very dear to Stephen the young artist whose role as "priest of the eternal imagination" is to "forge the uncreated conscience of his race." His role as artist is to forge a new Irish identity that is not harsh and oppressive but confident and free.

In the Cyclops chapter of *Ulysses*, Joyce's Bloom clashes with the nationalist denizens of Barney Kiernan's pub, echoing the difficulties Moses experienced with his own Hebrew people whom God had commissioned him to liberate. Bloom is sarcastically referred to as "A new apostle to the gentiles,"[9] and utters the words, "Your God was a jew. Christ was a jew, like me," to which the nationalist "citizen" who persecuted Bloom for being charitable (defending the tormented Josie Breen[10] and voicing reservations about the use of armed force[11]) responds with threats of murder in the name of Christ: "By Jesus . . . I'll brain that bloody jewman for using the holy name. By Jesus, I'll crucify him so I will."[12] Bloom is thus likened to Moses, Christ, and St. Paul (apostle to the gentiles), suffering the same fate of persecution.

Scripture indicates that Moses was approximately Bloom's age when he fled to the desert, and his experiences at that same age are loudly echoed in the experiences of Bloom (and of Stephen) on 16 June 1904, as related in the Book of Acts 7: 23-29. No less striking than the age coincidence between Moses and Bloom is the fact that the mini-biography of Moses in the relevant passage of the Book of Acts is narrated by none other than Christianity's first martyr, namesake of Stephen Dedalus, who like Moses would choose flight and exile. Stephen the Protomartyr suffered the same fate as Moses the Lawgiver—that of rejection—just as Joyce's Bloom would suffer the same fate as his Stephen (Dedalus), namely rejection: "Now when they heard these things they were enraged, and they ground their teeth against him . . . Then they cast him out of the city and stoned him" (Acts 7:54, 58). The analogies between Stephen the martyr and Stephen Dedalus, and between Bloom and Moses, are no less rewarding of attention and unfolding than the Homeric parallels. They help us to understand the realization of Joyce's mission to forge the uncreated conscience of his race.

The liberation of the Irish from imperialist occupation, like that of the Israelites from Egypt, is not achievable solely in the sphere of the political or solely by military force. This is at most a preliminary step, and the main challenge, which is the de-colonization of the mind, remains. This was the experience of Moses, and by evoking the experience of Moses, Joyce is drawing clear parallels with his own experience. The obvious resonances between the biblical narration and Joyce's *Ulysses* suffice to establish that there is a serious and sophisticated dialogue going on between Joyce and Irish Catholics.

The Joycean aesthetic is not a matter of simple rejection of rigid rules in favor of sexual revolution. Instead, it is a complex network of conversations about what needs to be emphasized and de-emphasized and lived in order for the rebirth or the growth and maturation of a flourishing Ireland. Joyce's Ireland is passing from slavery under the Pharaoh to being an independent nation, and Joyce's question is *how can Ireland exercise a healthy self-dominion?* In the *Dubliners* stories and *Portrait*, Joyce has exposed that one bad habit a recently emancipated slave can pick up is to inherit the ex-master's heavy reliance on rules and formulas, angrily imposed under the threat of punishment. This may produce a certain initial success, but at some point there is a backlash, as occurred in the case of Moses.

IV.2.2: The Path to Plenitude

Moses began his liberating career with an act of violence, killing an Egytian overseer, only subsequently to be rejected by his own people. As Christ-like mediator between God and man, Moses will have to suffer the perversity of man's resistance to his own liberation, with the resultant diminishment of their own personhood: "Yet they acted presumptuously and . . . sinned against thy ordinances, by the observance of which a man shall live . . . Nevertheless in thy great mercies thou didst not make an end of them or forsake them" (Neh 9:29b, 31a). It is true that the Hebrew people have much to learn, but so does Moses himself, and one of the things he must learn is precisely this great mercy that will never destroy or forsake. The dominant defect of Moses is anger, and he must learn gentleness. Moses must himself undergo a process of exodus by way of preparation for his mission to lead his people on the same journey.

The spiritual journey of Moses serves as a Scriptural paradigm of all journeys of human maturation; we should therefore find in him the harmonization of the feminine and masculine that we have seen in the Joycean paradigm of the humane. And so it is. Having commenced his mission of liberation with violence and murder, Moses, over time and through much suffering, in obedience to the spirit of wisdom, acquires a paternal and maternal heart: "Now the man Moses was very meek, more than all men that were on the face of the earth" (Num 12:3). His meekness, though, does not entail emasculation: even in old age, "his eye was not dim, nor his natural force abated" (Deut 34:7b). Not unlike Leopold Bloom, the personality of Moses eventually harmonizes meekness and vigor.

In Joyce's writings we have perceived the protagonism of an elusive spirit which, alternating encouragement and correction, enables human maturation, and we have seen that for Joyce human maturation is about reconciling *anima* and *animus* in a strong and serene identity. This theme of sexual identity is neither alien nor antithetical to biblical and Catholic anthropology. St. Edith Stein is a Catholic contemporary of Joyce who has reflected on this subject and articulated the Catholic position:

> Christ embodies the ideal of human perfection: in Him all bias and defects are removed, and the masculine and feminine virtues are united and their weaknesses redeemed; therefore, His true followers will be progressively exalted over their natural limitations. That is why we see in holy men a tenderness and a truly maternal solicitude for the souls entrusted to them while in holy

women there is manly boldness, proficiency, and determination.[13]

The diverse qualities of boldness and tenderness are united in Moses. The synthesis envisaged by Stein is the culmination of a process of sanctification, the goal of life's pilgrimage. Stein's understanding of sexual identity articulates something not much considered in Joyce's Irish environment or its Catholic interpretive community; but, even so, it has demonstrable Scriptural roots. Given that he was thinking in these very terms, the veterotestamentarian harmonization of *animus* and *anima* would not have escaped Joyce's notice as he read the Moses story. In the personal maturation of Moses, Joyce found a dynamism, an openness to mystery, and a flexible docility to the Spirit that constituted a convenient corrective to the legalistic rigidity and intellectualism of the religiosity seemingly presented to him in the name of Catholicism. Positively, he found in the Moses story a support for his own belief, epiphanized in *Portrait*, in an instinct of the soul docile to the enlivening inspirations of an unnamed spiritual principle.[14] In Augustine he found an explication of the dynamics that attracted him to the figure of Moses.

IV.3: Joyce's Interest in Augustine

IV:3.1: Sensualism and Intellectualism

The depiction of the self journeying from childhood through conversion to maturity is typical of the

Bildungsroman, or coming-of-age novel, a literary genre that flourished in the 19th and 20th centuries, but which in Augustine's *Confessions* has ancient roots. This is what Hugh Kenner meant when he spoke of the *Confessions* as "the chief archetype"[15] of Joyce's *Portrait*. We know that Joyce was "puzzled and fascinated" by St. Augustine's teachings on grace and remained interested in this doctrine even after leaving the Church.[16] Even though Joyce does not make direct references to the *Confessions*, there is in his writings a clear attempt to grapple with substantive ideas that are traceable to Augustine. In chapter I of this study we have seen Thornton's presentation of self-determining individualism and over-confidence in the power of rational consciousness as typical characteristics of the Modernist Syndrome, exemplified in Stephen and critiqued by Joyce. The presence of these same characteristics in the youthful Augustine indicates that they are perennial perils of human rationality. Both Augustine, in the *Confessions*, and Stephen Dedalus, in *Portrait*, have in common that they must, in their journey towards maturity, navigate their way by the perils of sensualism and intellectualism.

Both Stephen and Augustine abandon themselves to the tide of passion at the age of sixteen. In both cases the passion for thinking, revising, and internal debate is initially presented as a key to the formation of personality as much as if not more than the influence of the external world of action, but it is a key that ultimately fails to open the way to integration. In both cases the very manner of conducting this interior debate, the *modus operandi* of thought itself, will require "conversion."

As a young adult Augustine approached the Bible with intellectual curiosity and fruitlessly: "I was not then fitted to penetrate it . . . for my swollen pride shunned their manner, and my keen wit could not penetrate their depths . . . Blown up with pride, I saw myself a great man."[17] Youthful confidence in his own intellectual prowess is an impediment rather than an advantage. When Augustine approaches the Scriptures again later in life, he has changed interiorly from a position of over-confident intellectuality to one of quiet receptivity; a change brought about by God: "Then, Lord, little by little, with most gentle and merciful hand, you touched and quieted my heart."[18]

Like Joyce's *Portrait*, Augustine's *Confessions* narrate the drama of opposition between prideful male intellectualism and feminine wisdom; the latter represented by the mother figure. Augustine's mother Monica, like Stephen's (by her death and the legacy of her love and her words), will have a role to play in the reorientation and reintegration of mind and heart. When the young, proud, and brilliant Stephen is about to depart Ireland with the mission to forge the uncreated conscience of his race, his mother prays that he may learn "in my own life and away from home and friends what the heart is and what it feels."[19] This prayer that loneliness will bring humility, contact with the heart, and true understanding, is very like something Monica might have said—probably did say, more than once, one way or another—to the young Augustine, who, like Stephen, was afflicted by something we might call cerebral gigantism, i.e., a cumbersome and over-confident intellectualism. Augustine wrote: "Did you really say nothing to me then? Whose words were they but yours, which through my faithful mother you chanted in my ears? Nothing went down compellingly to my heart."[20] Augustine's intellect, like Stephen's, will be painfully and therapeutically humbled by life experiences.

Augustine suffers the death of a friend, separation from his lover, professional insecurity, migration from one city and situation to another; all part of the divine *admonitio* and preparation of mind, will, and heart. His description of his pain and self-pity at the loss of a dear friend could be applied without substantial change to Stephen's reaction to the loss of his mother: "I wept most bitterly, but in bitterness found relief. Thus was I unhappy, but I held my unhappy life more dear than my friend himself."[21] Failure, emotional trauma, and insecurity are humbling, and humility is prerequisite to readiness to listen and receptivity. In Gabriel Conroy's humbling epiphany at the end of "The Dead," we have seen the paradoxical action of an Ariel-like "impalpable and vindictive being" from whose imminent onslaught Gabriel instinctively shrinks, but its designs are ultimately benign and affirmative.[22]

IV.3.2: Admonitio and Delectatio in the Life of Augustine

Augustine frequently describes, with paradoxical aphorisms, a similar phenomenon: "And by the hidden hand of your healing . . . the dimmed and darkened eyesight of my mind was daily healed by the stinging balm of healthy sorrows."[23] In treating Joyce's writings earlier in this study we have seen reflections of Augustine's teaching on the divine, two-pronged, gracious activity—*admonitio* and *delectatio*, admonition and enticement—and its role in shaping the person.[24] Just as Gabriel Conroy shrinks from his inexorably advancing epiphany, a part of Augustine's being instinctively shrinks from the divine *admonitio*—"the nearer it drew to me, the greater dread did it beat into me"[25]—but, just as in Gabriel's case, its fruits in the end are healing and liberating and enriching.

In the *Dubliners* stories, especially in "The Dead," there is a sense of communion with a transcendent elfish being who plays a playful part in human affairs and yet is more than a puckish muse, although mischievousness is one of its characteristics. The sense of the presence of this "being" remains and develops throughout Joyce's work, expanding, especially in *Ulysses*, to God-like proportions. We have seen in the last chapter of this work that Stephen, in *Portrait* and in *Ulysses*, like all the other actors on the stage of life that is Joyce's Dublin on the 16th of June 1904, is being "acted upon" by a mysterious force; a force of which Joyce himself is the hidden servant and seer as "priest" of the imagination. Augustine explicitly "confesses" the saving machinations of a "force" that operates in a way similar to the one epiphanized by Joyce, and to similar ends.

Augustine is the Doctor of Grace, and Joyce's fascination with his doctrine arose from its congeniality with his own entelechial anthropology. The Joycean vision of the human struggle includes the possibility of heroism and growth by cooperation with the inner motions and circumstantial manoeuvres of an invisible agency, in life's ordinary, everyday realities. Augustine's *Confessions* are an exuberant canticle of praise to the God who mercifully and ingeniously engineered his salvation, availing even of the very concrete and "coincidental" detail of a child at play chanting "pick it up and read it" as he agonized over the demands of conversion.

Joyce may have had this moment in mind when he composed the exchange between Stephen Dedalus and Mr. Deasy in *Ulysses*: Deasy affirms that, "The ways of the Creator are not our ways . . . All history moves towards one great goal, the manifestation of God," and Stephen, jerking his thumb towards the window and the noise of school children playing outside, responds, "That is God . . . A shout in the street."[26] Joyce would have been drawn to this Augustinian instance of epiphany in the apparently trivial, and in the exuberance of Augustine's praise Joyce would also have found an interesting manifestation of *eros* in contrast to the *agape*-dominated religiosity depicted in "Eveline" and *Portrait*.

The Augustinian spirituality is about mutuality and union and personal enrichment. Augustine's eventual celibacy, in contrast to Mr. Duffy's in "A Painful Case," or Leopold Bloom's in *Ulysses*, is not another instance of repressed *eros*. On the contrary, it is a case of divine *Eros* ecstatically relativizing a lesser *eros*. This is an opportune point to recall Joyce's response to his brother Stanislaus' derisory dismissal of the "misty mystics": "'They interest me . . . In my opinion, they are writing about a very real spiritual experience you can't appreciate . . . And they write about it . . . with a subtlety that I don't find in many so-called psychological novels.'"[27] Joyce found that "very real spiritual experience" in Augustine's writings too.

Unlike Stephen's retreat leader in *Portrait*, Augustine returns time and again to Scripture and to the mystery of Christ, pontiff (from *pons*; bridge) between God and man. If Augustine eventually commits himself to *agape*-love, it is because his heart has previously been seduced and conquered by *eros*-love; and *eros*—reciprocity, union, mutual possession—is the beginning and end of his relationship with the divine. The divine pursuer has alternately employed *admonitio* and *delectatio* to re-orientate and attract the soul to enter a love-alliance that combines *agape* and *eros*, giving and receiving. Clearly, *agape* purifies *eros*, restraining it from self-destructive excess, and *eros* animates *agape* by providing joyful motivation and an ecstatic unitive goal. Each enables and perfects the other. Also, the harshness of *agape*-love is sweetened by *delectatio*, and the sweetness of *eros*-love is tempered and toughened—given "saltiness" (cf. Mk 9:50)—by the disciplining action of *admonitio*. This perfective dynamic of loving mercy, which synthesizes tenderness and exigency, gentleness and vigor, empathy and authority, describes the divine action as narrated by Augustine in his *Confessions*; it also describes the "fatherly" authorial intent that we have identified in Joyce's *Ulysses*.[28] We return now to Joyce's creative relationship with Aquinas.

IV.4: Joyce's Interest in Aquinas

IV.4.1: Fascination and Reservation

Ironically, the proponent of Catholic teaching whom we will now study, St. Thomas Aquinas, is accused by Umberto Eco and others of the kind of cerebralism we have seen critiqued in Augustine's *Confessions* and in Joyce's *Portrait*. Stanislaus Joyce remarks on his brother's ambivalent fascination with the perceived unforgiving perfectionism of Catholic theology: "My brother was undoubtedly interested more in the Catholic Church than in any other organized system in Europe. He found its theologians ruthlessly logical, granting their premises, and suggestive of thought even when he did not agree with them."[29]

We have already seen Joyce's declared indebtedness, never revoked, to Thomist aesthetics. In his biography of Joyce, Richard Ellmann relates how, in a discussion about philosophy, Joyce defended that St. Thomas Aquinas was the greatest of philosophers because his reasoning was "like a double-edged sword," and how he had the custom of reading him in the original Latin, "a page a day."[30]

Ellmann mentions no other author or book that Joyce had the habit of reading daily. In the library conversation of the Scylla and Charybdis chapter of *Ulysses*, Stephen, with respect and irreverence in equal measure, invokes the authority of Aquinas, "whose gorbellied works I enjoy reading in the original."[31]

Joyce found Aquinas to be intellectually convincing, but insufficient. In his reference to mercy as the preserve more of "vulgar" journalists than of theologians (in his essay on the Renaissance) there is a note of complaint in the midst of admiration. Ruthless logic may be admirable, but it is not enough and may even be anti-human. His position therefore is one of respect, but with reservations. He admires reason—Stephen Dedalus never ceases to be profoundly intellectual, and neither did Joyce—but he sees that reason can also be a limitation and a trap.

No less a Thomist authority than Josef Pieper concedes that Joyce had a point: "[I]t must be granted that scholasticism on the whole, by virtue of its basic approach, contained within itself the danger of an over-estimation of rationality, that is, of thinking by way of arguments and conclusions."[32] Of course, the rational employment of arguments and conclusions is a sound and fecund way of thinking, but it is not the only way. Pieper develops his point: "To simplify somewhat, human reason may be over-valued in two different ways: one way is the over-valuation of experience; the other is the overvaluation of logical deduction from general principles."[33] Human reason then will always oscillate between the opposite poles of materialism and idealism, empiricism and rationalism. The danger of theological rationalism that, according to Pieper, always threatens the Scholastic approach is twofold: to put God in a box and to put man in a box, i.e., to catalogue the divine and the human experience.

The perhaps inevitable solution, Pieper says, would be to focus on the factual and abandon the metaphysical: "[A]fter the tremendous intellectual effort of the century of the *Summa*, a certain weariness, a lack of energy for putting ideas in order, and probably a certain impatience with the system-building efforts of speculative philosophy, were only to be expected."[34] Joyce describes this weariness in his essay on the Renaissance.[35] He also identifies and describes the reaction against it: after rationalism, materialism—the pendulum effect. He perceived and rejected this error. In this same essay he laments that the "skin has replaced the soul in modern man,"[36] and in his essay on Blake he dismisses the pretensions of materialism as a response to idealism: "If we must accuse of madness every great genius who does not believe in the hurried materialism now in vogue with the happy fatuousness of a recent college graduate in the exact sciences, little remains for art and universal philosophy."[37]

IV.4.2: Defending Thomism

It should be noted in his defense that St. Thomas is before all else a mystic, caught up in the divine madness as a youth and paying the price of a year of imprisonment for it. Intense emotion is very much part of his every thought about God. Supernatural charity is palpable in everything Aquinas produces when it is read in the climate in which it is written, which is that of faith. The separation of knowledge from passion and emotion, wisdom from love, the knowable True from the desirable Good, is not a feature of the Gospel or of the Catholic tradition.[38] As Robin Young puts it, "In Christian philosophy and theology, not only does the human being long for the Good; the Good longs for man, too—as the narrative of salvation attests."[39]

The climate of Catholic theology, therefore, is one of

interpersonal love-driven search, and dialogue: "[W]ithout prayer there was no theology, which was really, at its core, the conversation of lovers."[40] The pursuit of truth occurs in a context not solely or primarily of study and analysis, but of relationship and dialogue. When Aquinas seeks with his reason to understand the truth he admires and is fascinated by, he is at the same time seeking with his will to unite himself to the Good he loves and worships, because he knows, Etienne Gilson points out, that "every act of knowledge supposes that the object known becomes present in the knowing subject."[41] When the object known is a personal incarnate God, science is subsumed into mysticism. Theological knowledge, then, is not about intellectual conquest and control; it is about mystical mutual inhabitation: God in the soul and the soul in God. In a word, it is about *eros*.

For Thomas, and for Augustine, and Catholic orthodoxy always, the Incarnation is not just an historical, in the sense of a *past*, event; it is historical in the sense of being perennially present: in Christ eternity has irrupted with all its transformative power and continues to irrupt daily, into time. And time, in turn, is perennially transmutable into and teleologically projected towards eternity. There is no indicator in the account of Stephen's conversion in *Portrait* that he knew this as a Catholic doctrine, at least not in all its scandalous incarnational immediacy and realism. Stephen in *Portrait* comes to know God the Creator, God the Organizer, but not the God of *eros* and *agape*. As we have seen, he experienced science-knowledge of the divinity, not faith-knowledge.[42]

However, despite the undeniable continuity of thought between Augustine and Aquinas in the Catholic tradition, the theological language of Aquinas does not contain the overt emotional power and existential intensity of the *Confessions*. Given the emotive restlessness described by Joyce as a feature of the Renaissance and the Modern age, it seems that, in order to make theology contemporarily relevant, it was necessary to recover the existential reference and the personal emotional charge so powerfully present in the writings of Luther, Kierkegaard, and Augustine's *Confessions*.

Neo-Thomist theologian Aidan Nichols, referring to the reaction against Thomism in early 20th century theology, expressed the challenge well: "Whereas for Thomists Thomas had improved on the *modus operandi* of patristic thought, for the [20th century] neopatrologists he had introduced a method that was too systematic and over-intellectual." Theology in general (like Joyce) reacted against this: "What was wanted was a more poetic, holistic theology full of person-to-person appeal."[43] Though not a Joyce scholar, Nichols thus adds to the accumulation of testimonies from diverse sources (one of whom is Joyce) confirming the sense of a theological hiatus and an eclipse of *eros* that needed to be redressed.

IV.4.3: Redressing the Theological Hiatus

But Nichols, referring to what he calls the "potted Scholasticism" that prevailed in Joyce's era, clarifies that this perception did not really do justice to Thomism, speaking of "a want of the imagination that alone could translate these ideas into other idioms of reflection and experience." Having noted the shortcomings of decadent Scholasticism, Nichols proceeds to describe the corrective concerns of the 20th century Thomistic renaissance: "[D]istinguishing features of the new movement include a self-conscious guarding against 'woodenness' in expression, and a desire to integrate the philosophy more thoroughly within an essentially theological vision."[44]

Now, with the benefit of a century of hindsight, Catholic thinkers begin to recognize, and sometimes even to overstate, the inevitable limitations of Thomism. Dr. Peter Huff, for example, has described the tensions between the classical and modern ways of doing theology. Huff's description of the *Nouvelle Theologie* of the 20th century is unerring: "The 'new theology' explored another side of religion: the intersection of nature and grace in concrete life situations."[45] This last clause would serve as a good description of Joyce's epiphanies. Huff's description of the second Vatican Council's task of harmonizing the classical and modern ways of doing theology sounds not altogether unlike the Joycean project: "Drawing from the more poetic outlook of Scripture and patristic literature, the movement sought to understand the drama of faith in the dynamic contexts of historical change and human experience."[46]

Incorporation of the personal, emotional, and existential struggle is a necessary feature of the contemporary theology that attempts to build upon the Thomist contribution, availing of its perennial evangelical potential. We have seen Joyce's essay on the Renaissance concerning the need to unite the power of Scholasticism with the counterpower of the Renaissance.[47] This would mean reintegrating skin and soul, that is, body and spirit, intellectuality and emotion, in a more holistic vision and expression of human personhood, without minimizing the great drama of human fallibility, struggle, and uncertainty.

Joyce's art, as interpreted on the basis of textual evidence in chapter III of this work, epiphanizes the daily drama of the human struggle without ultimately compromising in the areas of theological and anthropological truths. As Levy points out, Joyce was not among those who reacted with unequivocal negativity towards the Scholastic contribution or with unequivocal enthusiasm towards the Enlightenment; he would combat "with drawn sword" the foolish optimism of modernism. But he would add "a new personal experience," to use the words he gives to Stephen in *Portrait*, to the Thomist achievement: "So far as this side of esthetic philosophy extends, Aquinas will carry me all along the line[48] . . . When we come to the phenomena of artistic conception, artistic gestation, and artistic reproduction I require a new terminology and a new personal experience."[49]

Joyce's relationship with Thomas, and with Catholicism, is not one of radical and total separation. There is continuity in the essentials. Joyce's "Catholic categories"—epiphany and ontology, the workings of grace, the Eucharist—demonstrate that he is not as far from the essential Catholic position as is commonly supposed. What Eco calls the "Joycean Thomism" does not demand a total discarding of the religious dimension or even of the Thomist theology; rather, it recognizes the necessity to discover anew the ever-surprising protagonism of mystery in the ordinary personal present, a project that is entirely consonant with the Thomist one. Next, we will discern if, despite initial discouraging signs, there might be a possibility of continuity between the Joycean project and the Ignatian spirituality.

IV.5: Joyce's Interest in Saint Ignatius

IV.5.1: Jesuitical Intellectualism and Rigidity

So far in this chapter we have approached the Moses story, Augustine, and Thomas with a view to discerning the outcome of Joyce's engagement with these voices of the Catholic tradition. In general, we have found continuity in essentials, and misunderstandings and discrepancies on the surface. A trajectory of increasing negativity may also be identified: Joyce's engagement with the Moses story is explicit and positive; his engagement with Augustine is implicit and largely positive; his engagement with Aquinas is explicit and ambivalent, perhaps more positive than negative; and his engagement with the Jesuits is also explicit, but largely negative. Moses and Augustine can scarcely be accused of rigidity and intellectualism, and such criticisms are at most partially valid in the case of Aquinas. Those same criticisms arise again in Joyce's treatment of the Jesuits.

In his biography, Richard Ellmann relays Joyce's positive remarks concerning his Jesuit teachers: from them he had learned "how to arrange things in such a way that they become easy to survey and to judge."[50] Mary Lowe-Evans, referring to the Joycean portrayal of his

Jesuit formation, states that: "The implication is clear. To be brought up in a Jesuit college is to be intellectually superior to the ordinary Protestant and even the ordinary Catholic."[51] This deduction, although it contains a strong element of accuracy, misses the point in the way that it was missed by Ellmann when he wrote: "If Joyce retained anything from his education, it was a conviction of the skill of his Jesuit masters, the more remarkable because he rejected their teaching. 'I don't think you will easily find anyone to equal them,' he said long afterwards."[52]

Here there is a fundamental misreading of Joyce's position: it was not *in spite of* the impressive intellectual thoroughness of his religious formation that Joyce initially rejected Catholicism, it was *because of* it; this intellectuality is critiqued and rejected by Joyce. He sees it as a hyper-masculine, anti-natural exaggeration of *logos* and *agape* that asphyxiates *eros* and the "impulses of my nature."[53] Even in his words of praise—they taught him how to "arrange" and "survey" and "judge"—there is a vague hint of backhanded compliment. These words are heavily weighted in the direction of discipline and order and, like the Joycean portrayal of Thomist cerebralism, suggest ruthless intellectual precision at the expense of natural vitality and emotional freedom. The accusation against the Jesuits is similar if not identical to the one leveled at Aquinas: intellectualism. Jesuit spirituality—more derisively and perhaps aptly called "Jesuitical"—denotes a neurotic obsessiveness with order. It is *agape* without *eros*; joyless, unrequited self-immolation; all head and no heart. To refute this, it is necessary to demonstrate that what is portrayed is not, in fact, Jesuit spirituality.

Let us turn now to *Portrait of the Artist* to see how Joyce depicted Jesuits and his understanding of their spirituality. Just before Stephen's interview with the college director in which he is invited to consider a vocation to the priesthood, we are privy to Stephen's interior reminiscences about his Jesuit teachers. The portrayal of Stephen's teachers in this passage is at first glance gracious and benign. There is a sense of magnanimous gratitude towards masters whose education by word and deed has been helpful but limited and now surpassed. But there is also a hint of dehumanization in the figures contemplated; an impoverishment of humanity in the direction of mechanical rigidity and uniformity—"men who washed their bodies briskly with cold water and wore clean cold linen"[54]—a diminishment of individuality and flexibility that ends in products more than persons. There is also a sense in the language at the end of the passage that this world is something he is going to leave behind or grow out of. It is going to become a foreign world to him.

This intuition crystallizes in his interview with the college director about his vocation. Wisdom, Stephen comes to understand as he reflects on the interview afterwards, is best achieved in solitude and autonomy; and obedience is antithetical to freedom: "His destiny was to be elusive of social or religious orders . . . He was destined to learn his own wisdom apart from others or to learn the wisdom of others himself wandering among the snares of the world."[55] A third passage, in chapter five, describes the Jesuit dean of studies at the university. At this point Stephen has effectively broken with Catholicism: "Like

Ignatius he was lame but in his eyes burned no spark of Ignatius's enthusiasm . . . *Similiter atque senis baculus*, he was, as the founder would have had him, like a staff in an old man's hand."[56]

IV.5.2: Ignatian Enthusiasm

Here as above, albeit with less subtlety, Stephen's perception of the dean of studies depicts a man stunted in his humanity by fidelity to the Rule of St. Ignatius, a man with no spark of enthusiasm, no fire of apostolic energy; a man without love, mechanically committed to obedience and silent service. The word "enthusiasm," as a wordsmith like Joyce would have known, proceeds from the Greek "theos" meaning God. A Jesuit who has lost the "enthusiasm" of his founder, therefore, cannot be said to be "as the founder would have had him." If enthusiasm is gone, God is gone. The insinuation here, frequent throughout the history of Christianity,[57] is that religious obedience instrumentalizes and diminishes the human person. Interpreters generally pick up on this insinuation and go no further, but the fact that Joyce (Stephen) distinguishes between the Jesuit dean of studies and Ignatius himself—"in his eyes burned no spark of Ignatius's enthusiasm"[58]—is a hint that Joyce's critique is aimed not at religion itself but at a degenerate religiosity which has "abandoned the love you had at first" (Rev 2:4).

There is another indicator that Joyce understood that Stephen's critique of the Jesuits was a critique of a distortion of the teaching of Ignatius. When Stephen, while contemplating the movements of the university dean, makes passing reference to the "fabled books of secret subtle wisdom,"[59] it is logical to suppose that the Spiritual Exercises of Ignatius would feature in first place among these books. There is an inconsistency here in Stephen's thought, given that the third chapter of *Portrait* narrates his terrifying experience of a three-day "Spiritual Exercises" retreat which preached little else but eternal damnation. St. Ignatius proposes that meditation for one day, in a context of a four-week retreat. This contrast suggests that "secret subtle wisdom" has degenerated into gross clumsiness, and that Joyce's depiction of the Jesuits in *Portrait* is an accurate depiction of an inaccurate spirituality. It is this misrepresentation that I wish to address, by explicating the centrality of religious *eros* in the thought of Ignatius, connected to his understanding of religious obedience.

Obedience, for Ignatius, is an act of love that leads to union with God: "Obedience is a holocaust, in which man in his entirety, without interior division, offers himself in the fire of charity to his Creator and Lord through the hands of his ministers."[60] The finality of religious obedience is nothing less than the fullness of divine filiation and the indwelling of the Trinity in the soul: "If a man loves me, he will keep my word, and my Father will love him, and we will come to him and make our home with him" (Jn 14:23). It was in the Eucharist more than anywhere else that Ignatius was swept up in the vortex of the Trinitarian circuminsession. He is a witness of Eucharistic *eros* and enthusiasm: "Then, suspended midway or over mid-way in the Mass . . . alternating between great fire and water . . . many motions and tears come to me, and intermittently, for prolonged periods of time, great commotions, sobs and effusions of tears."[61]

In faith, Ignatius perceived obedience as a way of ecstasy, of going out of self into union with the divine. His spirituality, therefore, is marked by intelligent docility (which is essential to the "divine madness" of obedience) rather than by rigidity and intellectualism. What I have called the "mysterious principle" in Joyce's writings, never explicitly named but always at work within and around his fictional characters, provoking and facilitating a perfective dynamism—the principle which Stephen and Bloom "instinctively" obey—is not alien to the "principle" that Catholics call God. The life of Ignatius was devoted, after conversion, to cooperation with this "principle," and the Ignatian Spiritual Exercises are designed to create the conditions for intelligent and joyful surrender to it.

IV.5.3: The Ignatian Journey

The purpose and goal of the Ignatian Spiritual Exercises is stated at the beginning of the first week, under the title "Principle and Foundation." Far from frustrating human personhood with stagnating formulae, the Ignatian vision provokes man to growth, preparing him to undergo maximal apparent insecurity by relativizing all things in favor of the one authentic but invisible security that is God: "[M]an should avail of them insofar as they aid him in the achievement of his end, and should put them aside insofar as they impede him from doing so."⁶² Faith is the most intelligent and adventurous of risks. Man is called to a continual exodus out of self into self-fulfillment via communication with the divine Other and human others. He is challenged to live by the power of grace in the ambit of the humanly impossible—the divine will—and thereby to become fully human and to become divine by participation.

The climax of the Exercises is in the famous Ignatian prayer of total self-surrender in the fourth and final week: "Take, Lord, and receive all my liberty, my memory, my understanding and my entire will, all that I have and possess; it was You who gave it to me, to You, Lord, I return it; it's all Yours now, dispose of it according to Your will; give me Your love and grace, that is enough for me."⁶³ Ignatius perceived this moment not as a passive dehumanizing instrumentalization of the person but as an active holocaust of love in the form of self-donation to the Divine Persons by way of response to the discovery of the self-donating holocaust of God to the soul in Christ. The moment (just described) of radical and total detachment or inner freedom, of relativization of the relative in its multiplicity of forms and absolutization of the one and only Absolute, is preceded by three weeks of daily meditation in silence on the mysteries of faith: creation, sin, judgment, the Incarnation of Christ and his public life, his Passion, death and Resurrection, the mission of his Apostles and disciples.

Love finally, climactically, knows and responds to Love in a dynamic of mutual surrender, belonging, and inhabitation. The divine *Eros* for man expresses itself in the form of total *Agape*, thereby inviting, awakening, and enabling an ecstatic human love for God which also combines *eros* and *agape*. It is this element of *eros* that is notably absent from the story "Eveline" and other Joycean depictions of religiosity, including those of *Portrait*. The dynamic may not have been articulated in *eros-agape* terms in Joyce's time; it took the sharp challenges of Nietzsche to provoke their precise articulation, but the concepts are already present, and Joyce knew it to be a teaching of the Catholic tradition. He had discovered it and recognized it as a "very real spiritual experience" in the teachings of the "misty mystics" derided by his brother Stanislaus.[64]

Ignatius' personal journey took him, like Moses, Peter, Paul, James, and John (the *Boanerges* brothers), from violent beginnings to consummate, contemplative gentleness, without loss of vigor; a combination familiar to Joyce readers. The aging Ignatius affectionately scolded diminutive flowers, urging them to be quiet because they spoke to him so movingly of God;[65] a gesture with implications beyond the merely anecdotal, reminiscent of the theology of Molly Bloom who saw nature, specifically flowers, as a proof of God.[66] This is the same man who commenced his spiritual journey with homicidal impulses towards a Muslim who dared to cast doubt upon the virginity of Mary.[67] The Ignatian Exercises are consummately crafted to enable life, and their fruits are visible in the life of their author, fruits of maturity which Joyce, judging from what we have seen of the values he extols, would have admired.

The true Ignatian spiritual theology is about total trusting surrender to and active collaboration with the mysterious dispositions of a humanizing "principle" similar in its means and ends to the one that operates in the human experience as depicted in Joyce's fiction. We have already identified similarities of operation and aspiration. It is Godlike in its *modus operandi* and its *telos*; i.e., in the way it works and in the end towards which it works. This vital principle is remarkable by its *absence* in the Joycean portrayal of Jesuitry. Magisterial developments during Joyce's own lifetime and afterwards have clarified and responded to the challenges Joyce faced without contradicting previous teachings or introducing essentially incompatible concepts. In the next section we will see how, in areas like explaining *eros* and *agape* and uniting the sacred and the profane, Catholic orthodoxy has dealt with what I have called the theological hiatus of Joyce's epoch, in a way that combines creativity and continuity.

IV.6: Tradition as Creativity and Continuity

IV.6.1: Eros and Agape in the Recent Magisterium and in Joyce

Pope Benedict XVI's first encyclical, on divine love, articulates the harmonization of *eros* and *agape*. What Pope Benedict XVI describes as "the divine *eros* for man" culminates in the divine *agape* for man (without ever ceasing to be *eros* also; i.e., the loving desire to possess, to enjoy communion with the other), which in turn awakens the human *eros*, and then also *agape*, for God and for neighbor. This is what Benedict meant when he wrote that, "The Eucharist draws us into Jesus' act of self-oblation" (*DCE* 13). We are drawn in by the healing power of God's love in Christ and then capacitated to pour out that same healing love with Him to others, so that *eros* and *agape* are combined: "And all the crowd sought to touch him, for power came forth from him and healed them all" (Lk 6:19). Joyce's art attempts to actualize this same dynamic. Joyce's main theme is love, but his thinking about love is not at odds with Benedict's.

Disagreement among Joyce interpreters is attributable, at least partly, to the fact that Joyce is not as ideologically conditioned as many of his readers. Underlying secular humanism is the notion that the idea of God is an impediment to self-realization. The revelation of God as love exposes this opposition as a fallacy. It is in communion that man, as a religious and social being, achieves fullness: "[M]an, who is the only creature on earth which God willed for itself, cannot fully find himself except through a sincere gift of himself" (*GS* 24); "Whoever follows after Christ, the perfect man, becomes himself more of a man" (*GS* 41). Since God became Man in Christ, deification and humanization are synonyms. When man responds sacramentally and existentially to God's condescension in Christ, incorporation and ascension to God become available to him, and union with others. This is the "enthusiasm" of St. Ignatius: semantically and otherwise impossible without communion with a God who is love and life—not the sole preserve of the founder, but his perennially life-giving legacy to all of those who drink faithfully (in both senses of the term) from the sources he left to posterity.

The Ignatian Spiritual Exercises are crafted to cultivate in the soul the readiness required for the pilgrimage toward mutual possession. The spirit of combat and change has characterized Christian spirituality from its beginnings and remains part of the spiritual doctrine of the Catholic Church:

> This dramatic situation of 'the whole world [which] is in the power of the evil one' makes man's life a battle: The whole of man's history has been the story of dour combat with the powers of evil, stretching, so our Lord tells us, from the very dawn of history until the last day. Finding himself in the midst of the battlefield man has to struggle to do what is right, and it is at great cost to himself, and aided by God's grace, that he succeeds in achieving his own inner integrity.[68]

These words aptly describe the milieu in which Stephen Dedalus and Leopold Bloom must forge their identity and in which Bloom's *caritas* shines out with Christ-like force. We have seen that Joyce was not an acritical champion of unmitigated *eros* and that his eventual anthropology, in *Ulysses*, combines *eros* and *agape*.

Nor was Joyce an unreflecting enemy of *agape* in his own life. Stanislaus Joyce describes his brother's capacity for martyr-like *agape* commitment to an ideal even after apparent apostasy: "Not only was he still capable of setting an ideal aim above his happiness and his career; such an unquestioning sacrifice was even essential to his character."[69] Joyce's dedication to his craft in the midst of tremendously adverse circumstances and personal sufferings, at the cost of exhausting effort, did in fact border on the martyrial, as we know also from Ellmann's biography. Joyce's stories and novels were produced in conditions of extreme financial insecurity, constant migration from one apartment to another, one city to another, one country to another; in later life, though financially more secure, he had to deal with the commonplace upheavals of a war-torn Europe. Later still, he suffered with a gradual and painful blindness, and the even more painful mental illness of his daughter Lucia, whose "episodes," in spite of many and varied remedies, steadily increased in frequency and intensity until, eventually, she was definitively committed to an institution of psychiatric care.

Such tireless exertion on Joyce's part in itself calls for inquiry as to the cause that motivated it. Perhaps such religious zeal was provoked by and devoted to a cause not altogether irreligious. He remarked to Valery Larbaud that it might be the "influence of *ad maiorem dei gloriam*,"[70] by which, as self-defined "priest of the eternal imagination,"[71] he may have meant exactly what he said. Although likely to stir protestations from secularist Joyceans, the possibility cannot easily be discounted. Joyce was not a secularist.

The reconciliation of *eros* and *agape* is one major Joycean theme; the reconciliation of the sacred and the profane is another. Both themes are essential to what Joyce perceives as healthy, humanizing individuation. We have seen already that Benedict's thinking on the subject of *eros* and *agape* builds upon the reflections of thinkers like Pieper and Lewis. On the subject of reconciling the sacred and the profane, St. Josemaria Escriva de Balaguer is arguably one of the most important Catholic voices of the 20th century.

IV.6.2: Joyce and Escriva

IV.6.2.1: Uniting the Sacred and the Profane

Escriva is a Catholic interlocutor whose spirituality may be introduced connaturally to the Joycean discussion because, like Joyce, he relates the "ordinariness" of the Eucharist to those fleeting epiphanies of divine truth and love in the secular realities which all too often go unnoticed, in a way that coincides with, and responds to, Joyce's abhorrence of an exclusivist monopolization of the sacred by the guardians of the temple. As a partial contemporary of Joyce who faced similar challenges, it is illuminating to put them in dialogue with one another.

Joyce sought to overcome repression and open a way to human fullness, epiphanizing the actuations of a humanizing principle in ordinary life and ordinary people. He turned to the Eucharist, as we will see in detail in the next chapter, to show that an ordinary meal, in the midst of human limitations, can be an image of a greater reality. Escriva, in re-vitalizing the universal call to holiness, also held up the ordinariness of the Eucharistic species of bread and wine as a proof that the divine is present in commonplace realities.

It is eyebrow-raising that an immanentist humanist like Richard Ellmann should choose the title "Towards Lay Sanctity" for a chapter in his book, *Ulysses on the Liffey*.

It seems safe to say that Ellmann's understanding of the word "sanctity" would have little to do with the Catholic understanding of that same word, but one wonders what it might be about Joyce's prose that prompted Ellmann to think along such lines. It would not be overly farfetched to imagine that Ellmann's choice of words suggests that "laity" is *contrary* to what Catholicism typically considers sanctity. But Escriva's description of "lay sanctity" may not, in fact, be so far from Joyce's understanding of how the divine works in the profane, this-worldly realities.

In 1968 *The Furrow* published a homily given the previous year by Escriva under the title, "Passionately Loving the World," in which he repeats and summarizes a doctrine he has insisted upon against "false spiritualisms," as he himself puts it, for forty years.[72] The homily begins with and returns to the mystery of the Eucharist, which he calls "the most sacred and transcendent act which man, with the grace of God, can carry out in this life." However, this act is distorted, "whenever men have tried to present the Christian way of life as something exclusively *spiritual*, proper to *pure*, extraordinary people, who remain aloof from the contemptible things of this world, or at most tolerate them as something in necessary juxtaposition to the spirit."[73]

Escriva often described himself as anticlerical, for love of the priesthood: "From his seminary days . . . he had been repelled by the clericalism that characterized large parts of the Spanish Church."[74] The clericalist distortion of Christianity leads to sacerdotal mystification and religious aristocratism, to the detriment of lay (and priestly) spirituality: "When things are seen in this way, churches become the setting *par excellence* of the Christian life." This gives rise to a false dichotomization of temple and marketplace, of the sacred and the secular, the holy and the profane. Two distinct worlds are formed, each opposed to or at best separated from the other: "And being a Christian means going to church, taking part in sacred ceremonies, being taken up with ecclesiastical matters, in a kind of segregated *world*, which is considered to be the ante-chamber of heaven, while the ordinary world follows its own separate path."[75] By way of antidote to this distortion, Escriva proposes a "Christian materialism."

IV.6.2.2: A Christian "Materialism"

Escriva wishes to flatly reject this deformed spiritualist vision of the Eucharist and of Christianity. He employs terms familiar to us after reading Joyce: "[T]here is something holy, something divine hidden in the most ordinary situations, and it is up to each one of you to discover it . . . We discover the invisible God in the most visible and material things. There is no other way."[76] To negate the material and the secular would be neither natural nor supernatural but *anti-natural* and therefore anti-human and anti-Catholic: "That is why I can tell you that our age needs to give back to matter and to the most trivial occurrences and situations their noble and original meaning."[77]

This insistence on physicality and practicality is to be found in St. Teresa also, who spoke of God being found "among the pots and pans"[78] of everyday life. It is essential to the authentic Christian tradition. The doctrine of the Incarnation precludes both immanentism and spiritualism, as Escriva insists: "We can, therefore, licitly speak of a *Christian materialism*, which is boldly opposed to those materialisms which are blind to the spirit."[79] We have seen that Joyce's "materialism" is by no means blind to the spirit. Escriva's description of the disposition required of Catholics living in "the hustle and bustle of the workaday world," recalls the Dedalan (and Aquinan) interest in everyday epiphanies of *claritas*: "Blended into the mass of their companions, they try at the same time to detect the flashes of divine splendour which shine through the commonest everyday realities."[80]

We will see in the next chapter that Joyce availed of Catholic teachings on the Eucharist to invest *Ulysses* with a sacred, or quasi-sacred, significance. Escriva, in a way similar to Joyce, sees the Eucharist as the apotheosis of sacramental elevation of the apparently trivial and banal. Escriva refers his "materialist" vision to the mystery of the Eucharist. The Eucharist is a sacred, transcendental act, but it is also plain and simple *matter*. He advocates a *profane* spirituality; a spirituality that is alive and alert outside as well as inside the temple: "Leave behind false idealisms . . . Instead turn seriously to the most material and immediate reality, which is where our Lord is."[81] It was Christ himself, according to Catholic doctrine, who invested the Eucharistic Mystery with visceral, flesh and blood realism.

Joyce was drawn to the Eucharist because he saw coalesce there the themes that most interested him: the search of the son for the father, the union of bride and bridegroom, the union of the sacred and the profane, of the material and the spiritual, of body and soul. Like no other writer, he would harness these Eucharistic teachings artfully to vitalize and enrich the mundane and the quotidian with subtle resonances of the sublime. One thinks of Bloom's Eucharistic encounters with Stephen when one reads Escriva's insistence that "discovering that 'divine something' contained in these details, finds a special place in that vital sphere in which human love is enclosed."[82]

IV.6.3.3: Joyce's Ireland and Escriva's Spain

Escriva and Joyce responded to somewhat similar situations in somewhat similar ways. Some parallels can be identified between the fortunes of Catholicism in Spain and its fortunes in Ireland during the respective (and partly contemporaneous) lifetimes of Escriva and Joyce. Ireland passed from a period of anti-Catholic religious persecution through the trauma of famine to emerge into a period of political autonomy and the apparent triumph and prosperity of Catholic spirituality. Spain passed from a situation of political turbulence and decadence, in its colonies and at home, in the 19th century, to one of increasing anti-Catholic hostility, culminating in a civil war from which, apparently, Catholicism emerged triumphant. In both countries a politicization of faith occurred in reaction to persecution. In Ireland the persecuting forces were not indigenous. Ireland had a war of independence closely followed by a civil war, Spain underwent a civil war, but the dynamics and results were not entirely dissimilar.

In the closing paragraphs of an article on Catholicism in Spain in the 1920s, Dr. Federico Requena speaks of the need "to overcome a certain clericalism," and of a "fracture established, in some Catholics, between spiritual life and temporal action." He attributes that fracture to the influence of liberal propaganda promoting the "total fracture between faith and activity in the public sphere."[83] To this it might be added that the tendency to bifurcate the spiritual life and temporal action is a perennial danger inherent in Christianity without the influence of liberalism. It is addressed frequently in the Gospels. Similarly, the temptation to confuse political, economical and spiritual messianism is as old as the Gospel itself.

James Joyce's life coincided, approximately, with the time of crisis in Ireland, and St. Josemaria Escriva's with the time of crisis in Spain. Both men knew and abhorred clericalism, and both responded to it in diverse and comparable ways. In both countries the social mainstream became politically Catholic and an embittered defeated liberal and anticlerical minority turned more anti-Catholic than before. Although on the surface it may seem that "Catholicism won," it never wins when it is politicized. Joyce did not align himself unequivocally to the mainstream or to the minority; rather, there is evidence that he sought aesthetically to subvert a perceived politicoclerical oligarchy and to champion the presence of the sacred in the secular. *Mutatis mutandis*, Escriva labored for the same goal. His theology of the mystical life in the midst of the secular realities is an evangelical antidote to the danger of a Catholicism reduced to ideology.

This comparison should not be pushed beyond very

narrow limits, but the extent of the likeness, however limited, does reinforce the impression—hinted at also by Pope Benedict XVI and overtly argued by others as we have seen in chapter II—that Catholicism in parts of Europe in the late 19th and early 20th centuries was subject to a two-pronged assault on its holistic, sacramental vision of reality: on the one hand, an aversion to the material proper to Puritanism, and on the other hand, an aversion to the supernatural typical of liberal secularism.[84] Otherwise Escriva would not have felt the urgent need to redress this imbalance by re-affirming the Catholic sacramental synthesis of the spiritual and the profane. If the synthetic interpretation of Stephen's exclamation—"'Heavenly God!' . . . in an outburst of profane joy"—is correct, then Joyce perceived a similar need and Escriva's spirituality is an aid to discern the motivating factors underlying the Joycean project and to provide an orthodox Catholic response to Joyce's questions and critiques. On the subject of everyday epiphanies, at least, the two would have had grounds for interesting discussion.

IV.7: Conclusion of Chapter IV

For all five of the paradigms of Judeo-Christian anthropology that we have briefly studied—Moses, Augustine, Aquinas, Ignatius, Escriva—temporal existence is not only a time and place of probation, but also one of enthusiastic opportunity, and to each one of them without exception Joyce's own admiring description of Giordano Bruno as a "God-intoxicated" man could readily be applied: "Inwards from the material universe,

. . . his opportunity for spiritual activity, he passes, and from heroic enthusiasm to enthusiasm to unite himself with God."[85] There is abundant textual corroborative evidence that Joyce sought artistically to associate the material universe with spiritual activity and union with God. He was interested in mystical *eros* and enthusiasm. But was it Joyce's project to secularize the Catholic mysteries? Was Joyce an immanentist or pantheist, a disbeliever in God as a transcendental Being?

In his encyclical letter *Pascendi*, Pius X remarks upon the difficulty of defining what is meant by immanentism. The Pontiff identifies three versions of immanentism. One version, secularism, simply denies the supernatural order. Another version, instead of denying the supernatural order and naturalizing everything, denies the natural order and pantheistically supernaturalizes everything. There is a version of immanentism, however, that has an orthodox interpretation: "Some understand it in the sense that God working in man is more intimately present in him than man is in even himself, and this conception, if properly understood, is free from reproach"

Much later, Pope John Paul II elaborated on God's simultaneous transcendence and immanence, explaining that the Triune God is "wholly transcendent" regarding the "visible world," but is also "present in it, and in a sense immanent, penetrating it and giving it life from within." This immanent presence of the transcendent God in the visible world acquires a special intimacy in relation to the human person: "God is present in the intimacy of man's being, in his mind, conscience and heart: an ontological and psychological reality, in considering which St. Augustine said of God that he was 'closer than my inmost being'" (*Dominum et vivificantem* 54).

Does Joyce's vision respect the distinction as well as the mutuality of the immanent and transcendental realms? The merciful actuations epiphanized in Joyce's writings, which so intelligently combine *admonitio* and *delectatio* to effect humanization, bespeak a transcendental and personal Being that is present and operative in immanent reality but that is also irreducibly distinct from it. The ingenuity and unpredictability of its operations testify to a principle that is indefinable by immanentist categories, *beyond* human comprehension, and transcendental. Its readiness medicinally to confound and perfect natural inclinations and expectations suggests that Joyce's art is more than an aesthetic laicization of Christianity or naturalization of religion.[86]

Stanislaus mentions his brother's brief flirtation with pantheistic theosophy: "Theosophy may have been the only intellectual adventure of his nonage that he regarded as pure waste of energy."[87] But Joyce certainly found interlocutors in the Catholic tradition with whom he maintained a dialogue that interested him, in the areas of grace and growth, dynamism and pilgrimage, *eros*, ecstasy, epiphany and enthusiasm, not to mention the Eucharist. Lightly to dismiss his engagement with Catholicism is to impoverish one's reading of his art, and to miss an opportunity better to understand Catholicism in its historical circumstances. This conviction is based on the evidence accumulated thus far regarding Joyce's engagement with Aquinas on the subject of aesthetics and epiphany, and on the basis of his adaptation of Augustinian doctrine on the gracious machinations of divine mercy in ordinary, immanent scenarios.

Joyce sympathized with Giordano Bruno's interest in science, humanism, and immanent manifestations of the divine, but did not pursue the Dominican heretic to the point of serious interest in alchemy and black magic, or to the point of explicit denial of the transcendental. In his conversation with Cranly in the final chapter of *Portrait*, Stephen cryptically remarks to Cranly that, "I tried to love God . . . It seems now I failed. It is very difficult. I tried to unite my will with the will of God instant by instant. In that I did not always fail. I could perhaps do that still."[88] This comment strongly suggests continued belief in God and hints at another way of serving Him. The immanent activity of the divine that Joyce advocates does not contradict the correct Catholic positions regarding God's immanent activity and the material universe not only as a place of probation but also as man's opportunity for spiritual activity and union with God.

The conviction that Joyce and Catholicism are mutually illuminating will be reinforced further by an examination of the Joycean treatment of the Eucharist. Now, in chapter V, with the aid of Joyce critics, I will follow Stephen's climactic cry in *Portrait*—"'Heavenly God!' . . . cried Stephen's soul in an outburst of profane joy"[89]— and his stated project of "transmuting the daily bread of experience into the radiant body of everliving life"[90] to their Eucharistic and artistic culminations in Joyce's aesthetic adaptations of the Mass. Joyce's Eucharistic art may be the realization of Stephen's speculative musings about another way of serving God.

Chapter V: Eucharistic Mutations and Permutations

V.1: Introduction

V.1.1: Joyce and the Eucharist

On the 2nd of February, 1932, the occasion of his fiftieth birthday, Joyce was presented with a cake shaped and decorated to replicate his novel *Ulysses*. His spontaneous response to this surprise, related by Eugene Jolas who was present on the occasion, is revealing: "Called on to cut the cake, Joyce looked at it a moment and said: *Accipite et manducate ex hoc omnes: Hoc est enim corpus meum*."[1] A younger Joyce remarked to his brother Stanislaus, in a conversation related by the latter in his memoir, "Don't you think, said he reflectively, choosing his words without haste, there is a certain resemblance between the mystery of the Mass and what I am trying to do?"[2] These are important extra-textual, biographical proofs of Joyce's Eucharistic intentions, authorial affirmations that *Ulysses* was for him the fulfillment of the artistic ambition expressed by Stephen Dedalus in *Portrait* to be "a priest of eternal imagination, transmuting the daily bread of experience into the radiant body of everliving life."[3]

Stephen frames his artistic ambition in clearly Eucharistic terms. In our opening chapter we have seen Richard Ellmann's reading of Joyce's artistic transmutation of Catholicism: Joyce "converted the temple to new uses instead of trying to knock it down, regarding it as a superior kind of human folly and one which, interpreted by a secular artist, contained obscured bits of truth."[4] Ellmann's biography is itself a kind of Joycean "temple" which has not been knocked down, but, over time, clear gaps have emerged, one of which is the treatment of Joyce's Catholic imagination. We have seen Lernout's attempt to defend Ellmann's reading and de-authorize Catholic scholarship, and we have seen John McCourt on the necessity of Catholic scholarship to fill an obvious gap in Joyce studies in Ellmann's aftermath.[5]

In fact, Ellmann's failure to exploit the rich thematic implications of Joyce's Catholic categories has been addressed, and redressed, by more recent scholarship. The comments of Joyce at his birthday party and to his brother have given rise to a Eucharistic thread in the vast tapestry of Joycean criticism. As critic Harry Levin put it, Joyce retained Catholic categories after loss of faith: "That Joyce felt the intellectual attraction of theology as well as the emotional appeal of ritual, is evident in everything he wrote;"[6] and, as critics have delighted in discovering, Catholic liturgy provided his aesthetic enterprise with a rich metaphorical goldmine.

Beginning with Dr. Paul Briand's 1968 article, "The Catholic Mass in James Joyce's *Ulysses*,"[7] the *James Joyce Quarterly* to this day has devoted space to the subject of Joyce's treatment of the Eucharist. This Eucharistic thread has continued to the present, surfacing again in Declan Kiberd's 2009 book, *Ulysses and Us*. We will examine Briand's article and Kiberd's book and a selection of the scholarly contributions to the debate in between these two. Inevitably, as we shall see, much of this literary criticism is also sacramental theology. It represents an attempt to respond to the Catholic *lacuna* in Joyce studies, but the attempt has succeeded only partially and in the midst of errors and inaccuracies. The task of this chapter is to correct those errors and inaccuracies, theologically to reinforce the accurate interpretations (especially by Jesuit Joyce scholar Robert Boyle), and, eventually, to offer a more complete reading of Joyce's Eucharistic intentions with an explanation of an important aspect of the Eucharist that has been overlooked by Joyce scholars; namely, the Eucharist as nuptial union between Bridegroom and Bride.

In Joyce's treatment of the Eucharist there is further evidence that his agendum was one of revitalization by synthesis rather than rupture. Kevin Sullivan, in his book *Joyce among the Jesuits*, expresses an intuition that there is continuity between Catholic categories and Joyce's work. Sullivan argues that Joyce as artist "secularizes this function [the Mass] of the priest, and his sacrament is a celebration of the communion of humanity," and then succinctly formulates this suggestive thought: "This is not substitution, it is simultaneity."[8] Ellmann and others, as we are about to see, interpret it as substitution, not simultaneity. Having already added elements to our understanding of the Catholic imagination of Joyce, we will now focus on the Eucharist in his imagination, further revealing the insufficiencies of Ellmann's hermeneutic. By comparing the Joycean treatment of the Eucharist with the truths of faith in the Catholic tradition concerning this mystery, one comes to a fuller appreciation of Joyce's aesthetic achievement, and to a fuller understanding of his philosophy.

V.1.2: Contours of the Eucharistic Debate

Roy Gottfried, developing Ellmann's hermeneutic, articulates the Joycean project in terms of secularizing metaphorization of Catholic teachings. His reading serves as a useful introduction to the debate about Joyce's aesthetic employment of the Eucharist. Contradicting Stephen's claim to have received the guidelines for his aesthetic task from Aquinas, Gottfried presupposes that Catholic orthodoxy in general is somehow antagonistic to art. He argues that Joyce's aesthetic vision is not unitary and that it is heretically and schismatically opposed not only to the Catholic (i.e., Universal) vision but to authority itself, in whatever manifestation: "To . . . be a misbeliever . . . was, for Joyce, to be always mindful of orthodoxy while attempting to break its hold of unitary meaning, its narrow sense, and to open up personal possibilities that led to artistic ones of rebellious challenge and freedom."[9] Sebastian Knowles, himself an established Joyce scholar, in his Foreword to Gottfried's book, endorses this view: "Gottfried is good on all the heresies in the catalog; by situating Joyce within the heretical margins, he shows Joyce's abiding contempt for all forms of authority."[10]

Etymological reminders literally bring us back to basics: the word "authority" stems from the Latin *augere*, meaning to create and to increase, giving us also the words "author" and "augment." If Joyce despised all forms of authority he should have written nothing. What Gottfriend perceives as a condemnation of all religious authority was really in the mind of Joyce a critique of the way in which that authority was concieved of and exercised in the clerical circles of Ireland in the 19th century. For Gottfried orthodoxy and opportunity are antithetical, while heresy and schism are conducive to creativity. Ratzinger's explanation presented in the first chapter of this work exposes the falsity of these premises, but Joyce's art does so also, in general and particularly in his employment of Catholic Eucharistic teachings.

Gottfried argues that Joyce found in Protestantism a liberating alternative to Catholic authoritarianism, citing as an example the case of Eucharistic theology and "the unorthodox reformist position that the elements of the Mass are emblematic rather than actual." In the line of Ellmann and Eco, who perceive the Joycean achievement in terms of a metaphorization of rituals, emptying these of their original substance to avail of them as evocative aesthetic signs now in the service of other ends, or in the service of the same ends but to better effect, Gottfried sees the Protestant position as more favorable to Joyce's intent: "This unorthodox view of the Eucharist as a system of resemblances and metaphors enters Joyce's stories as a very close association of religion with art."[11]

Gottfried makes Catholic Eucharistic orthodoxy sound like pedestrian logic when in fact it contains a subversive realism that most people find scandalous and that Joyce would surely have found attractive, given its sacramental reconciliation of the historical and the eternal, the material and the spiritual, that he wishes aesthetically to achieve. Gottfried claims Joyce preferred the Protestant interpretation of the Eucharistic mystery, but, in fact, the emptying of incarnational content and the consequent separation of matter from metaphor, of substance from symbol, results in an impoverishment of the sacrament and of the literature that seeks aesthetically to reproduce its synthesizing effect.

The subversiveness and imaginative fecundity inherent to Catholic orthodoxy has escaped Gottfried's notice. It did not escape the notice of James Joyce. We have seen that Joyce abhors the Puritanism that denies real human drives and needs, biological and otherwise, but the separation of matter and spirit that the Protestant Eucharistic theology advocates, *promotes* that etherealization and idealization, achieving its most extreme dualistic form in Puritanism. Joyce did not make Gottfried's doctrinal error of reducing the Eucharist to symbol and separating matter from metaphor; Joyce understood the mysterious but real materiality of the Eucharist and for that very reason was drawn to it and made aesthetic use of it not only in his project to reintegrate body and spirit but also to "transcendentalize" the ordinary. The connection between Catholic Eucharistic theology and Joyce's art is radical and substantial, not superficial and symbolic; it is ontological, not emblematic, as we will now see.

V.2: Key Moments in the Joycean Trajectory

V.2.1: Eucharistic Intimations in Portrait

The Eucharistic thread in Joyce criticism has arisen out of obvious Eucharistic moments in *A Portrait of the Artist as a Young Man* and *Ulysses*. Two climactic declarations in *Portrait* provide a Eucharistic key for reading

Ulysses. The first declaration occurs when Stephen beholds a girl knee-deep in the waters of the sea on Sandymount strand—"A girl stood before him in midstream, alone and still, gazing out to sea"—and Stephen reacts explosively: "'Heavenly God!' cried Stephen's soul, in an outburst of profane joy."[12] Later on, Stephen declares his ambition to be "a priest of eternal imagination, *transmuting the daily bread of experience into the radiant body of everliving life*"[13] [emphasis added]. In *Ulysses*, these two declarations are fulfilled in a "Eucharistic" coalescence of the heavenly and the profane, the quotidian and the radiant. To this affirmation it may be objected that Stephen's grand pretentions are subsequently thrown into crisis, an objection with some evidence in its favor.

Between the end of *Portrait* and the beginning of *Ulysses*, Stephen's mother has died and he has refused to pray by her bedside. He has seen his moribund mother spew green bile into a bowl in her final agonies even as he refuses to bend his knee for God's sake or for hers. His spirit is in shock and his sensibility still raw from the recent trauma. His earlier aesthetic optimism concerning the celebration of matter is thrown into crisis: "Houses of decay, mine, his and all . . . Come out of them, Stephen. Beauty is not there."[14] He has discarded institutional religion in favor of art, but he has as yet written nothing. He has found in the writings of St. Thomas Aquinas an aesthetic theory with which to chart his writing career, but his creative impulse has not yet found a way out of the intellectualism that dominates his approach to reality, an intellectualism now thrown into utter confusion by the apparent banality and squalor of life, death, and human relationships. He is immobilized by anguish and depression.

But in *Ulysses* Stephen emerges from this darkness, and the death-and-resurrection and father-son aspects of Eucharistic theology are crucial motifs in the transmission of that emergence. There are six major Eucharistic references in *Ulysses* that we should be aware of before we begin to participate in the Joycean Eucharistic discussion, which may be subdivided into three "Eucharistic moments" and three "communion scenes." We will look at these briefly now.

V.2.2: Three Eucharistic Moments in Ulysses

In the opening lines of the opening chapter (Telemachus) of *Ulysses*, Buck Mulligan, in the living quarters of the Martello Tower overlooking the Irish Sea which he shares with Stephen Dedalus and the Englishman Haines, satirically celebrates his matutinal shaving ritual in the form of the Mass: "He held the bowl aloft and intoned: *Introibo ad altare Dei.*"[15] On one level, Mulligan is mocking the opening words customarily recited by the priest as he approaches the altar at the beginning of Mass; on another level, Joyce, by beginning his novel with these words on its first page, is intimating the Eucharistic intentions of his art.

Later, in the Oxen of the Sun episode Stephen proposes a Eucharistic toast over his round of beer:

> About that present time young Stephen filled all cups that stood empty... praying for the intentions

of the sovereign pontiff . . . Now drink we, quod he, of this mazer and quaff ye this mead which is not indeed parcel of my body but my soul's bodiment. Leave ye fraction of bread to them that live by bread alone.[16]

There are several Mass references in this short passage. Customarily, the first of the intercessory prayers of the Mass, after the proclamation of the Gospel, is for the Pope's intentions. Then the priest proceeds to prepare the offerings of bread and wine in the sacred vessels, before offering the same in sacrifice to the Father in the Consecration, and then as spiritual food to the people. Stephen's toast in the pub irreverently and jocosely recollects these moments of the Mass, but, as in the case of Mulligan's mockery, Stephen's satire also expresses Joyce's own more serious Eucharistic intentions.

The consecration scene of the Black Mass in the Circe episode of *Ulysses* is another Eucharistic moment. I have paraphrased the episode in the third chapter of this work from the perspective of Bloom; here I will do so focusing on Stephen. The "Mass" is protagonized by Stephen's arch-enemies. In this episode, Stephen confronts his interior demons. On the level of external fact, he enters Dublin's Nighttown in a drunken state accompanied by the untrustworthy Lynch and followed by Leopold Bloom who joined the group earlier, first in a hospital maternity ward and then in a nearby pub to which he accompanied them. Bloom is motivated by a desire to protect the younger man, having empathized with his inner situation and fearing for his well-being. Bloom knows Stephen's father and is aware of his mother's recent death. Bloom is not drunk because earlier he has surreptitiously emptied the contents of his glass during the medical students' ribald conversation; Odysseus, in the Homeric parallel, prayed while the men consumed the sacred cows. He is therefore at his lucid and sober best when it comes to coping with the crisis that will occur in the brothel.

Stephen, on the other hand, is anything but sober and lucid, and in the brothel all kinds of negative dynamics come to a head. Persons who have been present in the life and consciousness of Stephen and Bloom appear and blend and dissolve into one another throughout the scene, which is one of bizarre burlesque mixed with blasphemy and nightmarish tension, dramatizing especially the inner tensions of Stephen and Bloom, in whose psyches differing forces and influences clash and compete for predominance. Still bearing the pain of his mother's death, Stephen also contends with tensions between himself and his group of false friends, led by Buck Mulligan. Haunted by his mother's ghost screaming at him to repent under the threat of hell—"Repent! O, the fire of hell!"[17]—Stephen's inner tensions erupt in the brothel where, in a fit of drunken rage, he smashes a chandelier with his cane. Bella Cohen, the brothel madam, confronts him, seeking to exploit the situation for monetary gain, and Bloom intervenes on Stephen's behalf.

It is in this climactic moment of Bloom's rescue of Stephen that the Black Mass consecration takes place, presumably in Stephen's drunken and highly stressed imagination: "Father Malachi O'Flynn, in a long petticoat and reversed chasuble, his two left feet back to the front, celebrates camp mass. The Reverend Mr. Hugh C. Haines Love M.A . . . his head and collar back to the front, holds over the celebrant's head an open umbrella."[18] Fr. Malachi O'Flynn is a composite figure of Buck (Malachi) Mulligan and the Fr. O'Flynn of Joyce's short story "The Sisters" in *Dubliners*. Haines is his English companion. Both of them feature also in the first episode; they temporarily share living quarters with Stephen in the Martello Tower, in the midst of simmering tensions. The script continues in the mode of hallucinatory melodrama and chaotic, blasphemous parody of the consecration:

FATHER MALACHI O'FLYNN:
Introibo ad altare diaboli.

THE REVEREND MR HAINES LOVE:
To the devil which made glad my young days.

FATHER MALACHI O'FLYNN:
(*Takes from the chalice and elevates a blooddripping host*) *Corpus Meum.*[19]

The "Mass" script continues in similar vein: the Eucharistic (or anti-Eucharistic) sacrifice coincides with Stephen's "persecution" in the brothel and his flight out onto the street where his "crucifixion" occurs in a clash with a British soldier who punches him and knocks him to the ground: "PRIVATE CARR: (*With ferocious articulation*) I'll do him in, so help me fucking Christ! I'll wring the bastard fucker's bleeding blasted fucking windpipe!"[20] Private Carr's murderous inclinations are thwarted. Bloom, having intervened on Stephen's behalf before Bella, the brothel madam, now intervenes again to defend him from the British soldiers and to pacify a passing police constable, taking Stephen into his charge and escorting him away from this "crucifixion scene" and towards what critics have interpreted as "communion scenes," in which the Eucharistic analogies continue.

V.2.3: Three Communion Scenes

The first of the communion scenes occurs in the Eumaeus chapter (the sixteenth), when Bloom accompanies Stephen to the cabman's shelter: "The keeper of the shelter in the middle of this tete-a-tete put a boiling swimming cup of a choice concoction labeled coffee on the table and a rather antediluvian specimen of a bun, or so it seemed . . . pushing the socalled roll across,"[21] and a few pages later Bloom encourages Stephen to eat and drink: "Can't you drink that coffee, by the way? Let me stir it and take a piece of that bun. It's like one of our skipper's bricks disguised. Still, no one can give what he hasn't got. Try a bit."[22] Critics have seen Eucharistic imagery in the "cup" of coffee and the "bun" pushed "across" the "table," representing, in their own prosaic way, the chalice of wine, the bread, the cross and the altar. It is in this moment that Stephen recognizes Bloom as his savior, musing inwardly to himself in acceptance of Bloom's ministrations: "*Christus* or Bloom his name is, or, after all, any other, *secundum carnem.*"[23]

The second communion scene occurs in Bloom's

home in the penultimate chapter of the novel, the Ithaca episode. After their collation in the cabman's shelter, Bloom takes Stephen to his home, and there, in his own kitchen, serves Stephen from his own favorite cup: "Relinquishing his symposiarchal right . . . he substituted a cup identical with that of his guest and served extraordinarily to his guest . . . Epp's massproduct, the creature cocoa."[24] In this shared consumption of "Epp's massproduct" critics have seen a typically Joycean wordplay with Eucharistic associations. The communion between Bloom and Stephen seems mundane to the point of trivial, but the semantic resonances of sharing the same cup and "massproduct" invest it with a hint of holiness.

The third communion scene occurs between Bloom and Molly in Molly's reminiscences of their courtship: "the day I got him to propose to me yes first I gave him the bit of seedcake out of my mouth and it was leapyear like now yes 16 years ago my God."[25] Molly's exclamation of "my God," like Stephen's of "Heavenly God," is more than a matter of gratuituous swearing. It contains an element of prayer. Of this third communion moment Ellmann has written that, "Moist with spittle, the seedcake offers its parallel . . . to the host, and the lovers' rite is contrasted with the black mass of *Circe*."[26] Joyce's intention is not sacrilegiously to debase something sacred; rather, his intention is to avail of Catholic imagery to epiphanize the presence of something sacred in profane realities.

In the trajectory of critical commentary on these scenes there has been a discernible escalation of depth, richness, and density. Joyce critics, in their diverse readings, have enabled a penetration of the original Joyce texts, gradually deepening the Eucharistic discussion. But a full and fair treatment of Catholic Eucharistic theology is required in order to understand what Joyce is accepting in Catholic imagery and what he is rejecting. It offers a way to navigate the problems raised by literary critics, problems that have sometimes been solved, sometimes half-solved and sometimes compounded by critical interpretations. Having seen the Eucharistic moments in the original Joyce texts, we will now navigate our way through the critical commentary, comparing and contrasting that commentary with Catholic sacramental theology on the Eucharist, the better to understand Joyce's artistic intentions and his religious mind.

V.3: Joyce's Eucharistic Imagery

V.3.1: Stephen between Portrait and Ulysses

V.3.1.1: Joyce's "Catholic Emancipation"

In 1968, Paul Briand ignited the debate about Joyce's Catholic imagination, especially in relation to the Mass. Briand presents Joyce as an uncomplicated anti-Catholic apostate, prone to sacrilegious mockery: "His mimicry of the Mass is sacrilegious, perhaps, from the Catholic point of view; but the mockery serves as another interesting parallel of insight into reality, from the aesthetic point of view."[27] Three years later, in 1971, Ruth Walsh recognized Brand's contribution but feared the danger of exaggeration: "Religion is everywhere in dear dirty

Dublin, but like the snow in 'The Dead,' it covers everything but never penetrates beneath the surface."[28] This statement surely undervalues the significance of snow in "The Dead" as much as it does that of religion in Joyce's writings. If Walsh's contention was that Joyce critiques a skin-deep religiosity hardly deserving of the name religion, claims could be made in its favor, but this does not seem to be her position. Walsh sees Joyce's writings in terms of gradual emancipation from the ties of Catholicism in particular and religion in general.

Walsh states that Stephen's "out-growing" of Catholicism was not fully achieved by intellectual rejection and must be completed by an emotional purgation. She sees it as a process. Individuation by means of art is presented as the higher alternative. Walsh assumes, I believe mistakenly, that Joyce intends us to take seriously Stephen's so-called "great spiritual renewal in terms of conventional religion," and that Joyce shares Stephen's elitist esteem for art: "Art became religion to Stephen and Stephen moved from a religion which had a reality for many to one that had a reality for very few." In effect, Walsh approaches Joyce from the same philosophical position as Ellmann, i.e., post-Christian atheistic humanism: "[T]o Joyce, the literary 'god of creation,' Catholicism was reduced largely to the level of artistic grist."[29]

Walsh assumes that Joyce overcame and outgrew his love of God by replacing it with a love of art. The question often left unasked by critics is, art in service of what and/or whom? Art in the service of art itself, mere Wildean aestheticism, may be discounted. A more probable answer seems to be, art in the service of the spirit of man. But Joyce is not an acritical humanist. He is often critical of the so-called spirit of man left to its own devices, and his art epiphanizes the independent and unpredictable operations of a principle that perfects, and often corrects, the spirit of man. In fact, that is precisely what occurs in the case of Stephen's juvenile religiosity. Stephen's adolescent spiritual awakening is a valid but incomplete religious experience, and Joyce's project is not to negate but to perfect it.

Beginning with the social macrocosm of *Dubliners*, Walsh maintains that the Mass is merely "a naturalistic and realistic detail ironically analogous with a theme of spiritual paralysis." The Mass is simply a naturalistic detail of Joyce's Dublin, without an essential thematic role. In *Portrait*, Walsh maintains, the Mass does fulfill a thematic function: "In *Portrait*, the Mass helps to communicate the transubstantiation of Stephen-Christ into the God of artistic creation. *A Portrait* sees the achievement of Stephen's intellectual transformation."[30] Walsh unabashedly employs two terms here—God and transubstantiation—in ways which Joyce studiously avoids. Joyce does not speak of transubstantiation of the artist into the God of artistic creation; he speaks of the artist as priest, *like* the God of creation, whose business it is not to transubstantiate but to *transmute*. These distinctions have important theological and ontological ramifications. The term transubstantion is unique to the Eucharist. If Joyce had used this term in reference to his aesthetic project, this would have been a clear declaration of intent to supplant rather than unite religion with art and priesthood with artist.

Walsh concludes with the claim that, whereas Stephen's emancipation in *Portrait* is solely intellectual, "his emotional emancipation from Catholicism, and consequent selfhood—wholeness, personal integration—takes place in *Ulysses* where Joyce again re-enacts the death-resurrection ritual as symbolized by the Mass."[31] Before studying the validity of the claim that in *Ulysses* Stephen somehow achieves emancipation from Catholicism with the symbolic aid of the Catholic Mass, we should pause to consider the claim that Stephen intellectually rejects Catholicism in *Portrait*. Joyce is not nearly as clear in this matter as many of his critics are.

V.3.1.3: A Decidedly Ambivalent Apostasy

Walsh leads us to raise the question whether it was intellectual disbelief in the Eucharist or sin and vice that led Stephen to desist from receiving communion. It is important, therefore, to take a step back from our discussion of the Eucharist to understand the difference between these two human actions, one being a mental action and the other being a physical action related to the virtue of purity and the vice of lust. Both could lead to the same result: not taking communion. But reasons for that result are quite different, as are its implications regarding the religious mind of Joyce.

It was nothing so clear and simple as intellectual disbelief that prevented Stephen in *Portrait* from receiving communion:

'Do you believe in the eucharist?' Cranly asked. 'I do not,' Stephen said.

'Do you disbelieve then?'
'I neither believe in it nor disbelieve in it,' Stephen answered . . . [32]

'And is that why you will not communicate,' Cranly asked, 'because you are not sure . . . because you feel that the host . . . may be the body and blood of the son of God and not a wafer of bread? And because you fear that it may be?' 'Yes,' Stephen said quietly, 'I feel that and I also fear it.' [. . .]

'Do you fear then,' Cranly asked, 'that the God of the Roman catholics would strike you dead and damn you if you made a sacrilegious communion?'

'The God of the Roman catholics could do that now,' Stephen said. 'I fear more than that the chemical action which would be set up in my soul by a false homage to a symbol behind which are massed twenty centuries of authority and veneration.'[33]

There is a double scrupulosity in Stephen's position: the fear of dire punishment by an irate divinity on the one hand, but on the other hand, more importantly for him, the fear of the consequences of frivolous betrayal of his conscience by mechanical recognition of a rite he refuses to pay the price to receive. The price is repentance, as

Stephen later records in his diary: "Then she [Stephen's mother] said I would come back to faith because I had a restless mind. This means to leave church by back door of sin and re-enter through the skylight of repentance. Cannot repent. Told her so and asked for sixpence. Got threepence."[34]

There is no evidence of intellectual disbelief in Stephen's position. His "I neither believe in it nor disbelieve in it," coupled with his "Cannot repent," indicates a moral and sexual rather than an intellectual position, and a policy of avoidance rather than of rejection. In this, Stephen's position, or lack thereof, is an accurate reflection of Joyce's. This is borne out by Ellmann's report that "he declared flatly . . . to a friend, that sexual continence was impossible for him. He felt he must choose between continual guilt and some heretical exoneration of the senses."[35] There is no need to turn to heresy to exonerate the senses. There is no inherent opposition between divine love and sexual love. Once again, *eros* is the artificial problem. Over-indulgence of the senses at the expense of human dignity and responsibility would be another matter, but denial of the dignity proper to the senses would be as heretical as pseudo-rationalized over-indulgence of them. Joyce did not seek to rationalize sexual over-indulgence.

But there is biographical evidence that sexual intemperance was a factor in Joyce's abandonment of the Church. Fr. Bruce Bradley S.J. refers perspicaciously to the letter that Joyce wrote to Nora Barnacle on 29 August 1904 about having left the Catholic Church, "'hating it most fervently,' because he found it impossible to remain in it 'on account of the impulses of my nature' (*SL* 25-16).″ To pass over this declaration without reflective pause is to waste a valuable hermeneutical opportunity. Bradley sees this text as "pivotal for understanding Joyce's early religious experience."[36] The intimation here is that Joyce's initial rejection of Catholicism was at least as much hormonal and temperamental as intellectual, and that his later relationship with it uses aspects of its own sacramental doctrine to defy the dualistic demonization of physicality that he had supposedly encountered. Stephen's position is not clearly iterated in order to avoid the kind of false simplifications which less circumspect thinkers sometimes superimpose.

Stephen's position regarding religion is as complex, and sometimes even contradictory, as his sexual morality. In this, too, he is an accurate reflection of Joyce. As we have seen, the structure of *Portrait* shows that Stephen has overcome, thanks at least partly to his faith, the addictiveness of crude sensualism to which he succumbed in early adolescence.[37] There are indicators, however, that he has not entirely escaped its clutches: in *Ulysses* he is still frequenting brothels, and Ellmann provides biographical evidence that neither had Joyce, at Stephen's age and older, fully freed himself from them. In any event, Stephen's conversation with Cranly shows that the matter is not as easily reduced and understood as painted by Walsh. On the one hand, Stephen has determined to avoid the Eucharist; on the other, he has taken the Eucharist as paradigm of his aesthetic mission. As we continue to examine Joyce's attitude towards religion and the role of the Eucharist in *Ulysses*, we will see that the aspect of "determination to avoid" becomes increasingly problematic while that of "paradigm" acquires escalating importance.

V.3.1.4: The Eucharist as Paradigm

In the conversation revolving around religion and receiving communion that we have just seen in *Portrait*, there is already a hint that Joyce's break with religion is not radical and total. Stephen tells Cranly: "I tried to love God... It seems now I failed. It is very difficult. I tried to unite my will with the will of God instant by instant. In that I did not always fail. I could perhaps do that still."[38] This last remark does not mean a repetition of the previous failed attempt; rather, it hints at the possibility of another approach along the lines described in chapter III of this work: Joyce will epiphanize the divine "sense of mercy" in his art; a form of mercy that, combining and alternating *admonitio* and *delectatio*, gently and strongly favors personal development. The conversation with Cranly was Joyce's opportunity to pronounce, through Stephen, a position of disbelief or at least agnosticism; instead, continuing belief is tacitly assumed by Stephen, as he muses aloud on an alternative way of uniting his will with God's.

The Eucharist is central to Joyce's alternative religious and aesthetic way of uniting his will with the will of God. Secularist Joyceans assume that there has been a radical break with religion in favor of art, but the reality is more nuanced. In a later article on the Mass in *Ulysses*, Walsh maintains the position that Joyce abandoned religion in favor of art, observing that "Joyce started *Ulysses* with a Mass because it must have seemed to him an entirely appropriate opening keynote from every point of view."[39] Among "every point of view" she includes: the linking of *Ulysses* with *A Portrait of the Artist as a Young Man* and its themes of struggle with faith, family, and fatherland in the pursuit of self-identity, development of the dominant theme of *Ulysses,* which is the search of the son for the father and of the father for the son, introduction of the theme of man's need for social communion. That Joyce realized that all of these themes coalesce in the Eucharist is significant in itself, testifying to a hermeneutic of continuity rather than rupture.

Walsh, while maintaining a hermeneutic of rupture and opportunism, provides evidence of thematic continuity between the Catholic Eucharist and Joyce's art. Catholicism somehow provides Joyce with the liturgical motifs best suited to his thematic concerns, while constituting at the same time a force from which he feels the need to be freed. This ambiguity is exemplified in Walsh's interpretation of Stephen's psychological liberation from the trauma of his mother's death and the guilt he experiences at having made his mother suffer. Stephen is tormented by his mother's recent death and by his own refusal to kneel at her bedside and pray. Joyce will use the Mass, Walsh explains, as a point of reference in his trajectory of maturation: "Before the novel ends, what Joyce will show is—not communion necessarily with another—but integration of the self. As one of many means to illustrate self-integration, Joyce uses the Mass to show Stephen's mental adjustment toward religion."[40] This claim falsely opposes communion and self-integration, which Thornton's and other readings of *Ulysses* contradict and correct, showing that relationship is essential to individuation.[41]

But, more pertinently to the present argument, there is an unexplained opposition also underlying Walsh's affirmation that the Catholic liturgy is at one and the same time the metaphorical vehicle of Stephen's liberation and a force of psychological imprisonment. We have taken a step back from Joyce's implicit aesthetic treatment of the Eucharist to look at Stephen's explicit statements concerning religion and the Eucharist, sin and personal guilt, because these ancilliary realities help to refine our understanding of the complexity of Stephen and of Joyce's religious imagination. Now, with a more vivid sense of the tension in Joyce's relationship with Catholicism, we will proceed to a sequential analysis of the Mass scenes in *Ulysses*, beginning with Buck Mulligan's "Mass" in the first chapter of that novel. If Joyce, like Mulligan, knowingly and maliciously ridicules what the Church holds most sacred, the Holy of holies, then he is sacrilegious and blasphemous and his rejection of Catholicism is total. Joyce's authorial disposition towards his fictional invention, Buck Mulligan, will shed light on the matter.

V.3.2: Joyce's Stance in Relation to Buck Mulligan

V.3.2.1: Mere Mockery

To the blasphemous Buck Mulligan who "celebrates Mass" in the opening chapter of *Ulysses*, the Mass is an object of parody; to Stephen, and to Joyce, it is something different, we may even say something much more, than that. Walsh, quoting McNelly, argues that, "Mulligan's behavior in blessing the mountains, tower, and surrounding countryside 'serves as a Joycean device of ridicule against the Church and characterizes Mulligan as a jocund blasphemer.'"[42] There is an important distinction here: Joyce's intention to distance himself from Mulligan is notorious.[43] Far from sympathizing with Mulligan's mockery, Joyce's intention is to expose its superficiality. Walsh maintains that Joyce wishes both to mock and to condemn mockery.

Walsh is not alone among Joyce critics in wishing simultaneously to hold contradictory positions in this and other areas. Lernout labors under the same ambiguity. On the one hand, he bows unavoidably to the reality of Joyce's rejection of Mulligan's cavalier blasphemy, but then: "The fact that Stephen distances himself from his friend's mockery does not necessarily mean that he is offended or that he takes the church's side; Joyce only seems to think that mockery is not the right weapon in the fight against religion."[44] But Lernout then devotes several pages (cf. pp. 181-185) to an account of the Catholic theological debate in the Middle Ages on the fate of the foreskin of Christ purportedly retained as a relic from the time of his boyhood circumcision.

As Lernout points out, the subject of the destiny of Christ's circumcised foreskin was subsequently taken up as an attractive target—for mockery—in anti-Catholic literature. Lernout maintains that the Catholic idea "that the Divine Foreskin will become a constellation at the end of time" is also a target for Joyce's anti-Catholic irony.

In his reading of the scene in the Ithaca chapter where Bloom and Stephen urinate in unison in Bloom's garden while contemplating the nocturnal firmament, Lernout imputes to Joyce a spirit of mockery akin to Mulligan's: Bloom and Stephen witness, "just before they part, the assumption of the divine prepuce into heaven."[45] This hypothesis, which Len Platt finds "deliciously blasphemous,"[46] if correct, may also be read as further evidence that Joyce shared (in his own comical way) Catholicism's curious interest in the ultimate fate of human flesh.

In Lernout's hypothesis and in Platt's response to it, there is a tacit presupposition that Catholicism would find Joyce's joke blasphemous; but, at least objectively, there is nothing blasphemous in it. Malicious or contemptuous subjective intent, however, could render blasphemous an objectively inoffensive joke. Evidence suggests that this is Mulligan's disposition in general, and in particular when he "celebrates" Mass; whether or not it is also Joyce's position, as Lernout assumes, is not so clear. There is evidence to suggest that it is not, and that Joyce's attitude towards corporality, be it human and divine as in the case of Christ or solely human as in all other cases, is closer to the Catholic position than to the Puritan or materialist ones.

V.3.2.2: Puritanism, Materialism & Catholic Orthodoxy

Declan Kiberd states that, "For Joyce the body was at once dignified and comic, sacred and soiled."[47] Kiberd's view of Buck Mulligan tallies with what we have seen so far in the light of his liturgical buffoonery: "All through *Ulysses* Mulligan as medic has adopted a brazenly materialist approach to human life, whereas Stephen has sought a balance between the spiritual and the physical."[48] Joyce's commitment to a wholesome celebration of corporality is described by Kiberd with the aid of an interesting affirmation by Joyce himself: "'For too long were the stars studied and men's insides neglected,' said Joyce: 'An eclipse of the sun could be predicted many centuries before anyone knew what way the blood circulated in our bodies.'"[49]

How then should we understand Mulligan's Mass, if it does not express Joyce's position? An article by Frances Restuccia displays an in-depth understanding of the Catholic Mass and argues that Joyce understood the Mass too—"James Joyce did not approach the subject of the Eucharist as a dilettante. We know that he was familiar with Aquinas' rigorous questions concerning the Eucharist"[50]—citing evidence in *Portrait* and *Ulysses* in support of this observation. She maintains that Joyce in *Ulysses* navigates his way through varying versions of the Eucharist, including Mulligan's versions in the Telemachus and Circe episodes, ultimately to affirm the orthodox one.

The orthodox Mass is Joyce's model for his art, and he rejects other versions: "What these false views appear to share (we shall observe) is an overemphasis on matter; they all, it might be said, involve what Jacques Maritain has called the 'sin of materialism.'"[51]

Restuccia's argument concurs with Weldon Thornton's hermeneutic of Joyce as an artist who negotiates his way through the polar perils of naturalism and symbolism, materialism and idealism. The Catholic Mass provides the background that enables and supports the Joycean synthesis: Joyce "makes clear finally that he remains faithful—artistically—to the Church's Eucharist."[52] The purpose of Restuccia's article is to demonstrate this, and Buck Mulligan's "Mass" is the starting-point for doing so.

Mulligan, unconsciously or otherwise, is a proponent of the "sensualistic" heretical interpretation of the Eucharist: an overly literal and materialistic understanding of the mystery. Restuccia argues that this is not the Catholic position. Aquinas, she says, was "unable to accept this gross realism." There follows a brief exposition of "transubstantiation" according to St. Thomas, and then: "What the sensualists . . . fail to understand . . . is that it is 'the accidents of the bread and wine [that] remain after the consecration.'"[53] Restuccia's familiarity with Aristotelian and Thomist doctrines enables her to grasp the implications of important distinctions between substance and accidents, distinctions with which Joyce would also have been familiar: "[W]e can make physical contact with them alone. It is true that the accidents of Christ's body are also in the Eucharist, but only 'by means of the substance . . . Christ's body is substantially present in this sacrament.'"[54]

Although it is reality's most "real" substratum, substance is invisible, as Thomas explains: "But substance, as such, is not visible to the bodily eye, nor does it come under any one of the senses, nor under the imagination, but solely under the intellect, whose object is what a thing is."⁵⁵ Only those who are sensitive to epiphany may perceive it. Buck Mulligan is not one of them: "In the opening scene of *Ulysses*, Buck Mulligan falsifies the Eucharist, then, by assuming that through his conversion, Christ's 'body and soul and blood and ouns' will enter his shaving bowl chalice."⁵⁶ Catholic orthodoxy navigates a middle way between Puritan scorn of corporality and materialist exaltation of it. The Catholic Eucharist is propitious to Joyce's project to unite the spiritual and the material, and Joyce distances himself from Mulligan's scientism and sensualism.

V.3.2.3: Scientism and Sensualism

Buck is a scientist and a sensualist whose intention, Restuccia observes, is "to scoff at the idea of the Real Presence."⁵⁷ His exaltation of science and senses restricts him to the world of accidents and excludes him from the world of substance: "But as all Catholic theologians would doubtless assert, 'Transubstantiation . . . is a religious reality, not a natural phenomenon.'"⁵⁸ Buck Mulligan uses science to ridicule realities that are beyond the scope of science. He numbers among those materialists who, as the Vatican Council II puts it, employ the scientific method "to scrutinize the question of God" in such a way "as to make it seem devoid of meaning," and who, "unduly transgressing the limits of the positive sciences, contend that everything can be explained by this kind of scientific reasoning alone" (*GS* 9).

Restuccia's description of Mulligan's approach echoes the Council's: "By mingling the two heresies—sensualist and scientific—Buck displays a talent for theological legerdemain: the modern, realist, and arguably respectable scientific point of view arrives at an ancient absurdity." Realities that operate on different registers are falsely opposed: "Thus the operation of *reductio ad absurdum* has been performed on the whole doctrine of the Eucharist, under a scientific aegis."[59]

Mulligan, a medical student, is a scientist in theory and, logically, a sensualist in practice: if all is matter, morality does not matter. This is Mulligan's position. Joyce, without scorning science or sensuality, is neither a scientist nor a sensualist, and the contrast between Stephen and Mulligan is his way of distancing himself from the latter's position. In another example of confusing ambiguity among Joyce scholars regarding Joyce's position vis-a-vis Mulligan, Frances Devlin-Glass, in an otherwise incisive commentary which includes awareness of Joyce's antipathy towards Gogarty (and therefore Mulligan), speaks of Joyce "celebrating" the spirit of Buck Mulligan: "However, he does not fail to celebrate anarchy, deviance and performative excess for its own sake in both *Circe* and the representation of a high-camp Buck Mulligan."[60]

Joyce's thinking regarding homosexuality, as described by David Norris,[61] gives the lie to this interpretation by Devlin-Glass, as does Joyce's known disposition towards Gogarty. To read Mulligan's celebration of the Mass in the Telemachus episode as an instance of Joycean mockery of the Church and at the very same time as a critique of mindless Mulliganesque mockery, is a self-contradictory and impossible predicate. Similarly, the depiction of Mulligan in the Black Mass of the Circe episode is either celebration or critical caricature; it cannot be both at the same time.

To misread the tone, content, and intention of Joyce's depiction of Mulligan would be to miss a main point of the Joycean project. The Joycean anthropology is about harmonious reconciliation of the feminine, which Joyce associates with *eros*, and the masculine, which Joyce associates both with *logos*-rationality and with *agape*-love's capacity for self-sacrifice. Mulligan is a character in whom there is exaggeration of sensualism to the point of homosexuality (as indicated in his depiction in the Circe Black Mass), which we know Joyce saw as a threat to individuation, or pansexuality. We have seen similar sensualist tendencies in Bloom, as Restuccia also observes.

V.3.2.4: Bloom's Sensualism

Having analyzed Buck Mulligan's version of the Mass, Restuccia focuses on the Mass according to Leopold Bloom: "His 'rum idea' of the Eucharist as cannibalism (*U* 80) . . . is sensualism taken to absurd lengths."[62] Restuccia quotes Aquinas by way of response to Bloom's naïve Eucharistic naturalism. Aquinas argues that Divine Providence conceived the sacrament in such a way as to preclude cannibalism and avoid derision. Bloom's scandal echoes that of his biblical ancestors who responded, "This is a hard doctrine; who can accept it" (cf. Jn 6), when Christ first explicitly preached the doctrine of the Eucharist as the eating of his body and drinking of his blood.

This coincidence between Bloom and Buck has important implications for our interpretation of Joyce's entire aesthetic project: "In the hands of Buck and Bloom, the sensualist heresy reduces to a predisposition to dwell on matter at the expense of spirit." The Joycean aesthetic is about the reconciliation of matter and spirit. He will not react against disincarnate spiritualism by championing immanentist materialism. Restuccia makes the challenging point that Bloom shares the sensualist perspective of Mulligan, from whom Joyce clearly wishes to distance himself: "[T]hat Bloom, a character with whom Joyce is more closely associated, commits the same heresy, primarily because he lives naturally in the material world, should give us pause."[63]

If we assert that Joyce identifies himself unequivocally with Bloom, we must ineluctably deduce therefrom, as secularist Joyceans tend to do, that Joyce is a naturalist in his thinking and writing and therefore has "no conception of another world, substantial or spiritual, beyond the accidents."[64] Restuccia observes that many critics describe *Ulysses* as a work of the naturalist kind. She argues, however, that if this were the case and nothing more were to be said, the Eucharist would not feature in *Ulysses* other than in the blasphemous and derisive form employed by Buck Mulligan, with whom Stephen and Joyce are in manifest discord, and in the naturalist ignorance and indifference displayed by Leopold Bloom.

However, a prolonged perusal of the Eucharistic motif in *Ulysses* reveals that Joyce is neither a sensualist in the mold of Mulligan nor a naturalist like Bloom: "We may get deeply enmeshed in *Ulysses* before we are able to distinguish Joyce's view from Buck's. Even a scene as late as the Last Supper scene in 'Oxen' may strike us as burlesque." In the scene Restuccia refers to, Stephen presides in a bar "as a Christ figure over a 'holy' meal of beer and sardines."[65] We will look at this irreverent moment now.

V.3.2.5: Stephen's Toast

On the subject of Stephen's irreverent toast, Joyce critic Patrick McCarthy builds upon Paul Briand's reading: "At the Holies Street hospital Stephen, thoroughly inebriated by this time, parodies the consecration after he proposes a toast to the pope with his beer, a cheap substitute for sacramental wine."[66] McCarthy introduces the notion of Joyce's art as "Eucharistization" or transubstantiation: "The important point is that Stephen, who is both priest and victim, is distributing his 'soul's bodiment' to the people—just as an artist gives of his soul each time he releases to the public a new creation."[67] The parallels between priest and artist and the Eucharistic/artistic communion realized through sharing of the "soul's bodiment," is an important insight that will be taken up and developed by other critics.

Stephen's self-identification as priest of the imagination is satirically present in the passage quoted by McCarthy, but there is also more to his distinction of "parcel of my body," and "my soul's bodiment," and to the cursory dismissal of "fraction of bread"—"Leave ye fraction of bread to them that live by bread alone"—than McCarthy seems to recognize. On one level, Stephen is simply, sadly, and comically saying that he prefers to spend his money on getting drunk than on satisfying his hunger, but on another level the distinction between "fraction of bread" and "soul's bodiment" has a larger significance that Joyce readers have sometimes failed to grasp. Kiberd, for example, by maintaining that Joyce is critiquing a Catholic aversion to materiality, commits a serious theological *faux pas*: "Stephen suggests that Christians made a terrible error in denying the material reality of the host at the consecration of the Mass . . . For Stephen body and soul must be placed in equilibrium."[68] The "terrible error" made by Christians and supposedly suggested by Stephen, is this: "Both the Catholic belief in transubstantiation and the Protestant doctrine of consubstantiation are wrong because they deny the material nature of the human body."[69]

If it was Stephen's belief that Catholic Eucharistic theology denies the material nature of the human body, it is an erroneous one: Catholicism has always defended the *Real Presence* of Christ's glorified material body in the Eucharist. Furthermore, the accidents of the bread—which constitute its materiality, as Restuccia has explained—remain; as do the accidents of Christ's risen body, sacramentally and mysteriously but also literally and materially. We may speak, to coin a phrase, not of consubstantiation but of "conaccidentation." The divine and the mundane are conjoined: "I am the living bread which came down from heaven" (Jn 6:51).

Kiberd interprets Stephen's toast in *Ulysses* as a "bitter parody of this exclusion" (i.e., of the body, the material): "'Quaff ye this mead which is not indeed parcel of my body but my soul's bodiment. Leave ye fraction of bread to them that live by bread alone.'"[70] In fact Stephen's toast is perfectly orthodox. The heresy of Capernaumism—so called because it was in Capernaum that a numerous contingent of Christ's followers committed this error and abandoned Him (cf. Jn 6)—is that which would reduce the Eucharistic mystery to cannibalism, misinterpreting it as an invitation to eat a "parcel" of his historical, pre-Resurrection body rather than to receive his "soul's bodiment," i.e., as "fraction of bread" rather than as corporal and spiritual communion with the entire risen Christ truly present under both species.

Stephen's toast is therefore a rejection both of materialism and of spiritualism. It may constitute comical irreverence but if it is "bitter parody" of "Catholic" spiritualism or materialism, then it is Stephen himself whom Joyce is placing in error, which is always possible but not likely in this instance. There is no evidence that Stephen rejected the Eucharist because of its failure to incorporate materiality. In fact, in the Black Mass of the Circe episode, which is the next major Mass reference in *Ulysses*, Joyce critiques both mockery and materialism, and, according to Restuccia, likens his art to the orthodox Catholic Eucharist precisely because it conjoins the material and the spiritual in a way that his art also aspires to do. Restuccia's reading eventually emerges from a background of other hermeneutics as the most authoritative interpretation.

V.3.3: The Black Mass

V.3.3.1: The Freudian Reading

In the Black Mass of the Circe episode, it is the choice of location, according to Briand, that makes this aesthetic adaptation of the mystery of the Mass blasphemous: "Joyce, in profane travesty and sacrilegious mockery, has his consecration in a black mass, in a house of prostitution."[71] Certainly, a Black Mass in a brothel is a disconcerting scenario, not readily identifiable as compatible with Catholic orthodoxy. But Joyce's use of the Black Mass is not sacrilegious satire for its own sake. The purpose is to dramatize the interplay of the forces of psychic darkness with which Stephen and Bloom struggle (e.g. their personal bereavements: Bloom's loss of his son, Stephen's of his mother), and satirically to over-dramatize the events that actually occur in the brothel. Equally significant as far as concerns sacrilegious intent is the fact that neither Stephen nor Bloom—the two characters with whom we are most intended to sympathize—is a chief protagonist in the Mass.

Ruth Walsh provides a summary of the events of the Circe episode and its climax: "The 'Circe' black Mass concludes with Stephen's being knocked out physically. When he recovers consciousness after being violently freed from his own oppression, Stephen finds himself in the hands of Bloom, his secular savior."[72] According to Walsh, Stephen's recognition of Bloom as savior evinces a secularization of religion. With Ellmann and others, she sees Bloom as a secular supplantation of Christ:

"Stephen's ability to see Bloom as '*Christus*' is evidence of his change in attitude toward religion. Bloom is now the secularized Christ."[73]

This reading contains an unspoken either/or assumption that should be confronted. In other words, Stephen's "savior" must be either Christ or Bloom, either sacred or secular, either religious or real. It seems clear from the conclusions drawn by some critics that they operate according to these false polarities as unconsciously assumed principles. The possibility that they might in fact be false polarities is not addressed. Nor is the possibility that Joyce might have operated from a both/and perspective. We will bear this possibility in mind as we proceed, while pointing out that Catholicism, operating from a both/and perspective, would see no reason why Christ in Bloom could not come to Stephen's rescue, in spite of Bloom's obvious imperfections.

V.3.3.2: Bloom's Imperfections

Critics too optimistically assume that Bloom is Joyce's paradigm of a good and complete man from the moment of his first appearance in the novel, rather than a "work in progress" like Stephen, as we have seen earlier.[74] In fact, Joyce is as interested in correcting Bloom's sensualism as he is in correcting Stephen's intellectualism. Walsh succumbs to this very over-optimism about Bloom: "Bloom's philosophy is one of reality and practicality, tempered with true Christian charity . . . Bloom's mind is pleasantly preoccupied with life."[75] This is true, but it is also the case that Bloom's natural optimism has been dealt a severe blow with lasting effects by the death of his son, Rudy, and by the suicide of his father. This is central to the theme of the novel and to the theme of religion in it.

Walsh concludes that "The source of charity in Joyce's hero stems plainly from the heart, not from the concepts of organized religion . . . Joyce is making definite and absolute the fact that Bloom's goodness has no causal relationship with his admitted Catholicism."[76] We have seen that Bloom's goodness is incomplete until his intervention on Stephen's behalf in the Circe episode. His natural benevolence, weakened by sensualism, is toughened and perfected by this initiative. The weakness of his will is rectified by an act of *agape*-love. The source of his potential "charity" is the heart, as Walsh rightly says, but it has to be actualized by a conspiracy of external circumstances. There is no point in denying, or need to deny, that Catholicism has had little or no overt formative influence on Bloom, negative or positive, as it has undoubtedly had on Stephen. With Bloom, Joyce has another purpose in mind: to dramatize the dynamic of a humanizing instinct at work in the human consciousness, independently of doctrinal knowledge. Walsh is touching upon, but overstating, an important Joycean theme about instinctive goodness and the human condition. Walsh maintains that Bloom's goodness is natural and instinctive. We have considered this in chapter III; Walsh's observations develop and confirm the point. She observes that, as an apostate Jew by way of an unsuccessful attempt to integrate himself into Dublin's Catholic social milieu, Bloom is, like Stephen, something of a social and religious outcast; but, she maintains, "Bloom, the Jew, is Dublin's only true Christian."[77] Walsh deduces that Bloom is Joyce's paradigm of "secularized Christianity" or natural humaneness without need of any external perfective influence.

Walsh's secular humanist hermeneutic perceives Bloom as Joyce's ideal father for the motherless and fatherless Stephen, and perceives the Joycean adaptation of the Eucharist as a secularized motif of that secularist theme: "Stephen learns to secularize and to realize the precepts of his religion through Bloom's example . . . Bloom needs no religion to teach him to love mankind, a response which he instinctively understands."[78] Walsh is partially correct in saying that Bloom's goodness and charity is "instinctive," but Joyce is not an optimistic sentimentalist in the mold of Rousseau. He believes in the natural, or instinctive, benevolence of the human spirit but is critically aware also of negative forces, internal and external, that compete against that benevolence. His writings recurringly expose these dynamics. He believes also in an elusive Ariel-like principle that masterminds circumstances to bring the best out of the human spirit; his "humanism" is not therefore immanentist.

The secular humanist hermeneutic argues that Joyce's aim is to make religion relevant by "secularizing" it, stripping religion of its transcendental reference. The elusive Ariel-like spirit in Joyce's world has eluded some of his readers, perhaps because they unconsciously, and mistakenly, associate religion exclusively with other-worldliness. Christianity proclaims God's irruption in the secular sphere with Christ's Incarnation. Catholicism does not deny that divine grace is active outside the visible parameters of its structures and rituals; on the contrary, the ubiquitous activity of grace is a truth of the Catholic faith, and one with which we know Joyce was familiar to the point of fascination, a fascination that expressed itself in his work.

Given that Christ was commonly accused of consorting with prostitutes (cf. Mt 9:11), there is no reason to suppose that the ubiquitous activity of grace would cease at the doors of a brothel. The benefits that accrue to Stephen and Bloom in the Black Mass scene testify to the actuation of a humanizing principle at work even in the most degrading of human situations—prostitution and drunkenness—and may be interpreted in theological terms as fruits of actual grace. The mission of Joyce's artistic priesthood is to epiphanize this dynamic. Frances Restuccia's reading of the Black Mass scene offers further evidence that Joyce's abhorrence of spiritualism and his determination to restore the dignity of the corporal and material and sensual did not impel him to a reactionary materialism that negates the world of the spirit.

V.3.3.4: Stephen's Catharsis and the Black Mass

In the drama of the black Mass, Restuccia discovers a tension in Stephen (and perhaps in Joyce) between the "desire to be a realist . . . to present the material world as sufficient—and his urge to write a kind of figural realism—to regard the real world as only mediately important." Here Restuccia is getting to the very heart of the central Joycean debate concerning the extent of his naturalism. The "tension" which she identifies is present also in Joycean criticism as we are seeing. The Circe chapter dramatizes the antagonism between spirit and matter: "[I]n the world of black masses, one not only resides in the real world—the world of matter—but to do so is necessarily to be contemptuous of the spiritual."[79]

The question that continues to badger the world of Joycean criticism concerns the extent to which his rejection of the institutional face of the Catholic Church led him to reject Catholicism itself, Catholic theology, Catholic philosophy, religion itself and spirituality, belief in the supernatural: "The conflict between modern realism and figural realism that Joyce has left unresolved to this point thus comes to a head: his immersion in the naturalistic world has led him, by an apparently inevitable logic, to vicious mockery of the Catholic Church." After providing ample and convincing evidence of the connections between the Mass of the Telemachus chapter and that of Circe, Restuccia concludes: "We can say, therefore, that brought to its extreme, but logical, end in the black mass of 'Circe,' Buck's eucharist is rendered at the very best distasteful, at the very worst, perverse and bestial." But mockery fails to exorcise the insistent logic of religion. Mockery is *not* Joyce's aesthetic position—"Translated to literary terms, the black mass thus expresses Joyce's own rejection of naturalism"[80]—and we may deduce that nor is it his religious position.

Evidence suggests that the Circe Black Mass is a satiric rejection not of the Mass itself, but of its diametrical opposite. It is a rejection of all that is ignoble, disordered, and diabolical; and indicates a turning point for Bloom,

Stephen, and Joyce. The aesthetic and philosophical position that Joyce ultimately champions is evident in the remaining chapters of the book and, again, the Eucharist provides the motif by which it is represented: "Having wrestled with and having finally disavowed naturalism, *Ulysses* is free to present a series of secular eucharists (one stands out in each of the three remaining chapters) modeled on the proper—not a sensualist—version of the Church Eucharist."[81] (I will look at these in the next section.) It took the literary world decades to see beyond the initial impressions provoked by the Black Mass in *Ulysses* and to reach Restuccia's concluding insight: "By exploding the sensualist eucharist . . . thus suggesting that his artistic model be seen as the official Church Eucharist (as Aquinas defines it), Joyce reveals that he secularizes the mysteries and rituals of the Church without devaluing the spiritual."[82]

Restuccia's interpretation captures what I have earlier called the subversiveness of Catholic orthodoxy. At the time when *Ulysses* was published there were morally insurmountable obstacles to a reading like this one, which claims that Joyce's artistic employment of the Eucharistic mystery is in fact dependent upon and compatible with Catholic teaching. The expression that he "secularizes the mysteries and rituals of the Church without devaluing the spiritual" is disconcerting: again, in the light of the Incarnation and the realism of the Real Presence in the Eucharist, Catholicism has never envisaged the secular as separable from the spiritual. Even in the light of the doctrine of Creation, the secular and the spiritual are inherently, sacramentally connected. Therefore, the concept of "secularizing" mysteries and rituals "without devaluing the spiritual" is a redundancy and a self-contradiction. There are indicators, however, that this false dichotomization was somehow promoted in the name of Catholicism. Joyce's pontifical (that is, bridge-building) work as priest of art involves the correction of that dichotomy and the restoration of sacramental unity between the secular and the spiritual. This is nowhere more evident than in the "communion scenes" of *Ulysses*.

V.3.4: The Communion Scenes

V.3.4.1: Communion of Father, Son, and Spouses

Paul Briand, in his seminal article, affirmed that communion occurs when Bloom and Stephen share tea in Bloom's home: "This drinking of the cocoa . . . marks the end of the search for the father by the son, the finding of the son by the father, the attainment of identification for both." Furthermore, it betokens the revival of Bloom's marriage. It is the moment in which all is resolved and new life becomes possible for all three protagonists: "Vivified Bloom will now assert himself with his wife for the first time in ten years; Molly will prepare breakfast for Bloom." Stephen is also renewed by the encounter: "[H]aving broken from his precious, priggish shell of selfish aestheticism, [he] can now go forth to create as an objective artist." Stephen, concludes Briand, has accepted Bloom the Christ figure and way to the Father, and is thus "born anew into the world of man."[83]

Subsequent critical consensus has gradually accepted

that these communion scenes contain demonstrable Mass references. We know on the one hand that Joyce was more than capable of investing the word "massproduct" with Eucharistic significance, and we know on the other hand that among his main aesthetic aims was numbered that of redressing a perceived removal of the sacred from the secular and the mundane. This he would achieve by rediscovering the sublime in the apparently banal and by reuniting the sensual and the spiritual, with the aid of the Catholic Eucharist.

Frances Restuccia argues that Joyce distances himself from the heretical sensualism of Buck and Bloom in favor of an approach to reality that recognizes an active translucent otherworldly presence, a mysterious substantiality accidentally visible: "It must be stressed . . . that Joyce's secularization of Catholicism is not tantamount to boiling down reality to the merely secular."[84] This short statement, correct in its essence, also contains a confusion of concepts and presuppositions that calls for clarification. If Joyce's "secularization of Catholicism" does not "boil down reality to the merely secular"—i.e., if it retains the sense of the sacred and the spiritual in the secular—then how may it be said to differ from Catholicism itself? Restuccia finds evidence of this presence of the spiritual in the temporary and the mundane in the remainder of *Ulysses*, providing a thorough analysis of the communion scenes and of the language in which they are expressed.

The arguments she provides are rigorously grounded in the text: semantic, imaginative, and persuasive. The Eucharistic symbolism, artfully woven into the text, is unobstrusive, but unavoidable:

> It is because religious language . . . is so highly concentrated in these scenes that critics come to regard them as communion scenes . . . Because the religious terms of these episodes are first grasped as secular terms (since their religious meanings are so often disguised), and thus can be viewed as accidents holding religious substances within them, each of the scenes as a whole may be readily conceived of, eucharistically, as (ordinary) accidental reality embodying (extraordinary) substantial meaning.[85]

The Eucharistic moments here described are "secular," but it is Catholic doctrine that invests them with rich sacramental significance. When Ellmann uses an expression like "secularized host," and Restuccia "secular communion," one wonders if they grasp their compatibility with Catholic doctrine. Rather than denying religion in these supposedly "non-religious" communions that occur outside the temple walls, Joyce is calling attention to the presence of the transcendental in the apparently profane and mundane.

In the conclusion of her analysis, Restuccia indicates that she does grasp the connection between Catholicism and Joyce's art: "Joyce meant the accidents-substance structure to be taken as the proper model for his entire novel."[86] This implies that the worldview of *Ulysses* is Eucharistic and incarnational. In these Catholic doctrines Joyce found the means to overcome the shortcomings of naturalism on the one hand and symbolism on the other, and to harness and synthesize their virtues. As we pursue the trajectory of critical commentary on these texts, we will observe an ever deepening and expanding coincidence between the Joycean Eucharistic aesthetic and orthodox Catholic Eucharistic theology.

V.3.4.3: Ulysses *as a Novel about Communion*

Some of the critical insights that we have seen concerning the Eucharist in Joyce's work are by now "canonical," that is, generally accepted. This is evident in Kiberd's recent book about *Ulysses* and the art of everyday life. His commentary, always lively and provocative, gathers together the best of what has preceded while also offering original readings. By ascribing to the scene in Barney Kiernan's pub in the Cyclops chapter a climactic importance, for example, Kiberd seems to suggest that this scene corresponds to the proclamation of the Gospel and the homily in the structure of the Mass. It is proclaimed by Bloom: "'Force, hatred, history, all that. That's not life for men and women, insult and hatred. And everybody knows it's the very opposite of that that is really life.' 'What?' says Alf. 'Love,' says Bloom, 'I mean the opposite of hatred. I must go now.'"[87]

There is a Christ-like poignancy and power to Bloom's words and conduct in this scene and it is one of the most dramatic in the book. His depiction as a Christ figure is at once a joke and more than a joke: "Moments earlier the Citizen had disparaged him as the new messiah for Ireland; but now, that same Citizen gives credence to the mocking title by throwing a biscuit tin at Bloom with the cry, 'I'll crucify him so I will.'"[88] The idea of Bloom as Gospel witness is further reinforced later when, reflecting on the incident, he thinks, "Suppose he hit me. Look at it other way round. Not so bad then. Perhaps not to hurt he meant."[89] *Ulysses* contains multiple resonances that ensure that the Mass and the Gospel are never far from our thoughts.

In Joyce's work the Eucharist provides an analogical eloquence in service of the aesthetic redemption and recreation of experience in art. But in the Eucharist Joyce found also a sacramental dramatization of the main theme of *Ulysses*, that of paternity and filiation and identity, the restoration of communion between father and son. Identity is achieved in exodus out of self and relationship with the other, especially with the father. The encounter between Stephen and Bloom in the Eumaeus chapter is now serenely accepted in critical circles as a "communion scene":

> Bloom offers to stir Stephen's putrid coffee, and he also offers him a bun, while joking that it now looks more like a brick from a nearby building site. 'Couldn't' (773) is Stephen's strained reply. Here the idea of transubstantiation—that the body and blood of Jesus are presented at the consecration of the Mass under the appearance of bread and wine—is recreated, in the bread roll that looks like a brick and in the coffee which may well be something else. This is Joyce's heavily ironic climax to *Ulysses*. After all the fake consecrations, this is the true one, a real attempt at communion.

Here Bloom becomes the distributing priest, as an act of common kindness tilts the moment towards the Eucharistic. The young Stephen had refused the Eucharist, saying he must wait for it to come to him—and now it has. In this moment both Eucharist and epiphany are rejoined—the sudden showing-forth of a hidden symbolic meaning of a seemingly banal exchange between two tired men.[90]

To describe this moment as "heavily ironic" is to miss the ultimate grandeur of Joyce's achievement, for here we find Joyce's attempt to reflect, with deft discretion, the possibility of redemption. If it is read as satiric banalization of the sacred and sublime, then yes, it may be described as heavily ironic. But if it is read as an aesthetic transmutation "of the daily bread of experience into the radiant body of everliving life," then it is to be found on the opposite end of the spectrum from "heavily ironic." In Bloom, Stephen has finally found the lowly Christian loveliness, humanity at its humble best. In this Eucharistic coalescence of the mundane and the sublime Joyce fulfills the task expressed in *Portrait* to become priest of the eternal imagination.

V.3.4.4: Eucharistic Radiance in Quotidian Realities

In a post-Christian humanist moment reminiscent of Ellmann, Kiberd perceives the Ithaca communion incident in terms of supplantation of religious ritual: "Bloom will offer his coffee and bun in a revised, gentler version.

If sacrifice was once designed by humans to propitiate gods, now it is propounded by godlike humans as an offering made ultimately to themselves."[91] It is hard to envisage how any version of the Eucharistic sacrifice could be gentler than God's giving of himself in Christ to humans under the appearance of bread and wine, empowering them to give themselves in a "God-like" way to God and to one another. The "communion" between Stephen and Bloom is perfectly admissible as a dynamic not of supplantation of the Catholic Eucharist but of simultaneity, as Kevin Sullivan suggested.[92] Kiberd recognizes this simultaneity when he observes, "This is the deeper meaning of that Eucharist around which not only the life of Jesus but also the meeting of Bloom and Stephen is organized."[93]

Towards the close of the next chapter of his book, Kiberd distinguishes between true religion and an infirm religiosity: "The Catholicism in which Joyce was raised was a rule-bound affair of external proprieties meticulously observed, and any infraction filled the sinner with scruples."[94] This is a good description of the "Catholicism" of *Portrait*. Kiberd argues that Joyce proposed an alternative spirituality. His description of that spirituality has distinctly Catholic resonances to the minimally trained theological ear: "Bloom . . . draws Stephen, all unconsciously, into a Eucharistic fellowship, offering Stephen his own cup, that supreme image of the known world."[95]

By these subtle evocations of the Eucharistic mystery Joyce indicates that, within the context of ordinary-looking events, if our spiritual eyes are open, we may catch glimpses of the divine. The intention is not to secularize, relativize or banalize the Eucharist. Instead, Joyce believes that, somehow, mysteriously and beautifully and meaningfully, whatever is real in religion must be connected to such mundane realities. The critical attention that we have seen thus far has focused predominantly on the Eucharistic species of bread, which becomes Christ's body; it will now focus on the species of wine, which turns to blood. With this, the visceral realism of Joyce's Eucharistic art reaches a still deeper level.

V.4: Body and Blood in Ulysses

V.4.1: Molly's Menstruation

According to Joyce's biographer, Richard Ellmann, Joyce's achievement was "to convert Christianity from a dogma to a system of metaphors."[96] In 1972 Ellmann gave further impetus to critical investigation of the Eucharistic motif in Joyce's writing, making what is later seen to be an important contribution to Joyce studies:

> Joyce is establishing a secret parallel and opposition: the body of God and the body of woman share blood in common. In allowing Molly to menstruate at the end Joyce consecrates the blood in the chamberpot rather than the blood in the chalice ... It is human blood, not divine. Menstruation is Promethean.[97]

With this Eucharistic reading of Molly's menstruation,

Ellmann apparently considers that he is discovering in Joyce's writing an anti-dualistic improvement upon the Catholic doctrine of human redemption, an unthinkable innovation which utilizes "the Catholic myth" while surpassing it and rendering it obsolete except as metaphorical vehicle of a greater vision. In saying, "It is human blood, not divine," and "Menstruation is Promethean," Ellmann indicates that he has not thought through to its ultimate consequences the radical innovativeness of the doctrine of the Incarnation: Christ, as "God's Prometheus," has taken blood from woman and returned it, divinized but still human, in the Eucharist.

As another, similar, example, Ellmann offers this typically "post-Christian humanist" interpretation of Stephen's experience on the beach in *Portrait*: "That girl had constituted for him a vision of secular beauty, a pagan Mary beckoning him to the life of art which knows no division between soul and body."[98] Christianity's greatest and most controversial claim to originality is the Incarnation of God. Christ is human and divine, a sharer in our nature in all things but sin, the new Adam. To affirm a division between soul and body, either in the name of Christianity or in accusation against it, would indicate a failure to grasp its most fundamental and revolutionary truth and perennial novelty: the mystery of God made flesh.

The "religious Mary" is no less "secular" or historical—that is, no less real, no less physical, no less incarnate in time and space and matter—than the girl Joyce saw paddling in the water or than the menstruating Molly. Her soul is not divided from her body. In fact, by a curious quirk of faith, according to Catholicism it never has been, not even in death. It is true that in the Catholic anthropology of fallen human nature there exists a certain tension (as opposed to division) within the soul-body duality (a tension that is experientially evident already in this life), but it is no less true that this same anthropology conceives of man's original prelapsarian soul-body state as being tension-free and conceives his final destiny as one of glorious and eternal reconciliation of the postlapsarian tension. In Mary's case, that tension was present too but within a unique, unprecedented and unrepeated harmony. Soul and body are more undivided in Mary than in any other woman, and no woman's beauty is as sacred or as secular.

The difference between many Joyceans and James Joyce is that Joyce *did* attempt—evidence suggests—to think through the inexhaustible mystery of the Incarnation to its ultimate consequences. Joyce pushed to unseen limits the incarnational logic of intrinsic unity between the sacred and the secular, but he did not push that logic to the point of rupture. Without incurring in heresy, Joyce explored the legitimate reaches of Catholic orthodoxy in ways unthinkable in his time. By this I do not mean that he probed the periphery. Rather, within the dynamic described by Ratzinger (of creativity within continuity), Joyce went to the heart of the doctrine of the Incarnation (and its prolongation in the Eucharist) to a point that provokes the reaction of shock that spurred the Jewish elders to crucify Christ for the very same "blasphemy."

So, contrary to critical consensus, Stephen in Circe

is not purged of religion but of a purist religiosity, and Joyce's anti-Catholicism is skin-deep. Medieval Catholicism, as we have seen in the case of speculation concerning Christ's circumcision, was more comfortable with bodily realities than post-Puritan Catholicism, and Joyce's project is partly about restoring that healthy disinhibition. This he will do by celebrating in his art the presence of the sacred in bodily realities, menstruation included, with the aid of Catholic Eucharistic theology.

V.4.2: Eucharistic Art

Fr. Robert Boyle declares indebtedness to Ellmann's insight on Joyce's "image of art as Eucharist" upon which his own reflections will build: "This is his perception of Molly's (and the other Dublin women's) menstruation as intimately allied to the various consecrations throughout Dublin of Christ's blood and body."[99]

Boyle will confront the issue of crude naturalistic realism to the point of apparent blasphemy in Joyce's art. The charge of blasphemy rests on the assumption not only of mockery by Joyce (like Mulligan), but also on the assumption that it is sacrilegious or blasphemous to associate what is human, Molly's menstruation, with what is divine, Christ's blood.

Boyle, as theologian and Joycean literary critic, is well equipped to interpret Joyce's aesthetic adaptation of the Eucharist. In *Portrait*, Boyle explains, Stephen, perhaps in an act of modest realism, substitutes the word transubstantiation for that of *transmutation* in describing himself and his aesthetic project.[100] The term transubstantiation is unique to the Eucharistic context. Boyle offers a theologically exact summary of the Thomist doctrine of transubstantiation, which, transmuted to transmutation, will be applied to Joyce's art:

> Christ, as it were, comes across ('trans') the void to replace the substance of the bread, though the accidents (or appearances) of bread remain, inhering in no substance at all, but somehow sustained in existence by divine power in some relation to Christ's body. Thus when I move the appearances of bread I really move Christ's sacramental body. Thus I can eat the living Christ as divine nourishment and a source of ever-living life.[101]

This communion with the living body of Christ enables new "conscience"—meaning "to know with"—in the receiver, just as the "communion" with the artist through the reading of his work written in ink enables introduction through, with and in him to a new form of knowing: "A new conscience—a knowing-with Christ, like what I take to be Stephen's basic meaning in forming a new conscience for his race, a knowing with the artist—is thus nourished."[102]

As priest of art, Joyce will share with humanity his nourishing knowledge of the human condition. The human condition has its dark side as well as its capacity for goodness, a fact of which Joyce is acutely aware; his humanism is not ingenuous. Boyle explains that the term "subsubstantiality" describes those forms of human communion that produce degradation and bestiality, exemplified by Buck Mulligan's "eucharist" and general worldview, blasphemously dismissive of divinity and cynically scornful of humanity. Stephen, in contrast, seeks a "consubstantiality" that would celebrate humanity even in its physicality and a transubstantiality that would make the divine human and the human divine.

Boyle's reading does not succumb to the dichotomization of sacred and secular, divine and human, matter and spirit that we have seen in other readings. His interpretation, if it is correct, indicates that in maturity Joyce has succeeded in returning to and fulfilling the young Stephen's aesthetic intention of transmuting the raw material of his "father's house"—the "rotted cabbage . . . this disorder, the misrule and confusion of his father's house and the stagnation of vegetable life"[103]—into the radiant material of art. Stephen as artist (not theologian) appropriates the Eucharistic mystery in metaphorical service of his own literary endeavour. This will bear fruit in a form of art that combines a realism that is visceral to the point of scandal with a radiance that, according to Boyle, may be called sublime.

V.4.3: Visceral Eucharistic Realism

Under the auspices of the Eucharist, Joyce disconcertingly combines the visceral and the sublime. Equally disconcerting is the scale of his priestly and Eucharistic artistic pretentions: "[H]is ultimate aim, as I conceive it, is to prepare for the image of the multilocation of the life-giving artist under the accidents of ink."[104] As Godlike artist operating through the accidents of ink, Joyce's art is scatological and eschatological, eucharistic and artistic, and finds its fullest expression, according to Boyle, in *Finnegans Wake*, where Shem prepares "a caustic ink out of his own body wastes."[105] The Catholic faith-perspective experiences shock at finding the Eucharist discussed in association with menstruation by an agnostic humanist—Ellmann[106]—and with body wastes by a Jesuit priest—Boyle—but the shock factor is tempered somewhat by the recollection that Christ, contrary to Mosaic prescriptions concerning ritual and legal impurity, allowed himself to be touched by the hemorrhaging woman (cf. Lk 8:43-48), and spoke freely of the process of ingestion, digestion, and defecation (cf. Mk 7:18-19).

A certain squeamishness about our own humanity is a curious human tendency, of which squeamishness concerning the humanity of God and of God's Mother is a natural extension, but Mary menstruated and Jesus of Nazareth went to the bathroom (euphemism intended). In drawing attention to these facts there may be a subjective irreverent or blasphemous intention, but objectively the facts themselves are an uncontroversial incarnational consonant. *Gaudium et spes* 14, for example, states that "[M]an is not allowed to despise his bodily life, rather he is obliged to regard his body as good and honorable since God has created it and will raise it up on the last day." As Weldon Thornton has written, "Joyce felt that the artist had an obligation far beyond that of the 'ordinary person' to face up to every aspect of life, including those that might seem coarse or sordid."[107]

To confront and somehow transmute the mystery of material flux is a legitimate philosophical and aesthetic enterprise. Joyce's response to the corruptibility of matter is emphatically *not* that of Sartre's atheistic *Nausea*. The involvement of the Eucharistic mystery in this endeavour provokes initial shock but to call it blasphemous may be a knee-jerk reaction, given that in a faith context redemption of what seems destined to corruption (human flesh and blood) is in fact what the Eucharistic mystery realizes.

Stephen's refusal in *Portrait* to discount rotten cabbage as the stuff of radiant art, developed in Joyce's ongoing preoccupation with the hidden potentiality of apparent waste in *Ulysses*, assumes in *Finnegans Wake* associations within stark and shocking contrast.[108] Following this ever-expanding trajectory from the corruptible to the incorruptible, Boyle finds fuller metaphorization of the Eucharist in Joyce's later work: "The fullest development of the eucharistic image, with all its possibilities and all of its positive and negative elements operative, can be found on pages 185-86 of *Finnegans Wake*."[109] I remit to Boyle's article for the English translation. Material doesn't get much more raw than this and, in Boyle's judgment, nor does art get much more radiant: "The Catholic dogma of the Incarnation most deeply implies that both words and flesh can be divinized and more beautiful than reason . . . can comprehend, and . . . Joyce developed that implication to almost divine artistic achievement."[110]

V.4.4: The Visceral and the Sublime

Catholics might find Joyce's Eucharistic synthesis ugly and unamusing, but if it is intended comically to convey the potential immortality of corruptible matter, then it is not objectively blasphemous or even theologically incorrect, given that the Eucharist is God's promise to man that what is destined to putrefaction and death is destined also to eternal glorification. Without scorning the most seemingly squalid human realities, Joyce's literary eucharist eventually achieves cosmic and sublime proportions. The Eucharist is essential to Joyce's life-giving and life-affirming project to "bring forth his literary race to carry life, livable and unlivable, into the world" and to prove "literature's cosmic worth to the human race."[111] Boyle's article fulfills its stated intention to build upon Ellmann's insight. To dismiss it as a mere "Catholic exposition," a "contribution to theology, not to literary criticism,"[112] is not only to fail honestly to confront the sources and implications of Boyle's interpretation—that is, Catholic theology—but is to fail also to confront the inspirations and intentions of Joyce's art.

The Joycean aesthetic enterprise has much to do with the reconciliation of the material and the sublime, of spirit and flesh, the temporal and the eternal. Joyce's early option in *Portrait* in favor of the corporal and the material leads logically to confrontation in *Ulysses* with the mystery of disintegration and apparent waste. The aesthetic mission joyfully to redeem solid matter is challenged by the crude spectacle of its liquid corruption, its dissolution into flux and apparent ultimate disappearance. The initially shocking "Eucharistic" synthesization of death, decomposition, waste, life, and glory that Boyle finds in *Finnegans Wake* is an orthodox Catholic Eucharistic insight, given that it is in the Eucharist that corruptible flesh is gloriously redeemed.

The spirit-flesh opposition was a Manichean doctrine, unintentionally resurrected by Descartes. The soul-body dualist opposition was resolved by the Eternal Word's Incarnation in Christ and the perpetuation of his glorified corporal presence in the Eucharist. Joyce was aware of this fact and therefore favored the Catholic over the Protestant interpretation, in a time during which, apparently, the influence of purist doctrines prevailed even in Catholic circles.

As Josef Pieper puts it, responding to the same spiritualist error perceived by Joyce, "the great teachers of Christendom would scarcely have dared to espouse the idea of the complete existential unity of body and soul and carry it to its ultimate conclusions had it not been reinforced by the doctrine of the 'Incarnation.'" Here we have a timely reminder of the perennial originality and audacity of Catholic orthodoxy, to which Pieper adds a nice etymological nuance: "Strictly speaking, the term [Incarnation] means, after all, not 'God becoming man' but 'God becoming *flesh*.'"[113]

As Aquinas flatly puts it, "[T]he body of Christ was not a heavenly, but a carnal and earthly body."[114] An avid reader of Aquinas, Joyce perceived and aesthetically appropriated the inexhaustible potential of this astonishing doctrine that is unique to Christianity, and in its Eucharistic prolongation unique to Catholicism. Other Joyce critics besides Boyle have divined more of the rich sacramental resonances of his art.

V.4.5: Sacramental Resonances

Dennis Shanahan develops a rich analysis of the phenomenon of blood in *Ulysses*. Shanahan, like Ellmann, sees Joyce's art in terms of substitution of Catholic dogma rather than simultaneity. He begins his article with a reference to the Letter to the Hebrews. Stephen's priesthood supersedes Christ's as Christ's superseded Melchisedec's: Stephen "renders the Catholic priesthood old and refuses that legal, temporal, and inherited order. Art is now, in the rest of *A Portrait* and in *Ulysses*, the 'better testament' and requires a 'blood sacrifice.'"[115] But Shanahan then proceeds to describe Joyce's artistic priesthood in terms that, instead of displacing Christ's priesthood, depend on it.

The priesthood of Stephen, like that of Christ, must confront the great challenges of life and death. As artist, Stephen must transmute into art the raw material of life. This vision is expressed in a living testament written in blood: "As a priest of art . . . Stephen would participate in and witness life and execute a testament of blood, as Joyce has created a testament of blood in *Ulysses*." The Eucharist, as prolongation of Christ's Passion, will serve as prototype. Joyce perceived and capitalized upon its enormous aesthetic potential.

Curiously, in Shanahan's analysis, Catholic claims are made for Joyce's art that seem to presuppose failure of those claims on the part of Catholicism itself: "*Ulysses* employs this Catholic formula of the passion in order to universalize and secularize the Incarnation and the sufferings of Calvary; the eucharist is the aesthetic (sacramental) expression of the universal passion."[116]

Joyce's art achieves an everyday relevance for the Eucharistic mystery that the Eucharist itself is assumed not to have. Shanahan presupposes and suggests that the "Catholic formula of the passion" and the mystery of the Eucharist that it describes and enacts, have failed to "universalize and secularize the Incarnation and the sufferings of Calvary," whereas Joyce's *Ulysses* succeeds in doing so; in which case *Ulysses* invites a kind of "faith" that Catholicism can no longer claim. Catholic theology is availed of to unpack the sacramental riches of Joyce's art, while at the same time the invalidity of that theology is asserted, and Joyce's rejection of it assumed. But if that theology is invalid, then so too must be Joyce's sacramental worldview. Conversely, if Joyce's artistic vision is valid, then the sacramental theology upon which it depends is also valid, and Joyce is a believer. Let us look more deeply now at the congruity and interdependence between Catholic theology and Joyce's aesthetic, and the thematic implications thereof for a correct understanding of Joyce's art and his religious mind. Shanahan's hermeneutic is a useful bridge for this task.

V.5: Joyce's Theological Intentions

V.5.1: Agape in Joyce's Art

Shanahan aspires to complete Boyle's hermeneutic. Boyle focused on ink; Shanahan will focus on blood and its crucial role in Stephen's priest-artist analogy, showing how Joyce's preoccupation with blood in *Ulysses* aesthetically exploits the ascetical and sacrificial dimension of the Eucharist; that is, the giving of life at the cost of the spilling of blood: "Within the particular historical and environmental situation, the body struggles and thereby gains a 'spirit,' a consciousness of eternal truth, and within that struggle (passion) the body 'bleeds' that spirit onto the page as ink." The artist's struggle culminates in his art and bears fruit in a quasi-immortalizing mode of expression: "The blood-ink expresses the soul, the eternal verities apprehended or formed in the body's passion."[117]

Blood runs through Joyce's book as it runs through the human body: "*Ulysses* is a blood-drenched novel. The word 'blood' and forms of the word occur at least two hundred times," not including the multiple occurrences of blood-related words and phenomena. This is only to be expected: "If *Ulysses* is a 'body' consisting of chapter-organs, it is appropriate that blood would course throughout; the novel expresses the body, but its means of expression is the body's blood." Shanahan, whether consciously or not, shares the Judaic, and subsequently the Christian, understanding of blood as bearer of life. He also shares the bibilical anthropology of human personhood as a unity in the soul-body duality. In Joyce's art, Shanahan explains, Word and Flesh, spirit and matter, become one, and blood is bearer of the spirit: "*Ulysses* represents the body of naturalistic fact, but the Word that makes the representation a meaningful one is formed out of the body's blood."[118]

Shanahan develops his blood-passion-lifegiving hermeneutic in a direction that coincides remarkably with recent Eucharistic orthodoxy. The sacrificial theology of the Letter to the Hebrews, to which he refers at the beginning of his article, informs his reading of Joyce's work. We have seen the biographical evidence that Joyce approached his artistic mission with *agape* zeal;[119] Shanahan, with the aid of the Letter to the Hebrews, discovers evidence of that martyr-like zeal written deeply into the works themselves. Cardinal Albert Vanhoye is a leading contemporary expert on the Letter to the Hebrews. His theological explanation of the Letter resonates with Shanahan's hermeneutic and, indirectly but impressively, enriches our reading of Joyce.

V.5.2: Agape in the Letter to the Hebrews

In his prologue to Vanhoye's published commentary on the Letter to the Hebrews, Pope Benedict XVI expressed gratitude to Vanhoye for teaching that "the blood of Jesus was, on account of his prayer, 'oxygenated' by the Holy Spirit. In this way, it has become the power of resurrection and the source of life for us."[120] Vanhoye pointed out in the course of a retreat to the papal household that the Hebrew word for Spirit and for breath—*ruah*—are one and the same, and that in the Hebrew mentality blood is sacred because it carries the spirit of life. This Judeo-Christian intuition has been reaffirmed by modern science: "Our blood is intimately related to our 'breath.' In order to live it is necessary that our 'breath' enter our blood . . . enriching it with oxygen, so that the blood may communicate this oxygen to all the cells of the body to vivify it."[121]

Vanhoye does not fail to draw out the biological and theological implications of this body-soul sacramental synthesis: "Christ in his passion by means of intense prayer has 'breathed in' the Holy Spirit . . . The blood of Christ has become for human nature the vital principle which has communicated to it the new life, communion with God and with our brothers."[122] The dynamic outlined here by Vanhoye in terms of incarnation and passion, inblooding and communication of the Spirit, is almost replicated in Shanahan's description of the dynamic at work in Joyce's art. For Joyce, Shanahan explains, blood evokes the mystery of death, life and communion or "consubstantiality" of the artist with humanity.[123]

It would be difficult to find a description of the Catholic theology of art and literature more consonant with the following description of Joyce's art in *Ulysses* at the end of Shanahan's article: "A true artistic eucharist raises the limited and individual life and vision to a particular enactment of the general *via crucis* . . . For Joyce, art elevates everyday life, as does *Ulysses*, a eucharist representing the passion, the drama of the human body."[124] Joyce's art culminates in an expression of the Eucharistic realities that is entirely homogenous with orthodox Catholic theology. It is orthodox Catholic sacramental theology that gives this interpretation its full expressive force. Vanhoye's interpretation of the Eucharist draws from the Letter to the Hebrews and from the findings of modern science to explain more fully and deeply what Catholicism has always taught about the Eucharist as prolongation of Christ's Incarnation, Passion, death, and Resurrection and perpetuation of his Real Presence so that his Body, Blood, and the Spirit may be communicated to us in Holy Communion.

As Frances Restuccia has explained, there is no clash between the Catholic and Joycean Eucharistic theologies. We are often asked to choose between faith in Christ and the Church's Eucharist, or faith in Joyce's Eucharistic art, even though no inherent conflict is presented between Christ's gospel and Joyce's art to justify such a requirement. Moreover, Joyce's art draws seamlessly from Catholic Eucharistic theology and thematically depends upon it. This same disconcerting pseudo-dilemma recurs in the discussion of the Joycean "trinity" of Bloom, Stephen, and Molly. We will look now at Joyce's use of Trinitarian theology in search of evidence of authorial intention to break from Catholic theology by heresy or parody.

V.5.3: Trinitarian Analogues

V.5.3.1: Orthodoxy or Heresy?

The discussion of Joyce's use of Trinitarian theology arises connaturally out of the discussion of his use of the Eucharist motif. Paul Briand raised the idea of Bloom, Stephen, and Molly as a secular supplantation of the Holy Trinity. Briand's theory is that Joyce uses the Mass to portray not the union of Christ as Head and Church as Body, but of Intellect (Stephen) and Flesh (Molly) in an Intellect-Flesh synthesis represented by Leopold Bloom: "What is achieved in the novel is the trinity of the one substance of humanity in the united identities of the persons of Stephen, Bloom, and Molly." In Joyce's human trinity, Briand sees Molly as a reverse idealization of a "third principle," a Joycean comical representation of the Holy Spirit, a representative of feminine wisdom: "the earth-mother, the everlasting female, the eternal she."[125]

In the chapter of his book on *Ulysses* entitled "Towards Lay Sanctity," Ellmann interprets Molly as the symbol of the flesh in Joyce's construction of a new earthly city, intended to parody and replace the heavenly Jerusalem: "Freed from supernatural trappings, Bloom and Stephen offer profane salvation, The New Bloomusalem."[126] Again, we see here the dichotomization of the supernatural and the profane. In this new "terrestrial paradise," Molly "constitutes the third in a new, three-in-one being, a human improvement upon the holy family as upon the divine trinity. To confirm it, she is accorded the same birthday as the Virgin Mary."[127]

Umberto Eco concurs with this hermeneutic of a Trinitarian parallel, and imputes to Fr. William Noon an attempt "to attenuate the Trinitarian parody in its most blasphemous aspects," without identifying the blasphemy. He insists upon "the mediatory function of Molly," against Fr. Noon's agenda, allegedly, to erase her: "importance is . . . given to the mediatory function of Molly which Noon's interpretation leaves more in the shade, almost in an attempt to attenuate the Trinitarian parody in its most blasphemous aspects."[128]

There is an important misunderstanding here which is easily elucidated with a moment of patristic theology. St. Augustine wrote in his seminal book on the Trinity that, "It will be clear that I do not find the opinion very convincing, which supposes that the trinity of the image of

God, as far as human nature is concerned, can be discovered in three persons . . . composed of the union of male and female and their offspring."[129] There is no need here to go into Augustine's reasons for not endorsing the idea of the human family as analogue of the Holy Trinity. For our purposes, it is sufficient to note that Augustine rejects the idea not as blasphemous but simply as unconvincing.

V.5.3.2: The Family as Image of the Trinity

The idea of the human family as analogue of the Trinity would much later be taken up by Hans Urs Von Balthasar, who would maintain, in disagreement with Augustine, that the conjugal and familial nucleus "remains, in spite of all the obvious dissimilarities, the most eloquent *imago Trinitatis* that we find woven into the fabric of the creature."[130] The analogue has subsequently been integrated into the ordinary Magisterium by Pope John Paul II. For example: "God in his deepest mystery is not a solitude, but a family, since He has in Himself fatherhood, sonship, and the essence of the family, which is love. This subject of the family is not, therefore, extraneous to the subject of the Holy Spirit."[131] Similarly, no. 2205 of the *Catechism of the Catholic Church* states that: "The Christian family is a communion of persons, a sign and image of the communion of the Father and the Son in the Holy Spirit."

God the Father is not "married" to the Holy Spirit and we cannot speak of the Holy Spirit as being of female gender. The Church has therefore been reticent about applying the human analogy to the Trinitarian reality in strictly conjugal terms, but as a *familial* analogy which evidently includes woman as spouse and mother, it is not foreign to Catholic thought. Why Eco should consider it blasphemous, or consider that Catholicism considers it so, is something of a mystery; it might be symptomatic of the erroneous notion of absolute polarization of the divine and the human. The possibility of analogue between the human and divine families is a logical extension of the twin truths of man's creation in God's image and likeness and of God's Trinitarian and relational identity: if God is Trinitarian and relational, and man is created in God's image and likeness, then Trinitarian resonances and relations will naturally be found in and between human persons.

Catholicism has no difficulty with admitting an analogue between the Holy Trinity and the human family. It would, however, have obvious difficulties with the claim of replacing one with the other. Whether this was *Joyce's* intention or not, is the recurring question. The sharp distinction that some critics establish between the supernatural and the profane is not a feature of Catholic theology. One aspect of the Eucharistic mystery which has gone largely unnoticed in Joycean criticism and which most probably did not pass unnoticed by Joyce himself, clearly demonstrates this analogical and sacramental connection between the human and the divine: the Eucharist as nuptial union between the Bridegroom and the Bride.

V.5.4: The Nuptial Motif

V.5.4.1: In the Judeo-Christian Tradition

It may be the case that Molly is intended implicitly and imperfectly to represent the Holy Spirit, as Joyce critics have suggested. However, following the Eucharistic logic of Joyce's art, it is more likely that Molly primarily represents humanity itself as fallen bride of Bloom the fallen bridegroom. This latter parallel is closer to the Joycean text than the former one. The Trinitarian analogue requires an imaginative leap that might be accused of forcing the text, whereas Molly is, after all, a bride, and Bloom a bridegroom. Since Joyce likens Bloom to Christ (Stephen recognizes him as *Christus*), it seems plausible that Molly, Bloom's bride, may be likened to the Bride of Christ. Reconciling the sexes belongs, as we have seen throughout chapter III, not just to the warp and woof of *Ulysses* but to the thematic drive of Joyce's entire corpus.

Curiously, the nuptial dimension of the Eucharist and the possible parallels between Bloom as Christ the Bridegroom and Molly as Church the Bride has not been developed. Joyce critics have failed to consider the possibility that the union of Christ as Head and Church as Body may find a parallel not in Bloom alone as the center who unifies Stephen and Molly in an intellect and flesh synthesis, but in Bloom's reunion with Molly (bridegroom with bride) following upon his encounter with Stephen.

The nuptial aspect of God's relationship with humanity was propitious to Joyce's aesthetic, as a perusal of its biblical trajectory promptly reveals. The prophet Hosea was told by God to take a prostitute (Gomer) to be his bride—"Go, take to yourself a wife of harlotry . . . for the land commits great harlotry by forsaking the Lord" (Hos 1:2b)—so that God's people would see in his prophet what they were doing to Him. Here is an example of a spiritual truth being taught in the midst of apparently blasphemous conditions, according to the minds of many literary critics, and if Joyce had a blasphemous mind in the way imputed to him, the Hosea story would be an attractive imaginative trope for him to incorporate into his literary imagination. The Hosea story is characteristic of the alliances that God serially forms with his chosen people, who serially break them. The Hebrew word used for sin is *thanah*, meaning adultery, indicating the aspect of nuptial betrayal inherent in sin.

The nuptial image continues into the New Testament with Christ's first miracle—the Eucharistic transformation of water into wine—at the wedding feast of Cana (cf. Jn 2:1-12). St. John the Baptist perceives his role in terms of the Bridegroom's "best man" (Jn 3:29). Christ develops the image in the parable of the vigilant virgins awaiting the Bridegroom's return (cf. Mt 25:1-13), and openly refers to himself as the Bridegroom (cf. Lk 5:35). Later, St. Paul would explicate the theology of matrimony in terms of sacramental participation in the relationship between Christ the Bridegroom and his Bride the Church (cf. Eph 5:21-33).[132] Coincidentally, resonances of the biblical nuptial motif may be found in Joyce's writings.

V.5.4.2: The Nuptial Motif in Joyce

It seems more than coincidental that Martin Cunningham, who in the short story "Grace" and in *Ulysses* is depicted as a devout Catholic, has to suffer, like Bloom, the ongoing pain of a difficult marriage. In the light of the theology of Christ as Bridegroom and Head of his Bride and Body the Church, indissolubly joined in one Flesh at the wedding feast of Calvary, a Christ-like quality is present in Bloom's stubborn love for a faithless spouse (Molly), who repeats her "yes" in the midst of her infidelities. It seems likely that the Hosea imagery, which culminates in the Bride/Bridegroom Ecclesiology and Eucharistic theology, is part of Joyce's literary imagination, serving the themes of personal individuation and harmonization of the masculine and feminine: dynamism via alliance.

Given on the one hand Joyce's known thematic preoccupation with harmonizing the sexes, and on the other hand the prominence of the nuptial doctrine in the Old Testament, in the Gospel, in Pauline and Augustinian teachings, and in Magisterial declarations throughout the Church's history—a prominence comparable in all of these sources to that given to the theology of Christ as Head and the Church as Body (to which the Bridegroom and Bride theology is closely connected),[133] and arguably superior to the theology of the Eucharist as reunion of Father and Son—it seems highly probable that Joyce is aware of this dimension of Catholic Eucharistic Ecclesiology, and wishes aesthetically to exploit it for his own conception of personal individuation.

Kiberd has spoken of Joyce's conception of personality "as process rather than product,"[134] as *dynamis* rather than *stasis*, which corresponds with the biblical and Christian anthropology of man as pilgrim towards plenitude via search, suffering, and relationship. Homer's epic is about the longing for union of bridegroom and bride and of father and son, a longing inscribed in human nature. It is central to Christianity too—its apotheosis occurs in the Eucharist—and to *Ulysses*. Some critics discover signs in *Ulysses* which promise the restoration of relationships just described; paternal-filial bonds are formed between Bloom and Stephen, and marital bonds are renewed between Bloom and Molly. Many Joyce critics have identified the Joycean employment of the Eucharist motif as vehicle for the theme of paternity, but this aspect of the Eucharist is inextricably related to the nuptial aspect: the union of Christ with his Bride the Church depends upon his prior union with the Father; his rescue of the Bride and the consummation of his nuptial union with her occurs through his reunion with the Father, and vice versa. These dynamics merge in the Eucharist.

Bloom's marital reunion with Molly is conditional upon his assimilation of the death of Rudy and his transformative encounter with Stephen. The parallel between Molly and the Virgin Mary is intentional: Molly's birthday is the 8th of September. Mary is the prototype of the Church, Bride of Christ. Throughout *Ulysses*, as we have seen in chapter III, Bloom, although in some ways Christ-like, is depicted as an incomplete man. He is not yet Moses or Christ, father, son, or spouse. He must win back his bride with an act of *agape*-love. If the nuptial aspect of the Eucharistic mystery holds nearly as much weight in the cryptic designs of *Ulysses* as do the other aspects of that mystery, it provides a further argument in favor of finding reconciliation, resurrection, and hope in Joyce's "post-Catholic" novel, which draws so richly on Catholic categories.[135]

V.5.5: Catholic Categories and Joyce's Intentions

The recurring question is: what was Joyce's intention? Was it to satirize and separate, or was it to synthesize and vitalize? Ultimately, the matter of authorial intention is unknowable and perhaps inessential. What matters is the end result. The end result is that, if Joyce intended radically to break from Catholic Ecclesiology and Eucharistic theology in his art, he did not succeed. If, in the end, it may be established that Joyce's art, whether intentionally or otherwise, is largely reconcilable with Catholic theology and anthropology, then we have achieved our purpose of better understanding the permanence of Catholic categories in Joyce's "apostate mind." The external evidence is sufficient to establish continuity.

The external evidence reveals deeper aspects of the Eucharistic mystery, not overtly treated in Joyce or Joyce studies, which indicate an intrinsic compatibility between the Catholic and Joycean worldviews, independently of whether or not Joyce intended to exploit the correspondencies in his art. Knowledge of these aspects enriches our literary understanding of Joyce's Eucharistic art. In the literary discussion that we have followed, the Mass, although eventually properly understood (after shaky beginnings) in orthodox Catholic terms as liturgical ritual, is insufficiently understood in terms of activity, dynamism, and alliance. The rich expressiveness of the Eucharistic mystery as a motif in the artistic endeavor to discover the sublime in the ordinary is perceived by Joyce and by Joyceans, from Boyle to Ellmann.[136] The same may be said concerning the dignity that the Eucharist confers upon human corporality, although Fr. Boyle perceives the visceral incarnational realism of this more clearly than those who interpret the Eucharist as mere symbol or metaphor, void of material content.[137]

However, the Catholic understanding of the Eucharist as essentially relational and dynamic—as *dynamism via alliance* (growth through relationship) and as synthesis of mystical *eros* and *agape*—while also present in Joycean literary discussion (insofar as it addresses the theme of reconciliation of father and son), is nonetheless understated and apparently underestimated, at least by Joyceans if not by Joyce. Biographically, we know that Joyce experienced this "erotic" Eucharistic attraction on some level: hence his lifelong participation, however limited, in the Easter Triduum. And, of course, Joyce frequently returns to the Eucharistic mystery in his art.

In the closing lines of "The Dead," as we have seen in chapter III, Michael Furey's death evokes Christ's crucifixion and a Christian synthesis of *agape* and *eros* which Gabriel recognizes as authentic: "he knew that such a feeling must be love."[138] Gabriel's recognition of authentic love echoes Christ's pronouncement, "Greater love has no man than this, that a man lay down his life for his friends" (Jn 15:13). Later in the same chapter we have seen strong indicators of this *agape-eros* synthesis recurring in Leopold Bloom.[139] The Eucharist is the divine and human perpetuation of the *eros-agape* synthesis. A full understanding of Catholic doctrine on the Eucharist helps the literary critic to make a judgment about the Eucharistic scenes in Joyce's art, and ultimately, to understand the mind of Joyce with respect to these scenes. Joyce's *agape-eros* synthesis in *Ulysses* aesthetically replicates the Catholic Eucharistic synthesis.

V.6: The Eucharist as Culmination of Eros and Agape

V.6.1: Eros and the Eucharist

The Catholic understanding of two recurring themes in Joyce's work—the dynamic of personal individuation and the synthesis of *eros* and *agape*—has been articulated by Pope Benedict XVI in relation to the Eucharist. Catholic doctrine has always maintained that the Eucharist contains the Body, Blood, Soul and Divinity of the risen glorified Jesus Christ. This affirmation is a truth of faith but it does not exhaust the Eucharistic mystery, and fails perhaps to evoke its dynamism. The bodily Presence of Christ in the Eucharist has dynamic, vivifying implications.

Pope Benedict XVI's Eucharistic theology begins from the premise of Christ's bodily Eucharistic Presence, but from this premise of living Presence there flows a dynamic and dynamizing reality of nuptial union, which is natural as well as supernatural, and not solely spiritual but bodily too. It incorporates man in his entirety. The

Eucharistic relationship, drawing us into bodily fellowship, synthesizes *eros* and *agape* as well as body and spirit. To disregard this dimension of the Eucharist as relationship, Benedict says, would have reductive consequences: "The Eucharist . . . would be relegated to the status of a thing, and the true Christian plane of existence would not be attained."[140]

When Christ said of himself and the Father that They are "working still" (cf. Jn 5:17), He was referring implicitly to the Eucharist, which would soon become the place *par excellence* of his divine and human, ever-present, all-reaching activity. Therefore, the presence of Christ in the Eucharist is more than the presence of body and blood, as Pope Benedict explains: "The ancient world had dimly perceived that man's real food—what truly nourishes him as man—is ultimately the *Logos*, eternal wisdom: this same *Logos* now truly becomes food for us— as love. The Eucharist draws us into Jesus' act of self-oblation" (*DCE* 13). The key expression here for present purposes is "draws us into." Now we are speaking of a material presence that is spiritually dynamic, attractive and expansive, combining *eros* and *agape*: "More than just statically receiving the incarnate *Logos*, we enter into the very dynamic of his self-giving" (*DCE* 13).

The dynamic of mutual donation leads logically to the nuptial aspect of the Eucharistic mystery: "The imagery of marriage between God and Israel is now realized in a way previously inconceivable: . . . now it becomes union with God through sharing in Jesus' self-gift, sharing in his body and blood" (*DCE* 13). This corrects the idea of faith as a tangential reality which fails to touch the world intimately and lacks existential engagement and relevance. It is, of course, a truth of faith and not of reason, that the Eucharist is not only alive but infinitely and eternally so. Its contagious vitality knows no bounds; its dynamism is personally and universally relational. Joyce harbored artistic aspirations to achieve something similar.

V.6.2: The Eucharist and Individuating Dynamism

Joyce's Eucharistic art aspires aesthetically to produce a world-embracing, life-communicating effect, epiphanizing the daily drama of contention between life-negating and life-enabling dynamics, availing of Eucharistic doctrines about communion and transubstantiation, the spilling of blood and the sharing of the spirit, as thematic vehicles in his endeavour to represent how human beings become more fully human. Catholic doctrines were propitious to his vision and task, perhaps more propitious even than the Church of his time fully realized.

The Church has traditionally defended the realism of the Eucharist as *substance*, i.e., what the Eucharist *is*; Benedict, as we have just seen, wishes to emphasize also the *dynamic* of what the Eucharistic Presence *does*, i.e., how, as the Source of all Grace, it perfects human nature in nuptial relationship. Catholicism teaches that the Incarnate and Eucharistic Christ is the presence of the eternal in time so that, in time, time itself—history, corporality, all—may be introduced into the eternal: "so that God may be everything to every one" (1 Cor 15:28). That fullness has already been realized in the God-Man

Christ, and by virtue of his resurrection it is now open to all, through the perpetuation of his ever enticing incarnated presence, now glorified, in the Eucharist: a Presence that is at once the culmination and the continuation of a relational dynamism.

The nuptial aspect of the Eucharistic mystery, realizing and expressing the reconciliation of Bridegroom and Bride, *agape* and *eros*, *animus* and *anima*, shares much in common with the Joycean anthropology of the individuating dynamism that leads to human plenitude. Regardless of whether Joyce intentionally used the nuptial theology of Christ as Bridegroom and Church as Bride in his portrayal of Bloom and Molly, the fact is that the Joycean theme of growth concurs with this theology: human development happens through alliance. For Joyce, it is in relationship (with the human other and with a mysterious unnamed Other) that the human person passes from potency to act, from potentiality to full personhood.

Christ's own words, "I, when I am lifted up . . . will draw all men to myself" (Jn 12:32), refer principally to his Eucharistic Presence. Pope Benedict XVI affirms as much when he speaks of the Eucharist as "the mystical heart of Christianity, in which God mysteriously comes forth, time and again, from within himself and draws us into his embrace,"[141] relating this dynamic presence to the verse of St. John's gospel just cited. The Eucharistic Presence is unceasingly active: attracting and invigorating. The term "state of grace" is a regrettable misnomer, given that grace is anything but static. The seminal principle of divine filiation, introduced to the soul in baptism, subsequently unfolds and flowers into fullness in the existential dynamic of pilgrimage.

Man, to borrow Gabriel Marcel's celebrated expression, is *homo viator*, journeying towards plenitude between what Christ has won and man must still conquer. The Eucharist is spiritual food for that journey. Joyce's employment of Eucharistic imagery in his representation of the meals between Stephen and Bloom indicates that he understood the spiritual significance of the Eucharist as food for the human journey. It is the Eucharist motif that invests these "secular" moments with a rich and radiant significance. Rather than blasphemously "secularizing" the sacred, Joyce's project in his communion scenes is to epiphanize the presence of the divine in the most ordinary realities, and the Eucharist, along with Catholic teachings about grace and sacrifice (*caritas* or *agape*), is a constant interpretive key to discovering his thematic intent.

V.6.3: The Question of Blasphemy

The critical consensus in relation to the Circe chapter of *Ulysses* is that the Black Mass is used to dramatize distortion and negativity—as opposed to *celebrating* the same—and is not therefore sacrilegious. George Orwell (a neutral, perhaps even anti-Catholic, observer) noted in 1945 that "an intelligent Catholic is able to see that the blasphemies of . . . James Joyce are not seriously damaging to the Catholic faith."[142] In order to settle the question as to whether Joyce wished to commit blasphemy, let us turn to the most probable blasphemous scene in the Joycean corpus, namely that of the Nausicaa chapter in which Gerty MacDowell's self-exposure is interwoven with Benediction at the nearby Church of St. Mary, the explosion of fireworks at a nearby charity bazaar and Bloom's excited voyeurism, masturbation, and ejaculation.

The juxtaposition of Benediction, fireworks, exhibitionism, voyeurism, and masturbation seems on first sight to prove that Joyce saw this particular expression of piety, having lost his own faith in it, as a form of self-centered and sterile escapism. If the scene is intended to entail equation of these realities, it is, for the Catholic sensibility, the moment in which Joyce comes most disturbingly close to mockery of Eucharistic adoration and offensive blasphemy.

Kiberd offers a nuanced interpretation which would mitigate if not eliminate the charge of blasphemy: "On Sandymount, the merely spiritual worship of the host in the sacred monstrance was contrasted with the merely physical pleasure taken by Bloom in the display of the human body." Again, there is dichotomization of spirit and body as opposed to synthesis: "But the division between the two types of experience remained absolute—so absolute that one could add both to the growing list of fake consecrations in *Ulysses*."[143] Kiberd has thus provided the Catholic context for understanding the supposed blasphemy, given that Catholicism condemns the artificial separation of the corporal and the spiritual, not only in the sexual sphere. Kiberd interprets the scene as Joyce's juxtaposition of two aberrational extremes: spiritualism and fetishism. If it is ethereal and escapist pseudo-piety that is satirized on the one hand, as opposed to adoration of the Blessed Sacrament, and voyeuristic fetishism on the other, as opposed to conjugal sexuality, then there is no question of blasphemy or libertinism. The Christian incarnational body-soul synthesis—especially in the Catholic understanding of the Eucharist—exposes both by contrast as dualistic distortions.

In this scene, Joyce is denouncing an escapist pseudo-piety bereft of profane (outside the temple) expression. By implicitly associating it with Bloom's sin, he is accusing Christians of often reducing Eucharistic adoration to what he sees as a form of spiritual voyeurism and masturbation. To employ the words of Pope Benedict XVI, by this false form of worship, "The Eucharist . . . would be relegated to the status of a thing, and the true Christian plane of existence would not be attained."[144] Instead of spreading the divine fire, all is thus reduced to all too human fireworks. By associating the twin deformities with fireworks, Joyce's comic perspective tempers the condemnation. We are not intended to view the perpetrators of either form of "masturbation," the physical or the spiritual, with contempt.

Contempt is not a characteristic of the Joycean perspective. Joyce wished to show the richness and the wretchedness of life through a prism of a mercifulness that is extended to all, even in the most bizarre of circumstances and most perverse behaviors. Joyce is not condemning Eucharistic adoration as such, any more than he is condemning human sexuality as such. While recognizing with pain the dehumanizing deformity, we know that Bloom's sexuality is capable of greater things (Bloom knows it too, as we have seen),[145] and so is Christian piety. To view the episode as gratuitous blasphemy on the one hand and smiling indulgence of sexual fetishism on the other is a gross distortion of Joyce's purpose. As usual, he is critiquing deformities at both ends of the spectrum, corporal and spiritual, while proffering by implication a paradigmatic synthesis of the sacred and the profane.

V.7: Conclusion of Chapter V

Joyce's project was about reconciling the secular and religious registers of reality rather than about celebrating the emancipation of one from the other. Joyce critic Michael O'Shea claims that in Joyce's art "the liturgy is a source of ideas and images which can be used apart from the sacred mysteries conventionally supposed to underlie them."[146] In fact, there is no objective conflict between the "sacred mysteries" of the liturgy and the "ideas and images" in Joyce's art of which, according to O'Shea, the liturgy is a source. The sacramental, synthesizing import of the Catholic worldview was compatible with the Joycean worldview and conducive to his art. The danger of the secularist perspective is to respond to a perceived religious hostility towards the secular sphere with a reactionary monopolization of secularity that is hostile and exclusivist towards religion. Alienation is no solution to alienation.

The following from Roy Gottfried is a similar example of the secularist error: "A focus on religious schism gave Joyce intellectual freedom from dogma and papal authority, and those ruptures freed him from all analogous constraints."¹⁴⁷ In fact, the Catholic sacramental worldview, by virtue of its synthesization of the material and spiritual, *liberates* analogy from the constraints of reductive materialism on the one hand and from the etherealism of ersatz symbolism on the other; therefore it *provided* Joyce with the freedom conducive to his analogous aesthetic aims. So, there is no conflict between the original "dogmatic meaning" and the Joycean one, and therefore no need for "liberation" from authority. The alternative would be a kind of aesthetic necrophilia and parasitism with unavoidable negative implications: if the Eucharist is a living Body, then the art it feeds is a valid and living art; if the Eucharist is a dead body, then the art that feeds upon it loses any claim to vitality and validity.

In response to Jeffrey Segall's observation quoted in my Introduction, that Catholic intellectuals tend to "soft pedal" Joyce's blasphemy and general anti-Catholicism,¹⁴⁸ it may be said that nonbelieving Joyce critics tend to downplay or silence the implications of Joyce's profound, far-reaching compatibility in many points with Catholic orthodoxy. The argument of subjective projection applies both ways. Both Joyce and Catholicism are more complex than secularists tend to recognize. It is a Catholic teaching, for example, that even saints sin. Also, Alighieri Dante placed popes in hell without ceasing to be Catholic. The French writer Francois Rabelais, and the English Chaucer, would be other, more apposite, references. Chaucer, without ceasing to be a Catholic or an artist, contemplated the Church with a comical and critical spirit.

Joyce also contemplates humanity with a comical

and critical spirit. He may have ceased to be a Catholic, but he retains Catholic categories and a belief in the divine. He conceives of human fulfillment as the fruit of interaction with others and instinctive receptiveness to an elusive individuating agency. There are clear parallels between this perspective and the Catholic position that human fulfillment is the fruit of response to grace, God's necessary nourishment for body and soul. Joyce does not negate the religious dimension of human nature. His aesthetic employment of the Eucharist confirms a philosophical position in favor of epiphany and ontology and not one of relativism and scepticism. Joyce's persistent ontological bent argues, in turn, in favor of some form of religious belief and against outright atheism. It is Catholic theology as it informs his literary imagination that gives the climactic moments of Joyce's *Ulysses*—like the communion scene between Bloom and Stephen—their artistic potency, as several Joyce critics have recognized.

Joyce critics have identified Joyce's exploitation of several aspects of the Church's Eucharistic doctrine in his art, but there is an important *lacuna* which has been addressed in the latter part of this chapter: the nuptial aspect of the Eucharistic mystery with its concomitant dynamics of mystical *eros* and *dunamis*. A Joyce reader with a full set of Catholic imaginative categories, enriched by recent Magisterial statements and scholarship, would expect Joyce's literary imagination to include the nuptial aspect of the Eucharistic mystery in his central Eucharistic scenes. We have seen in chapters I, II, and III that *eros* and dynamic potentiality were enormously important to Joyce. The missing element in the religiosity of "The Sisters" and "A Painful Case," of "Eveline" and *Portrait*, is the same dimension of "erotic" and entelechial dynamism that is notably absent from Joycean commentary on the mystery of the Eucharist.

Joyce did not explicitly employ the terms *agape* and *eros*, and neither do Joyce critics in their critiques of Joyce and of Catholicism, but the concepts which these terms represent are prominently present in Joyce's writings and have been explicated in the post-Joycean Catholic Magisterium. The correspondencies between Catholic teachings on these aspects of love and the Joycean anthropology are there to be seen in Joyce's writings. However, Joyce criticism up to this point has arrived only at a stern critique of distorted *agape* without *eros*,[149] mistakenly assuming this to be the Catholic position. This has included an often acritical acceptance of a deformed material or sensualistic *eros* without *agape*,[150] mistakenly assuming this to be the Joycean position, and thus missing the Joycean synthesis, which happens to coincide with the Catholic position, as Joyce himself was aware. The reality of that synthesis enables us to draw some modest conclusions about Joyce's religious position.

Final Summary and Conclusion

1: Apostasy and Afterwards

1.1: A Catholic Apostate

The constant peril of the Catholic Joyce reader, as secularists rightly affirm, is to exaggerate similarities to the point of eliminating difference. Nevertheless, a close study of Joyce's writings prompts one to ask: could a believing Catholic have written Joyce's *Dubliners* stories, *Portrait of the Artist as a Young Man,* and *Ulysses*? The answer to this question is yes, in spite of initial appearances. Moreover, it may be added that a writer not intimately familiar with Catholicism could not have written these works. And a reader or critic not intimately familiar with Catholicism is in many ways ill-equipped to interpret them. The Joycean vision is not closed to religion, and a strong argument may also be made that it is positively religious.

The intent of this study has been to discern the nature and extent of Joyce's apostasy and/or heresy. There are two clear polarized possibilities: firstly, that Joyce sought to "materialize" and revitalize the Catholic worldview in art and thereby to surpass and supplant it as artist, prophet, and high priest of a post-Christian secularist humanism; secondly, that Joyce perceived that his own vision in its essence harmonized uncontroversially with Catholicism (or controversially, from the secularist perspective). A third possibility somewhere between these two is that in the course of his writing career and accompanying intellectual investigations, having begun and advanced quite far with the former project, the latter realization gradually crystallized. Hence the ambivalence of his typically hide-and-seek response to the question, put to him after the publication of *Ulysses*, as to when exactly he had left the Catholic Church: "That is for the Church to say,"[1] and hence the difficulty in ascertaining his ultimate position and the conflicting perspectives in Joycean criticism.

With this evasive response to the Catholic question, Joyce is saying, perhaps, that he considers the matter of belief and non-belief as only tangentially relevant to his aesthetic task and responsibility. His task as artist is not to produce an art that provides answers or even asks questions but simply to "recreate life out of life."[2] His aesthetic simulacrum of the human experience is not hermetically closed to the secularist or to the religious position, just like life itself. This being so, it would be rash to define Joyce as a secularist or as a religious writer. He defies facile categorization by either side, hence the frequency of ambiguity and controversy surrounding this point in Joyce studies.

1.2: The Secularist Prism

Umberto Eco, for example, states that, though Joyce abandoned faith, "religious obsession does not abandon Joyce." Eco admits that the term Catholicism may be applied to Joyce, but only in the sense we have seen argued by Richard Ellmann. The term is valid, he says, only in the sense that Joyce, "having rejected a dogmatic substance and having uprooted himself from a certain moral experience," retains a disposition of "fascination with liturgical rules, rites and images."[3] Referring to Joyce's aesthetic use of Catholic liturgical ritual, Eco discovers a form of blasphemy that pays paradoxical tribute to its orthodox source of inspiration. The orthodox source is rejected, and one is left with "the sense of blasphemy celebrated in accordance with liturgical ritual."[4] If I have succeeded in suggesting persuasively that this perspective constitutes an underestimation both of Catholic orthodoxy and of Joyce's engagement with the same, perhaps this in itself would be no mean contribution to the Joycean debate.

When Joyce's favorite aunt declared *Ulysses* unfit to read, presumably finding it blasphemous like Eco but from a faith perspective, Joyce's pained response—"If *Ulysses* isn't fit to read, life isn't fit to live"[5]—suggests that the book is *not* a blasphemous provocation, but rather a picture of life in all its messy richness; unless he thought life itself to be blasphemous, which seems very unlikely. Joyce was demonstrably interested throughout his life in what believers have to say, esteeming belief as a valuable conversation partner. He is an ex-Catholic apostate writer in whose writings orthodox Catholic categories play an essential thematic role. While his ongoing Easter attendance at church would hardly earn him the title of practicing Catholic, nevertheless, to exclude this from the frame of reference, to exaggerate incompatibilities to the point of radical and total rupture, is also a distortion.

The standard image of Joyce as an emblematic

anti-Catholic freethinker requires revision, since it fails to account for the complexity, richness, and profundity of his relationship with religion. Joyce was interested in the great mystics of the Catholic tradition and in the doctrine of grace, which perfects human nature. In them and in Aquinas he read of the correcting of negative inclinations and the overcoming of natural limitations by grace in relationship with God; he read of human reason, will, affectivity, and sensuality acquiring new grace-inspired possibilities without ceasing to be human.

American Catholic writer Flannery O'Connor stated that her artistic focus was the "action of grace in a territory held largely by the devil";[6] Joyce's focus is the actuation of grace in the terrain of the world and the flesh. When Stephen, in the context of a conversation with his mother about repentance, asked for sixpence and got threepence,[7] it seems improbable that we are intended to understand that he will settle for half—the threepence of actual over the sixpence of sanctifying grace—but there are less improbable indicators that this or something like it was Stephen's and Joyce's choice.

1.3: Actual Grace in an Apostate World

Pope Benedict XVI, overcoming a black and white approach to the inscrutable mystery of the human heart and divine judgment, describes a "category" of persons not unlike those who populate Joyce's fiction:

> Yet we know from experience that neither case [extremes of malice or saintliness] is normal in

human life. For the great majority of people—we may suppose—there remains in the depths of their being an ultimate interior openness to truth, to love, to God. In the concrete choices of life, however, it is covered over by ever new compromises with evil—much filth covers purity, but the thirst for purity remains and it still constantly re-emerges from all that is base and remains present in the soul.[8]

This is an indirect but accurate description of the Joycean drama. Joyce's work gives center stage to the anonymous mass of "ordinary" human beings, neither saints nor Satanists, who defy what he perceived as the neat and reductive categorizations of a theological and anthropological perfectionism.

The actuations of grace are notoriously resistant to theological categorization. We know that disputes on the subject in the 16th century reached such a fever pitch that, at the beginning of the 17th century, Dominicans and Jesuits were silenced by papal decree. More recently, Karl Rahner controversially hypothesized about the "anonymous Christian" whom he defined as "the pagan . . . who lives in the state of Christ's grace through faith, hope and love, yet who has no explicit knowledge of the fact that his life is orientated in grace-given salvation to Jesus Christ."[9] Leopold Bloom's obvious ignorance of Christian doctrine and Stephen Dedalus' distorted knowledge of it, combined with their occasionally Christ-like behaviors, might, at a stretch, qualify them in Rahner's judgment as implicit Christians.

The merits and demerits of Rahner's theory are not relevant to the task in hand; it *is* relevant to the task in hand, however, that Rahner felt moved to theorize on this matter in a Europe inexorably becoming post-Christian. The Fathers of Vatican Council II felt similarly moved to declare the possibility of salvation outside the visible parameters of the Church. When Joyce is situated in his greater historical context, as we have attempted to do in this work, there is a sense of a theological hiatus in certain areas, such as *eros* and *agape* and the ubiquitous actuation of grace. The Church subsequently corrected the deficiency, articulating doctrines that were present in the tradition, sometimes latently and others patently, but that were forgotten, undeveloped or under-emphasized by Joyce's immediate Catholic intellectual predecessors and contemporaries. It is an important factor in our reading of Joyce to know that he is writing in, and responding to, this vacuum.

Joyce, writing out of the same European context that provoked Rahner's reflections, seems to be saying that a Christianizing instinct is innately present and operative in the human soul, independently of Christian Revelation; indeed, it may even coincide with intellectual rejection of Revelation. None of this is to deny that the fullness of grace—albeit often eclipsed by anti-testimony—is present in the Eucharist and in communion therewith. The fact of his abandonment of this sacrament (except aesthetically) must be taken into account when it comes to ascertaining the nature of Joyce's final religious position *vis-a-vis* Catholicism, even as we also take into account the common ground between his vision and the Catholic one. If Joyce aesthetically championed with consummate craftsmanship the divine activity in ordinary human experience at the personal cost of communion with the Eucharist, we would have to say from a Catholic perspective that he paid a high and unnecessary price.

The Eucharist is the ultimate paradigm of how the extraordinary can be at once hidden and revealed, mysteriously and really present, in the ordinary; nowhere else are corporality and spirituality, matter and soul, the secular and the sacred, so sacramentally harmonized. It is difficult to reconcile Joyce's rejection of this great sacramental mystery with his "Eucharistic" approach to reality, humanity, and art. The inescapable biographical fact that he did, however, reject it, enables us to suggest that Catholicism out-Joyces James Joyce. Then again, it should be borne in mind that Joyce *did* continue to attend Holy Week services all his life, which suggests that he was not entirely cut off from the Eucharist and must have been receiving something from this tenuous contact: something more than a by-then redundant intellectual confirmation of its symbolic value. And the enigma of his apostasy stubbornly resurfaces.

1.4: Emotional Apostasy; Intellectual Orthodoxy

In the light of the overwhelming accumulation of evidence that we have seen in favor of continuity between Catholicism and Joyce's art, the outstanding question is, why did Joyce leave the Church? It would be easy and erroneous to underestimate the significance of the historical context of Joyce's apostasy. He became an apostate in a unique time and place—late 19th and early 20th century Dublin—in which by many accounts Catholicism was hyper-scholastic and hyper-masculine. Yet he returned ceaselessly and happily to the "nets" of family, nation and religion which in early adulthood he determined to transcend. His early expressions on these themes are marked by anger and a determination to escape, while his later intellectual engagement with Catholic doctrines in his art is rich and nuanced; as is his engagement with the subjects of nation and family. It is difficult to reconcile the vehemence of his early rejection of Catholicism with the depth and density of his later engagement with it.

Matters are complicated still further by the fact that Joyce shows signs of being aware, as early as the *Stephen Hero* draft of *Portrait*, that Catholicism was bigger (in size and in spirit) than its Irish context. Stephen wonders to himself if it was "anything but vanity which urged him to seek out the thorny crown of the heretic,"[10] speaking of himself as a heretic, not an atheist. Joyce represents Stephen battling with temptations—to which he gives no answer—that his project could in fact be accommodated within the Catholic tradition: "In temper and in mind you are still a Catholic. Catholicism is in your blood . . . A revolution such as you desire is not brought about by violence but gradually: and, within the Church you have an opportunity of beginning your revolution in a rational manner."[11]

Joyce depicts a conflict in Stephen between emotion and reason. On the one hand, there is anger and sensuality and the longing to be free of sentient and emotional restrictions; on the other hand, there is intellectual conviction concerning the rationality of Church teachings. Joyce did not permit his sexual impulses to distort his rationality and dictate his intellectual positions. As one contemporary social commentator, E. Michael Jones, has put it, "The most insidious corruption brought about by sexual sin is the corruption of the mind." All too often, Jones observes, "One moves all too easily from sexual sins, which are probably the most common to mankind, to intellectual sins, which are the most pernicious."[12] But we have seen that Joyce did not attempt to construct a pseudo-rationalized "justification" of his sexual misbehavior.[13]

Also in *Stephen Hero*, Stephen's mother seeks advice from a priest on her son's irreligious conduct, and is warned by the priest that the consciences of her younger children are in danger of being scandalized by their elder brother's bad example. Upon learning of this exchange, Stephen distances himself from his mother in anger, "persuaded that he could have no satisfactory commerce with her so long as she chose to set the shadow of a clergyman between her nature and his."[14] This incident is based upon historical fact,[15] and Joyce and his mother, with whom he had been very close,[16] were still estranged on this major point when his mother died. Family psychological dynamics may be one of the possible explanations for Joyce's break with the Catholic Church and his refusal to return. Perhaps, given his outburst about "black magic" so much later in life, the wounds of his upbringing remained raw to the end.

Perhaps in his contradictoriness Joyce is also emblematic of the apostate mind. Augustine shows in his *Confessions* that intellectual conviction of the truths of Catholicism, though helpful, is not always sufficient to ensure return to Christ and Church. Perhaps many apostates, having eventually separated the wheat from the chaff in their relationship with God and Church after a long period of time filled with life experiences and observation and reflection, remain nonetheless fossilized in an ambiguous state of residual resentment, indecision and apathy. But the conflict between mind and heart is resolved in Joyce's art, if not in private religious practice, in the form of a synthesis of sensuality and intellectuality, emotion and reason.

1.5: The Remedy: Artistic Synthesis

From the outside, all that may be said, again, is that, objectively, there is no major inherent clash between the Joycean worldview and orthodox Catholicism. We have seen that the Joycean enterprise celebrates the human capacity to grow. Anything, therefore, that stifles that capacity, anything that causes stagnation, is considered and depicted as enemy. Joyce mercilessly exposes and critiques a false and dehumanizing religiosity; his position is not negative towards a religion that truly humanizes. There is much common ground between him and St. Augustine, St. Thomas, and St. Ignatius in all that is affirmatively human and open to the divine. The worldview that Joyce champions is closer to Catholicism than the "Catholicism" that he rejects.

Catholicism is a religion of redemption, victory, and hope. It is therefore of its nature dynamic, festive, and affirmative. When it is stagnant, joyless, and repressive it is because it has failed to be faithful to its own message. In the human experience inside and outside the Church, the ludical dimension easily degenerates into the Dionysian and the Apollonian dimension into the draconian. The maintenance of equilibrium is a perennial challenge. In the Irish context there were factors that exacerbated the difficulty. We cannot discount the possibility that Joyce's statement to the Church of his time (particularly but not exclusively the Irish Church) is this: "I have God, you do not." Or better still: "I have *your* God, you do not."

In this sense of competing with Catholicism over a "sense of mercy," it may well be true that Joyce strove to out-do Catholicism. But as Stephen himself saw and said, Joyce could have made his critiques from within the Church. Perhaps Joyce saw the speck in his brother's eye insofar as he perceived the deficiencies of a Church that emphasized devotion and vocations but was overly attached to rules, and failed to see the plank in his own eye, not so much insofar as concerns sexual sin, but rather in misunderstanding an Irish Catholic error of emphasis rather than of essence, a misapplication of principles in an extraordinarily difficult situation. In any event, Joyce's entire *oeuvre* may be seen as a corrective response to a disordered religiosity.

As Levy observes, Joyce found a way of "turning Aquinas's ideas against the teaching of his Jesuit masters"[17] in the matter of aesthetics, but he employed this tactic in other areas too, so that he may be described as a prophetic apostate or a heretical prophet. Such an open-ended, polyvalent "conclusion" seems quintessentially Joycean.

It also seems fitting somehow, before proceeding to offer some closing words on the potentialities present in Joyce studies for the faith-culture dialogue, to allow St. Thomas Aquinas the last word, so to speak, on what might have been Joyce's post-apostasy position.

2: Vestigial Belief According to Aquinas

Even after apostasy, religious categories may and often do remain in the soul. Aquinas trained his analytic intelligence on this very subject, and the fruits of his ruminations are interesting. Aquinas says that when the theological virtues of faith, hope, and charity are lost through mortal sin, certain after-effects nonetheless remain. He considers even dead faith to be a gift from God, and that, by God's grace, the soul's capacity for good actions remains even after the loss of faith and charity: "and as lifeless faith is from God, so too, acts that are good generically, though not quickened by charity, as is frequently the case in sinners, are from God."[18]

Sometimes God even grants special gifts to the subject who has lost living faith and charity: "the gift of prophecy, or the like, is given to some without charity."[19] And, after the loss of living faith (vitalized by supernatural charity), the soul may retain a certain immunity to the error of idolatry and a vestigial appreciation of the divine: "Even lifeless faith excludes a certain impurity which is contrary to it, viz. that of error, and which consists in the human intellect, adhering inordinately to things below itself, through wishing to measure Divine things by the rule of sensible objects."[20] In other words, even after apostasy and/or the loss of living faith and charity through unconfessed mortal sin, the soul, having once had faith, will not easily be deceived by materialist counterfeits of the divine.

In summary, then, the soul with lifeless faith may still be capable of good actions, may have the gift of prophecy and other gifts, and may retain the capacity to distinguish between false and true worship, between false gods and the truly divine. Joyce attended Easter Mass throughout his life with intentions and attitudes evidently not reducible to the sacrilegious and blasphemous. His position therefore is not definable solely in terms of blasphemy and is more complex than non-believing Joyce readers sometimes wish to recognize. Aquinas takes into account the nuanced complexity of the human heart and God's action in it.

Secularist critics read Joyce's art as an attempt to surpass the religious dimension of human nature and to supplant the divine. In reality, Joyce's aim was to correct the way the divine was presented so that, with his new understanding, religion could better serve its purpose of linking the ordinary to the divine. Joyce waged war on a distortion of the spirit-matter binary and sought to rework the dynamics to achieve a better harmony, so that one aspect would not predominate tyrannically at the expense of the other. Joyce wants us to see how the divine operates and is manifest in the ordinary events of life and how the human experience is the "place" where the mundane and the divine meet, so that "profane joy" and the "Heavenly God" may be synthesized.

The strongest argument of all in favor of Joyce's

unitive—rather than divisive—agendum is Stephen's climactic cry of "Heavenly God!" with "profane joy" in *Portrait*. In chapter III we have seen how a dynamic akin to grace produces unity of *eros* and *agape* and of *anima* and *animus* in the self. In chapter V we have seen the unitive agendum carried through to sublime reaches in Joyce's Eucharistic art in *Ulysses*. Owing to its fusion of the earthly and the heavenly, and its numerous other aspects, Joyce perceived the Eucharistic bread that "came down from Heaven" (cf. Jn 6:51) as the ideal motif for his unitive message. Despite initial appearances, his aesthetic employment of the Eucharistic mystery is orthodox, and serves Joycean themes that are compatible with Catholic doctrine. He critiques materialism and spiritualism and promotes a sacramental view of reality, putting his Catholic categories to use in ways that do not contradict the Catholic position, fulfilling Stephen's aspirations to artistic priesthood as aesthetic mediator between God and man.

3: Joyce and the Faith-Culture Dialogue

3.1: Categories of Atheism

St. Justin spoke in the second century of *logoi spermatokoi*—seeds of the Word, whisperings of the spirit of truth—present in preChristian philosophies, which justified dialogue with them not only to teach but also to learn, based upon the premise that wherever there is love, the Holy Spirit is present. As Aquinas put it, *Omne verum, a quocumque dicatur, a Spiritu Sancto est*.[21] An atheistic skepticism that denies the possibility of access to the truth would render dialogue impossible by eliminating indispensable foundations. In the case of Joyce, there are signs of belief in love and life, in humanity and in a mystery seeking to break through in order to make communication and communion possible. Such a worldview is of interest to Catholicism, and dialogue with it is possible and fruitful, even though some secularist Joyce readers prefer a hermeneutic of division. Given the common ground between Joyce's "Catholicism" and his humanism, the term "Catholic humanism" might serve to describe his position.

The words of Vatican Council II's reflections on atheism that seem most nearly applicable to the Joycean anthropology are these: "Some laud man so extravagantly that their faith in God lapses into a kind of anemia, though they seem more inclined to affirm man than to deny God" (*GS* 19). But Joyce's celebration of the spirit of man is neither acritical nor extravagant. His comic-merciful approach to man does not fit easily into a triumphant secular humanist vision. He recognizes the value and interest of the mystics and writers on grace; he does not dismiss them as delusional. There are grounds to argue that the Joycean aesthetic is about celebrating the action of God in man rather than about affirming man and denying God.

Certainly, in Joyce's work there is a daring handling of sacred material, but sacrilegious things also happen in the bible, and sufficient evidence is present in his work, albeit with exquisite discretion, to support a strong argument in favor of belief in the presence and action of a non-immanent principle in the midst of immanent realities. The writer's vehement declaration of faith in the human soul—"All things are inconstant except the faith in the soul . . . I have found no man yet with a faith like mine"[22]—bespeaks belief in a non-materialist entity and a convinced openness to a non-immanent reality. While insisting that none of this necessarily and definitively entails a return to faith and Church on the part of the author himself, and that the possibility of outright apostasy still remains, it is clear in either event that Catholicism is so essential to Joyce's writing as to render ignorance of it a serious handicap to authoritative literary critical interpretation. Moreover, the better we understand Catholicism, the better we will understand James Joyce. The fact that the converse is also to a great extent true is a sign of his vast but incomplete catholicism.

Joyce is, at the very least, a highly sophisticated humanist with a worldview in many ways profoundly compatible with the Catholic one, and the field of Joyce studies offers the opportunity to learn much about the roots and spirit of 20th century secularism, and to say much to that milieu about Catholicism. This book has been an attempt to define, in the case of an emblematic apostate of the 20th century, the extremely complex character of this kind of apostasy, and, having taken—to the degree possible—the measure of his religious position, to enter into dialogue with him, looking for common ground and also for a better understanding of both the Catholic faith and his difficulties with it. In the course of pursuing this task, if I have succeeded only in more effectively complicating a 20th century figure who has been artificially simplified by ideological lenses, perhaps this in itself is a helpful and worthwhile contribution. Joyce has much to contribute to the faith-culture dialogue, to Catholicism's understanding of itself, and to Christian aesthetics.

3.2: A Christian Aesthetic of the Ordinary

In the course of writing this book, important issues beyond its immediate scope have emerged, which lead one to see Joyce as a key figure on the frontier not only between secularity and faith but also between literature (aesthetics) and theology. Fr. John Paul Wauck, in an article closely related to our subject, published in 2005, describes a Christian aesthetic which is remarkably similar to the Joycean one. He speaks of "epiphanies" of beauty as a "mode of addressing the theme of ordinary life," and lists examples which Stephen Dedalus would surely not have discounted: "renewed visions of ordinary, familiar things, usually brought about by some traumatic experience . . . or captured in unusual language . . . moments of exceptional vision within everyday life: memorable encounters with romance in relatively ordinary settings."[23]

Homecoming, Wauck points out, is a major theme of many great works of literature: "It is natural that this should be so, since home and work are, as it were, the hallmarks of the quotidian . . . We tend to take for granted that so many stories end with someone returning home, but it does not cease to be a striking fact." The homecoming ending is often seen as a kind of return to monotonous normality, a form of epilogue, a cessation and rest in the aftermath of the real substance of adventure. Perhaps this is reductive of the hidden richness of ordinary life: "But there is also the possibility of seeing it as the end in a richer sense: as the goal, destination, and purpose of the narrative."[24] This might serve without any necessity of adaptation as a description of the ending of Joyce's *Ulysses*.

Wauck concludes with an expression of "hope for a new kind of writing." He makes the point that "Christian theology provides reasons to find beauty, drama and sublime importance in ordinary life," lamenting the fact that "in practice, ordinary life . . . has been slow to receive its due in the realm of Christian aesthetics," and in his closing statement calls for "a Christian aesthetic of the ordinary."[25]

On the basis of what we have seen of James Joyce's self-described "Mass-like" aesthetic, it may be said that no Christian writer intent on responding to Wauck's call could afford to ignore Joyce's achievement, which is so essentially indebted to the Catholic worldview and so consonant with the Catholic theology of the ordinary. The Joycean anthropology is particularly interesting and challenging by virtue of its pervasive Catholic inheritance and a complexity that defies facile categorization and demands atom-splitting discernment and nuance as well as the courage and humility to be silent in the presence of the unfathomable.

BIBLIOGRAPHY

PRIMARY SOURCES

AQUINAS, THOMAS. *Summa Theologica*. New York: Christian Classics, 1981.

AUGUSTINE OF HIPPO. *Confessions*. Translated by E.M. Blaiklock. London: Hodder and Stoughton, 1983.

AUGUSTINE OF HIPPO. Tractatus in evangelium Iohannis, tr. 26, 4: PL 35, 1609. *New Advent*. Accessed November 11, 2013. http://www.newadvent.org/fathers/1701026.htm.

AUGUSTINE OF HIPPO. *The Trinity*. Edited by Edmund Hill. New York: New City Press, 1991.

IGNATIUS OF LOYOLA. *Obras Completas de S. Ignacio de Loyola*. Edited and Annotated by Fr. Ignacio Iparraguirre, S.I., and Fr. Candido de Dalmases, S.I., Edicion Manual. Madrid: B.A.C., 1952.

When Joyce's works are cited in quotations from the critical commentaries of others, the editions cited are retained; when they are cited directly in my own analyses, these are the editions cited:

JOYCE, JAMES. *The Critical Writings of James Joyce*. Edited by Ellsworth Mason and Richard Ellmann. London: Faber and Faber, 1959.

JOYCE, JAMES. *Dubliners*. Edited and introduced by Robert Scholes & A. Walton Litz. New York: Penguin, 1996.

JOYCE, JAMES. *Portrait of the Artist as a Young Man*. Edited by Chester G. Anderson. New York: Viking Press, 1968.

JOYCE, JAMES. *Selected Letters*. Edited by Richard Ellmann. London: Faber & Faber, 1975.

JOYCE, JAMES. *Stephen Hero*. Edited by Theodore Spencer, John J. Slocum, and Herbert Cahoon. New York: New Directions, 1963.

JOYCE, JAMES. Vols. I, II, and III of *Letters of James Joyce*. Edited by Stuart Gilbert and Richard Ellmann. New York: Viking Press, 1966.

JOYCE, JAMES. *Ulysses*. Introduction by Declan Kiberd. London: Penguin Books, 2000.

MAGISTERIUM

BENEDICT XVI. *Deus caritas est*, 2005. *Spe salvi*, 2007. *Sacramentum caritatis*, 2007.

DENZINGER-SCHONMETZER. *Enchiridion Symbolorum, definitionum et declarationum de rebus fidei et morum* (1965).

JOHN PAUL II. *Dominum et vivificantem*, 1986. *Fides et ratio*, 2001. *Vita consecrata*, 1996.

PAUL VI. *Humanae vitae*, 1968. *Lumen ecclesiae*, 1974.

PIUS X. *Pascendi Dominici gregis*, 1907.

VATICAN COUNCIL II. *Gaudium et spes*, 1965.

SECONDARY SOURCES

BECK, WARREN. *Joyce's Dubliners: Substance, Vision, and Art.* Durham: Duke University Press, 1969.

BENEDICT XVI. *Light of the World.* Translated by Michael J. Miller and Adrian J. Walker. San Francisco: Ignatius Press, 2010.

BENEDICT XVI. *Jesus of Nazareth: From the Baptism in the Jordan to the Transfiguration.* Translated by Adrian J. Walker. San Francisco: Ignatius Press, 2007.

BENEDICT XVI. *Jesus of Nazareth: Holy Week: From the Entrance into Jerusalem to the Resurrection.* Translated by Philip J. Whitmore. San Francisco: Ignatius Press, 2011.

BENEDICT XVI. *The Yes of Jesus Christ: Exercises in Faith, Hope, and Love.* Translated by Robert Nowell. Indiana University: Crossroad Publishing Company, 1991.

BENNETT, JANICE. *St. Laurence and the Holy Grail: the Story of the Holy Chalice of Valencia.* San Francisco: Ignatius Press, 2002.

BERRONE, LOUIS. *James Joyce in Padua.* Edited, translated and introduced by Louis Berrone. New York: Random House, 1977.

BOYLE, ROBERT, S.J. *James Joyce's Pauline Vision: A Catholic Exposition.* Carbondale: Southern Illinois University Press, 1978.

BRADLEY, BRUCE, S.J. *James Joyce's Schooldays.* New York: St. Martin's Press, 1982.

BRIVIC, SHELDON. *Joyce Between Freud and Jung*. Port Washington: Kennikat Press, 1980.

BUDGEN, FRANK. *Joyce and the Making of Ulysses*. Oxford: Oxford University Press, 1972.

CANTALAMESSA, RANIERO. "The Two Faces of Love: Eros and Agape." *ZENIT: The World Seen From Rome*. March 25, 2011. https://zenit.org/articles/father-cantalamessa-s-1st-lenten-sermon--2/.

COLUM, MARY & PADRAIC. *Our Friend James Joyce*. London: Victor Gollancz, 1958.

CONNELL, K. H. *Irish Peasant Society*. Gloucestershire: Clarendon Press, 1968.

CORISH, PATRICK. *Maynooth College: 1795-1995*. Dublin: Gill & MacMillan, 1995.

COVERDALE, JOHN F. *Uncommon Faith: The Early Years of Opus Dei*. Princeton: Scepter Publishers, 2002.

ECO, UMBERTO. *The Aesthetics of Chaosmos: the Middle Ages of James Joyce*. Translated by Ellen Esrock. Tulsa: University of Tulsa Press, 1982.

ECO, UMBERTO. *The Aesthetics of Thomas Aquinas*. Cambridge: Harvard University Press, 1997.

ECO, UMBERTO. *Le poetiche di Joyce*. Milan: Bompiani, 2002.

ELLMANN, RICHARD. *James Joyce*. Rev. ed. New York: Oxford University Press, 1982.

ELLMANN, RICHARD. *Ulysses on the Liffey*. New York: Oxford University Press, 1972.

EPSTEIN, EDMUND. *The Ordeal of Stephen Dedalus.* Carbondale: Southern Illinois University Press, 1971.

ESCRIVA DE BALAGUER, JOSEMARIA. *Christ Is Passing By.* Dublin: Veritas Publications, 1974.

FRENCH, MARILYN. *The Book as World: James Joyce's "Ulysses."* Cambridge: Harvard University Press, 1976.

GILSON, ETIENNE. *The Christian Philosophy of St. Thomas Aquinas.* Notre Dame: University of Notre Dame Press, 1994.

GOTTFRIED, ROY. *Joyce's Misbelief.* Introduction by Sebastian Knowles. Florida: University Press of Florida, 2008.

GRODEN, MICHAEL, ed. (et al.). *James Joyce Archive.* New York: Garland, 1978.

HEATH, JEFFREY. *The Picturesque Prison: Evelyn Waugh and His Writing.* Kingston: McGill-Queen's University Press, 1982.

HENKE, SUZETTE A. *Joyce's Moraculous Sindbook: A Study of "Ulysses."* Columbus: Ohio State University Press, 1978.

HUFF, PETER A. *Vatican II: Its Impact on You.* Liguori: Liguori Publications, 2011.

JOHN PAUL II. *Crossing the Threshold of Hope.* Edited by Vittorio Messori and translated by Jenny McPhee and Martha McPhee. New York: Knopf, 1994.

JOHN PAUL II. *Puebla: A Pilgrimage of Faith.* Edited by the Daughters of St. Paul. Boston: St. Paul Editions, 1979.

JOYCE, STANISLAUS. *Dublin Diary.* Edited by George Harris Healey. New York: Ithaca, 1962.

JOYCE, STANISLAUS. *My Brother's Keeper.* Edited with notes by Richard Ellmann. Cambridge: Da Capo Press, 2003.

JUNG, CARL. *Aspects of the Feminine.* New Jersey: Princeton University Press, 1982.

KIBERD, DECLAN. Introduction to *Ulysses: Annotated Student Edition* by James Joyce. London: Penguin Classics, 2000.

KIBERD, DECLAN. *Inventing Ireland: The Literature of the Modern Nation.* London: Vintage Books, 1996.

KIBERD, DECLAN. *Ulysses and Us: The Art of Everyday Life in Joyce's Masterpiece.* New York: W.W. Norton & Company, 2009.

LEVIN, HARRY. *James Joyce: A Critical Introduction.* Norfolk: New Directions, 1941.

LERNOUT, GEERT. *Help My Unbelief: James Joyce and Religion.* London: Continuum International Publishing Group, 2010.

LEWIS, C.S. *The Four Loves.* Harcourt: Mariner Books, 1971.

LOWE-EVANS, MARY. *Catholic Nostalgia in Joyce and Company.* Florida: University of Florida Press, 2008.

LOWE-EVANS, MARY. *Crimes Against Fecundity: Joyce and Population Control.* New York: Syracuse University Press, 1989.

MACCARTHY, M.J.F.. *Priests and People in Ireland.* London: Hodder and Stoughton, 1908.

MARITAIN, JACQUES. *Art and Scholasticism and The Frontiers of Poetry.* Translated by Joseph W. Evans. New York: Charles Scribner's Sons, 1962.

MARITAIN, JACQUES. *Three Reformers: Luther, Descartes, Rousseau.* London: Sheed & Ward, 1966.

NICHOLS, AIDAN, O.P. *Discovering Aquinas.* Grand Rapids: Wm. B. Eerdmans Publishing Co., 2003.

NIETZSCHE, FRIEDRICH. *The Anti-Christ.* Translated by H.L. Mencken. Maryland: Serenity Publishers, 2009.

NIETZSCHE, FRIEDRICH. *Beyond Good and Evil.* Edited by William Kaufman and translated by Helen Zimmern. London: Dover Thrift Editions, 1997.

NOON, WILLIAM T., S.J. *Joyce and Aquinas.* Connecticut: Archon Books, 1970.

NOON, WILLIAM T., S.J. "The Religious Position of James Joyce." In *James Joyce: His Place in World Literature*, edited by Wolodymyr T. Zyla, 7-21. Lubbock: Texas Tech Press, 1969.

NYGREN, ANDERS. *Agape and Eros.* Texas: University of Chicago Press, 1982.

O'BEIRNE RANELAGH, JOHN. *A Short History of Ireland.* Cambridge: Cambridge University Press, 1994.

O'CONNOR, FLANNERY. *The Habit of Being: Letters of Flannery O'Connor.* Edited by Sally Fitzgerald. New York: Vintage Books, 1980.

O'CONNOR, FLANNERY. *Mystery and Manners: Occasional Prose.* Edited by Sally & Robert Fitzgerald. New York: Farrar, Straus & Giraux, 1969.

Ó RÍORDÁIN, JOHN J. *Irish Catholic Spirituality: Celtic and Roman*. Dublin: The Columba Press, 1998.

OWENS, COILIN. *James Joyce's Painful Case*. Florida: University Press of Florida, 2008.

PIEPER, JOSEF. *Death and Immortality*. Translated by Richard and Clara Winston. South Bend: St. Augustine's Press, 2000.

PIEPER, JOSEF. *Enthusiasm and the Divine Madness*. Translated by Richard and Clara Winston. South Bend: St. Augustine's Press, 1999.

PIEPER, JOSEF. *Faith, Hope, Love*. Translated by Richard and Clara Winston. San Francisco: Ignatius Press, 1997.

PIEPER, JOSEF. *Leisure: the Basis of Culture*. Translated by Gerald Malsbary. South Bend: St. Augustine's Press, 1998.

PIEPER, JOSEF. *Scholasticism, Personalities and Problems of Medieval Philosophy*. Translated by Richard and Clara Winston. South Bend: St. Augustine's Press, 2001.

POWERS, JOSEPH M., S.J. *Eucharistic Theology*. New York: Herder and Herder, 1967.

RAHNER, KARL. *Ecclesiology, Questions in the Church, the Church in the World*. Vol. 14 of *Theological Investigations*. Translated by David Bourke. London: Darton, Longman & Todd, 1976.

RAO, JOHN C. *Americanism and the Collapse of the Church in the United States*. St. Paul: Remnant Publications, 1984. http://jcrao.freeshell.org/Americanism.html.

RATZINGER, JOSEPH. *Introduction to Christianity*. Translated by Foster & Miller. San Francisco: Ignatius Press, 1990.

RATZINGER, JOSEPH CARDINAL. *The Spirit of the Liturgy*. Translated by John Saward. San Francisco: Ignatius Press, 2000.

SCHOPENHAUER, ARTHUR. Vol. 2 of *The World as Will and Representation*. New York: Dover Publications, 1966.

SEGALL, JEFFREY. *Joyce in America: Cultural Politics and the Trials of 'Ulysses.'* Berkeley: University of California Press, 1993.

STEIN, EDITH. *Woman*. Vol. II of *The Collected Works of Edith Stein*. Edited by L. Gebler and Romaeus Leuven and translated by Freda Mary Oben. Washington: ICS Publications, 1996.

SULLIVAN, KEVIN. *Joyce Among the Jesuits*. New York: Columbia University Press, 1958.

TERESA OF AVILA. *The Book of Her Foundations: a Study Guide*. Edited by Marc Foley, O.C.D. Washington: ICS Publications, 2011.

TERESA OF AVILA. *The Life*. Translated by J.M. Cohen. London: Penguin, 1988.

THORNTON, WELDON. *The Antimodernism of Joyce's Portrait of the Artist as a Young Man*. New York: Syracuse University Press, 1994.

THORNTON, WELDON. *Voices and Values in Joyce's Ulysses*. Florida: University Press of Florida, 2000.

TINDALL, WILLIAM YORK. *The Literary Symbol.* New York: Columbia University Press, 1955.

TWOMEY, D. VINCENT. *The End of Irish Catholicism?* Dublin: Veritas, 2003.

VANHOYE, ALBERT CARDINAL. *Accogliamo Cristo Nostro Sommo Sacerdote, Esercizi Spirituali con Benedetto XVI.* Citta del Vaticano: Libreria Editrice Vaticana, 2008.

VON BALTHASAR, HANS URS. *Seeing the Form.* Vol. I of *The Glory of the Lord: A Theological Aesthetics.* Edited by Joseph Fessio and John Riches and translated by Erasmo Leiva-Merikakis. San Francisco: Ignatius Press, 2009.

VON BALTHASAR, HANS URS. *The Truth of God.* Vol. II of *Theo-Logic: Theological Logical Theory.* Translated by Adrian J. Walker. San Francisco: Ignatius Press, 2004.

DICTIONARIES, JOURNALS, PERIODICALS, MAGAZINES

BALAZS, THOMAS. "Recognizing Masochism: Psychoanalysis and the Politics of Sexual Submission in *Ulysses.*" *Joyce Studies Annual* 13, no. 1 (2002): 160-91.

BEEBE, MAURICE. "*Ulysses* and the Age of Modernism." *James Joyce Quarterly* 10, no. 1 (1972): 172-88.

BOYLE, ROBERT, S.J. "Miracle in Black Ink: A Glance at Joyce's Use of His Eucharistic Image." *James Joyce Quarterly* 10, no. 1 (1972): 47-60.

BRADLEY, BRUCE, S.J. "Book Review of *Ulysses and the Irish God,* by Frederick K. Lang." *James Joyce Quarterly* 33, no. 2 (1996): 300-05.

BRIAND, PAUL. "The Catholic Mass in James Joyce's *Ulysses.*" *James Joyce Quarterly* 5, no. 4 (1968): 312-22.

BRIVIC, SHELDON. "Joyce's Consubstantiality." In *James Joyce: The Centennial Symposium*, edited by Morris Beja, Philip Herring, Maurice Harmon, and David Norris, 149-57. Urbana: University of Illinois Press, 1986.

BRIVIC, SHELDON. "Joyce and the Metaphysics of Creation." *The Crane Bag* 6, no. 1 (1982): 13-19.

DEVLIN-GLASS, FRANCES. "Writing in the Slipstream of the Wildean Trauma: Joyce, Buck Mulligan and Homophobia Reconsidered." *The Canadian Journal of Irish Studies* 31, no. 2 (2005): 27-33.

ELLMANN, RICHARD. "Joyce's religion and politics." *The Irish Times* (Dublin, Ireland), Feb. 2, 1982.

ESCRIVÁ DE BALAGUER, JOSEMARÍA. "Passionately Loving the World." *The Furrow* 19, no. 5 (1968): 269-77.

FITZGERALD, ALLAN D. "Commentary on St. Augustine's 'In Epistulam Johannis ad Parthos tractatus, 7.8.'" In *Augustine Through the Ages: An Encyclopaedia*, edited by Allan Fitzgerald, 310-11. Grand Rapids: Wm. B. Eerdmans Publishing Co., 1999.

GRODEN, MICHAEL & VICKI MAHAFFEY. "Silence and Fractals in 'The Sisters.'" In *Collaborative Dubliners: Joyce in Dialogue*, edited by Vicki Mahaffey and Jill Shashaty, 23-47. Syracuse: Syracuse University Press, 2012.

GROSSI, VITTORINO, O.S.A. "Correction." In *Augustine Through the Ages: An Encyclopedia*, edited by Allan D. Fitzgerald, O.S.A., 24244. Grand Rapids: Wm. B. Eerdmans Publishing Co., 1999.

HIBBERT, JEFFREY. "Joyce's Loss of Faith." *Journal of Modern Literature* 34, no. 2 (2011): 196-203.

HUGHES, EAMONN. "Joyce and Catholicism." In *Irish Writers and Religion*, edited by Robert Welch, 116-37. Gerrards Cross: Colin Smythe, 1992.

JOLAS, EUGENE. "My Friend James Joyce." In *James Joyce: Two Decades of Criticism*, edited by Seon Givens, 3-17. New York: Vanguard Press, 1948.

JONES, DAVID E. "The Essence of Beauty in James Joyce's Aesthetics." *James Joyce Quarterly* 10, no. 3 (1973): 291-311.

KENNER, HUGH. "Book Review of Ulysses *on the Liffey*, by Richard Ellmann." *James Joyce Quarterly* 10, no. 2 (1973): 276-80.

KENNER, HUGH. "The Cubist *Portrait*." In *Approaches to Joyce's Portrait: Ten Essays*, edited by Thomas F. Staley and Bernard Benstock, 171-213. Pittsburgh: University of Pittsburgh Press, 1976.

KENNER, HUGH. "Molly's Masterstroke." *James Joyce Quarterly* 10, no. 1 (1972): 19-28.

KENNER, HUGH. "The *Portrait* in Perspective." In *Joyce: a Collection of Critical Essays*, edited by William M. Chace, 29-49. New Jersey: Spectrum, 1974.

LARKIN, EMMET. "The Devotional Revolution in Ireland, 185075." *The American Historical Review* 77, no. 3 (1972): 625-52.

LEVIN, HARRY. "James Joyce." *Atlantic Monthly* CLXXVIII, December 1946.

LEVY, ANTOINE, O.P. "Great Misinterpretations: Umberto Eco on Joyce and Aquinas." *Logos: A Journal of Catholic Thought and Culture* 13, no. 3 (2010): 124-63.

LUFT, JOANNA. "Reader Awareness: Form and Ambiguity in James Joyce's 'Eveline.'" *The Canadian Journal of Irish Studies* 35, no. 2 (2009): 48-51.

MAHAFFEY, VICKI & JILL SHASHATY. Introduction to *Collaborative Dubliners: Joyce in Dialogue*, edited by Vicki Mahaffey and Jill Shashaty, 1-22. Syracuse: Syracuse University Press, 2012.

MAHON, JOHN W. "Joyce Among the Brothers." *Christianity and Literature* 53, no. 3 (2004): 349-59.

MANGANIELLO, DOMINIC. "The Beauty that Saves: *Brideshead Revisited* as a Counter-*Portrait of the Artist*." *Logos: A Journal of Catholic Thought and Culture* 9, no. 2 (2006): 154-70.

MANGANIELLO, DOMINIC. "Book Review of *Crimes Against Fecundity: Joyce and Population Control*, by Mary Lowe-Evans." *Canadian Journal of Irish Studies* 17, no. 2 (1991): 116-19.

MARTIN, AUGUSTINE. "Reviewed Works: *Joyce's Ulysses: An Anatomy of the Soul* by Theoharis Constantine Theoharis; *Ulysses as a Comic Novel*, by Zack Bowen; *Joyce and the Law of the Father*, by Frances L. Restuccia." *Irish University Review* 20, no. 2 (1990): 378-80.

MERCANTON, JACQUES. "The Hours of James Joyce." In *Portraits of the Artist in Exile: Recollections of James Joyce by Europeans*, edited by Willard Potts, 206-52. New York: Harcourt Brace Jovanovich, 1986.

MCCARTHY, PATRICK A. "Further Notes on the Mass in *Ulysses.*" *James Joyce Quarterly* 7, no. 2 (1970): 132-37.

MCCOURT, JOHN. "Reading Ellmann Reading Joyce." In *Joyce's Audiences*, edited by John Nash, 41-59. New York: Rodopi, 2002.

NEEDLETON ARMINTOR, MARSHALL. "Book Review of *Voices and Values in Joyce's* Ulysses, by Weldon Thornton." Criticism 44, 1 (2002): 111. (Available at: http://digitalcommons.wayne.edu/criticism/vol44/iss1/4).

NOON, WILLIAM T., S.J. "A Delayed Review." *James Joyce Quarterly* 2, no. 1 (1964): 7-12.

NORRIS, DAVID. "The 'Unhappy Mania' and Mr. Bloom's Cigar: Homosexuality in the Works of James Joyce." *James Joyce Quarterly* 31, no. 3 (1994): 357-73.

NORRIS, MARGOT & VINCENT D. PECORA. "Dead Again." In *Collaborative Dubliners: Joyce in Dialogue*, edited by Vicki Mahaffey and Jill Shashaty, 343-78. Syracuse: Syracuse University Press, 2012.

Ó FLOINN, DONNCHADH. "The Integral Irish Tradition." *The Furrow* 15, no. 12 (1954): 756-68.

O'ROURKE, FRAN. "Joyce's Early Aesthetic." *Journal of Modern Literature* 34, no. 2 (2011): 97-120.

O'SHEA, MICHAEL J. "Catholic Liturgy in Joyce's *Ulysses.*" *James Joyce Quarterly* 21, no. 2 (1984): 123-35.

PLATT, LEN. "Book Review of *Help My Unbelief* by Geert Lernout." *James Joyce Quarterly* 47, no. 4 (2010): 664-67.

RATZINGER, JOSEPH CARDINAL. *Pilgrim Fellowship of Faith: The Church as Communion*. Edited by Stephan Otto Horn and Vinzenz Pfnur and translated by Henry Taylor. San Francisco: Ignatius Press, 2005.

RATZINGER, JOSEPH CARDINAL. *On the Way to Jesus Christ*. Translated by Michael J. Miller. San Francisco: Ignatius Press, 2005.

RATZINGER, JOSEPH CARDINAL. *The Nature and Mission of Theology: Essays to Orient Theology in Today's Debates*. Translated by Adrian Walker. San Francisco: Ignatius Press, 1995.

RATZINGER, JOSEPH CARDINAL. "The Theological Locus of Ecclesial Movements." *Communio: International Review* 25, no. 3 (1998): 480-504.

REQUENA, FEDERICO. "Vida religiosa y espiritual en la Espana de principios del siglo XX." *Anuario de Historia de la Iglesia* 11 (2002): 3968.

RESTUCCIA, FRANCES. "Transubstantiating *Ulysses*." *James Joyce Quarterly* 21, no. 4 (1984): 329-40.

RODGERS, W.R., ed. *Irish Literary Portraits*. London: British Broadcasting Corporation, 1972.

SCHORK, R.J. "James Joyce and the Eastern Orthodox Church." *Journal of Modern Greek Studies* 17, no. 1 (1999): 107-24.

SHANAHAN, DENNIS M. "The Eucharistic Aesthetics of the Passion: The Testament of Blood in *Ulysses*." *James Joyce Quarterly* 27, no. 2 (1990): 373-86.

STEINBERG, ERWIN R. "The Bird-Girl in *A Portrait* as Synthesis: The Sacred Assimilated to the Profane." *James Joyce Quarterly* 17, no. 2 (1980): 149-63.

THORNTON, WELDON. "The Greatness of *Ulysses*." *New Hibernia Review* 7, no. 4 (2003): 26-37.

VAN BAVEL, TARCISIUS J. "Discipline." In *Augustine through the Ages: An Encyclopedia*, edited by Allan D. Fitzgerald, 273-76. Grand Rapids: Wm B. Eerdmans Publishing Co., 1999.

WALSH, RUTH. "In the Name of the Father and of the Son . . . Joyce's Use of the Mass in *Ulysses*." *James Joyce Quarterly* 6, no. 4 (1969): 321-47.

WALSH, RUTH. "That Pervasive Mass: In *Dubliners* and *A Portrait of The Artist As A Young Man*." *James Joyce Quarterly* 8, no. 3 (1971): 20520.

WALZL, FLORENCE L. "Gabriel and Michael: The Conclusion of 'The Dead.'" *James Joyce Quarterly* 4, no. 1 (1966): 17-31.

WALZL, FLORENCE L. "Joyce's 'The Sisters': A Development." *James Joyce Quarterly* 10, no. 4 (1973): 375-421.

WAUCK, JOHN PAUL. "Christianity and the Poetics of Ordinary Life." In *Poetica & Cristianesimo*, edited by Rafael Jimenez Catano & Juan Jose Garda-Noblejas, 149-78. Roma: Edizioni Universita della Santa Croce, 2005.

WILSON, EDMUND. "James Joyce." In *Joyce: a Collection of Critical Essays*, edited by William M. Chace, 50-66. New Jersey: Spectrum, 1974.

YEATS, W.B. "Anima Hominis." In *The Collected Works of W.B. Yeats*, edited by William H. O'Donnell, 1-34. New York: Charles Scribner's Sons, 1994.

YOUNG, ROBIN DARLING. "Theologia in the Early Church." *Communio* 24 (1997): 681-90.

NOTES

INTRODUCTION

1. Antoine Levy, O.P., "Great Misinterpretations: Umberto Eco on Joyce and Aquinas," *Logos: A Journal of Catholic Thought and Culture* 13, no. 3 (2010): 137.

2. Jeffrey Segall, *Joyce in America: Cultural Politics and the Trials of 'Ulysses'* (Berkeley: University of California Press, 1993), 168.

3. Augustine Martin, "Reviewed Works: *Joyce's Ulysses: An Anatomy of the Soul* by Theoharis Constantine Theoharis; *Ulysses as a Comic Novel* by Zack Bowen; *Joyce and the Law of the Father* by Frances L. Restuccia," *Irish University Review* 20, no. 2 (1990): 37-8.

4. Harry Levin, *James Joyce: A Critical Introduction* (Norfolk: New Directions, 1941), 25.

5. Geert Lernout, *Help My Unbelief: James Joyce and Religion* (London: Continuum International Publishing Group, 2010), 211.

6. Mary and Padraic Colum, *Our Friend James Joyce* (London: Victor Gollancz, 1958), 207.

7. Lernout, *Help My Unbelief*, 214.

8. James Joyce, *Letters of James Joyce*, vol. II, edited by Stuart Gilbert and Richard Ellmann (New York: Viking Press, 1966), 48.

9. Stanislaus Joyce, *My Brother's Keeper*, edited with notes by Richard Ellmann (Cambridge: Da Capo Press, 2003), 227.

10. Lernout, *Help My Unbelief*, 2.

11. Declan Kiberd, *Ulysses and Us: The Art of Everyday Life in Joyce's Masterpiece* (New York: W.W. Norton & Company, 2009) 255.

12. Dominic Manganiello, "The Beauty that Saves: *Brideshead Revisited* as a Counter-*Portrait of the Artist*," *Logos: A Journal of Catholic Thought and Culture* 9, no. 2 (2006), 154.

13. Umberto Eco, *The Aesthetics of Thomas Aquinas* (Cambridge: Harvard University Press, 1997), 249.

14. Levy, "Great Misinterpretations," 133.

15. Richard Ellmann, *James Joyce*, rev. ed. (New York: Oxford University Press, 1982), 298.

16. Hugh Kenner, "The *Portrait* in Perspective," in *Joyce: a Collection of Critical Essays*, edited by William M. Chace, 29-49 (New Jersey: Spectrum, 1974), 39.

17. Roy Gottfried, *Joyce's Misbelief* (Florida: University Press of Florida, 2008), 25.

18. Frances Restuccia, "Transubstantiating *Ulysses*," *James Joyce Quarterly* 21, no. 4 (1984): 329.

19. "James Joyce," *Wikipedia*, last modified 22 April 2013. https://es.wikipedia.org/wiki/James_Joyce.

20. Ibid., quoting Maurice Beebe, "*Ulysses* and the Age of Modernism," *James Joyce Quarterly* 10, no. 1 (1972): 176.

21. Hugh Kenner, "Book Review of *Ulysses on the Liffey* by Richard Ellmann," *James Joyce Quarterly* 10, no. 2 (1973): 276.

22. On the 17th of December 1982, the *Times Literary Sup-*

plement published Kenner's response to Ellmann's biography of Joyce, in an article bearing the title, "The Impertinence of Being Definitive."

23. See William T. Noon, S.J., "A Delayed Review," *James Joyce Quarterly* 2, no. 1 (1964): 7-12.

24. See Pope Benedict XVI, "Dictatorship of Relativism," in *Light of the World*, translated by Michael J. Miller and Adrian J. Walker, 50-59 (San Francisco: Ignatius Press, 2010).

25. Atheists are often "religious writers" and thinkers in the sense that they think and write a great deal about the subject of religion and negatively define themselves in relation to it, but here I mean "religious writer" in the sense of positive openness to a reality not reducible to the immanent and material, a believer in some form of transcendental or supernatural reality typically thought of as God.

26. Lernout, *Help My Unbelief*, 180.

27. Declan Kiberd, *Inventing Ireland: The Literature of the Modern Nation* (London: Vintage Books, 1996), 454.

28. Charles Moeller, *Literatura del Siglo XX y Cristianismo, I; El Silencio de Dios* (Madrid: Editorial Gredos, 1981), 30. My translation; the original French version, *Litterature du XX' Siecle et Christianisme; I Silence de Dieu*, was first published by Casterman, in Tournai, Belgium, 1954.

29. Josef Pieper, *Leisure: the Basis of Culture*, translated by Gerald Malsbary (South Bend: St. Augustine's Press, 1998), 68-69.

30. Ibid., citing St. Thomas Aquinas, *Commentary on Aristotle's Metaphysics* I, 3, par. 55.

31. St. Augustine, *Confessions*, 9.1.

32. Hans Urs Von Balthasar, *Seeing the Form*, vol. I of *The Glory of the Lord: A Theological Aesthetics*, edited by Joseph Fessio and John Riches and translated by Erasmo Leiva-Merikakis (San Francisco: Ignatius Press, 2009), 18.

33. Ibid.

34. Joseph Cardinal Ratzinger, *On the Way to Jesus Christ*, translated by Michael J. Miller (San Francisco: Ignatius Press, 2005), 36.

35. Michael Polanyi, *Personal Knowledge: Towards a Post-Critical Philosophy* (Chicago: University of Chicago Press, 1974), 199.

36. Ibid., 67.

37. James Joyce, *Portrait of the Artist as a Young Man*, edited by Chester G. Anderson (New York: Viking Press, 1968), 215.

38. Ibid., 221.

39. Joyce, *My Brother's Keeper*, 105.

40. R.J. Schork, "James Joyce and the Eastern Orthodox Church," *Journal of Modern Greek Studies* 17, no. 1 (1999): 107.

41. Ibid., citing Jacques Mercanton: 'The Hours of James Joyce,' in Willard Potts, ed. *Portraits of the Artist in Exile: Recollections of James Joyce by Europeans* (New York: Harcourt Brace Jovanovich, 1986), 214.

42. Ibid.

43. Kiberd, *Ulysses and Us*, 296.

44. Ibid., citing Potts, ed., *Portraits of an Artist in Exile*, 35.

45. Ibid., citing W.R. Rodgers, ed. *Irish Literary Portraits* (London: British Broadcasting Corporation, 1972), 29.

46. Ibid., citing Joyce, *My Brother's Keeper*, 159.

47. Flannery O'Connor, *Mystery and Manners: Occasional Prose*, edited by Sally & Robert Fitzgerald (New York: Farrar, Straus & Giraux, 1969), 44-45.

48. Flannery O'Connor, *The Habit of Being: Letters of Flannery O'Connor*, edited by Sally Fitzgerald (New York: Vintage Books, 1980), 130.

49. Ellmann, *James Joyce*, 107, citing *Letters*, vol. I, 53.

50. Weldon Thornton, *Voices and Values in Joyce's* Ulysses (Florida: University Press of Florida, 2000), 62.

51. Ibid. 62-63.

CHAPTER 1

1. See subsection 1.5.1 of the Introduction, which gives a clarification of terms used in this study.

2. James Joyce, *Stephen Hero*, edited by Theodore Spencer, John J. Slocum, and Herbert Cahoon (New York: New Directions, 1963), 77. In 1911 Joyce threw this manuscript in the fire in a fit of pique; his sister Eileen rescued it and, though eventually radically transformed, it remained useful as a draft for *Portrait of the Artist* (See Ellmann, *James Joyce*, 314).

3. Ibid., 95.

4. Ibid., 104.

5. Ibid., 205.

6. Ibid., 211.

7. Ibid.

8. Joyce, *Portrait of the Artist*, 207.

9. Ibid., 209.

10. Ibid., 211.

11. Fran O'Rourke, "Joyce's Early Aesthetic," *Journal of Modern Literature* 34, no. 2 (2011): 97.

12. Umberto Eco, *The Aesthetics of Chaosmos: the Middle Ages of James Joyce*, translated by Ellen Esrock (Tulsa: University of Tulsa Press, 1982), 18.

13. Levy, "Great Misinterpretations," 129.

14. Ibid., 130.

15. Ibid., 132.

16. Gottfried, *Joyce's Misbelief*, 18.

17. William T. Noon, S.J., *Joyce and Aquinas* (Connecticut: Archon Books, 1970), 21.

18. Eco, *The Aesthetics of Thomas Aquinas*, 249.

19. Levy, "Great Misinterpretations," 133.

20. Ibid., 134.

21. Ibid., 136. The debate is partly a modern resurgence of ancient philosophical categories: Heraclitus, a relativist, believed that all was flux; Parmenides saw everything in terms of unchanging, motionless being, excluding the possibility of change; Empedocles saw reality as debated

between the poles of love and strife; the realists—Socrates, Plato, Aristotle, and later Aquinas—break the polar deadlock by identifying matter, form, being, substance, accidents, potentiality and act, as a way of recognizing the reality of motion and change while also reconciling it with what is stable and unchanging.

22. Ibid., 131.

23. Ibid., 137.

24. Ibid., 148.

25. Ibid., 156.

26. See Levy, "Great Misinterpretations," 157. He suggests, in fact, that there may be evidence of change in Eco's own position: Roberto Pellerey, in a contribution to a book edited by Eco, has shown "that the principles of Eco's theory of semiotic interpretation are thoroughly isomorphic to Aquinas's theory of knowledge."

27. Joyce, *Portrait of the Artist*, 212.

28. Kiberd, *Inventing Ireland*, 345.

29. I will return to this point with the guidance of Weldon Thornton in section I.6 of this chapter on Joyce as a realist, and again in chapters III and IV; especially subsection III.3.3.3 on Stephen between *Portrait* and *Ulysses*, and subsection IV.3 on St. Augustine.

30. Joyce, *Portrait of the Artist*, 209.

31. Ibid., 211.

32. Jeff Israely, "A Resounding Eco," *Time Magazine*, June 2005.

33. Levy, "Great Misinterpretations," 138.

34. Eco, *The Aesthetics of Chaosmos*, 39.

35. Frank Budgen, *Joyce and the Making of Ulysses* (Oxford: Oxford University Press, 1972), 21.

36. Eco, *The Aesthetics of Chaosmos*, 55.

37. Levy, "Great Misinterpretations," 142.

38. Ibid., 144. (It was discovered as recently as 1975, by Louis Berrone in the archives of the University of Padua, and was published in 1977: *James Joyce in Padua*, edited and translated by Louis Berrone (New York: Random House, 1977).

39. Ibid., 145-146, quoting *James Joyce Archive*, ed. Michael Groden, et al. (New York: Garland, 1978).

40. Ibid., 145.

41. Ibid., 146.

42. Ibid.

43. Umberto Eco, *Le poetiche di Joyce* (Milan: Bompiani, 2002), 18. (My translation).

44. Ibid., 18-19.

45. Ibid., 11.

46. Joseph Cardinal Ratzinger, *The Nature and Mission of Theology: Essays to Orient Theology in Today's Debates*, translated by Adrian Walker (San Francisco: Ignatius Press, 1995), 82.

47. Ibid., 93.

48. Ibid., 95.

49. Ibid.

50. Ibid., 96

51. Ibid., 97.

52. Ibid., 98.

53. Fourth Lateran Council, Canon 2.

54. Joseph Ratzinger, *Introduction to Christianity*, translated by Foster & Miller (San Francisco: Ignatius Press, 1990), 20.

55. H. L. Mencken, *A Mencken Chrestomathy* (New York: Knopf, 1949), 624.

56. Ratzinger, *Nature and Mission of Theology*, 97.

57. Joseph Cardinal Ratzinger, *The Spirit of the Liturgy*, translated by John Saward (San Francisco: Ignatius Press, 2000), 156.

58. Ibid., 159

59. Ibid., 168.

60. Ibid., 169.

61. Gottfried, *Joyce's Misbelief*, 9.

62. Ibid., 2.

63. Ibid., 3.

64. Dr. Lernout, Professor of English and Comparative Literature at the University of Antwerp, Belgium, and Director of the Antwerp James Joyce Centre, is a respected authority on Joyce. It has been written of his book, *Help My Unbelief: James Joyce and Religion*, that it is, "as full an account of Joyce's atheism as one could desire," Len Platt, "Book Review of *Help My Unbelief* by Geert

Lernout," *James Joyce Quarterly* 47, no. 4 (2010): 666, and, "an indispensible starting point for an extended examination of religion in Joyce's works and his always intricate perspectives," Jeffrey Hibbert, "Joyce's Loss of Faith," *Journal of Modern Literature* 34, no. 2 (2011): 203.

65. Lernout, *Help My Unbelief*, 30. Ratzinger's theology of development in continuity responds to this charge. In 1878 Cardinal Newman presented and responded to the same charge in his over 200-page essay on the development of doctrine. (Both in youth and in maturity Joyce considered Newman the greatest prose-writer in the English language. Ellmann, separating form and substance, insists that Joyce's admiration was solely "stylistic" (Ellmann, *James Joyce*, 40). St. Vincent of Lerins, in the 4th century, responded to the accusation in *Commonitory*, Chapter XXIII, "On the Development of Doctrine in the Church," no. 54.

66. Ibid.

67. Ibid., 215.

68. See CCC no. 127 2; Rom. 8:29; Council of Trent (1547): Denzinger-Schonmetzer [Hereafter abbreviated as DS], 1609-19.

69. Lernout, *Help My Unbelief*, 217.

70. See ibid., 2-3.

71. Eamonn Hughes, "Joyce and Catholicism," in *Irish Writers and Religion*, edited by Robert Welch, 116-37 (Gerrards Cross: Colin Smythe, 1992), 120.

72. See ibid., 135.

73. Lernout, *Help My Unbelief*, 120.

74. James Joyce, *Ulysses* (London: Penguin Books 2000), 23: 32-33.

75. Lernout, *Help My Unbelief*, 49, quoting M.J.F. McCarthy, *Priests and People in Ireland* (London: Hodder and Stoughton, 1908), 625.

76. Ibid., 50.

77. Joyce, *Ulysses*, 732:14-19.

78. Ibid., 733:1-3.

79. Lernout, *Help My Unbelief*, 179.

80. See Ellmann, *James Joyce*, 259.

81. CCC 36 and Vatican Council I, *Dei Filius* 2: DS, 3004; Vatican Council II, *Dei Verbum*, 6.

82. Here is the moment in context: "[T]hose things are good which yet are corrupted which neither if they were supremely good nor unless they were good could be corrupted. Ah, curse you! That's saint Augustine." Joyce, *Ulysses*, 180:15-18.

83. James Joyce, *The Critical Writings of James Joyce*, edited by Ellsworth Mason & Richard Ellmann (London: Faber and Faber, 1959), 134.

84. Lernout, *Help My Unbelief*, 180-81, citing Joyce, *Ulysses*, 817:31-818:4.

85. Joyce, *Ulysses*, 733:1-3: "O, that, Stephen expostulated, has been proved conclusively by several of the best known passages in Holy Writ, apart from circumstantial evidence."

86. Joyce, *Portrait of the Artist*, 172.

87. Joyce, *Ulysses*, 42:20-29.

88. Ibid., 931:17-28.

89. Richard Ellmann, *Ulysses on the Liffey* (New York: Oxford University Press, 1972), 168.

90. Lernout, *Help My Unbelief*, 188.

91. Ibid., 188-89.

92. Joyce, *Stephen Hero*, 210.

93. Ellmann, *James Joyce*, 66.

94. Kiberd, *Ulysses and Us*, 303.

95. Ibid., 307.

96. Ibid., 305.

97. Joyce, *Portrait of the Artist*, 221.

98. See Joyce, *Ulysses*, 511:8-10. This expression by Stephen will be addressed more fully in subsection I.6.2.5 of this chapter, on religion in the Oxen of the Sun episode of *Ulysses*.

99. W.B. Yeats, "Anima Hominis," in *The Collected Works of W.B. Yeats*, edited by William H. O'Donnell, 1-34 (New York: Charles Scribner's Sons, 1994), 8.

100. John McCourt, "Reading Ellmann Reading Joyce," in *Joyce's Audiences*, edited by John Nash, 41-59 (New York: Rodopi, 2002), 56, quoting a letter by Ellmann to Ellsworth Mason, 20 June 1953, Ellmann Collection.

101. Ibid.

102. Ibid., 58.

103. See Bruce Bradley, S.J., "Review of *Ulysses and the Irish God* by Frederick K. Lang," *James Joyce Quarterly* 33, no. 2 (1996): 302-03.

104. Ibid.

105. Kenner, "The *Portrait* in Perspective," 46.

106. Kenner's position will be expounded upon in chapter III; especially in section III.3 on *Portrait of the Artist*.

107. Prominent Joyce scholars have applauded Weldon Thornton's work. Zack Bowen has called him "one of the most respected critics in Joyce studies," Zack Bowen, foreword to *Voices and Values in Joyce's Ulysses* by Weldon Thornton (Florida: University Press of Florida, 2000), ix.

108. Weldon Thornton, *The Antimodernism of Joyce's Portrait of the Artist as a Young Man* (New York: Syracuse University Press, 1994), 37-38.

109. Ibid., 104.

110. Weldon Thornton, *Voices and Values in Joyce's Ulysses* (Florida: University Press of Florida, 2000), 16.

111. Weldon Thornton, personal correspondence, 31 October 2011; quoted with permission.

112. Weldon Thornton, personal correspondence, 2 May 2013; quoted with permission.

113. Thornton, *Voices and Values in Joyce's Ulysses*, 95.

114. Thornton, *The Antimodernism of Joyce's Portrait*, 2.

115. Ibid., 3.

116. Ibid., 4.

117. Ibid.

118. Ibid.

119. See section I.2 of this chapter on the debate about Joyce's aesthetic theory, and section I.3 on Joyce's views on Scholasticism and the Enlightenment.

120. Thornton, *The Antimodernism of Joyce's Portrait*, 40-41.

121. Ibid., 43, citing Hugh Kenner, "The Cubist *Portrait*," in *Approaches to Joyce's Portrait: Ten Essays*, edited by Thomas F. Staley and Bernard Benstock, 171-213 (Pittsburgh: University of Pittsburgh Press, 1976).

122. Ibid.

123. See sections I.2 and I.3 of this chapter for a fuller exposition of the debate about Joyce's aesthetic theory and views on Scholasticism and the Enlightenment.

124. Thornton refers clearly to the "outerness" of the so-called religious experience, but does not develop its full meaning as I will do in this study.

125. Thornton, *The Antimodernism of Joyce's Portrait*, 156-57.

126. Jacques Maritain has described this dichotomization well: "The retreat of the human mind on itself, independence of the reason with respect to the sensible origin of our ideas, to the object as the rule of our science, to real natures as the immediate term of our intellection—absolute intellectualism, mathematicism, idealism—and, finally, irremediable breach between intelligence and Being—that, then, is how Descartes revealed Thought to itself." *Three Reformers: Luther, Descartes, Rousseau* (London: Sheed & Ward, 1966), 78-79.

127. Martin, "Reviewed Works: Joyce's *Ulysses*, ect.," 378.

128. Thornton, *The Antimodernism of Joyce's Portrait*, 101.

129. Ibid., 133.

130. Joyce, *Portrait of the Artist*, 233.

131. Thornton, *The Antimodernism of Joyce's Portrait*, 135.

132. Josef Pieper, *Death and Immortality*, translated by Richard and Clara Winston (South Bend: St. Augustine's Press, 2000), 32, citing St. Thomas Aquinas, *ST* I, q. 75, a. 4, co.: *Homo non est anima tantum*.

133. Ibid., citing St. Thomas Aquinas, *Quest. Disp. De spiritualibus creaturis*, a. 2, ad. 5.

134. Ibid.

135. Ibid.

136. Thornton, *Voices and Values in Joyce's Ulysses*, 23.

137. Ibid., citing Ellmann, *James Joyce*, 471.

138. Joyce, *Portrait of the Artist*, 215.

139. Thornton, *Voices and Values in Joyce's Ulysses*, 50, quoting Sheldon Brivic, "Joyce's Consubstantiality," in *James Joyce: The Centennial Symposium*, edited by Morris Beja, Philip Herring, Maurice Harmon, and David Norris, 149-57 (Urbana: University of Illinois Press, 1986), 149.

140. Kiberd, *Inventing Ireland*, 339.

141. Thornton, *Voices and Values in Joyce's Ulysses*, 16.

142. Ibid., 42.

143. Ibid., 95.

144. Ibid., 18, citing Joyce, *Critical Writings*, 220.

145. Ibid., 19, citing Budgen, *Joyce and the Making of Ulysses*, 71.

146. Ibid., 39.

147. Ibid.

148. Ibid., 40.

149. Ibid.

150. Ibid., 52-53. This echoes an observation by Fr. William T. Noon. It embryonically expresses a view that I will develop in chapter III: "The comic attitude imposes a kind of withdrawal from the maelstrom of life, but its laughter saves it from misanthropy. It may not conduce to pity of weak human nature, but it can and frequently does lead us to love the erring mortal." The reaction of loving enjoyment is another aspect of the Joycean reading experience that is common to readers of diverse ideological perspectives, but Joyce's comic spirit is not acritical and indulgent. Noon continues: "To come back to *Ulysses*, we see that though Joyce succeeds in presenting a searching and exhaustive critique of contemporary society . . . the tone of the novel is nowhere that of *saeva indignatio* . . . there is an absence of anger." Noon, *Joyce and Aquinas*, 101-03.

151. Ibid., 138.

152. A fuller treatment of the Circe episode will be given in Chapters III and V of this study.

153. Thornton, *Voices and Values in Joyce's Ulysses*, 160.

154. Ibid., 164.

155. Marshall Needleton Armintor, Review of Thornton's *Voices and Values in Joyce's Ulysses* in "Criticism," (2002)

Vol. 44, Iss 1, Art 4: Book Reviews: 111. Available at: http://digitalcommons.wayne.edu/criticism/vol44/iss1/4.

156. Thornton, *Voices and Values in Ulysses*, 164, citing Budgen, *Joyce and the Making of Ulysses*, 231.

157. Ibid.

158. Ibid., 147.

159. Ibid., 149.

160. Joyce, *Portrait of the Artist*, 221.

161. Thornton, *Voices and Values in Joyce's Ulysses*, 149.

162. Ellmann, *James Joyce*, 537.

CHAPTER II

1. Segall, *Joyce in America*, 168.

2. Lernout, *Help My Unbelief*, 3.

3. Gottfried, *Joyce's Misbelief*, 83.

4. Ibid., citing Joyce, *Letters*, vol. II, 191-92. The statement in full is: "By the way, they are still at the 'venereal excess' cry in Sinn Fein. Why does nobody compile statistics of 'venereal excess' from Dublin hospitals? *What* is 'venereal excess?'. . . . Anyway, my opinion is that if I put down a bucket into my own soul's well, sexual department, I draw up Griffith's and Ibsen's and Skeffington's and Bernard Vaughan's and St. Aloysius' and Shelley's and Renan's water along with my own. And I am going to do that in my novel (inter alia) and plank the bucket down before the shades and substances above mentioned and see how they like it: and if they

don't like it I can't help them. I am nauseated with their lying drivel about pure men and pure women and spiritual love and love for ever: blatant lying in the face of the truth."

5. Ultimately, I propose to demonstrate that the *eros-agape* synthesis Joyce eventually achieves is in fact a Catholic doctrine; this will be the content of the next chapter.

6. Joanna Luft, "Reader Awareness: Form and Ambiguity in James Joyce's 'Eveline,'" *The Canadian Journal of Irish Studies* 35, no. 2 (2009): 51.

7. Ibid., citing Warren Beck, *Joyce's Dubliners: Substance, Vision, and Art* (Durham: Duke University Press, 1969), 120.

8. Ibid., citing Beck, *Joyce's Dubliners*, 121.

9. Ibid., citing Beck, *Joyce's Dubliners*, 31.

10. Ibid., 51.

11. Hugh Kenner, "Molly's Masterstroke," *James Joyce Quarterly* 10, no. 1 (1972): 21.

12. James Joyce, *Dubliners*, edited and introduced by Robert Scholes & A. Walton Litz (New York: Penguin, 1996), 39.

13. Lernout, *Help My Unbelief*, 122.

14. See Mencken, *A Mencken Chrestomathy*, 624.

15. Ellmann, *James Joyce*, 731.

16. Lernout, *Help My Unbelief*, 110.

17. Joyce, *My Brother's Keeper*, 147.

18. Ibid., 238.

19. Joyce, *Portrait of the Artist*, 189.

20. See Emmet Larkin, "The Devotional Revolution in Ireland, 1850-75," *The American Historical Review* 77, no. 3 (1972): 625-52.

21. In later life Larkin (who died on March 19, 2012) believed that the Catholic Church in Ireland "provided an impoverished and oppressed people with consolation, hope, discipline, and cultural and national identity," as well as "social, medical and educational services when the state was indifferent to their poverty and ignorance." Larkin concluded that "the general effect of Irish Catholicism has been more positive than negative." William Harms, "Emmet Larkin, prominent scholar of Irish history, 1927-2012," *UChicagoNews*, March 27, 2012, http://news.uchicago.edu/article/2012/03/27/emmet-larkin-prominent-scholar-irish-history-1927-2012.

22. Larkin, "The Devotional Revolution in Ireland," 652.

23. Fr. D. Vincent Twomey, *The End of Irish Catholicism?* (Dublin: Veritas, 2003), 24. In fact, the temptation to confuse political, economical, and spiritual messianism is as old as the Gospel itself.

24. Ibid., 183-84n 40, citing John J. Ó Ríordáin, *Irish Catholic Spirituality: Celtic and Roman* (Dublin: The Columba Press, 1998), 104.

25. W.B. Yeats, *Collected Poems* (Hertfordshire: Wordsworth Editions, 2000), 86.

26. Ibid., 152.

27. Fr. Donnchadh O Floinn, "The Integral Irish Tradition," *The Furrow* 5, no. 12 (1954): 766.

28. John C. Rao, *Americanism and the Collapse of the Church in The United States* (St. Paul: Remnant Publications, 1984), sec. I, http://jcrao.freeshell.org/Americanism.html.

29. K. H. Connell, *Irish Peasant Society* (Gloucestershire: Clarendon Press, 1968), 86.

30. Patrick Corish, *Maynooth College: 1795-1995* (Dublin: Gill & MacMillan, 1995), 122.

31. Kiberd, *Inventing Ireland*, 184.

32. Ibid., citing Frantz Fanon, *The Wretched of the Earth* (New York: Grove Press, 2005), 119-49.

33. Joyce, *Portrait of the Artist*, 202.

34. Twomey, *The End of Irish Catholicism*, 91.

35. See Bruce Bradley, S.J., *James Joyce's Schooldays* (Dublin: Gill and MacMillan, 1982), 82-83.

36. Joyce, *My Brother's Keeper*, 23.

37. Ellmann, *James Joyce*, 49-50.

38. Joyce, *Letters*, vol. II, 48.

39. Friedrich Nietzsche, *Beyond Good and Evil*, edited by William Kaufman and translated by Helen Zimmern (London: Dover Thrift Editions, 1997), 45.

40. Ibid., 53.

41. Friedrich Nietzsche, *The Anti-Christ*, translated by H.L. Mencken (Maryland: Serenity Publishers, 2009), 12-13.

42. Ellmann, *James Joyce*, 142, citing Joyce, *Letters*, vol. I, 56.

43. Stanislaus Joyce, *Dublin Diary*, edited by George Harris Healey (New York: Ithaca, 1962), 47-50.

44. Ellmann, *James Joyce*, 142.

45. Lernout, *Help My Unbelief*, 129.

46. Coilin Owens, *James Joyce's Painful Case* (Florida: University Press of Florida, 2008), 78.

47. Thornton, *The Antimodernism of Joyce's Portrait*, 97.

48. As Cardinal Ratzinger has explained: "There is a permanent basic structure of the Church's life . . . and there are the ever renewed irruptions of the Holy Spirit, which ceaselessly revitalize and renew this structure . . . The Church must constantly check its own institutional structure in order to keep it from taking on too much weight—to prevent it from hardening into an armor that stifles its real, spiritual life," from Joseph Cardinal Ratzinger's "The Theological Locus of Ecclesial Movements," *Communio:International Review* 25, no. 3 (1998): 481.

49. Kenner, "The *Portrait* in Perspective," 46.

50. Joyce, *Portrait of the Artist*, 8.

51. See Ibid. and 40.

52. Ibid., 18.

53. Ibid., 50-51.

54. Ibid., 61-62.

55. Ibid., 62.

56. Ibid., 65.

57. Ibid., 79.

58. St. Augustine, *Confessions*, 2.2.

59. Joyce, *Portrait of the Artist*, 103.

60. Ibid., 103-04.

61. Ibid., 105.

62. Ibid., 148.

63. Joyce, *Critical Writings*, 36-37.

64. Joyce, *Portrait of the Artist*, 149-50.

65. Ibid., 243.

66. St. Thomas Aquinas, *Expositio et lectura super Epistolas Pauli Apostoli: II ad Corinthos*, 2, lect. 3, par. 73 with a citation of Gen. 27: 27. Cited in Aidan Nichols, O.P., *Discovering Aquinas* (Grand Rapids: Wm. B. Eerdmans Publishing, 2003), x. In section II.4.5 of this chapter I will present evidence that Joyce was, in fact, aware of the important differences between Christianity and Deism.

67. St.Thomas Aquinas, *ST* I, q. 12, a. 6.

68. Joyce, *Portrait of the Arist*, 149.

69. See Ellmann, *James Joyce*, 342. In his biography of Joyce, Ellmann relates how, in a discussion about philosophy, a 32-year-old Joyce defended St. Thomas Aquinas as the greatest of philosophers because his reasoning was "like a double-edged sword," and declared that he had the custom of reading him "a page a day" in the original Latin.

70. See St. Thomas Aquinas, *ST* II-I, q. 2, arts. 1, 2, 4, 6.

71. Joyce, *Portrait of the Artist*, 160.

72. Ibid., 160-61.

73. Ibid., 169-70.

74. Ibid., 172.

75. Ibid., 162.

76. Ibid., 172.

77. Ibid., 99.

78. Ibid., 106. If, as seems likely, Joyce suffered for decades from the ravages of syphilis—See Kathleen Ferris, *James Joyce and the Burden of Disease* (Lexington: University Press of Kentucky, 1995), and Kevin Bermingham, *Ulysses: The Most Dangerous Book* (London: Penguin Press, 2014)—he had good reason to abhor the horrors of sensualism.

79. See Chapter I of this work, section I.2 on the aesthetics debate, and especially subsection I.2.1.

80. Joyce, *Stephen Hero*, 171.

81. Joyce, *Portrait of the Artist*, 182-83.

82. Ibid., 220.

83. Ibid., 238.

84. Levy, "Great Misinterpretations," 146, quoting *James Joyce Archive*, edited by Michael Groden et al. (New York: Garland, 1978).

85. Joyce, *Portrait of the Artist*, 252.

86. Thornton, *The Antimodernism of Joyce's Portrait*, 101: "Though Jung had not yet articulated his ideas of the anima and the animus when *Portrait* was published . . . Joyce is . . . thinking in such terms."

87. Carl Jung, *Aspects of the Feminine* (New Jersey: Princeton University Press, 1982), 65.

88. Maritain, *Three Reformers*, 41.

89. Ibid., 42.

90. Ibid., 41.

91. Ibid., 42.

92. Ibid., 44.

93. Kenner, "The *Portrait* in Perspective," 40.

94. Ibid.

95. Joyce, *Portrait of the Artist*, 253.

96. See Anders Nygren, *Agape and Eros* (Texas: University of Chicago Press, 1982).

97. Pope Benedict XVI, *The Yes of Jesus Christ: Exercises in Faith, Hope, and Love*, translated by Robert Nowell (Indiana University: Crossroad Publishing Company, 1991), 88.

98. Ibid., 130n.

99. See Josef Pieper, *Faith, Hope, Love*, translated by Richard and Clara Winston (San Francisco: Ignatius Press, 1997), 139-283.

100. Raniero Cantalamessa, "The Two Faces of Love: Eros and Agape," *ZENIT: The World Seen From Rome*, March 25, 2011, https://zenit.org/articles/father-cantalamessa-s-1st-lenten-sermon--2/. See especially his citation of St. John Climacus, *La scala del paradiso*, XV, 98 (PG 88, 880).

101. Ibid.

102. Joyce, *My Brother's Keeper*, 131-32.

103. St. Augustine, *Confessions*, 9.1, 10.27.

104. Vittorino Grossi, O.S.A., "Correction," in *Augustine Through the Ages: An Encyclopedia*, edited by Allan D. Fitzgerald, O.S.A., 242-44 (Grand Rapids: Wm. B. Eerdmans Publishing Co., 1999), 242.

105. Ibid., Tarcisius J. van Bavel, "Discipline," *Augustine Through the Ages*, 273. When we see this process of alternating admonition and delight unfold in Stephen's individuating itinerary (subject of the next chapter) we will discover also Joyce's final position on the subject of *eros* and religion.

106. St. Augustine, *Contra duas epist. Pelag. II* 21 (PL 44, 586): "Ergo benedictio dulcedinis est gratia Dei, qua fit in nobis ut nos delectet et cupiamus, hoc est, amemus quod praecepit nobis." (My translation).

107. St. Augustine, Io. ev. tr. 26, 4: PL 35, 1609, *New Advent*, accessed November 11, 2013, http://www.newadvent.org/ fathers/1701026.htm.

108. Pope Benedict XVI, *Jesus of Nazareth: Holy Week: From the Entrance into Jerusalem to the Resurrection*, translated by Philip J. Whitmore (San Francisco: Ignatius Press, 2011), 60.

109. Pope John Paul II, *Crossing the Threshold of Hope*, edited by Vittorio Messori and translated by Jenny McPhee and Martha McPhee (New York: Knopf, 1994), 90.

110. G.K. Chesterton has described this in *The Everlasting Man* (San Francisco: Ignatius Press, 1993), 222: "Nothing

is more common . . . than to find such a modern critic writing something like this: 'Christianity was above all a movement of ascetics, a rush into the desert, a refuge in the cloister, a renunciation of all life and happiness; and this was a part of a gloomy and inhuman reaction against nature itself, a hatred of the body, a horror of the material universe, a sort of universal suicide of the senses and even of the self. . . It is not true of the Church; but it is true of the heretics condemned by the Church."

111. First published in *The Times Literary Supplement* on 20 October 1921.

112. Maritain, *Three Reformers*, 89; we will return to this idea of rupture and impoverishment of thought in Chapter IV, especially section IV.4 on Joyce's interest in Aquinas.

113. C.S. Lewis, *The Four Loves* (Harcourt: Mariner Books, 1971), 2.

114. Kiberd, *Inventing Ireland*, 329.

115. Levy, "Great Misinterpretations," 144.

CHAPTER III

1. Ibid, 147, quoting *James Joyce Archive,* ed. Michael Groden, et al.

2. Declan Kiberd, introduction to *Ulysses: Annotated Student Edition* by James Joyce (London: Penguin Classics, 2000), 1.

3. James Joyce, *Dubliners*, ed. Robert Scholes and A. Walton Litz (New York: Penguin, 1996), 12-18.

4. Fr. Flynn's fate resonates interestingly with the historical case of Fr. Vicente Frigola, the priest who dropped and

broke the chalice allegedly used by Christ at the Last Supper—the Holy Grail—in the year 1744 and died shortly afterwards from grief. When Fr. Vicente dropped and damaged the chalice, there was nothing in it; Joyce goes to subtle lengths to highlight this same detail in the episode that traumatized Fr. Flynn. It is possible that Fr. Frigola's story somehow reached Joyce's ears, ever alert to epiphanical opportunities. He would surely have seen it as an epiphany of murderous scrupulosity. See Janice Bennett, *St. Laurence and the Holy Grail: the Story of the Holy Chalice of Valencia* (San Francisco: Ignatius Press, 2002), 238, 282.

5. Joyce, *Dubliners*, 18.

6. Joyce, *Portrait of the Artist*, 158-59.

7. Joyce, *Stephen Hero*, 228.

8. Florence L. Walzl, "Joyce's 'The Sisters': A Development," *James Joyce Quarterly* 10, no. 4 (1973): 397-98.

9. Gottfried, *Joyce's Misbelief*, 24.

10. Walzl, "Joyce's 'The Sisters,'" 415.

11. See Ruth Walsh, "That Pervasive Mass: In *Dubliners* and *A Portrait of the Artist as a Young Man*," *James Joyce Quarterly* 8, no. 3 (1971): 209, citing Brewster Ghiselin, "The Unity of Joyce's Dubliners," *Accent* XVI (1956): 75-88, 196-213.

12. Joyce, *Dubliners*, 17.

13. Joyce, *Stephen Hero*, 210.

14. Michael Groden and Vicki Mahaffey, "Silence and Fractals in 'The Sisters,'" in *Collaborative Dubliners: Joyce in Dialogue*, edited by Vicki Mahaffey and Jill Shashaty,

23-47 (Syracuse: Syracuse University Press, 2012), 42.

15. Joyce, *Dubliners*, 117.

16. Ibid.

17. Lernout, *Help My Unbelief*, 123.

18. See Owens, *James Joyce's Painful Case*, 154-57.

19. The word *eros* is in fact rare in Nietzsche's writings. He does write that, "Love to one only is a barbarity; for it is exercised at the expense of all others. Love to God also!" *Beyond Good and Evil*, 46. The incompatibility of *eros* with Nietzsche's philosophy is thoroughly treated by Eve Tushnet in "Nietzsche's Rejection of Eros," *blogspot.it*, accessed February 14, 2014, http://eveseniore-say.blogspot.it/.

20. Joyce, *Dubliners*, 111.

21. Arthur Schopenhauer, vol. 2 of *The World as Will and Representation* (New York: Dover Publications, 1966), 534.

22. Joyce, *Dubliners*, 115.

23. Ibid., 109

24. Ibid., 110.

25. Ibid., 112.

26. Owens, *James Joyce's Painful Case*, 9.

27. Ibid., 10.

28. Ibid., 212.

29. Ibid., 129.

30. Ibid., 129-30.

31. Jesus described the state of ultimate perfection in terms of integration of masculinity and femininity: "For when they rise from the dead, they neither marry nor are given in marriage, but are like angels in heaven" (Mk 12:25).

32. St. Augustine, "In Epistulam Johannis ad Parthos tractatus, 7.8," commentary by Allan D. Fitzgerald, in *Augustine Through the Ages: An Encyclopaedia*, edited by Allan Fitzgerald and John C. Cavadini, 310-11 (Grand Rapids: Wm. B. Eerdmans Publishing, 1999), 311: "Love and do what you will."

33. Vicki Mahaffey and Jill Shashaty, introduction to *Collaborative Dubliners*, edited by Vicki Mahaffey and Jill Shashaty, 14.

34. Ibid., 15.

35. Pope Benedict XVI, *Jesus of Nazareth: From the Baptism in the Jordan to the Transfiguration*, translated by Adrian J. Walker (San Francisco: Ignatius Press, 2007), 256-57.

36. Mahaffey and Shashaty, introduction to *Collaborative Dubliners*, 16.

37. Declan Kiberd, personal correspondence 11 September, 2011.

38. Joyce, *Dubliners*, 224.

39. Florence L. Walzl, "Gabriel and Michael: The Conclusion of 'The Dead,'" *James Joyce Quarterly* 4, no. 1 (1966): 29.

40. Margot Norris and Vincent D. Pecora, "Dead Again," *Collaborative Dubliners*, 359.

41. Ibid., 369.
42. Ibid., 358.
43. Joyce, *Dubliners*, 178.
44. Ibid., 189.
45. Ibid., 179.
46. Ibid., 210.
47. Ibid., 214.
48. Ibid., 215.
49. Ibid., 220
50. Ibid., 221.
51. Ibid., 222.
52. Ibid., 223.
53. Ibid.
54. Ibid.
55. Ibid, 224
56. Levy, "Great Misinterpretations," 147, quoting *James Joyce Archive*, edited by Michael Groden, et al.
57. Joyce, *Dubliners*, 220.
58. Joyce, *Critical Writings*, 41.
59. James Joyce, *Selected Letters*, edited by Richard Ellmann (London: Faber & Faber 1975), 7.
60. Dominic Manganiello, "The Beauty that Saves," 154.
61. Ibid., 155.

62. Joyce, *Portrait of the Artist*, 172.

63. David E. Jones, "The Essence of Beauty in James Joyce's Aesthetics," *James Joyce Quarterly* 10, no. 3 (1973): 296.

64. Ibid., 310.

65. Manganiello, "The Beauty that Saves," 155.

66. Ibid., 156.

67. Josemaria Escriva de Balaguer, *Christ Is Passing By* (Dublin: Veritas Publications, 1974), 112.

68. Manganiello, "The Beauty that Saves," 158.

69. Ibid., 167n 4. See Jeffrey Heath, *The Picturesque Prison: Evelyn Waugh and His Writing* (Kingston: McGill-Queen's University Press, 1982), 162.

70. Erwin R. Steinberg, "The Bird-Girl in *A Portrait* as Synthesis: The Sacred Assimilated to the Profane," *James Joyce Quarterly* 17, no. 2 (1980), 149-50, citing William York Tindall, *The Literary Symbol* (New York: Columbia University Press, 1955), 80.

71. Ibid., 158, citing Joyce, *Portrait of the Artist*, 172.

72. Ibid., citing Edmund Epstein, *The Ordeal of Stephen Dedalus* (Carbondale: Southern Illinois University Press, 1971), 99.

73. Ibid., 158-59.

74. Joyce, *My Brother's Keeper*, 131-32.

75. Joyce, *Critical Writings*, 134.

76. St. Irenaeus, *Adversus Haereses* 2, 30, 9; 4, 20, 1: PG 7/1, 822, 1032.

77. See Robert Klawitter, "Henri Bergson and James Joyce's Fictional World," *Comparative Literature Studies 3*, no. 4 (1966): 429-37.

78. Joyce, *Portrait of the Artist*, 221.

79. Ibid., 162.

80. Josef Pieper, *Enthusiasm and the Divine Madness*, translated by Richard and Clara Winston (South Bend: St. Augustine's Press, 1999), 94.

81. Pieper, *Death and Immortality*, 104-05, citing Plato, *Phaedrus*, 246c.

82. Ibid., 105.

83. Pieper, *Enthusiasm and the Divine Madness*, 95.

84. Ibid.

85. Ibid.

86. St. Teresa of Avila, *The Life*, translated by J. M. Cohen (London: Penguin, 1988), 157.

87. Pieper, *Enthusiasm and the Divine Madness*, 95-96.

88. Ibid.

89. Joyce, *Portrait of the Artist*, 166.

90. John W. Mahon, "Joyce Among the Brothers," *Christianity and Literature* 53, no. 3 (2004): 349.

91. Ibid., citing Joyce, *Portrait of the Artist*, 253.

92. Joyce, *Portrait of the Artist*, 253.

93. See *Confessions*, 2.3. This similarity will be noted again in Chapter IV, section IV.3, on Augustine.

94. Ellmann, *James Joyce*, 299.

95. Kenner, "The *Portrait* in Perspective," 44.

96. Thornton, *The Antimodernism of Joyce's Portrait*, 106.

97. Ibid.

98. Ellmann, *James Joyce*, 169.

99. Joyce, *Ulysses*, 3:29-30.

100. Budgen, *Joyce and the Making of Ulysses*, 107.

101. Kenner, "The *Portrait* in Perspective," 39.

102. Noon, *Joyce and Aquinas*, 25, citing Joyce, *Ulysses*, 49:1-5.

103. Joyce, *Portrait of the Artist*, 162.

104. Kiberd, *Inventing Ireland*, 346.

105. We will return to this subject in sections IV.3 and IV.4 of the next chapter, on Augustine and Aquinas.

106. Joyce, *Critical Writings*, 64.

107. Marilyn French, *The Book as World: James Joyce's "Ulysses"* (Cambridge: Harvard University Press, 1976), 225.

108. Joyce, *Ulysses*, 614:1.

109. Declan Kiberd, introduction to *Ulysses* by James Joyce (London: Penguin Books, 2000), lxiv.

110. Kiberd, *Inventing Ireland*, 380.

111. Noon, *Joyce and Aquinas*, 117, citing Louis Gillet, "Stele for James Joyce," in *A James Joyce Yearbook*, 1949, 42.

112. Joyce, *Ulysses*, 74:33, 76:12-14.

113. Ibid., 871:14-15.

114. Edmund Wilson, "James Joyce," in *Joyce: a Collection of Critical Essays*, edited by William M. Chace, 50-66 (New Jersey: Spectrum, 1974), 54.

115. Ellmann, *Ulysses on the Liffey*, 160.

116. Ibid., 161.

117. Kiberd, *Inventing Ireland*, 338.

118. Budgen, *Joyce and the Making of Ulysses*, 18.

119. Kiberd, introduction to *Ulysses: Annotated Student Edition*, ix.

120. Ibid., x.

121. Joyce, *Ulysses*, 405:13-19.

122. See ibid., 230-32.

123. See ibid., 416:11-12.

124. Weldon Thornton, "The Greatness of *Ulysses*," *New Hibernia Review* 7, no. 4 (2003): 27.

125. Budgen, *Joyce and the Making of* Ulysses, 284-85.

126. Joyce, *Ulysses*, 504:13-15.

127. Ibid., 510:18-20.

128. See ibid., 554:14-16.

129. Joyce, *Ulysses*, 213:15-16.

130. Ibid., 510:5-9.

131. Ellmann, *Ulysses on the Liffey*, 133.

132. Joyce, *Ulysses*, 478:5-8.

133. Suzette A. Henke, *Joyce's Moraculous Sindbook: A Study of "Ulysses"* (Columbus: Ohio State University Press, 1978), 228-29.

134. Ibid., 229.

135. Joyce, *Ulysses*, 193:31-194:6.

136. Ibid., 345:2-3.

137. Ibid., 491:26-27.

138. Ibid., 670:16-18.

139. Ibid., 925:5-6.

140. Kiberd, introduction to *Ulysses: Annotated Student Edition*, l.

141. Ibid., liv.

142. Ibid., lxiii.

143. Budgen, *Joyce and the Making of Ulysses*, 315.

144. Levy, "Great Misinterpretations," 146-48.

145. David Norris, "The 'Unhappy Mania' and Mr. Bloom's Cigar: Homosexuality in the Works of James Joyce," *James Joyce Quarterly* 31, no. 3 (1994): 357.

146. Ibid., 373.

147. Sheldon Brivic, *Joyce Between Freud and Jung* (Port Washington: Kennikat Press, 1980), 20.

148. Norris, "Homosexuality in the Works of James Joyce," 373.

149. Frances Devlin-Glass, "Writing in the Slipstream of the Wildean Trauma: Joyce, Buck Mulligan and Ho-

mophobia Reconsidered," *The Canadian Journal of Irish Studies* 31, no. 2 (2005): 28, citing Joyce, *Critical Writings*, 202, 204.

150. Joyce, *Ulysses*, 508:21-25.

151. Ibid., 536:2-4.

152. Kiberd, *Ulysses and Us*, 206.

153. Ibid., 209.

154. Catholicism affirms the "primacy" neither of mother nor of child but the equal right to life of both, and the right to surgical intervention in the mother's favor which may have the undesired and unsought secondary effect of endangering the child's life.

155. Kiberd, *Ulysses and Us*, 208.

156. French, *The Book as World*, 173.

157. *Humanae vitae* speaks of "well-grounded reasons for spacing births" which would permit married couples to "take advantage of the natural cycles immanent in the reproductive system and engage in marital intercourse only during those times that are infertile, thus controlling birth in a way which does not in the least offend the moral principles . . . just explained." Pope Paul VI, *Humanae vitae*, Vatican Web site, July 25, 1968, http://w2.vatican.va/content/paul-vi/ en/encyclicals/ documents/hf_p-vi_enc_25071968_humanae-vitae.html, sec. 16. *Humanae vitae* is part of a tradition with roots in declarations of the Sacred Penitentiary concerning birth control in the mid-1800s, an important detail that is unlikely to have escaped Joyce's rigorous research ethic.

158. Joyce, *Ulysses*, 695:25-27.

159. Ibid., 696:5-7.20-21.

160. Joyce, *Stephen Hero*, 205.

161. Henke, *Joyce's Moraculous Sindbook*, 173.

162. Ibid.

163. Ibid., 175.

164. Mary Lowe-Evans, *Crimes Against Fecundity: Joyce and Population Control* (New York: Syracuse University Press, 1989), 1. The chief administrator of Irish famine relief was Charles Edward Trevelyan who "was convinced by Malthus' theory that any attempt to raise the standard of living of the poorest section of the population above the subsistence level would only result in increased population," John O'Beirne Ranelagh, *A Short History of Ireland* (Cambridge University Press, 1994), 116.

165. Ibid., 54.

166. Dominic Manganiello, "Book Review of *Crimes Against Fecundity: Joyce and Population Control* by Mary Lowe-Evans," *Canadian Journal of Irish Studies* 17, no. 2 (1991): 118.

167. Ellmann, *James Joyce*, 565n.

168. Joyce, *Ulysses*, 133:22-23.

169. Lernout, *Help My Unbelief*, 190.

170. Joyce, *Ulysses*, 614: 1.16.23.

171. Thomas Balazs, "Recognizing Masochism: Psychoanalysis and the Politics of Sexual Submission in *Ulysses*," *Joyce Studies Annual* 13, no. 1 (2002): 161.

172. Budgen, *Joyce and the Making of Ulysses*, 18: "Being an

orthodox agnostic I saw nothing illogical in admitting that what are called miracles might occur. I had no satisfactory evidence that any ever had occurred, but on my limited experience I felt I couldn't rule them out ... Joyce laughed and said: 'You are really more a believer than is many a good Catholic.'"

173. Ibid., 291.

174. Balazs, "Recognizing Masochism," 161. For example: "In his 1982 article 'A New Approach to Bloom as 'Womanly Man,'" Joseph Allen Boone explains Bloom's masochism as an attempt to purge himself of the internalized social stigma that attaches to him as an androgynous or 'womanly' man. A few years later, in *Joyce and the Law of the Father* (1989), Frances Restuccia characterizes Bloom's masochism as a psychosexual strategy—exemplifying a paradigm theorized by the postmodern psychoanalytic critic Gilles Deleuze—for undermining patriarchal power structures and achieving personal liberation. And in 1990, Suzette Henke in *James Joyce and the Politics of Desire* sees Bloom's masochistic encounters as part of a 'revolutionary narrative' that exposes the fiction of sexual difference (122). Others have seen Bloom's masochism as representing a more ambivalent posture with regard to gender." The list continues.

175. Budgen, *Joyce and the Making of Ulysses*, 248.

176. Ibid., 253.

177. Ibid., 254.

178. For a fuller explanation of this dynamic, see Chapter II of this work, section II.4: The *Eros* Controversy.

179. Joyce, *Ulysses*, 788:1-2.

180. Budgen, *Joyce and the Making of Ulysses*, 18.

181. Joyce, *Ulysses*, 815:20-22.

182. Ellmann, *James Joyce*, 162.

183. Thornton, "The Greatness of *Ulysses*," 33.

184. Levy, "Great Misinterpretations," 147, quoting *James Joyce Archive*, ed. Michael Groden, et al.

185. Joyce, *Ulysses*, 38:2-3.

186. As for example when Weldon Thornton coincides with Marilyn French on the subject of Bloom's *"caritas"* (See Thornton, *Voices and Values in Ulysses*, 38, citing French, *The Book as World*, 85).

187. See Joyce's *Ulysses*, 745:15-17: "*Christus* or Bloom his name is, or, after all, any other, *secundum carnem.*"

188. William T. Noon, S.J., "The Religious Position of James Joyce," in *James Joyce: His Place in World Literature*, edited by Wolodymyr T. Zyla, 7-21 (Lubbock: Texas Tech Press, 1969), 18-19.

189. Thornton, *The Antimodernism of Portrait*, 31.

190. Joyce, *Portrait of the Artist*, 221.

191. Sheldon Brivic, "Joyce and the Metaphysics of Creation," *The Crane Bag* 6, no. 1 (1982): 13.

192. Ibid., 14.

193. Ibid.

194. Ibid.

195. See Chapter II of this work, section II.4.2.3: Is this Christianity or Deism?

196. Brivic, "Joyce and the Metaphysics of Creation," 19.

197. Joyce, *Ulysses*, 265:11.

198. Kiberd, *Inventing Ireland*, 339.

199. Mt 23:1-11.

CHAPTER IV

1. See Chapter II of this work, section II.4.3.2, citing Jung, *Aspects of the Feminine*, 65: "Woman's psychology is founded on the principle of *Eros* . . . whereas from ancient times the ruling principle ascribed to man is *Logos*. The concept of *Eros* could be expressed in modern terms as psychic relatedness, and that of *Logos* as objective interest."

2. Joyce, *Critical Writings*, 134.

3. Joyce, *My Brother's Keeper*, 227.

4. Mary Lowe-Evans, *Catholic Nostalgia in Joyce and Company* (Florida: University Press of Florida, 2008), 8.

5. Ibid., 44.

6. Joyce, *Dubliners*, 174.

7. Joyce, *Stephen Hero*, 206.

8. Joyce, *Ulysses*, 181:8-18.

9. Ibid., 432:31.

10. See Ibid., 416:11-12.

11. See Ibid., 432:20-25.

12. Ibid., 445:9-10.

13. Edith Stein, "Separate Vocations of Man and Woman," in *Woman*, vol. II of *The Collected Works of Edith Stein*, edited by L. Gebler and Romaeus Leuven and translated by Freda Mary Oben, 59-86 (Washington: ICS Publications, 1996), 84.

14. See Chapter II of this study; section II.4.2.5, on Stephen's surrender to *Eros*.

15. Kenner, "The *Portrait* in Perspective," 46.

16. See Joyce, *My Brother's Keeper*, 227.

17. St. Augustine, *Confessions*, 3.5.

18. Ibid., 6.5.

19. Joyce, *Portrait of the Artist*, 253.

20. St. Augustine, *Confessions*, 2.3.

21. Ibid., 4.6.

22. See Chapter III of this study; section III.2.3 on "The Dead," citing Joyce, *Dubliners*, 220.

23. St. Augustine, *Confessions*, 7.8.

24. See Chapter II of this study; II.4.5 on *eros* in the Catholic tradition; and these sections in Chapter III: III.2.3.4 on *admonitio* and *delectatio*; III.3.3.1 on the unfinished ending of *Portrait*; III.3.3.2 on Stephen's relationships; III.3.3.3 on Stephen between *Portrait* and *Ulysses*; III.5, the conclusion of Chapter III.

25. St. Augustine, *Confessions*, 202:8.11.

26. Joyce, *Ulysses*, 42:20-28.

27. Joyce, *My Brother's Keeper*, 131-32.

28. See Chapter III of this work; section III.4.4: Resolution of the *Agape-Eros* Puzzle; especially subsections III.4.4.3 on Mercy and III.4.4.5 on Joyce and Fatherhood.

29. Joyce, *My Brother's Keeper*, 130.

30. Ellmann, *James Joyce*, 342.

31. Joyce, *Ulysses*, 264:2-3.

32. Josef Pieper, *Scholasticism, Personalities and Problems of Medieval Philosophy*, translated by Richard and Clara Winston (South Bend: St. Augustine's Press, 2001), 46.

33. Ibid., 61.

34. Ibid., 149-50.

35. See Chapter I of this study, section I.3.2 on Joyce and the Modern and the Medieval.

36. Levy, "Great Misinterpretations," 146.

37. Joyce, *Critical Writings*, 220.

38. See Chapter II of this work for a fuller discussion of this Cartesian dichotomization; especially subsection II.5 on a theological hiatus, and this quotation from Jacques Maritain: Descartes, he writes, "is an obstinate divider and he has not only separated modern and ancient, but he has set all things against each other—faith and reason, metaphysics and sciences, knowledge and love . . . The world sighs for deliverance; it sighs for wisdom, for the wisdom, I say, from which the spirit of Descartes has led us astray, for the wisdom which reconciles man with himself and, crowned with a divine life, fulfills knowledge in charity," *Three Reformers*, 89.

39. Robin Darling Young, "Theologia in the Early Church," *Communio* 24 (1997): 688.

40. Ibid., 689.

41. Etienne Gilson, *The Christian Philosophy of St. Thomas Aquinas* (Notre Dame: University of Notre Dame Press, 1994), 226.

42. See Chapter II of this work; especially sections II.4.2 on *Portrait* and II.4.2.3 on Christianity and Deism.

43. Aidan Nichols, O.P., *Discovering Aquinas* (Grand Rapids: Wm. B. Eerdmans Publishing, 2003), 141.

44. Ibid., 141-42.

45. Peter A. Huff, *Vatican II: Its Impact on You* (Liguori: Liguori Publications, 2011), 24.

46. Ibid., 24-25.

47. See Levy, "Great Misinterpretations," 146. See Chapter I of this study; especially subsection I.3.2 on whether in Joyce there is rupture or synthesis between the Medieval and the Modern.

48. Joyce, *Portrait of the Artist*, 209.

49. Ibid., 211.

50. Ellmann, *James Joyce*, 26.

51. Lowe-Evans, *Catholic Nostalgia*, 40.

52. Ellmann, *James Joyce*, 27.

53. Joyce, *Letters*, vol. II, 48.

54. Joyce, *Portrait of the Artist*, 156.

55. Ibid., 161-62.

56. Ibid., 186.

57. Hence *Lumen gentium*, sec. 46: "All men should take note that the profession of the evangelical counsels, though entailing the renunciation of certain values which are to be undoubtedly esteemed, does not detract from a genuine development of the human person, but rather by its very nature is most beneficial to that development."

58. Joyce, *Portrait of the Artist*, 186.

59. Ibid.

60. St. Ignatius of Loyola, "Letter 83: To the Fathers and Brothers of Portugal," in *Obras Completas de S. Ignacio de Loyola*, edited by Fr. Ignacio Iparraguirre, S.I., and Fr. Candido de Dalmases, S.I. (Madrid: B.A.C., 1952), 838. (My translation).

61. Ibid., 311.

62. St. Ignatius of Loyola, "Spiritual Exercises," *Obras Completas de S. Ignacio de Loyola*, 161-62.

63. Ibid., 205.

64. See Joyce, *My Brother's Keeper*, 131-32.

65. See Philip Caraman, S.J., *Ignatius Loyola: A Biography of the Founder of the Jesuits* (San Francisco: Harper & Row, 1990), 59; Jose Ignacio Tellechea Id^goras, *Ignatius of Loyola: The Pilgrim Saint*, translated, edited, and with a preface by Cornelius M. Buckley (Chicago: Loyola University Press, 1994), 146.

66. See Chapter I of this work; subsection I.5.3.3 on causality in Molly's soliloquy.

67. See St. Ignatius of Loyola, *Autobiografia, Obras Completas de S. Ignacio de Loyola*, 39-40.

68. CCC, no. 409.

69. Joyce, *My Brother's Keeper*, 153.

70. James Joyce, *Letters of James Joyce*, vol. III, edited by Stuart Gilbert and Richard Ellmann (New York: Viking Press, 1966), 84. Letter to Valery Larbaud.

71. Joyce, *Portrait of the Artist*, 221.

72. See Josemaria Escriva de Balaguer, "Passionately Loving the World," *The Furrow* 19, no. 5 (1968), 275-76.

73. Ibid. 269.

74. John F. Coverdale, *Uncommon Faith: The Early Years of Opus Dei* (Princeton: Scepter Publishers, 2002), 85.

75. Escriva de Balaguer, "Passionately Loving the World," 269.

76. Ibid., 270-71.

77. Ibid., 271.

78. St. Teresa of Avila, *The Book of Her Foundations: a Study Guide*, edited by Marc Foley, O.C.D. (Washington: ICS Publications, 2011), 43.

79. Escriva de Balaguer, "Passionately Loving the World," 271.

80. Ibid., 274.

81. Ibid., 272.

82. Ibid., 276.

83. Federico Requena, "Vida religiosa y espiritual en la Espana de principios del siglo XX," *Anuario de Historia de la Iglesia* 11 (2002): 67. (My translation).

84. Jacques Maritain, also a Joyce contemporary, but French, perceived a similar problem and proposed a similar solution with his universal call to contemplation amidst the everyday secular realities; See "Sur l'appel a la vie mystique et a la contemplation," in *De la vie d'oraison* (Paris: Louis Rouart et fils, 1924).

85. Joyce, *Critical Writings*, 134.

86. See Chapter III of this work, especially subsections III.2.3.3 on mercy and an Ariel-like being, and III.2.3.4 on *admonitio* and *delectatio*.

87. Joyce, *My Brother's Keeper*, 131.

88. Joyce, *Portrait of the Artist*, 245.

89. Ibid., 172.

90. Ibid., 221.

CHAPTER V

1. Eugene Jolas, "My Friend James Joyce," in *James Joyce: Two Decades of Criticism*, edited by Seon Givens, 3-17 (New York: Vanguard Press, 1948), 8.

2. Joyce, *My Brother's Keeper*, 103-04.

3. Joyce, *Portrait of the Artist*, 221.

4. Ellmann, *James Joyce*, 66.

5. See Chapter I of this work, especially sections I.5.4 on the secularist interpretation of Joyce and I.5.4.2 on critiques thereof.

6. Harry Levin, "James Joyce," *Atlantic Monthly* CLXXVIII, December 1946, 127.

7. Paul Briand, "The Catholic Mass in James Joyce's *Ulysses*," *James Joyce Quarterly* 5, no. 4 (1968): 312-22.

8. Kevin Sullivan, *Joyce Among the Jesuits* (New York: Columbia University Press, 1958), 146.

9. Gottfried, *Joyce's Misbelief*, 8.

10. Sebastian Knowles, introduction to *Joyce's Misbelief* by Roy Gottfried (Florida: University Press of Florida, 2008), ix.

11. Gottfried, *Joyce's Misbelief*, 25.

12. Joyce, *Portrait of the Artist*, 171-72.

13. Ibid., 221.

14. Joyce, *Ulysses*, 49:1-4.

15. Ibid., 1:5-6.

16. Ibid., 510:22-31.

17. Ibid., 682:16-17.

18. Ibid., 695:28-33.

19. Ibid., 695:34-696:4.

20. Ibid., 696:19-21.

21. Ibid., 717:19-25.

22. Ibid., 733:18-21.

23. Ibid., 745:15-17.

24. Ibid., 790:27-791:7.

25. Ibid., 931:30-33.

26. Ellmann, *Ulysses on the Liffey*, 169.

27. Briand, "The Catholic Mass," 312.

28. Ruth Walsh, "That Pervasive Mass: In *Dubliners* and *A Portrait of The Artist As A Young Man*," *James Joyce Quarterly* 8, no. 3 (1971): 208.

29. Ibid., 211.

30. Ibid., 218.

31. Ibid.

32. Joyce, *Portrait of the Artist*, 239.

33. Ibid., 243.

34. Ibid., 249.

35. Ellmann, *James Joyce*, 49-50.

36. Bruce Bradley, S.J., "Book Review of *Ulysses and the Irish God*," 305.

37. For a fuller account of the significance of the structure of Joyce's *Portrait of the Artist*, see Chapter III of this work, especially section III.3.2 on whether Stephen's experience on the beach is one of poisoned or pure *eros*, and subsection III.3.2.1 on the assimilation of the sacred and the profane.

38. Joyce, *Portrait of the Artist*, 245.

39. Ruth Walsh, "In the Name of the Father and of the-Son . . . Joyce's Use of the Mass in *Ulysses*," *James Joyce Quarterly* 6, no. 4 (1969): 3 23-24.

40. Ibid.

41. See Chapter I of this study, especially subsection I.6.1.3 on identity, evolvement and universality.

42. Walsh, "In the Name of the Father and of the Son," 326, citing Willis Everett McNelly's unpublished dissertation, "The Use of Catholic Elements As An Artistic Source in James Joyce's *Ulysses*" (Northwestern University, 1957), 20-21.

43. The character of Mulligan is based upon Oliver St. John Gogarty, former friend of Joyce. Ellmann relates their last encounter: "'I bear you no illwill . . . But I must write as I have felt.' Gogarty answered, 'I don't care a damn what you say of me so long as it is literature.' 'Do you mean that?' Joyce asked. He said, 'I do . . . Now will you shake hands with me at least?' Joyce replied, 'I will: on that understanding,' and left." Ellmann, *James Joyce*, 278.

44. Lernout, *Help My Unbelief*, 146.

45. Ibid., 185.

46. Len Platt, "Book Review of *Help My Unbelief* by Geert Lernout," *James Joyce Quarterly* 47, no. 4 (2010): 666.

47. Kiberd, *Ulysses and Us*, 88.

48. Ibid., 210.

49. Ibid., citing Willard Potts, ed., *James Joyce: Portraits of an Artist in Exile*, 159.

50. Restuccia, "Transubstantiating *Ulysses*," 329.

51. Ibid., citing Jacques Maritain, *Art and Scholasticism and The Frontiers of Poetry*, translated by Joseph W. Evans (New York: Charles Scribner's Sons, 1962), 123-24.

52. Ibid.

53. Ibid., 330.

54. Ibid., citing *ST* III, q. 76, a. 7.

55. Ibid.

56. Ibid.

57. Ibid., 331.

58. Ibid., citing Joseph M. Powers, S.J., *Eucharistic Theology* (New York: Herder and Herder, 1967), 116, 118. (For the sake of precision, Catholic theologians would in fact assert that the Eucharist is both a religious reality *and* a natural phenomenon).

59. Ibid.

60. Devlin-Glass, "Writing in the Slipstream of the Wildean Trauma," 32.

61. For a fuller discussion of this subject see Chapter III of this work, section III.4.3 on Joyce on homosexuality and contraception, and especially subsection III.4.3.1 on Joyce's views on homosexuality.

62. Restuccia, "Transubstantiating *Ulysses*," 331.

63. Ibid., 332.

64. Ibid., 333.

65. Ibid.

66. Patrick A. McCarthy, "Further Notes on the Mass in *Ulysses*," *James Joyce Quarterly* 7, no. 2 (1970): 132, citing Joyce's *Ulysses*, 391.

67. Ibid., 134.

68. Kiberd, *Ulysses and Us*, 210.

69. Ibid., 211.

70. Ibid.

71. Briand, "The Catholic Mass," 317.
72. Ibid.
73. Ibid., 335.
74. For a fuller discussion of this subject see Chapter III of this work, section III.4.2 on Leopold Bloom; especially subsection III.4.4.2 on the ending of *Ulysses*.
75. Walsh, "In the Name of the Father and of the Son," 337.
76. Ibid.
77. Ibid., 338.
78. Ibid., 341-42.
79. Restuccia, "Transubstantiating *Ulysses*," 333.
80. Ibid., 334.
81. Ibid., 334-35.
82. Ibid., 335.
83. Briand, "The Catholic Mass," 321.
84. Restuccia, "Transubstantiating *Ulysses*," 355.
85. Ibid., 339.
86. Ibid.
87. Kiberd, *Ulysses and Us*, 188.
88. Ibid., 190.
89. Joyce, *Ulysses*, 496:19-20.
90. Kiberd, *Ulysses and Us*, 238-39.
91. Ibid., 281.

92. Sullivan, *Joyce among the Jesuits*, 146. Sullivan argues that Joyce as artist "secularizes" the function of the priest, and that "his sacrament is a celebration of the communion of humanity." He concludes that: "This is not substitution, it is simultaneity." For a fuller context of his position, see the introduction of this chapter; subsection V.1.1 on Joyce and the Eucharist.

93. Kiberd, *Ulysses and Us*, 309.

94. Ibid., 329.

95. Ibid., 329-30.

96. Ellmann, *Ulysses on the Liffey*, 90. (Joyce's understanding of *metaphors* is more complex than commonly realized, as indicated in his sacramental use of the term epiphany, as described in chapter I, essentially to conjoin the material and the spiritual).

97. Ibid., 171.

98. Ellmann, *James Joyce*, 448.

99. Robert Boyle, S.J., "Miracle in Black Ink: A Glance at Joyce's Use of His Eucharistic Image," *James Joyce Quarterly* 10, no. 1 (1972): 47.

100. See Joyce, *Portrait of the Artist*, 221.

101. Ibid.

102. Boyle, "Miracle in Black Ink," 48.

103. Joyce, *Portrait of the Artist*, 160.

104. Boyle, "Miracle in Black Ink," 51.

105. Ibid., 53.

106. See Ellmann, *Ulysses on the Liffey*, 171. (See subsection V.4.1 on Molly's menstruation).

107. Thornton, *The Antimodernism of Joyce's Portrait*, 104.

108. See Boyle, "Miracle in Black Ink," 53: "Thus, under the accidents of this human ink, composed of faeces and urine as the Eucharist is composed of bread and wine, the artist makes himself available to his race, to give them conscience—to make them share, as the *FW* passage makes clear, in all human history by plunging with the individual artist into the dividual human chaos, substantiated in the verbal chaosmos of *Finnegans Wake*. So Joyce as a human being, like Dublin as a city containing all cities, contains in himself all humanity, as the particular contains the universal."

109. See Ibid., 56.

110. Robert Boyle, S.J., *James Joyce's Pauline Vision: A Catholic Exposition* (Carbondale: Southern Illinois University Press, 1978), 93.

111. Ibid., 59.

112. Lernout, *Help My Unbelief*, 16.

113. Pieper, *Death and Immortality*, 31.

114. St. Thomas Aquinas, *ST* III, q. 5, a. 2.

115. Dennis M. Shanahan, "The Eucharistic Aesthetics of the Passion: The Testament of Blood in *Ulysses*," *James Joyce Quarterly* 27, no. 2 (1990): 373.

116. Ibid.

117. Ibid., 376.

118. Ibid., 377.

119. See Chapter IV, subsection IV.6.1 on *Eros* and *Agape* (and on *agape* in Joyce's life and work).

120. Albert Cardinal Vanhoye, *Accogliamo Cristo Nostro Sommo Sacerdote, Esercizi Spirituali con Benedetto XVI* (Citta del Vaticano: Libreria Editrice Vaticana, 2008), 191. (My translation).

121. Ibid., 161.

122. Ibid., 161-62.

123. See Shanahan, "The Eucharistic Aesthetics of the Passion," 378.

124. Ibid., 384.

125. Briand, "The Catholic Mass," 315.

126. Ellmann, *Ulysses on the Liffey*, 149.

127. Ibid., 150.

128. Eco, *Le poetiche di Joyce*, 92-93.

129. St. Augustine, *The Trinity*, edited by Edmund Hill (New York: New City Press, 1991), 324.

130. Hans Urs Von Balthasar, *The Truth of God*, vol. II of *Theo-Logic: Theological Logical Theory*, translated by Adrian J. Walker (San Francisco: Ignatius Press, 2004), 62.

131. Pope John Paul II, *Puebla: A Pilgrimage of Faith*, edited by the Daughters of St. Paul (Boston: St. Paul Editions, 1979), 86.

132. For a fuller explanation of the nuptial dimension of Eucharist and Church in its biblical context see Scott Hahn, *The Lamb's Supper* (San Francisco: Doubleday Press, 1999).

133. See, for example: St. Augustine, *En. in Ps.* 74:4: PL 36, 948-49: *"as head, he calls himself the bridegroom, as body, he calls himself 'bride.'"*

134. Kiberd, *Ulysses and Us*, 74.

135. For a fuller account of this reconciliation see Chapter III of this work, section III.4 on *Ulysses*; especially subsections III.4.4.1 on Bloom's victory and III.4.4.2 on the ending of the novel.

136. See subsection V.4.3 on visceral Eucharistic realism, and subsection V.5.3 on Trinitarian analogues.

137. See subsections V.4.1 on Molly's menstruation; V.3.2.5 on Stephen's toast and V.5.2 on *agape* in the Letter to the Hebrews.

138. See Chapter III of this study; subsection III.2.3.2 on Gabriel's epiphany, citing Joyce, *Dubliners*, 223.

139. See subsection III.4.4.1 of Chapter III on Bloom's victory.

140. Joseph Cardinal Ratzinger, *Pilgrim Fellowship of Faith: The Church as Communion*, edited by Stephan Otto Horn and Vinzenz Pfnur and translated by Henry Taylor (San Francisco: Ignatius Press, 2005), 120.

141. Ibid., 122.

142. George Orwell, *Dickens, Dali and Others* (Florida: Mariner Books, 1970), 234.

143. Kiberd, *Ulysses and Us*, 210.

144. Ratzinger, *Pilgrim Fellowship of Faith*, 120.

145. See subsection III.4.2.3 of Chapter III on Bloom's defects.

146. Michael J. O'Shea, "Catholic Liturgy in Joyce's *Ulysses*," *James Joyce Quarterly* 21, no. 2 (1984): 133.

147. Gottfried, *Joyce's Misbelief*, 27.

148. See Introduction, section 1.1: "Joyce's humor, Joyce's obscenity, and Joyce's irrepressible irony are too frequently ignored or softpedalled by Catholic readers," Segall, *Joyce in America*, 168.

149. See Chapter II, subsection II.2.1 on the short story "Eveline" and critical interpretation.

150. See Chapter III, subsection III.4.3 on Joyce's views of homosexuality and contraception.

FINAL SUMMARY & CONCLUSION

1. Richard Ellmann, "Joyce's religion and politics," *The Irish Times* (Dublin, Ireland), Feb. 2, 1982.

2. Joyce, *Portrait of the Artist*, 172.

3. Eco, *Le poetiche di Joyce*, 12.

4. Ibid., 13.

5. Ellmann, *James Joyce*, 537.

6. O'Connor, *Mystery and Manners: Occasional Prose*, 118.

7. Joyce, *Portrait of the Artist*, 249: "Cannot repent. Told her so and asked for sixpence. Got threepence."

8. Pope Benedict XVI, *Spe salvi*, Vatican Web site, November 30, 2007, http://w2.vatican.va/content/benedict-xvi/en/encyclicals/documents/hf_ben-xvi_enc_20071130_spe-salvi.html, sec. 46.

9. Karl Rahner, *Ecclesiology, Questions in the Church, the Church in the World*, vol. 14 of *Theological Investigations*, translated by David Bourke (London: Darton, Longman & Todd, 1976), 283.

10. Joyce, *Stephen Hero*, 205.

11. Ibid., 206.

12. E. Michael Jones, *Degenerate Moderns* (San Francisco: Ignatius Press, 1993), 12.

13. This has been shown in Chapter III of this work; especially in subsection III.4 on *Ulysses*.

14. Joyce, *Stephen Hero*, 214.

15. See Joyce, *My Brother's Keeper*, 190: "Her confessor . . . advised her to put my brother and me out of the house 'before they corrupt the other children' . . . Jim was indignant."

16. See Ellmann, *James Joyce*, 292-94.

17. Levy, "Great Misinterpretations," 144.

18. St. Thomas Aquinas, *ST* II-II, q. 6, a. 2.

19. Ibid.

20. St. Thomas Aquinas, *ST* II-II, q. 7, a. 2.

21. St. Thomas Aquinas, *ST* I-II, q. 109, a. 1, ad. 1: "Whatever its source, truth is of the Holy Spirit" (cited and translated in Pope John Paul II's *Fides et ratio*, Vatican Web site, September 14, 1998, http://w2.vatican.va/content/john-paul-ii/en/encyclicals/documents/hf_jp-ii_enc_14091998_fides-et-ratio.html, sec. 45.

22. Ellmann, *James Joyce*, 107, citing Joyce, *Letters*, vol. I, 53.

23. John Paul Wauck, "Christianity and the Poetics of Ordinary Life," in *Poetica & Cristianesimo*, edited by Rafael Jimenez Catano & Juan Jose Garcia-Noblejas, 149-78 (Roma: Edizioni Universita della Santa Croce, 2005), 156.

24. Ibid.

25. Ibid., 178.

INDEX

AQUINAS, THOMAS

Commentary on Aristotle's Metaphysics, 18

Expositio et lectura super Epistolas Pauli Apostoli: II ad Corinthos, 140

Summa Theologica, 33-43, 52, 63, 93-94, 143, 146, 152-53, 296-303, 353-54, 356-57, 384, 414, 420-24

AUGUSTINE OF HIPPO

Confessions, 31, 136, 156-57, 160, 225, 290-95, 299-300, 303, 419-20

The Trinity, 392

Tractatus in evangelium Iohannis, 161, 189

BALÁZS, THOMAS

"Recognizing Masochism: Psychoanalysis and the Politics of Sexual Submission in Ulysses," 260-61

BECK, WARREN

Joyce's Dubliners: Substance, Vision, and Art, 114-15

BEEBE, MAURICE

"Ulysses and the Age of Modernism," 9

BENEDICT XVI

Deus Caritas Est, 14, 131-32, 171, 222-24, 261-62, 276-77, 311-12, 401-2

Jesus of Nazareth: From the Baptism in the Jordan to the Transfiguration, 190-91

Jesus of Nazareth: Holy Week: From the Entrance into Jerusalem to the Resurrection, 162

Light of the World, 13, 270

Spe Salvi, 414-15

BENNETT, JANICE

St. Lawrence and the Holy Grail: The Story of the Holy Chalice of Valencia, 173

BERRONE, LOUIS

James Joyce in Padua, 49

BOYLE, ROBERT, S.J.

James Joyce's Pauline Vision: A Catholic Exposition, 382

"Miracle in Black Ink: A Glance at Joyce's Use of His Eucharistic Image," 378-82, 399

BRADLEY, BRUCE, S.J.

"Book Review of *Ulysses and the Irish God*, by Frederick K. Lang," 80-81, 346

James Joyce's Schooldays, 128

BRIAND, PAUL

"The Catholic Mass in James Joyce's *Ulysses*," 328, 340-41, 361, 368-69, 390-91

BRIVIC, SHELDON

Joyce Between Freud and Jung, 247-48

"Joyce's Consubstantiality," 95

"Joyce and the Metaphysics of Creation," 269-72

BUDGEN, FRANK
Joyce and the Making of Ulysses, 48, 98, 104, 230, 239-40, 246, 260-61, 263

CANTALAMESSA, RANIERO
"The Two Faces of Love: Eros and Agape," 157-58, 220

CATECHISM OF THE CATHOLIC CHURCH
65, 70, 277, 313, 392-93

COLUM, MARY & PADRAIC.
Our Friend James Joyce, 3

CONNELL, K. H.
Irish Peasant Society, 124

CORISH, PATRICK
Maynooth College: 1795-1995, 125

COVERDALE, JOHN F.
Uncommon Faith: The Early Years of Opus Dei, 316-17

DENZINGER-SCHONMETZER (COUNCIL OF TRENT)
Enchiridion Symboloum, definitionum et declarationum de rebus fidei et morum, 65, 70, 120

DEVLIN-GLASS, FRANCES
"Writing in the Slipstream of the Wildean Trauma: Joyce, Buck Mulligan and Homphobia Reconsidered," 248, 355

ECO, UMBERTO
The Aesthetics of Chaosmos: the Middle Ages of James Joyce, 37, 47-48

The Aesthetics of Thomas Aquinas, 6, 40-41

Le poetiche di Joyce, 52-53, 331, 391-93, 412-13

ELIOT, T.S.
"The Metaphysical Poets," 163

ELLMANN, RICHARD
James Joyce, 7, 24-25, 70, 76, 79-80, 83, 108, 118, 128-31, 140, 226-27, 229, 237-38, 257, 296, 303-4, 327-31, 339-40, 345-46, 362, 370, 375-76, 381, 391, 399, 412-13, 419, 426

Ulysses on the Liffey, 10, 74, 242, 315-16

"Joyce's religion and politics," 412

EPSTEIN, EDMUND
The Ordeal of Stephen Dedalus, 214

ESCRIVÁ DE BALAGUER, JOSEMARÍA
Christ is Passing By, 212

"Passionately Loving the World," 283-84, 316-21

FITZGERALD, ALLAN D.
Augustine Through the Ages: An Encyclopedia, 189

FOURTH LATERAN COUNCIL
Canon II, 58

FRENCH, MARILYN
The Book as World: James Joyce's Ulysses, 233, 250

GILSON, ETIENNE
The Christian Philosophy of St. Thomas Aquinas, 299

GOTTFRIED, ROY
Joyce's Misbelief, 7, 39, 62, 111-12, 176, 330-32, 408

GRODEN, MICHAEL, & VICKI MAHAFFEY
"Silence and Fractals in 'The Sisters,'" 181, 437

GROSSI, VITTORINO, O.S.A
"Correction," 161

HEATH, JEFFREY
The Picturesque Prison: Evelyn Waugh and His Writing, 213

HENKE, SUZETTE A.
Joyce's Moraculous Sindbook: A Study of Ulysses, 242, 252-53

HIBBERT, JEFFREY
"Joyce's Loss of Faith," 63

HUFF, PETER A.
Vatican II: Its Impact on You, 301

HUGHES, EAMONN
"Joyce and Catholicism," 66-67

IGNATIUS OF LOYOLA
Obras Completas de S. Ignacio de Loyola, 307-13

ISRAELY, JEFF
"A Resounding Echo," 46

ST. IRENAEUS
Adversus Haereses, 217

JOHN PAUL II
Crossing the Threshold of Hope, 162

Dominum et vivificantem, 73, 322-23

Puebla: A Pilgrimage of Faith, 392

Veritatis Splendor, 31

JOLAS, EUGENE
"My Friend James Joyce," 327

JONES, DAVID. E.
"The Essence of Beauty in James Joyce's Aesthetics," 209-10, 419

JOYCE, JAMES
Critical Writings, 71, 138-39, 203, 216, 232-33, 281, 298, 314, 322

Dubliners, 105, 113-18, 124, 126-27, 129, 132, 145, 156, 172-88, 190-208, 228, 231, 247, 262, 272, 282-83, 287, 342, 396, 399-400, 410-11

"The Dead" (in *Dubliners*), 172, 193-208, 212, 228, 231, 268, 272, 292-94, 399-400

"Eveline" (in *Dubliners*), 113-118, 124, 126-27, 129, 132, 145, 156, 180, 185, 193, 267, 294, 310, 410

Finnegans Wake, 5, 27-28, 46, 49, 103, 381-82, 384

"Grace" (in *Dubliners*), 282-83, 396

"A Little Cloud" (in *Dubliners*), 206, 212

"A Painful Case" (in *Dubliners*), 172, 181-88, 191, 193, 205, 207, 212, 228, 231-32, 257, 272, 394, 410

"The Sisters" (in *Dubliners*), 172-181, 193, 205, 228, 231, 272, 410

Letters, 4, 111, 129, 204, 304, 346

"On the Worldwide Literary Influence of the Renaissance," 49-50, 202, 266, 298, 301

A Portrait of the Artist as a Young Man, 6-7, 10-11, 26, 32-45, 49, 52-53, 66, 76, 81, 84-90, 92-96, 98, 100, 105-9, 111, 113, 119, 125-27, 130, 132-50, 154-56, 161, 172, 175-77, 179-80, 182, 184, 203, 205, 207-18, 224-31, 235, 247, 262, 265, 267, 271-272, 287-297, 299, 302, 305-7, 310, 324-25, 327, 332-33, 342-48, 352, 373, 376, 379-80, 382-83, 385, 410-12, 414, 418, 423

Stephen Hero, 33-45, 75-76, 89, 145-47, 175, 178, 205, 252, 283, 418-19

Ulysses, 7, 9, 26, 41-43, 49, 67, 69-78, 81, 90-91, 95-100, 104-109, 154-56, 171-73, 203, 205, 226-53, 255-66, 268, 271-72, 274, 276-77, 284-86, 293-95, 310, 313, 318, 327, 332-41, 346-78, 382-83, 385-91, 394-98, 400, 402-7, 409-13, 415, 423

JOYCE, STANISLAUS

Dublin Diary, 130-31, 216

My Brother's Keeper, 5, 21-22, 24, 119, 128, 159, 281, 290,

294-96, 310, 313, 323, 327, 419

JUNG, CARL

Aspects of the Feminine, 151, 279-80

KENNER, HUGH

"Book Review of Ulysses *on the Liffey*, by Richard Ellmann," 10

"The Cubist *Portrait*," 89-90

in "The Impertinence of Being Definitive," 10

"Molly's Masterstroke," 115

"The *Portrait* in Perspective," 7, 81-83, 133, 154, 227, 230, 290

KIBERD, DECLAN

Introduction to Ulysses: *Annotated Student Edition*, 5, 233-34, 239, 245-46

Inventing Ireland: The Literature of the Modern Nation, 16, 44, 96, 125, 165, 170, 176, 231, 235, 238, 274

Ulysses *and Us*, 23, 76-77, 249-50, 328, 353, 359-60, 371-75, 397, 405-6

KLAWITTER, ROBERT

"Henri Bergson and James Joyce's Fictional World," 217

KNOWLES, SEBASTIAN

"Introduction" to *Joyce's Misbelief*, by Roy Gottfried, 330

LARKIN, EMMET

"The Devotional Revolution in Ireland," 119-20

LEVIN, HARRY

"James Joyce," 328

James Joyce: A Critical Introduction, 3

LERNOUT, GEERT

Help My Unbelief: James Joyce and Religion, 3, 5, 63-69, 72, 75, 81-83, 111, 117-18, 132, 165, 176, 182, 192, 257-58, 328, 350-51, 383

LEWIS, C.S.

The Four Loves, 157, 163-64

LEVY, ANTOINE, O.P.

"Great Misinterpretations: Umberto Eco on Joyce and Aquinas," 1, 6, 38, 39, 41-52, 149, 165, 169, 202, 246-49, 266, 298, 301-2, 421

LOWE-EVANS, MARY

Catholic Nostalgia in Joyce and Company, 282, 303-4

Crimes Against Fecundity: Joyce and Population Control, 253-4

LUFT, JOANNA

"Reader Awareness: Form and Ambiguity in James Joyce's 'Eveline,'" 114-17

MAHAFFEY, VICKI & JILL SHASHATY

"Introduction to *Collective Dubliners: Joyce in Dialogue*," 190-91

MAHON, JOHN W.

"Joyce Among the Brothers," 225-26

MANGANIELLO, DOMINIC

"The Beauty that Saves: *Brideshead Revisited* as a Counter-*Portrait of the Artist*," 6, 208-13, 231

"Book Review of *Crimes Against Fecundity: Joyce and Population Control*, by Mary Lowe-Evans," 254

MARITAIN, JACQUES

Art and Scholasticism and The Frontiers of Poetry, 353

Three Reformers: Luther, Descartes, Rousseau, 152-53, 163

MARTIN, AUGUSTINE

"Reviewed Works: *Joyce's* Ulysses: *An Anatomy of a Soul*, by Theoharis Constantine Theoharis; Ulysses *as a Comic Novel* by Zack Bowen; *Joyce and the Law of the Father*, by Frances L. Restuccia," 3, 92

McCARTHY, PATRICK A.

"Further Notes on the Mass in *Ulysses*," 358-59

McCOURT, JOHN

"Reading Ellmann Reading Joyce," 79

MENCKEN, H.L.

A Mencken Chrestomathy, 59, 117

MERCANTON, JACQUES

"The Hours of James Joyce" 22

MOELLER, CHARLES

Literatura del Siglo XX y Cristianismo, I: El Silencio de Dios, 17

NEEDLETON ARMINTOR, MARSHALL

"Book Review of *Voices and Values in Joyce's* Ulysses, by Weldon Thornton," 103-4

NICHOLS, AIDAN, O.P.

Discovering Aquinas, 140, 300-1

NIETZSCHE, FRIEDRICH

The Anti-Christ, 130, 166, 202
Beyond Good and Evil, 130-183

NOON, WILLIAM T., S.J.

Joyce and Aquinas, 40, 102, 230, 235

"The Religious Position of James Joyce," 268-69

"A Delayed Review," 11

NORRIS, DAVID

"The 'Unhappy Mania' and Mr. Bloom's Cigar: Homosexuality in the Works of James Joyce," 247-49

NORRIS, MARGOT & VINCENT D. PECORA

"Dead Again," 195-96, 356

NYGREN, ANDERS

Agape and Eros, 156-57

O'BEIRNE RANELAGH, JOHN

A Short History of Ireland, 254

O'CONNOR, FLANNERY

The Habit of Being, 24

Mystery and Manners: Occasional Prose, 24, 414

Ó FLOINN, DONNCHADH
"The Integral Irish Tradition," 122

Ó RÍORDÁIN, JOHN J.
Irish Catholic Spirituality: Celtic and Roman, 121

O'ROURKE, FRAN
"Joyce's Early Aesthetic," 37

ORWELL, GEORGE
Dickens, Dali and Others, 404-5

O'SHEA, MICHAEL J.
"Catholic Liturgy in Joyce's *Ulysses*," 407

OWENS, CÓILÍN
James Joyce's Painful Case, 133-34, 183, 185-89

PAUL VI
Humanae vitae, 250, 254-55

PIEPER, JOSEF
Death and Immortality, 93, 218-19, 384

Enthusiasm and the Divine Madness, 220-22

Faith, Hope, Love, 157

Leisure: the Basis of Culture, 18

Scholasticism, Personalities and Problems of Medieval Philosophy, 297

Pius X
Pascendi, 322

Platt, Len
"Book Review of *Help My Unbelief,* by Geert Lernout," 351

Polyani, Michael
Personal Knowlege: Towards a Post-Critical Philosophy, 19-20

Powers, Joseph M., S.J.
Eucharistic Theology, 354

Potts, Willard
Portraits of an Artist in Exile, 23-24, 352

Rahner, Karl
Ecclesiology, Questions in the Church, the Church in the World, 415-16

Rao, John C.
Americanism and the Collapse of the Church in the United States, 123

Ratzinger, Joseph Cardinal
Introduction to Christianity, 58-59

The Nature and Mission of Theology: Essays to Orient Theology in Today's Debates, 55-60, 331

On the Way to Jesus Christ, 19

Pilgrim Fellowship of Faith: The Church as Communion, 400-1, 403, 406

The Spirit of the Liturgy, 60-61, 77, 377

The Yes of Jesus Christ, 157

REQUENA, FEDERICO

"Vida religiosa y espiritual en la Espana de principios de siglo XX," 320

RESTUCCIA, FRANCES

"Transubstantiating *Ulysses*," 7, 352-61, 365-71, 390

RODGERS, W.R.

Irish Literary Portraits, ed., 24

SCHOPENHAUER, ARTHUR

The World as Will and Representation, 183

SCHORK, R.J.

"James Joyce and the Eastern Orthodox Church," 22-23

SEGALL, JEFFREY

Joyce in America: Cultural Politics and the Trials of Ulysses, 2, 111, 165, 408

SHANAHAN, DENNIS M.

"The Eucharistic Aesthetics of the Passion: The Testament of Blood in *Ulysses*," 385-90

STEIN, EDITH

Woman, 288-89

STEINBERG, ERWIN R.

"The Bird-Girl in *A Portrait* as Synthesis: The Sacred Assimilated to the Profane," 214-16

SULLIVAN, KEVIN

Joyce Among the Jesuits, 329, 374

TERESA OF AVILA, SAINT

The Book of Her Foundations: A Study Guide, 317

The Life of Saint Teresa of Avila, 221

THORNTON, WELDON

The Antimodernism of Joyce's Portrait of the Artist as a Young Man, 82, 84-89, 91-99, 133, 151, 227-29, 269, 290, 381-82

Voices and Values in Joyce's Ulysses, 27-28, 84-85, 95-109

"The Greatness of *Ulysses*," 240, 265

TINDALL, WILLIAM YORK

The Literary Symbol, 214

TWOMEY, D. VINCENT

The End of Irish Catholicism? 120-21, 128, 176

VAN BAVEL, TARCISIUS J.

"Discipline," 161

VANHOYE, ALBERT CARDINAL

Accogliamo Cristo Nostro Sommo Sacerdote, Esercizi Spirituali con Benedetto XVI, 388-90

VATICAN COUNCIL I

Dei filius, 70

VATICAN COUNCIL II

Gaudium et spes, 82, 281, 312, 355, 381, 425

VON BALTHASAR, HANS URS

"Seeing the Form," Vol. I of *The Glory of the Lord: A Theological Aesthetics*, 18-19

"The Truth of God," Vol. II of *Theo-Logic: Theological Logical Theory*, 392

WALSH, RUTH

"In the Name of the Father and of the Son . . . Joyce's Use of the Mass in *Ulysses*," 350, 361-64

"That Pervasive Mass: In *Dubliners* and *A Portrait of the Artist As A Young Man*," 177, 341-42, 347-49

WALZL, FLORENCE L.

"Gabriel and Michael: The Conclusion of 'The Dead'," 194

"Joyce's 'The Sisters': A Development," 175-77

WAUCK, JOHN PAUL

"Christianity and the Poetics of Ordinary Life," 427-28

WILSON, EDMUND

"James Joyce," 237

YEATS, W.B.

"Anima Hominis," 78

"Easter 1916," 121-22

"September 1913," 121-22

YOUNG, ROBIN DARLING

"Theologia in the Early Church," 298-99

ACKNOWLEDGMENTS

Writing this book has been more of a collective than a solitary task. It has been enriched by the input of many generous friends. It is a joyful duty, therefore, to convey heartfelt thanks to the following for their encouragement, aid, and insights: Fr. Jeff Langan, Fr. John Paul Wauck, Fr. Paul Callaghan, Fr. Jose Carlos Gimeno O.C.D., Jared Staudt, Joseph Pearce, Declan Kiberd, Mary Lowe-Evans, Fr. Antoine Levy O.P., Fr. Michael Paul Gallagher, Mary-Zoe Bowden, Kathy Dittus, Anne Breiling, Kristen Lancton, Deborah Choi, Terry Riordan, and Michael Kearney. I am grateful also to Joshua Hren, Kateri Krebs, Amelia Kumpel, Dominic Heisdorf, and all at Wiseblood Books Press, for the thoroughness and swiftness with which they produced the book, combined with an all-too-rare graciousness in personal communication. Special thanks are due to my religious Brothers, the Servants of the Home of the Mother, who so often animated me with their genuine interest in the project.

www.ingramcontent.com/pod-product-compliance
Lightning Source LLC
Chambersburg PA
CBHW062055280426
43673CB00073B/151